R

ART AND REPRESENTATION

ART AND REPRESENTATION

New Principles in the Analysis of Pictures

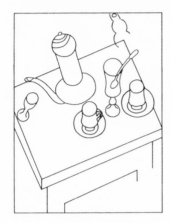
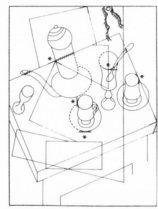
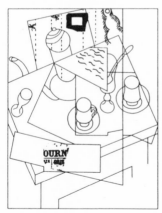

John Willats

PRINCETON UNIVERSITY PRESS

Princeton, New Jersey

© 1997 by Princeton University Press
Published by Princeton University Press, 41 William Street,
Princeton, New Jersey 08540
In the United Kingdom: Princeton University Press, Chichester, West Sussex
All Rights Reserved

Library of Congress Cataloging-in-Publication Data

Willats, John.
   Art and representation: new principles in the analysis of pictures /
John Willats.
         p.   cm.
   Includes bibliographical references and index.
   ISBN 0-691-08737-7 (alk. paper)
   1. Visual perception.   2. Perspective.   3. Optical illusions.   4. Oblique
projection.   I. Title.
   N7430.5.W55   1997
   701′.82—dc20   96-43335
                                                                              CIP

This book has been composed in Adobe Bembo and Galliard by Princeton
Editorial Associates, Princeton, New Jersey

Design by Diane Levy

Princeton University Press books are printed
on acid-free paper and meet the guidelines
for permanence and durability of the Committee
on Production Guidelines for Book Longevity
of the Council on Library Resources

Printed in the United States of America by
Princeton Academic Press

10   9   8   7   6   5   4   3   2   1

To Ruth and Bill

I found it absolutely necessary to consider this Subject entirely anew, as if it had never been treated of before; the Principles of the old Perspective being so narrow, and so confined, that they could be of no use to me in my Design: And I was forced to invent new Terms of Art, those already in use being so peculiarly adapted to the imperfect Notions that have hitherto been had of this Art, that I could make no use of them in explaining those general Principles I intended to establish.

—Dr. Brook Taylor
New Principles of Linear Perspective, 1719, pp. iv, v

Contents

PART V: CHANGES IN REPRESENTATIONAL SYSTEMS OVER TIME

Preface

During the 1960s a revolution took place in Western art schools. Art students were no longer content to learn—however imperfectly—the techniques of nineteenth-century academic drawing by imitating the examples of other students in the life class, as I had done while studying sculpture at the Royal College of Art. Instead they began to be influenced by many other kinds of pictures. Unfortunately, however, those of us who were teaching in the late 1960s came up against an unexpected problem: we found that when we attempted to discuss these pictures with the students, we literally had no words with which to describe the representational systems on which they were based. It was at this point that I realized that many of the projection systems with which I had become familiar in my earlier training as an engineer, and which I had always associated exclusively with engineering drawing, had formed the basis for artists' pictures in many other periods and cultures.

It was against this background that the painter Fred Dubery and I, who were teaching painting and drawing together, published our book on drawing systems in 1972. *Drawing Systems* was intended to serve simply as a kind of illustrated dictionary of the use of the projection systems in artists' pictures; but once the book had been published, people began to ask us why it was that artists in different periods and cultures had used these different drawing systems, and how children came to learn them—the kinds of psychological questions, in fact, that Professor Ernst Gombrich had asked at the beginning of *Art and Illusion*.

I went to see Professor Richard Gregory at the Brain and Perception Laboratory at the University of Bristol for advice on how to answer these questions, and he suggested that I should try to answer the question about children's drawings, at least, by carrying out some experiments: a novel idea so far as I was concerned, because at that time I knew nothing of the extensive scientific literature on children's drawings. I shall always be grateful to Professor Gregory for his suggestion, and also for his introduction to the then new field of artificial intelligence, from which I have drawn many of my ideas and much of my terminology.

I thus began the first modest researches which eventually led to my doctoral thesis, and almost at once I had the good fortune to meet Professor Stuart Sutherland, the head of Experimental Psychology at Sussex University. I owe a great debt of gratitude to Stuart for his help, encouragement, and criticism during the twenty-year period from the publication of my first paper on children's drawings, in the *Quarterly Journal of Experimental Psychology,* to his review of the first draft of this book.

My doctoral research during the first part of this period was guided by Professor Richard Wollheim, Grote Professor of Philosophy of Mind and Logic at London University, to whom I was introduced by Professor Gombrich, and to whose ideas and guidance I also owe a great deal. I was also fortunate at this period to meet Noam Chomsky at the Massachusetts Institute of Technology and, at his suggestion, the late David Marr, also at MIT, who had just published his revolutionary account of human vision; my admiration for their work is apparent throughout this book.

Anyone working in a field that spans more than one discipline is particularly dependent on the knowledge and willingness to help of other people. I cannot list here all the many people who have helped me, but I should particularly like to mention the help of John Matthews, David Pariser, Diana Korzenik, and Jim Victoria in art education; Marianne Teuber and Sue Malvern in art history; Jan Koenderink and Whitman Richards in artificial intelligence; Peter Denny in ethnolinguistics; Patrick Maynard and Nelson Goodman in philosophy; and Alan Costall, Harry Fisher, Norman Freeman, John Kennedy, Susan Somerville, Glyn Thomas, and Dennie Wolf in psychology. I am also very grateful to Jeff Pigott for his help in preparing the illustrations and to David Page for drawing my attention to fig. 7.7.

My special thanks are due to Patrick Maynard, who reviewed a later draft of this book; both he and an anonymous reviewer made many important suggestions for its improvement. I would also like to acknowledge the patient help of the staff of the Wiltshire Library Service, especially that of Jean Matthews and Susan Taylor, and the guidance of members of the Orthodox Church, especially Masha Springford of the University of Bristol and Mother Sarah of the Convent of St. John of Kronstadt, Bath, in the interpretation of icon paintings. Needless to say, I alone am to blame for any faults and omissions which the specialist reader may find.

Finally, my most grateful thanks are due to my wife Ruth and my son Bill, not only for the traditional family help and encouragement, but, in addition, to Ruth, whose help as an editor has been invaluable in the preparation of earlier versions of my manuscript, and to both Ruth and Bill for contributing many valuable and stimulating ideas.

CHAPTER ONE

Introduction

Ernst Gombrich (1960/1988) began *Art and Illusion,* his classic book on the psychology of pictorial representation, by asking the question that he called the "riddle of style": "Why is it that different ages and different nations have represented the visible world in such different ways?" As Gombrich pointed out, this is a question that has haunted the minds of art historians for many generations. But there are other equally puzzling questions associated with pictorial representation, and not all of them belong to the province of the art historian. Why is it that drawings by young children look so different from those by adults? Why do children take so long to learn to draw, and why do most adults find drawing so difficult? Are the odd-looking drawings produced by young children simply the result of their lack of skill in reproducing the appearance of objects, or do children see things differently from adults? Or is it that young children see things in the same way as adults, but use different pictorial systems for representing them? Are pictures from different cultures just different, much as English is different from Chinese, or are some pictures—pictures in perspective perhaps—better than other kinds of pictures? And why have pictorial styles changed during the course of art history? Do these changes constitute progress, as nineteenth-century art historians believed, or is the direction of stylistic change simply arbitrary?

Fascinating as these questions are, none of them can be answered, or even discussed in any meaningful way, without some clear account of the representational systems on which pictures are based. Before we can say *why* pictures have changed, we must be able to say *how* they have changed. The main aim of this book is to show that the different ways in which both artists and children represent the visible world can be described in terms of two representational systems: the drawing systems and the denotation systems. But in addition I shall try to show that analyzing pictures in terms of these two representational systems can be *useful:* useful, that is, in providing answers to some of the questions raised in the previous paragraph. In particular, I shall argue that differences in the representational systems found in different periods and cultures, and the changes that have taken place in these representational systems during the course of art history and that take place during the course of children's drawing development, are mainly determined by the different functions that representational systems are called on to serve.

The drawing systems are systems such as perspective, oblique projection, and orthogonal projection that map spatial relations in the scene into corresponding relations in the picture. In pictures in perspective, for example, like the drawing by Canaletto shown in fig. 1.1, objects that are further away in the scene are shown to a smaller scale than objects that are closer to the viewer, and the lines representing edges that lie perpendicular to the picture plane, or *orthogonals* as they are called, converge to a vanishing point. In pictures in oblique projection, like the twelfth-century Chinese painting shown in fig. 1.2, objects are shown to the same scale irrespective of their distance from the viewer, and the orthogonals are parallel and run at an oblique angle across the picture surface. In pictures in orthogonal projection, like the Greek vase painting shown in fig. 1.3 and the drawing of the

FIG. 1.1. Canaletto, *Venice: The Libreria and Campanile from the West,* mid-1730s. Ink over paper, 27 × 37.5 cm. The Royal Library, Windsor Castle. The Royal Collection, Her Majesty Queen Elizabeth II.

FIG. 1.2. *Lady Wenji's Return to China: Fourth Leaf,* c. A.D. 1100. Northern Sung Dynasty, twelfth century. Ink and colors on silk, 24.8 × 67.2 cm. Ross Collection. Gift of Denman Waldo Ross. Courtesy of Museum of Fine Arts, Boston.

FIG. 1.3. From an unsigned amphora by the chief painter of the factory of Andokides, *Herakles Feasting, with Athena,* sixth century B.C. Staatliche Antikensammlungen und Glyptothek, Munich.

locomotive shown in fig. 1.4, objects are shown to the same scale irrespective of distance, but there are no orthogonals. Instead, edges in the scene that lie perpendicular to the picture plane, such as the side edges of the table shown in fig. 1.3, are represented by points; and planes that are perpendicular to the picture plane, such as the top of the table and the ground plane, are represented by single lines.

These three drawing systems—perspective, oblique projection, and orthogonal projection—belong to a family of systems known as the projection systems. There are a number of others, but these three are the most important. Perspective is usually associated with Renaissance art, and oblique projection with Oriental art. Orthogonal projection is now usually associated with engineering drawing, but, as the last two examples suggest, the drawing systems in pictures can usually be described independently of their subject matter, or the period or country in which they were produced.

There are three classes of denotation systems: silhouettes, line drawings, and the optical denotation systems such as Pointillism. The denotation systems map features of the scene, or *scene primitives* as they are called, into corresponding *picture primitives* such as regions, lines, or points. In silhouettes, like the rock drawing of the gladiators in combat shown in fig. 1.5, the only recognizable features in the depicted scene are round lumps, like the men's heads; sticks, like their clubs; and, perhaps, discs or slabs if they are holding shields. All these features are represented in the picture by *regions:* either *round regions* or *long regions.* In line drawings, like Picasso's drawing of Stravinsky shown in fig. 1.6 and the drawing by a 9-year-old girl shown in fig. 1.7, the picture primitives are *lines* and these lines stand for, or denote, features such as edges or contours. Finally, in Pointillist paintings and pictures based on optical denotation systems, like the detail of a newspaper photograph shown in fig. 1.8, the picture primitives are *points,* and these

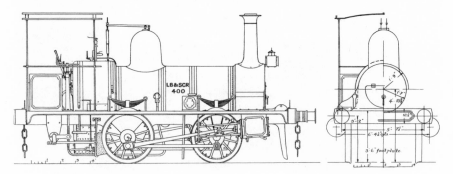

FIG. 1.4. F. C. Hambledon, *L.B. & S.C. Railway Locomotive No. 400.* From Hambledon (1948), courtesy of *Model Engineer* magazine.

denote optical features in the array of light coming from the scene, such as the colors and intensities of small bundles of light rays reaching the eye or the camera.

The three preceding paragraphs introduce a new and, for most people, unfamiliar vocabulary: few readers are likely to be familiar with terms like "denotation systems" and "picture primitives," and although words like "scene" and "picture" are familiar enough, they are used here in a special, technical sense. Using this special vocabulary is, however, unavoidable if we are to make any sense of the spatial systems in pictures. Physics as a science simply did not exist before the introduction of a precise terminology to describe such concepts as mass, weight, velocity, speed, and acceleration; and before this vocabulary was introduced, it was impossible to talk in any sensible or meaningful way about the motions of the planets or the movements of falling bodies. New words had to be introduced for new concepts, and old words, such as "mass" and "weight," had to be given a new and precise meaning. Similarly, it is impossible to talk in any meaningful way about the spatial systems in pictures without using a precise terminology.

Words such as "lines," "regions," "pictures," "scenes," and "primitives," which are used here in a special sense, come from the field sometimes known as "artificial intelligence," or "machine vision." In the 1960s, work began on the automatic analysis of pictures by computer as part of an attempt to understand the processes of visual perception. One of the most important insights to emerge from this early work was the absolute necessity of using one set of words to describe the three-dimensional world or *scene* and another, different set of words to describe two-dimensional *pictures*. Pictures can be so persuasive that it is all too easy to think of them as containing objects like people or tables, or shape features like edges and

FIG. 1.5. Rock drawing, Camonica Valley, *Gladiators in Combat,* c. 1000 B.C. From Anati (1964, detail of fig. 3.7).

FIG. 1.6.   Pablo Picasso, *Igor Stravinsky,* 1920. Pencil, 61.6 × 47.6 cm. Private collection, United States. Copyright Design and Artists Copyright Society 1997.

contours, whereas in reality pictures are made up of lines of ink or patches of paint. The central question in picture perception is: How do lines of ink or patches of paint come to *represent* features of real or imagined worlds?

The primitives of a system are the most elementary units of information available in a representation. Scene primitives are thus the most elementary units of shape information available in a scene, and picture primitives are the

FIG. 1.7. Joanne Hudson (9-year-old girl), *Self-Portrait with Dogs.* Courtesy of Doreen and Frank Hudson and Longman Education.

most elementary units of shape information available in a picture. Depending on the type of representation required, scenes may be defined in terms of a number of different kinds of primitives. Thus a very simple shape description of a table might be given by saying that it consists of a flat volume or slab standing on four long volumes or sticks. That is, a description of a table might be given in terms of three-dimensional or *volumetric* scene primitives. Alternatively, a more elaborate description of a table might be given in terms of two-dimensional scene primitives (faces) and their spatial relations, one-dimensional scene primitives (edges), or even in terms of the locations of a large number of zero-dimensional primitives (points) on the surface. Similarly, pictures can be described in terms of the spatial relations among two-dimensional picture primitives or regions, one-dimensional primitives or lines, or zero-dimensional primitives or points.

Scenes and pictures are relatively abstract concepts. Scenes provide abstract shape representations of physical objects such as tables and people: objects that have other, more complex attributes than just their abstract shapes. A similar distinction must also be made between pictures, which provide two-dimensional shape representations of scenes, and the way in which pictures are realized physically in paintings, drawings, mosaics, and so on by means of marks. It is necessary to make this distinction because it can sometimes be difficult to decide whether the variations in the marks in a

FIG. 1.8. Newspaper photograph of a hijacker (detail of fig. 2.4).

drawing or painting do or do not carry meaningful shape information: whether, for example, the variations in shape in the outline of a child's drawing, like the drawing of a man shown in fig. 1.12, are intended to carry information about the shape of the viewed object, or whether they are merely accidental. Moreover, physically different marks can carry similar shape information, and vice versa. Regions in a picture may be realized physically using areas of ink or paint, or they may be represented by blank areas enclosed by an outline. Conversely, lines in a picture may be realized physically using lines of stitches or mosaic, but the same marks may be used in hatching to represent optical features such as areas of shadow. It is therefore necessary to make a distinction between the *marks* in a picture and the more abstract notion of the picture primitives that these marks represent: a distinction akin to the distinction made in natural language between sounds and phonemes.

The terms "oblique projection" and "orthogonal projection" are terms used in engineering drawing. In 1963 a historian of engineering drawing, P. J. Booker, pointed out that many of the projection systems familiar to engineers, such as orthogonal projection, oblique projection, and isometric projection, had been used in other periods and cultures as a basis for the spatial systems in artists' pictures. For example, many Greek vase paintings, like the painting shown in fig. 1.3, are based on the system called orthogonal projection; but this system is now more familiar to us through its use in engineering working drawings, like the drawing of the locomotive shown in fig. 1.4. Today, oblique projection is not much used in engineering drawings, but in the nineteenth century it was often used to show what were called pictorial views. In artists' pictures, however, it was, until the advent of perspective, perhaps the most commonly used of all the drawing systems, and is found in Chinese paintings, Japanese prints, Persian miniature paintings, medieval paintings, and icon paintings.

Booker's suggestion that the projection systems could be used to describe the spatial systems in artists' pictures was taken a step further by Fred Dubery and myself in our book on drawing systems (Dubery and Willats, 1972). In it we illustrated the use of these systems in pictures from a wide variety of periods and cultures, and we also introduced names for two further projection systems—horizontal oblique projection and vertical oblique projection—which belong naturally to the mathematical family of projection systems but are not used in engineering drawing. Horizontal oblique projection is found in both Chinese paintings and icon paintings, and vertical oblique projection is found in Indian paintings and Cubist paintings. We also introduced the term "naive perspective" to describe a drawing system which is often found in naive painting and folk art, and which seemed to be a sort of halfway house between oblique projection and true perspective. In this system the orthogonals converge, but not in a regular way toward a single vanishing point.

All these systems can be found in children's drawings, and a number of experiments have shown that children use different projection systems at different ages. Fig. 1.9 shows the results of an experiment (Willats, 1977a, 1977b) in which English children were asked to draw a picture of a real scene consisting of a table with various objects on it. A few of the youngest children were unable to represent the spatial relations among the various objects, and their drawings were not classified in terms of their use of projection systems. The next oldest group of children, with a mean age of nearly 10 years, produced drawings of the table in orthogonal projection. Children in the next group, with a mean age of nearly 12 years, produced drawings in vertical oblique projection. This was the most commonly used system, and accounted for nearly 30 percent of all the drawings produced. In the next group were children who produced drawings in oblique projection (mean age 13½ years), while the oldest children produced drawings in either perspective or naive perspective (combined mean ages just over 14 years).

Booker (1963) also made an important distinction between what he called primary and secondary geometry. So far I have defined the projection systems in terms of secondary geometry and, in particular, in terms of the directions of the orthogonals. In orthogonal projection there are, somewhat paradoxically, no orthogonals; in horizontal oblique projection the orthogonals are horizontal; in vertical oblique projection the orthogonals are vertical; in oblique projection the orthogonals run obliquely across the picture surface; and in perspective they converge to a vanishing point. Booker described definitions of this kind as being given in terms of *secondary geometry:* the two-dimensional geometry of the picture surface. But ever since perspective was codified at the beginning of the Renaissance, theoretical writers on art had described perspective in terms of the three-dimensional geometry of the projection of lines or rays from the scene to the eye of a viewer, and the intersection of these rays with a plane, called the picture plane, to form a picture: much as the light reflected from objects forms an image on the film in a camera. Booker called this geometry *primary geometry.* In the nineteenth century, theoretical writers on engineering drawing adopted this approach as a basis for their descriptions of systems such as orthogonal projection and oblique projection, even though the idea of a notional viewer situated at infinity, necessitated by the fact that the projec-

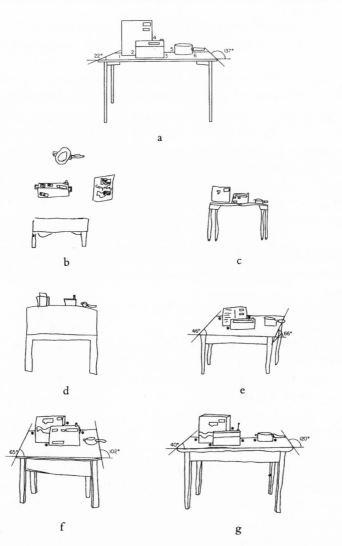

Fig. 1.9. Children's drawings of a table: typical drawings in each class. (a) The child's view of the table. (b) Class 1, no projection system, no overlap, mean age 7.4. (c) Class 2, orthogonal projection, overlap score 0, mean age 9.7. (d) Class 3, vertical oblique projection, overlap score 0, mean age 11.9. (e) Class 4, oblique projection, overlap score 3, mean age 13.6. (f) Class 5, naive perspective, overlap score 4, mean age 14.3. (g) Class 6, perspective, overlap score 6, mean age 13.7. From Willats (1977a), courtesy of *Quarterly Journal of Experimental Psychology.*

tion rays in these two systems are parallel, was rather a questionable one; this approach is still in use today. Because of this emphasis on primary geometry as a way of describing the spatial systems in pictures, it became difficult to think about these spatial systems, and the psychological processes by which pictures are produced, except in these terms. Booker's distinction between primary geometry and secondary geometry was important for three reasons. First, on a purely formal level, it makes it possible to give an account of a number of drawing systems, such as inverted perspective and systems based on topological geometry, which cannot be described in terms of the projection of light rays. Second, it provides a way of describing the actual mental processes by which pictures are produced that avoids the problem of supposing that all pictures are derived directly from views. Third, defining the drawing systems in terms of secondary geometry can lead to accounts of both children's drawing development and art-historical changes which are much more psychologically realistic than those given in terms of primary geometry.

Projection systems such as perspective, oblique projection, and orthogonal projection, and so on, can be defined in terms of both primary and secondary geometry. For example, orthogonal projection can be defined as the system in which the projection rays are parallel and intersect the picture plane at right angles: rather like taking a photograph of an object with a powerful telephoto lens from a considerable distance. But orthogonal projection can also be defined as the system in which there are no orthogonals, and the front faces of objects are drawn as true shapes. In this case, as I shall show in Chapter 2, the secondary geometry is a consequence of the primary geometry; and the same is true of all the other projection systems.

But there are two other kinds of drawing systems that cannot be defined in terms of primary geometry, although they can be defined in terms of secondary geometry. Of these the most important, at least so far as artists' pictures are concerned, is the system known as *inverted perspective* (or divergent perspective as it is sometimes called). In this system the orthogonals *diverge,* instead of converging as they do in normal perspective. Inverted perspective is sometimes found in Cubist paintings: in Braque's *Still Life: The Table* (fig. 1.10), for example, the lines representing the side edges of the table clearly diverge. But although inverted perspective is not uncommon in Cubist painting, it is not the commonest system, and Cubism was a relatively short-lived movement, so it is possible to argue that inverted perspective was simply an occasional aberration indulged in by a few eccentric modern artists. However, inverted perspective was, together with horizontal oblique projection, the system most commonly used in Byzantine art and Russian icon painting during a period extending over more than a thousand years. The orthogonals of the footstools in Andrei Rublev's *The Holy Trinity* (color plate 1), for example, diverge upwards.

The second group of pictures that must be defined in terms of secondary rather than primary geometry are those based on topological geometry. This class includes caricatures, schematic diagrams such as electric circuit diagrams, and route maps like the well-known map of the London Underground system (fig. 1.11). I shall argue that it also includes children's early drawings, like the drawing of a man by a 5-year-old boy shown in fig. 1.12. Topological geometry is based on the most elementary and general types of spatial properties, which include relations like touching, separation, spatial order, and enclosure. More special kinds of properties like straightness (preserved in projective projections) and the true (scale) sizes and shapes of faces (preserved in orthogonal projections) are not preserved in topological transformations. In the map of the London Underground, for example, the only spatial relations represented are the connections between the stations and their spatial order along the tracks. Similarly, in the child's drawing shown in fig. 1.12 the legs are only represented as *attached* to the body, and the eyes, nose, and mouth as *enclosed* within the region representing the face. Properties like true shape and true (scale) size are not preserved.

FIG. 1.10. Georges Braque, *Still Life: The Table,* 1928. Oil on canvas, 81.3 × 130.8 cm. Chester Dale Collection, National Gallery of Art, Washington, D.C. Copyright Design and Artists Copyright Society 1997.

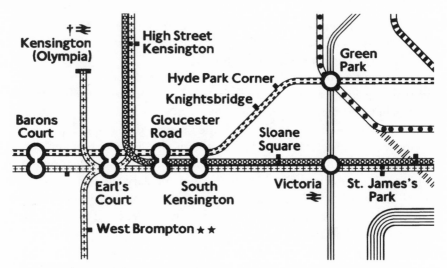

Fig. 1.11.   Map of the London Underground. Courtesy of London Transport Museum, LTR Registered User No. 94/E/643.

Chapter 2 of this book describes all the common projection systems in terms of both primary and secondary geometry, and also includes an account of inverted perspective and naive perspective, both of which can be satisfactorily described only in terms of secondary geometry. Chapter 3 describes two types of pictures based on topological geometry, and also includes an account of what is called *extendedness*. Extendedness is the most

Fig. 1.12.   *Drawing of a Man* by a five-year-old boy.

basic of all shape properties, and is used to describe the relative extensions in space of scene and picture primitives. For example, the simplest kind of scene primitive would consist of a roughly spherical volume, or *lump,* extended about equally in all three dimensions of space. If such a primitive were to be extended in one dimension but not the other two, it would take the form of an elongated volume or *stick;* while if it were to be extended in two dimensions but not the third, it would take the form of a *slab* (cf. Marr and Nishihara, 1978, p. 275). Informally, extendedness may be glossed by words like "round," "flat," and "long," but Chapter 3 also includes an account of a formal scheme for specifying the extendedness of scene and picture primitives. It is important to realize that the surface geometry of these primitives is not relevant to a specification of their extendedness: at this very basic level both spheres and cubes may be regarded as "round" lumps. For example, some of the stations in the map of the London Underground are represented by circles and others by squares, but this is not intended to tell us anything about the detailed shapes of the stations they represent. In terms of their extendedness, both these shapes may be regarded as round regions, representing round volumes or lumps. Thus the stations in this map are represented by round regions and the track by long regions. Similarly, in the rock drawing from Camonica Valley shown in fig. 1.5, round volumes or lumps in the scene, such as the heads of the gladiators, are represented by round regions in the picture; and long volumes like the legs are represented by long regions.

Extendedness also appears to play a part in children's early drawings. In their first drawings of people, the so-called tadpole figures like the drawing shown in fig. 1.12, children use lines or long regions to represent long volumes like the arms or legs, and round regions to represent round volumes like the head or head/body. This suggests that, at the very simplest level, children regard the human figure as a lump with sticks attached to it, and that they use the extendedness of the picture primitives in their drawings (the lines and regions) as a way of representing the extendedness of corresponding features in their internal shape descriptions of the human figure.

Part 1 describes all the common drawing systems: systems that map spatial relations in the scene into corresponding relations on the picture surface. Part 2 describes the denotation systems. At the risk of some repetition, it is necessary to emphasize again the difference between the drawing systems and the denotation systems. Whereas the drawing systems map spatial relations in the scene into corresponding spatial relations in the picture, the denotation systems map *scene primitives* into *picture primitives.* That is, whereas the drawing systems say where the picture primitives *go,* the denotation systems say what the picture primitives stand for, refer to, or *denote* (cf. Goodman, 1968). There are three main classes of denotation systems, based on two-, one-, and zero-dimensional picture primitives.

Parts 1 and 2 thus describe, at a purely formal level, the representational systems in pictures. There would be little point in describing these systems, however, unless such descriptions can be shown to be both useful and comprehensive: useful, in that they can enable us to solve at least some of the problems I outlined at the beginning of this chapter, and comprehensive to the extent that they allow us to describe the representational systems in a wide range of pictures. In order to demonstrate that the approach I propose is comprehensive, I have illustrated the various drawing and denotation systems using a very wide variety of types of pictures: maps, engineers' and architects' drawings, photographs, children's drawings, and artists' pictures from many different periods and cultures. In addition, these pictures deal with a very wide range of subject matter—among them, portraits, landscapes, still lifes, and religious subjects—and they are of very varied quality: some of them, like Picasso's drawing of Stravinsky and Andrei Rublev's *Trinity,* are acknowledged masterpieces, while others belong more to the realm of naive or folk art.

Thus, although the bulk of this book deals with artists' pictures, the methodology I have chosen to use is very different from that which would be adopted by an art historian: it is in fact much closer to the methodology that would be used by a modern linguist or psycholinguist. Typically, an art historian might choose to deal with paintings or drawings by an individual artist such as Paul Klee or Van Gogh, or within a particular *genre* such as landscape, portraiture, or still life, or produced in a particular country or period. But, above all, art historians are concerned with changes over *time:* either changes in style over a limited period within a particular culture or, perhaps, changes in the style of an individual artist over some or all of his or her working life. In contrast, the central focus of this book lies in an attempt to describe the representational systems in pictures, and the functions of these systems, independently of any historical or developmental considerations. It is true that in the last part of this book I have considered two kinds of changes over time: the developmental changes in children's drawings, and the changes—or lack of change—during two periods of art history. But I have done this for two reasons: first, to try to demonstrate the potential contribution which the approach I have described here might make to these two fields; and, second, in an attempt to provide an alternative to two theories of change which seem to me to be demonstrably wrong: Hagen's theory that "there is no development in art" (Hagen, 1985) (that is, that there are no significant changes in children's drawings over time except an improvement in mechanical skill, and that there are no directional changes in art history); and the evolutionary theory of art history, that art-historical changes present us with a more or less unified, lawful pattern of progress toward some single goal.

Apart from these two chapters, however, I have set out to describe the representational systems in pictures and their functions independently of any historical or developmental considerations. The kind of distinction I am trying to make here is thus analogous to the distinction made in the study of natural language between modern structural linguistics and the historical study of language, or philology. This distinction between two possible ways of looking at language was first articulated at the beginning of the twentieth century by Fernand de Saussure, one of the founders of modern linguistics. In contrast to the exclusively historical account of language that had held sway over the past hundred years, Saussure pointed out that it is possible to study language in two quite distinct ways, which he called "synchronic" and "diachronic." Synchronic linguistics studies the structure or "state" of a language as it exists at a given time within some particular group; while diachronic linguistics studies the changes in language over time. Thus a structural linguist might be concerned with the study of the structure of a language spoken by a particular group—say, native English speakers—irrespective of its historical context, while a philologist might study the historical changes that took place from Old English to Middle English (Crystal, 1971). Similarly, a linguist might attempt to describe the nature of a particular kind of "error" in children's speech, while a developmental psychologist or psycholinguist would be more concerned with the changes that take place in children's speech as they get older.

This distinction now seems fairly obvious, but the failure to draw it in the nineteeth century caused a good deal of confusion. Nowadays these two ways of studying language are generally regarded as complementary, but it is still necessary to draw a clear distinction between them. Similarly, although I hope that the approach I have followed here may be of interest to art historians and developmental psychologists, I want to emphasize that the methodology I have adopted is fundamentally different from that which underlies the study of art history.

Parts 1 and 2, then, describe the drawing systems and the denotation systems: the two systems involved in the representation of shape and space in pictures. Part 3 is concerned with the psychological reality of these systems: the question of the actual mental processes that underlie picture perception and picture production.

There is a persistent tradition that pictures are derived more or less directly from retinal images—or if not from retinal images, then from internal mental images that correspond more or less directly to possible views. The geometry of such images was thought to correspond to the geometry of a cross-section of the light reaching the eye; and the invention of the camera as a means of capturing and reproducing this geometry naturally reinforced this tradition. The problem with this kind of purely optical theory of pictures is that it makes it very difficult to account for a wide range of pictures whose geometry does not correspond to that of possible views except in terms of some kind of deficit theory: lack of skill on the part of children, and a similar lack of skill on the part of artists in earlier periods and other cultures.

I have already mentioned two kinds of pictures that are difficult to explain as being derived from views: drawings by young children like the tadpole figure shown in fig. 1.12, and pictures in inverted perspective. A third type of what I shall refer to as "anomalous" pictures—that is, pictures that do not provide possible views—are the so-called fold-out drawings. Pictures of this type are common in children's drawings, but they also appear in folk art and icon paintings. Somewhat similar forms appear in Cubist paintings, where they are sometimes referred to as providing multiple views or "shifting view-points" (Baxandall, 1985, p. 61). The so-called "split-style" or "double profile" pictures of animals in North West Coast Indian art may also belong to this group (Cox, 1992, pp. 97, 98). These kinds of pictures appear in their simplest form in children's drawings of rectangular objects such as boxes or cubes, as in the child's drawing of a box standing on the table in fig. 1.9d. It is as if the box had been cut down its edges and folded out flat onto the picture surface, hence the name. In terms of secondary geometry, pictures in horizontal or vertical oblique projection may be regarded as special cases of fold-out pictures in which only two faces of the object have been represented, and there are intermediate cases whose status is difficult to determine. For example, the folk art painting shown in fig. 8.12 and the icon painting shown in fig. 8.13 both show buildings in horizontal oblique projection, but in both cases the ground plane (which ought not to appear when this system is defined in terms of primary geometry) has been folded down onto the picture surface.

None of these types of anomalous pictures can be easily accounted for in terms of retinal images, or internal descriptions which correspond to possible views. I shall argue, instead, that they can be explained by supposing that they are derived from internal *object-centered* descriptions by the application of rules based on secondary rather than primary geometry.

The term "object-centered" is taken from Marr's account of visual perception (Marr, 1978; Marr and Nishihara, 1978; Marr, 1982). Marr's theory of vision revolutionized the study of three-dimensional shape recognition when it first appeared in the late 1970s and is still generally regarded as the most influential account of the operation of the human visual system. Marr's central question was: How can we obtain constant perceptions in everyday life on the basis of continually changing sensations? The answer that Marr proposed was that the function of the visual system is to take in local, unorganized, point sensations whose positions on the retina change with each new point or direction of view, and use them to compute three-dimensional internal shape descriptions that are independent of any particular point of view and unaffected by changes in the lighting conditions. These object-centered descriptions are then used in the recognition of objects when we see them again under different lighting conditions, or from a new position or direction of view. Marr called these relatively stable, three-dimensional shape descriptions "object-centered descriptions" because the frames of reference (or "coordinate systems") on which they are based are centered on the objects themselves, rather than being determined by the viewer's line of sight or position in space. Marr also argued that, for reasons of economy, such internal shape descriptions ought to be based on volumetric primitives, rather than on primitives consisting of points, edges, or surfaces: he pointed out that describing even the crude shape of a finger would require hundreds of point primitives distributed over the surface, whereas the same shape description could be accomplished with just one volumetric primitive.

However, the human visual system is not designed to take in object-centered volumetric shape descriptions directly. On the contrary, what we take in at the retina are point sensations whose positions on the retina change with each new position or direction of view. Marr called such images "viewer-centered" because they are dependent on a coordinate system defined in terms of the position of the viewer and the direction of the viewer's line of sight. Thus, using the terminology I have already described, much of which was introduced by Marr himself, the function of the human visual system is to take in viewer-centered images based on point primitives, and compute from them object-centered shape descriptions based on volumetric primitives. Much of this process, Marr contended, took place automatically and was independent of acquired knowledge or preconceptions about what we expect to see. So far as Marr's theory of shape recognition is concerned, the process ends here. But of course there must be a further stage or stages with humans in which we recognize objects and name them. This further process must depend on previously acquired knowledge: a knowledge of objects such as tables and people and their functions, and a knowledge of verbal language.

Thus, according to Marr, the human visual system must contain two kinds of internal representations of shape: viewer-centered and object-centered. *Viewer-centered* because we see things from particular points of view, and *object-centered* because we need to compute and store object-centered descriptions in order to recognize objects when we see them again from a new position or direction of view.

In Part 3 I propose that some pictures, particularly pictures that contain the characteristic types of anomalies I have described above, are derived from object-centered descriptions. This ought not to cause us any surprise because we already know that some kinds of pictures, such as engineers' drawings, are derived from object-centered descriptions rather than from views. Moreover, many, perhaps most, pictures produced by computer are derived from object-centered descriptions (fig. 8.2), and the computer provides us with a model for the process of picture production which is every bit as powerful, and much more psychologicaly realistic, than that provided by photography. It is only the predominance of perspective in Western painting that has, previously, allowed us to persuade ourselves that artists' pictures must be derived exclusively from views.

Part 4 is concerned with the various *functions* served by particular combinations of drawing and denotation systems: that is, with the question of what different representational systems are *for*. Here again, the predominance of Western realistic or illusionistic painting and the influence of photography can all too easily persuade us to suppose that the best kinds of pictures are those which provide us with an experience which is as similar as possible to the experience we have of seeing the real three-dimensional world. As Dr. Brook Taylor put it in his famous book on perspective, published in 1719:

> A Picture drawn in the utmost Degree of Perfection, and placed in a proper Position, ought so to appear to the Spectator, that he should not be able to distinguish what is there represented, from the real original Objects actually placed where they are represented to be. In order to produce this effect, it is necessary that the Rays of Light ought to come from the several Parts of the Picture to the Spectator's Eye, with all the same circumstances of Direction, Strength of Light and Shadow, and Colour, as they would do from the corresponding Parts of the real Objects seen in their proper Places. (Taylor, 1719, pp. 1, 2)

Almost two hundred and fifty years later the perceptual psychologist J. J. Gibson gave expression to very much the same idea in his definition of what he called a "faithful" picture: "A delimited surface so processed that it yields a sheaf of light-rays to a given point which is the same as would be the sheaf of rays from the original scene to a given point" (Gibson, 1954, quoted in Gibson, 1971, p. 28). It is very easy to slide from what was intended, in Gibson's account, to be a purely scientific definition of a faithful picture into supposing that artists' pictures that provide convincing illusions are *better* in some absolute sense than pictures that do not match up to this definition. And, because this attitude toward pictures is still very pervasive in our own culture, it is easy to look at children's drawings and pictures from other periods and cultures and see them as inferior judged by this standard. However, providing a convincing illusion is not the only function of pictures. What other functions do pictures serve, and how are these functions served by the various representational systems?

There are large classes of pictures that are clearly not intended to provide convincing illusions. These include, among others, engineers' and architects' working drawings, route maps, and road signs. Even these three classes of pictures, however, serve different kinds of functions; and are, in consequence, based on very different representational systems. Engineers' and architects' working drawings are intended to provide information about the shapes and sizes of objects in what Marr would call an object-centered description. In order to do this, such drawings are based on orthogonal projections that show the true shapes and (scale) sizes of the faces of rectangular objects or their cross-sections, rather than on perspective projections, which would show only the shapes and sizes of objects as they appear from a particular direction of view. In addition, because a single drawing would be ambiguous, such drawings show two, or more commonly three, related views. The denotation system used in these working drawings is usually a special version of line drawing, one in which edges and contours are represented by full lines, and hidden edges and contours, and lines relating one view to another, by broken lines.

Route maps, on the other hand, like the map of the London Underground shown in fig. 1.11, provide very little accurate shape information. Instead, they show only those spatial relations with which the traveler is concerned: the connections between stations, and the spatial order in which the stations occur along the route. Consequently, such maps are commonly based on a drawing system that preserves topological rather than projective or metric relations; and because only the most elementary shape properties need be represented, the shapes of the stopping places and the routes are represented only in terms of their relative extensions in three-dimensional space.

Finally, the prime requirement for road signs is that it should be possible to recognize the *objects* depicted in these signs under conditions of poor visibility or when the sign is seen from a considerable distance. Such pictures ought to be based on regions rather than lines, because lines are too thin to be seen under these conditions. In addition, projective relations must be at least roughly preserved, so that the image of the object does not appear to be too distorted. At the same time, however, regions in the silhouette must be distinct, and the extendedness of these regions should reflect the extendedness of the parts of the object they represent, so that even though the fine details of the outlines of the objects cannot be resolved, the object as a whole can still be recognized. Thus in all these cases the functions these pictures are intended to serve can be related to the formal properties of the drawing and denotation systems on which they are based.

All these functions are important, but the most basic function that pictures can serve is to provide what I shall call *effective shape representations.* The philosopher Richard Wollheim has defined representation in terms of "seeing in": the definition he gave (Wollheim, 1977, p. 182) was that a (pictorial) representation is a two-dimensional configuration in which something or other can be seen and, furthermore, one in which something specific can be *recognized.* Providing a representation in which something specific can be recognized can be seen as the most basic function of pictures. But how can an artist or draftsman give effect to this intention?

Recognizing objects in real scenes depends, in most cases, on our being able to recognize their *shapes,* although in some special cases color or texture may also be important (Biederman and Ju, 1988). The same argument applies to pictures: try to imagine what a picture of a table would look like if it did not represent its shape! Wollheim's definition can therefore be qualified by saying that if a picture is to provide an effective representation, it must be possible to recognize in it the *shapes* of the objects that the artist or draftsman intended to represent. I shall therefore define an *effective shape representation* as a pictorial representation in which the three-dimensional shapes of the objects that the artist or draftsman intends to portray can be seen, clearly and unambiguously.

Judged against this definition, engineering drawings like the drawing of the locomotive shown in fig. 1.4 do not as a rule provide particularly effective shape representations. The *two-dimensional* shapes of the faces of objects and their cross-sections are portrayed very clearly, but it is actually rather difficult to see the three-dimensional shapes of some parts of the locomotive, such as the shape of the smokebox, in the drawing. (The smokebox is the complex shape that connects the cylinders and the chimney.) As an extreme example, consider the "puzzle" drawing shown in fig. 1.13a, which is sometimes given to engineering students as a test of their powers of interpretation. This figure shows two related drawings in orthogonal projection: a front view above and a plan view below. There are no hidden edges. The question is: What object do these drawings represent? The answer is shown in fig. 1.13b, a pictorial view drawn in isometric projection. The related views shown in orthogonal projection contain the same information as the drawing in isometric projection, but only the drawing in isometric projection provides an effective shape representation, in the sense defined above.

The human visual system puts quite severe restraints on pictures if they are to be good as representations in this sense. Perhaps the most important of these constraints is that they should provide possible views: that is, their geometry must approximate to the geometry of a projection from a possible scene. The design of the visual system is such that it takes in shape information from real scenes in the form of projections to the retina, and picture perception appears to be parasitic on scene perception.[1] As a result, pictures are effective as representations only if they provide possible views, and in practice this means that they must be based on one or the other of the projection systems. If a picture is to provide an effective representation, however, it is not enough that it should provide a possible view: it must, in addition, provide a view taken from a *general position*. Huffman (1971), one of the pioneers in the analysis of line drawings in the field of artificial intelligence, defined a "general position" as one such that "a slight change of position would not change the number of lines in the picture or the configurations in which they come together" (p. 298). In the drawing shown in fig. 1.13b, for example, the object is drawn from a general position, and a slight change in the implied viewpoint from which the object was drawn would not change the number of lines in the drawing or the configurations in which they come together. This condition is intended to

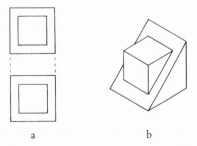

a   b

FIG. 1.13. Two drawings of the same three-dimensional body in (a) orthogonal projection and (b) isometric projection. Both drawings contain the same *shape information,* but only drawing (b) provides an *effective three-dimensional shape representation.*

prevent the representation of accidental alignments, such as a view in which one corner of an object appears to lie over another, unrelated corner. Accidental alignments are represented in pictures by what are called "false attachments": configurations in which, for example, two unrelated corners are represented by a single point. The two drawings shown in orthogonal projection in fig. 1.13a are full of false attachments—two unrelated edges of the triangular face on the left of the object, for example, are represented by a single line—and as a result these drawings are not effective as shape representations.

For objects such as buildings or tables, this constraint—that if a picture is to provide an effective representation, it should show such objects from a general position—is satisfied by pictures in perspective and the parallel oblique systems such as oblique projection and isometric projection, but not by pictures in orthogonal projection. This is why the discovery and rediscovery of these systems were such important turning points during the course of art history. Architects and engineers are well aware of this "general position" constraint: they use orthogonal projections for their working drawings because they show the true shapes of objects; but if they want to show their clients what their designs will look like, they produce pictorial views taken from a general position in systems like oblique projection, isometric projection, axonometric projection, or perspective.

Another constraint on pictures if they are to be good as representations is that they should be either line drawings or based on an optical denotation system. Silhouettes, especially silhouettes based on regions as picture primitives like the picture of the two gladiators in combat shown in fig. 1.5, do not normally provide effective shape representations because it is difficult to see in them the three-dimensional shapes of objects they represent. In this picture, for example, it is difficult to know whether the gladiators are holding weapons like swords or clubs, or whether they are also holding shields. In general, the impression of three-dimensional shape given by a line drawing like Picasso's drawing of Stravinsky (fig. 1.6) is much more vivid, and much less ambiguous, than the shape impression given by even a very detailed silhouette, like the silhouette shown in fig. 5.1.

If pictures of smooth objects such as the human figure are to provide effective shape representations, they should also show objects from a general position. However, this does not necessarily mean, as it does with rectangular objects, that they must be depicted in perspective or one of the parallel oblique systems. Because smooth objects do not have plane faces or straight edges, drawings in orthogonal projection, like the drawings of the figures in the Greek vase drawings shown in figs. 1.3 and 11.3a, can look very similar to drawings in perspective. What is important, if such drawings are to give an unambiguous impression of three-dimensional shape, is that they should contain examples of what are called "T-junctions" and "end-junctions." T-junctions in line drawings denote the points where an edge or a contour passes behind a surface, and can occur in drawings of both smooth objects and objects having plane faces. "End-junctions" occur only in line drawings of smooth objects and denote the points where contours end. Both types of junctions denote points of occlusion, where one surface occludes or hides another with respect to a viewer. Occlusion is one of the most powerful depth cues in the perception of scenes, and the representation of occlusion in pictures can give a strong impression of depth and shape. Picasso's drawing of Stravinsky (fig. 1.6), for example, and the *Self-Portrait with Dogs* by Joanne (fig. 1.7) both contain numerous examples of T- and end-junctions; as a result both drawings give a vivid impression of three-dimensional shape.

Providing effective shape representations is such a basic function of artists' pictures that it is often taken for granted, especially in a period like our own when effective representations are commonplace. In other periods and cultures, however, the artist's ability to produce an effective representation could not necessarily be assumed. The art historian Michael Baxandall traced the change, in fifteenth-century Italy, from an emphasis on the use of costly materials such as gold and ultramarine as the measure of a good painting at the beginning of the century, to an increasing emphasis on the artist's skill toward the end of the century. Basic to a patron's assessment of an artist's skill must have been the artist's ability to produce an effective representation, in the sense in which I have defined it. It was important, for example, in the context of Catholic religious painting, that the faithful should not only be able to recognize the objects portrayed in pictures of the lives of the saints, but that these objects should appear to be actually present. In support of his thesis that the religious function of pictures in the Quattrocento was to be "lucid, vivid and readily accessible," Baxandall quotes a sermon published in 1490 in which the Dominican Fra Michele da Carano observed that "images were introduced on account of our emotional sluggishness; so that men who are not aroused to devotion when they hear about the histories of the Saints may at least be moved when they see them, *as if actually present,* in pictures" (Baxandall, 1988, p. 41, my emphasis).

However, providing an effective representation is certainly not the only function that artists' pictures can perform. "Vivid," as Baxandall uses the word, means more than just providing an effective shape representation; it also means emotionally engaging, eye-catching, and memorable, and these requirements must be met by means, such as the portrayal of gesture and the direction of gaze, which go beyond the mere representation of shape and spatial relations. Moreover, it is necessary at this point to make a distinction between the cultural functions of pictures (such as a religious or aesthetic function) and the way these functions may be served within pictures by different representational systems and combinations of systems.

For example, engineering drawings are based on orthogonal projection because, as I have said, this system shows the true (scale) dimensions of objects and the true shapes of faces; the fact that this system does not provide a pictorial view, and can make objects look relatively flat, is a disadvantage. But Cubist paintings often contain individual objects represented in orthogonal projection—for example, the bottle on the right of Braque's *Still Life: The Table* (fig. 1.10)—and here the flattening effect of this system is an advantage, because one of the aims of the Cubist painters was to draw attention to the picture as a flat surface.

Two other drawing systems are found in Cubist painting: vertical oblique projection and inverted perspective. I have already mentioned the use of inverted perspective in Braque's *Still Life: The Table:* in this system the orthogonals diverge. The secondary geometry of vertical oblique projection may be summed up by saying that in this system a top view is added to a side view: in Braque's painting, the top of the wine glass at the center left is represented by a horizontal line, as it would be in orthogonal projection, but one half of a top view of the glass has been added to it. In Gris's *Breakfast* (color plate 6), vertical oblique projection is used much more exactly.

But inverted perspective is also found in Orthodox art—that is, in Byzantine art and Greek and Russian icon paintings—and the other most commonly used system in Orthodox art is horizontal oblique projection, the horizontal counterpart to vertical oblique projection. Again, I have already drawn attention to the diverging orthogonals in Andrei Rublev's *The Holy Trinity* (color plate 1), and other examples of the use of inverted perspective in Orthodox art can be found in the sixth-century mosaic of *Scenes from the Life of Abraham* at Ravenna (fig. 14.9) and the fourteenth-century mosaic of *The Numbering of the People* in Istanbul (fig. 14.11).

In horizontal oblique projection, the front and side views of objects are added together, and, like vertical oblique projection, using this system has the effect of flattening the picture surface. A good example of the use of this system appears on the left of the *Scenes from the Life of Abraham,* and another in the Greek icon painting shown in fig. 8.13.

Thus very much the same drawing systems appear in both Cubist paintings and Orthodox art. Clearly, the cultural functions of these two kinds of pictures are utterly different—aesthetic in one case and religious in the other—but the functions these systems serve within both kinds of pictures are, I shall argue, very much the same. The Cubist painters were anxious, for aesthetic reasons, to draw attention to their paintings as both symbol systems and physical objects rather than as illusionistic glimpses of the real world, hence the emphasis on the physical qualities of the paint surface and the use of drawing and denotation systems that destroy the illusion of three-dimensional space. But in Orthodox art, inverted perspective and horizontal oblique projection serve somewhat similar functions, although, as I have said, the cultural functions of these two kinds of pictures are quite different. On one hand, the employment of anomalous drawing systems enabled Orthodox artists to avoid the latent dangers of idolatry by providing pictures in which objects could be recognized, but in a symbolic form: images which belonged to another, spiritual world, rather than the three-dimensional material world of time and space. At the same time, by using systems that tended to draw attention to the picture as a physical object, icons reminded the faithful that the material world could be redeemed: "If flesh has become a vehicle of the Spirit, then so—though in a different way—can wood and paint" (Ware, 1993, p. 33).

Just as anomalous drawing systems can be used to destroy the illusion of three-dimensional space, so anomalous *denotation* systems can be used for the same purpose. In the context of artificial intelligence, Max Clowes in England and D. A. Huffman in the United States described rules governing the configurations in which lines in line drawings may and may not come together if they are to provide views of possible objects. Fig. 1.14 shows examples taken from Clowes (1971) and Huffman (1971) containing what

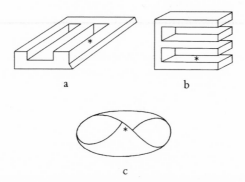

a   b

c

FIG. 1.14. Line drawings of impossible objects. Lines having two different meanings along their length are marked with an asterisk. (a) Adapted from Clowes (1971), courtesy of Elsevier Science. (b) and (c) Adapted from Huffman (1971), courtesy of Edinburgh University Press.

Huffman called "forbidden configurations." The result of including forbidden configurations of this kind in a drawing is that the shapes surrounding the forbidden configuration cannot be resolved by the visual system. For example, the lines on the left of the drawing shown in fig. 1.14a follow the rules described by Clowes and Huffman for pictures of possible objects, and as a result the left-hand part of the drawing gives a compelling impression of three-dimensional shape. But at the right of the drawing there is a forbidden configuration, and the reference of the line marked with an asterisk cannot be determined: at one end it denotes a convex edge, and at the other an occluding contour. At this point the eye is baffled, and locally the drawing appears relatively flat. Similar effects occur in drawings (b) and (c).

Forbidden configurations of this kind can also be found in artists' pictures. The patterns of lines denoting occluding contours in the folds of the angels' garments in Rublev's *The Holy Trinity* (color plate 1) contain numerous instances of such forbidden configurations: for example, in the folds of cloth covering the knee of the angel on the right of the picture. Picasso's drawing of Stravinsky (fig. 1.6) contains a number of even more obvious examples, particularly in the folds of the sleeves of Stravinsky's jacket. These anomalies seem quite deliberate, and it is known that Picasso went to Russia especially to study icon painting (Ouspensky and Lossky, 1994). In contrast, the *Self-Portrait with Dogs* by Joanne (fig. 1.7) follows the rules much more exactly, and contains only one anomalous T-junction where the head of the dog at the bottom right joins the body.

Yet another type of anomalous denotation system is found in both icon paintings and Cubist paintings: one in which the normal direction of tonal contrast is reversed. The painting by Braque shown in fig. 1.10 provides an example. Not only is the table shown in inverted perspective (an anomalous drawing system), but the normal direction of tonal contrast in the painted apples is reversed (an anomalous denotation system). Instead of the highlights being painted in a light tone on a darker ground, the highlights here are represented by black areas of paint on a yellow and white ground (Gombrich, 1960/1988).

This reversal of the normal direction of tonal contrast is also found in icon paintings, but in a rather more subtle form. As is well known, photographic negatives look less natural and are more difficult to interpret than photographic positives, even though both kinds of pictures contain exactly the same amount of information. Similarly, though in a more subtle way, white line drawings on a dark ground look less natural than black line drawings on a light ground. This effect is often found in icon paintings in the form of lines painted in a light tone or gold on a darker ground. In Rublev's *The*

Holy Trinity, for example, some of the lines denoting occluding contours in the folds of the angels' garments are painted in dark lines on a lighter ground, but other lines are painted in light tones on a darker ground, so that the normal direction of tonal contrast is reversed.

Thus a number of drawing and denotation systems can be used to flatten the picture surface, and prevent the viewer from experiencing the picture as if it provided an image of the three-dimensional, material world. Chapter 10 lists some of the pictorial devices that can be used for this purpose.

But as well as flattening the picture surface, anomalous drawing and denotation systems can also be for expressive purposes. The linguist Noam Chomsky used ungrammatical sentences as a way of investigating the structure of language, but he also pointed out that there are "degrees of grammaticalness," and that some sentences that are not completely well formed, such as "misery loves company," can often be given a metaphorical or allusive interpretation (Chomsky, 1965/1972, pp. 148–160). Thorne (1972) argued that such sentences have often been used for poetic or expressive purposes, and that the recognition of deviant or ungrammatical structures forms an essential part of our response to poetry or poetic speech. Similarly, I shall argue in Chapter 11 that some painters have used anomalous structures for expressive purposes, and I shall illustrate this argument with detailed analyses of three pictures: *Leave-taking,* by the Greek vase painter known as the Achilles painter (fig. 11.3); *Noli me Tangere,* by the fourteenth-century Florentine painter known as the Master of the Lehman Crucifixion (color plate 4); and Paul Klee's *Naked on the Bed* (color plate 5). All these painters introduced false attachments into their paintings, apparently for expressive purposes, although they perform this function in very different ways.

Finally, in Chapter 12, I shall show how some twentieth-century artists have used anomalous pictorial structures as a way of investigating the nature of depiction itself. As I have already mentioned, Chomsky had used un-grammatical sentences in the 1950s as a way of investigating the formal properties of language, and in the late 1960s and early 1970s a number of early workers in the field of artificial intelligence adopted the same approach: the anomalous drawings shown in fig. 1.14 were produced as part of the attempt to understand the formal properties of pictures. This approach had, however, already been anticipated by a number of artists such as Juan Gris, René Magritte, and Paul Klee.

Fig. 1.15 shows a drawing entitled TOWER used by Guzman (1968), a pioneer in the automatic analysis of pictures by computer, as a test for his program SEE. The object of this program was to decide automatically, without recourse to human intuitions, which of the numbered regions belong together as faces of separate objects. As Guzman pointed out, this picture contains a number of what he called "nasty coincidences," and these include two instances of false attachments (at the junctions surrounded by regions 2,4,5,6, and 9,16,17,23). Guzman introduced these "nasty coincidences" deliberately, as a test for the power and flexibility of his program. When pictures contain configurations of this kind, they are less effective as representations because it is more difficult to see in them the three-dimensional shapes of the objects they represent. Would the presence of these nasty coincidences make it difficult for SEE to interpret the picture?

Fig. 1.16 shows that the deliberate inclusion of false attachments in a similar picture had been anticipated nearly forty years before by Paul Klee in his *Town with Watchtowers*, 1929. Very much the same kind of anomalies appear in this drawing as in the drawing by Guzman: the corner of one object appears directly on the corner of another object, two parallel lines are merged into one, and so on. It seems probable that Klee introduced these anomalies deliberately, partly for compositional reasons and partly as a way of investigating depiction itself. As he wrote in his Bauhaus notebooks, "I have carried out many experiments with laws and taken them as a foundation. But an artistic step is taken only when a complication arises" (Klee, 1961, p. 454). However, Klee was himself influenced by much earlier work

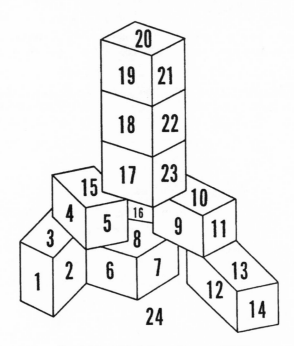

FIG. 1.15. *TOWER.* From Guzman (1968).

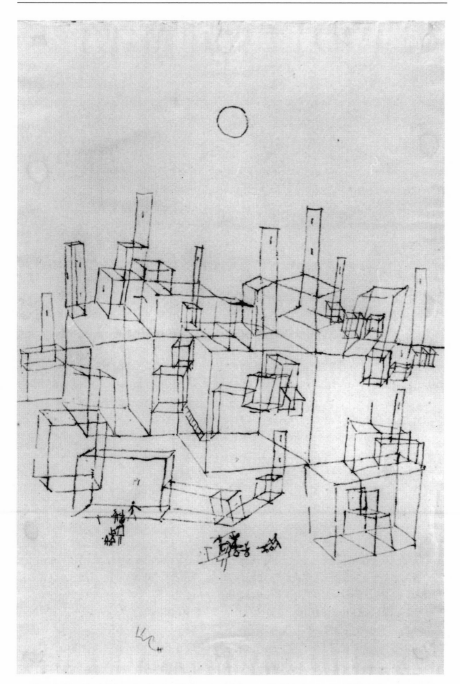

FIG. 1.16.   Paul Klee, *Stadt mit Wachttürmen (Town with Watchtowers)*, 1929. Ink on paper, 45.5 × 30.0 cm. Paul Klee-Stiftung, Kunstmuseum, Berne. Copyright Design and Artists Copyright Society 1997.

in scene perception: the diagrams in his Bauhaus notes closely resemble the diagrams illustrating perceptual effects in papers by the Gestalt psychologists Wertheimer and Fuchs (Teuber, 1976).

In Part 5, the last part of this book, I turn to two questions with which I began this chapter. Why do artists in different periods and cultures, and children of different ages, use different representational systems?

Drawings by older children are nearly always more effective as representations than drawings by younger children. Subjectively, the drawings of tables by the three groups of older children shown in fig. 1.9 are much more effective as representations of the shapes and spatial relations in the three-dimensional scene shown at (a) than the drawings by the three groups of younger children. Why is this? The answer is that the drawings by the older children are in oblique projection, naive perspective, or perspective, and thus show the table and the objects on it from a *general position*. Drawings by the younger children, in contrast, were in orthogonal projection or vertical oblique projection, and thus show the table from special positions. In addition, the drawings by the older children contained numerous T-junctions (marked here with asterisks) representing points of occlusion, whereas drawings by the younger children contained few, if any, such T-junctions.

Similarly, Joanne's *Self-Portrait with Dogs* (fig. 1.7) contains numerous instances of T- and end-junctions representing points of occlusion, and, consequently, it gives a vivid impression of three-dimensional shape. In contrast, the only T-junctions in the drawing by the five-year-old shown in fig. 1.12 do not represent points of occlusion but only the points where the legs are *attached* to the head/trunk. Consequently, the representation of shape in this drawing is ineffective.

Evidence of this kind suggests that what children are trying to do when they are learning to draw is produce pictures that are *more effective as shape representations*.[2] In order to do this, they have to learn to use more effective representational systems: that is, they have to acquire more effective drawing and denotation rules. In the drawings of tables shown in fig. 1.9, for example, the youngest children used a very simple rule: "Draw the front faces of objects as true shapes." This resulted in drawings in orthogonal projection, and the problem with this system is that it shows objects from a very special position. The next oldest group of children used a rather more complex rule: "Draw the front and top faces as true shapes and add them together." This resulted in drawings in vertical oblique projection, a system which still shows objects from a relatively special position. Moreover, this system is inherently ambiguous because vertical edges and side edges are represented by lines running in the same direction. In the next system in the developmental sequence, oblique projection, this ambiguity was resolved by using a much more complex rule: "Represent the front faces by true shapes, and the side edges by parallel oblique lines." This resulted in a much more effective representation because it shows the object from a general position, and allows the introduction of numerous T-junctions denoting points of occlusion. Finally, the two oldest groups of children used still more complex rules: "Represent the front faces by true shapes and the side edges by converging lines" (for naive perspective); and "Represent the front faces by true shapes and the side edges by lines converging to a central vanishing point" (for true perspective). This allowed these children to produce more effective representations, and at the same time to produce drawings whose geometry corresponded to that of the particular view which they were asked to draw.

Thus the rules used by the older children were much more complex than those used by younger children. These rules are not obvious, and acquiring them involves abandoning some of the earlier rules. For example, in order to learn to draw in oblique projection, children have to learn to use lines rather than regions as picture primitives, so that they can abandon the idea of representing all the faces of objects as true shapes. Presumably this is why children take so long to learn to draw.

A similar motive—the desire to produce pictures that are more effective as representations—seems to have prompted changes in styles of depiction during some periods of art history. For example, the earliest Greek vase paintings are pure silhouettes, rather like the rock drawing shown in fig. 1.5, and like these drawings appear to be based on regions as picture primitives. In the next phase of development, internal lines, painted in a lighter tone on the dark ground of the silhouette, were introduced in order to show internal details. However, the use of light lines on a darker ground in these black-figure paintings reversed the normal direction of tonal contrast for line drawings, and in the next phase a new technique, red-figure painting, made its appearance. In this technique, dark lines are painted on a lighter ground, still combining line drawing with silhouette but giving a more natural appearance to the paintings. Later paintings are either in this red-figure style, or are pure line drawings in the white-ground style. So far as the use of drawing systems is concerned, most Greek vase paintings are in orthogonal projection. In the earlier paintings, objects having plane faces, like tables or chairs, are shown from a special position in orthogonal projection. In the later paintings, such objects are shown either in foreshortened positions in orthogonal projection or in systems such as oblique projection or, in some rare cases, in naive perspective. As a result of the progressive discovery of these new drawing and denotation systems, the later Greek vase paintings provide more effective shape representations than the earlier paintings, and changes in Greek vase painting thus follow a systematic pattern of development directed toward this end.

Although the pattern of development in Greek vase painting is in many ways similar to the pattern of development in children's drawings, it is not necessary to explain this by supposing that children's drawing development recapitulates the course of art history in some evolutionary sense. What I am suggesting here is much more prosaic. Because children, and artists in some periods and cultures, have set out to solve the same problem—that of producing pictures that are more effective as representations—and because the human visual system sets such severe constraints on possible solutions to this problem, they have found very much the same solutions. Moreover, there are important differences in the patterns of development exemplified by children's drawings and Greek vase painting: children are accustomed, from an early age, to using pens or pencils that make dark marks on a light ground; whereas when the Greek vase painters started to use lines, they were obliged to use light lines within a dark silhouette. Consequently, the change from black-figure to red-figure painting has no counterpart in children's drawing development.

The effective representation of shape in pictures is not, however, the only function that pictorial systems can serve. Because pictures in some other periods and cultures have been intended to perform functions other than that of pure representation, they have been based on other combinations of drawing and denotation systems. In particular, artists in some periods and cultures have used anomalous drawing and denotation systems: systems that do not show possible views and subvert the normal rules that result in either an effective representation or a convincing illusion. Icon paintings and Byzantine mosaics provide particularly important examples of the use of anomalous pictorial systems because these systems appear to have been used during a period of well over a thousand years. I shall argue that these anomalous pictorial systems were used to serve quite specific functions: to enable icons to serve as images of the Incarnation, and to enable the icon painters to avoid the danger of idolatry by providing pictures in which Christ and his saints could be recognized, but in a form that belonged to another, spiritual world rather than the three-dimensional world of space and time.

Thus I shall argue that pictorial styles are not just arbitrarily different, in the way that English and Chinese are different. Nor is one style (the combination of perspective with an optical denotation system) better in some absolute sense, as nineteenth-century art historians believed. Instead, I shall argue that different representational styles—that is, different combinations of drawing and denotation systems—are suitable for different purposes, and that patterns of development—or in some cases lack of development—in both children's drawings and art history are determined by the different functions that these representational systems have to serve.

Part One

DRAWING SYSTEMS

CHAPTER TWO

Projection Systems

In Chapter 1, I introduced the idea of the projection systems as a basis for classifying the various ways in which the spatial relations between objects have been represented in pictures; and I also described Booker's distinction between the primary geometry of projection and the secondary geometry of the picture surface. In this chapter all the true projection systems are defined in terms of both primary and secondary geometry, and two further drawing systems are also described: naive perspective and inverted perspective. These two systems seem closely allied to the true projection systems— that is, to perspective, oblique projection, and so on—but they can in fact be defined only in terms of secondary geometry.[1]

A standard text on engineering drawing (British Standard 1192, 1969) defines projection as "the formal means adopted for representing the three-dimensional attributes of objects or arrangements on one or more planes of projection." The projection lines or rays are imagined as coming from objects in the scene, and these rays intersect a two-dimensional plane known as the plane of projection or picture plane. The geometry of these intersections forms the geometry of the picture.[2]

Three main types of projection systems are recognized in engineering drawing: perspective, oblique projection, and orthogonal projection (known in the United Kingdom as orthographic projection). In perspective projections the rays coming from objects in the scene converge to a point beyond the picture plane: this point is often identified with the eye of a viewer, and is referred to as the eye point or spectator point. The primary geometry of perspective thus corresponds in essence to the optical arrangement in a camera, or its predecessor the *camera obscura*.

In oblique projection the projection rays are parallel and intersect the picture plane at an oblique angle. This arrangement can never be fully realized optically, but the shadows thrown by the rays of the sun onto a flat plane set at an oblique angle approximate closely to oblique projections.

In orthogonal projections the rays are also parallel, but intersect the picture plane at right angles in both directions. Approximations to orthogonal projections can be obtained by using an ordinary camera fitted with a powerful telephoto lens, so that the rays from distant objects in the scene are nearly parallel and intersect the film at right angles.

These three main types of projection systems are then divided into subclasses according to the orientations of the objects represented relative to the plane of projection. In simple orthogonal projection, far and away the most commonly used system in engineering and architectural drawing, one of the principal faces of the object to be drawn—either the top, front, or side face—is normally set parallel to the picture plane. In the three subclasses of orthogonal projection recognized in engineering drawing—isometric, dimetric, and trimetric projection—the object to be drawn is shown in a foreshortened position: that is, its principal faces are set at oblique angles to the plane of projection.

In oblique projection the front face of the object to be drawn is always set parallel to the plane of projection, and in axonometric projection the top face is set parallel to the plane of projection. In these systems the object to be drawn is never normally shown in a foreshortened position, so the class of oblique projections has no subclasses.

Finally, in single-point perspective one of the principal faces is set parallel to the picture plane, while in the subclasses known as two-point and three-point perspective all three faces are inclined at an oblique angle to the picture plane. These definitions, framed in terms of primary geometry, lead to the classification scheme shown in fig. 2.1.

According to Booker (1963), however, definitions of the drawing systems given in terms of primary geometry have little practical significance or psychological reality. The modern method, described above, of defining the various drawing systems in terms of three-dimensional projective geometry was invented during the nineteenth century by textbook writers who wanted to give engineering drawing an air of authority by bringing it into line with Renaissance accounts of linear perspective. The idea of orthogonal projection as a variety of perspective with the object moved to an infinite distance away is a mathematical fiction, and engineers rarely, if ever, think of the system in this way. Instead, they think of orthogonal projection as the system in which the front, side, and top faces of objects are drawn as true shapes. That is, the regions representing these faces in the picture are the same shapes as the faces they represent, so that if the front face of an object is square it will be represented by a square region in the picture.

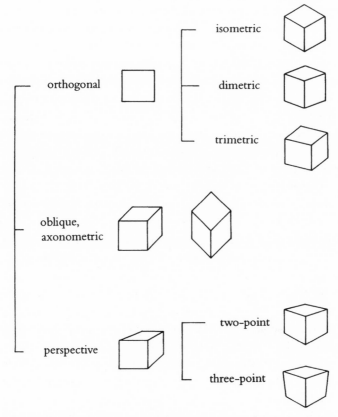

Fig. 2.1. Classification scheme for projection systems, based on primary geometry. Adapted from British Standard 1192 (1969).

Similarly, it was not until the late nineteenth century, when textbook writers felt obliged to fit every kind of drawing system into the format of projective geometry, that formal oblique projection appeared. It can be shown theoretically that a view in oblique projection can be obtained by projection using parallel rays inclined at an oblique angle to the plane of projection, but this kind of definition has never been shown to be of any practical use.

Moreover, defining the various projection systems in terms of their primary geometry leads to a classification scheme which seems counter-intuitive. In the scheme shown in fig. 2.1, which is based on definitions given in terms of primary geometry, drawings in isometric, dimetric, and trimetric projections, which show the three principal faces of a rectangular object, have to be defined as subclasses of drawings in orthogonal projection which show only one face. It would seem much more natural to assign drawings in isometric, dimetric, and trimetric projections, all of which show three principal faces of an object, and in which the orthogonals are parallel, to the same class as drawings in oblique and axonometric projections. In practice we recognize a drawing as being in one or other of the projection systems not by its primary geometry but by its secondary geometry: the number of faces shown in the drawing, and the directions of the orthogonals.

Engineers commonly speak of the drawings in the various projection systems as providing "views." This is true in the formal sense that the geometry of a picture in strict linear perspective corresponds to the geometry of a possible projection of a scene into what Marr (1982, p. 364) called the "frontal plane": a plane lying perpendicular to the line of sight. However, the correspondence between the geometry of the rays coming from a picture in perspective and the rays coming from a real scene holds good only if a picture in perspective is viewed from the correct spectator point.

If we accept the mathematical fiction of orthogonal projections as derived from objects situated at an infinite distance, then pictures in orthogonal projection, including the subclasses of isometric, dimetric, and trimetric projections, also provide possible views. The idea of pictures in oblique projection as providing possible views is perhaps a little more difficult to accept, because the directions of the projection rays, thought of as corresponding to the viewer's line of sight, would not intersect the frontal plane at right angles but at an oblique angle.

Thus we might want to question the psychological reality of referring to pictures in the various projection systems as providing possible views, in the sense of corresponding to what we actually experience when we view a scene. This issue is further complicated by the operation of the perceptual constancies. The tendency to see the face of an object as a true shape regardless of the viewing angle is referred to as shape constancy, and the tendency to see an object as its true size regardless of the viewing distance is referred to as size constancy. When we see an object at a distance, we might judge its size in one of three ways: first, according to its *perspective* size, that is, according to the geometry of perspective, seeing it as smaller as the distance from the viewer increases. Second, if size constancy were perfect, we might judge an object by its *object* size: that is, its true size in an object-centered description, independent of any particular point of view. In this event, objects would not appear smaller the further away they were. Third, we might compromise, and see objects as smaller at a distance, but not as much smaller as projective geometry dictates. This last possibility seems to correspond most closely to our actual experience. The same sort of thing seems to hold true for shape constancy: we see the shape of a circle, set at an angle to the line of sight, as a compromise between its true shape as a circle and its projected shape.

Thus, for all these reasons, we might want to question the psychological validity of equating the geometry of pictures in the various projection systems with the geometry of views of scenes as we *experience* such views. In this and the following four chapters, however, I shall try as far as possible to avoid psychological issues of this kind; instead, I shall give a purely formal account of the various drawing and denotation systems and discuss the question of the actual processes which underlie picture production and perception in Chapter 8.

The three main projection systems can also be defined in terms of secondary geometry: that is, the geometry of the picture surface. Definitions of this kind need not involve any references to mapping from *views,* although the pictures resulting from such operations may well provide possible views, in the engineering sense of corresponding to possible projections. The disadvantage of defining the projection systems in this way is that the definitions apply only to drawings of rectangular objects.

This kind of approach leads to the classification scheme shown in fig. 2.2. In orthogonal projection the front face of an object such as a cube is represented by a single region whose shape corresponds to the shape of the face to be represented. In oblique projection, and systems such as isometric and axonometric projection, the directions of either one or two edges of a cube are mapped into parallel oblique lines on the picture surface, and in perspective these edges—or some of these edges—are mapped into converging lines on the picture surface. Intuitively, this classification seems much more natural than the scheme based on primary geometry shown in fig. 2.1. For example, in the scheme shown in fig. 2.2, oblique projection, axonometric projection, and isometric, dimetric, and trimetric projection, all of which show three faces of the cube, are assigned to the same class, and orthogonal projection is reserved for drawings in which only one face is shown. This leaves a conceptual gap in the classification scheme for drawings showing *two* faces, and drawings of this kind are found in practice in children's drawings and pictures in non-Western cultures, although the system is not used in engineering drawing. Drawings of this kind, shown using dotted lines in the classification scheme, are described as being in horizontal oblique projection and vertical oblique projection (Dubery and Willats, 1972, 1983).[3]

In addition, this scheme seems to fit the developmental sequence found in children's drawings of rectangular objects. That is, the sequence of orthogonal projection, vertical oblique projection, oblique projection, and perspective, in which edges in the third dimension are first unrepresented and then successively represented by vertical lines, parallel oblique lines, and finally converging lines, corresponds to the developmental sequence found in children's drawings of rectangular objects such as tables (fig. 1.9).

Thus the projection systems can be defined in two different ways, in terms of either primary or secondary geometry. The following illustrations are intended to familiarize the reader with most of the common projection systems as they appear in pictures from a variety of disciplines, periods, and cultures, and to give examples of the different ways in which these systems

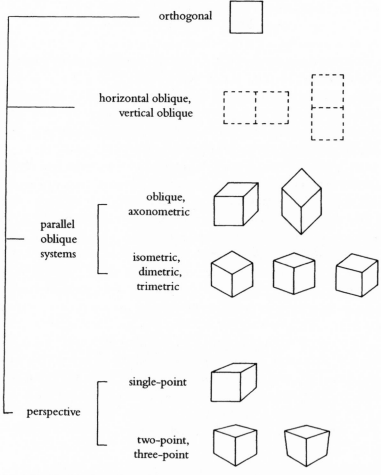

FIG. 2.2. Classification scheme for projection systems, based on secondary geometry.

may be defined. An account of the projection systems based only on primary geometry would, logically, begin by describing perspective as the most general case and then go on to describe the other, parallel, systems as special cases. However, because I shall argue in subsequent chapters that picture production is usually best described in terms of the rules of secondary geometry, I shall begin by describing systems like orthogonal projection and vertical and horizontal oblique projection which can be defined in terms of relatively simple rules, and then go on to describe systems like perspective which are based on more complex rules.

Orthogonal Projection

Defined in terms of primary geometry, orthogonal projection is the system in which the projection rays are parallel and intersect the picture plane at right angles in both directions (fig. 2.3). Pictures in orthogonal projection thus approximate to photographs taken with a powerful telephoto lens, like the newspaper photograph shown in fig. 2.4.

When orthogonal projection is defined in this way, there is no restriction on the shape of the object to be represented, or its orientation relative to the picture plane. It happens that the jumbo jet shown in fig. 2.4 has been photographed roughly end-on, but this is more or less a matter of chance. The air-conditioning truck, in contrast, appears to be set at an oblique angle to the picture plane: that is, it was photographed in a foreshortened position

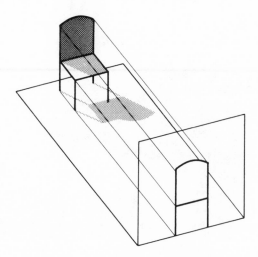

FIG. 2.3. Orthogonal projection: primary geometry. Copyright Fred Dubery and John Willats 1972.

relative to the camera. By convention, however, the principal axes of objects drawn in orthogonal projection are always aligned with the picture plane, as they are in fig. 2.3. As a result, the front, side, or top faces of rectangular objects are always projected as true shapes.

In terms of secondary geometry, orthogonal projection can thus be defined as the system in which the front, side, or top faces of objects are drawn as true shapes. For example, in the child's drawing of a table shown in fig. 1.9c, the front faces of the table, the box, and the radio are all drawn as true shapes, and in the child's drawing of a house shown in fig. 2.5 the front face of the house is drawn as a true shape. Alternatively, orthogonal projection can also be defined as the system in which vertical edges in the scene are mapped into vertical edges on the picture surface, and horizontal (side-to-side) edges in the scene are mapped into horizontal edges on the picture surface. Edges in the third (front-to-back) dimension in the scene are ignored. A characteristic feature of this system is that the ground plane is represented by a single line.

In orthogonal projection the dimensions of objects in the scene are defined relative to the principal axes of the object itself, rather than to any particular direction of view. Thus an engineer producing a drawing in orthogonal projection will begin with a list (implict or explicit) of the dimensions of the object in an object-centered description, such as the height of the footplate above the rails and the diameter of the boiler as specified in the drawing of the locomotive shown in fig. 1.4. Corresponding scale dimensions in the picture are defined relative to the vertical and

As the hijack bargaining goes on under the sweltering sun...

An armed guerrilla stands guard (right) as an airfield technician links up the supply line to the hijacked Jumbo from an air conditioning truck

FIG. 2.4. Newspaper photograph of a hijacked aircraft. Courtesy of *Express Newspapers*.

horizontal axes of the picture surface. The secondary geometry of the picture can thus be thought of as arising from rules mapping directions and dimensions in object-centered descriptions into the coordinate system of the picture surface. The mapping rules for orthogonal projection are very simple: "Map vertical dimensions in the scene into vertical dimensions in the picture, and horizontal (side-to-side) dimensions in the scene into horizontal dimensions in the picture."[4] If these mapping rules are applied to an object-centered description, the output will be a picture in orthogonal projection.

If the object to be drawn is rectangular, these dimensions will correspond to the dimensions of edges, like the edges of the coal bunker at the rear of the locomotive shown in fig. 1.4. Many parts of the locomotive, however, are either cylindrical (the boiler) or have a circular cross-section (the chimney and dome). Applying the mapping rule given above to such forms will result in a drawing corresponding to the shape of the cross-section.

It is, however, difficult to apply mapping rules based on secondary geometry to more complex forms such as the human figure, especially if the principal axes of such forms are not aligned with the picture plane. The table

Fɪɢ. 2.5. Child's drawing of a house in orthogonal projection. Courtesy of Claire Golomb (1992) *The Child's Creation of a Pictorial World* and the Regents of the University of California.

and the couch in the Greek vase painting shown in fig. 1.3 are drawn in orthogonal projection, and the ground plane is represented by a single line, like the ground plane in the drawing of the locomotive in fig. 1.4. The cylindrical columns at the ends of the couch are shown side-on, with their dimensions, like those of the locomotive boiler, corresponding to a longitudinal cross-section. When it comes to the drawings of the figures, the artist has tried as far as possible to avoid any foreshortening. Each part of the body is shown with its longest axis parallel to the picture plane, so that the shapes of the occluding contours correspond to the outlines of longitudinal cross-sections. Whereas the head is shown in profile, the upper part of the chest has been swung round to show a front view. Although there are differences in the ways in which Egyptian and Greek painters represented the human figure, distortions of this general kind are common in both Egyptian wall paintings and early Greek vase painting.

Horizontal Oblique Projection

Fig. 2.6 shows the primary geometry of horizontal oblique projection. In this system the projection rays are parallel and intersect the picture plane at an oblique angle in the horizontal plane. The front face of the object to be depicted is set parallel to the picture plane, and as a result this front face is projected as a true shape; and if the angle between the projection rays and the picture plane is 45°, the side face will also be projected as a true shape. If this angle is greater than 45°, the side face will be foreshortened.

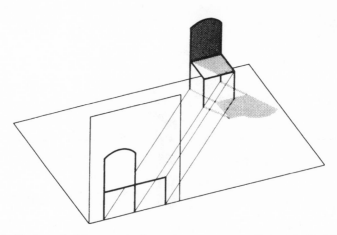

FIG. 2.6. Horizontal oblique projection: primary geometry. Copyright Fred Dubery and John Willats 1972.

This primary geometry is, however, of only theoretical interest. It would be difficult, though perhaps not impossible, to take a photograph corresponding to a horizontal oblique projection, because it would be difficult to arrange matters so that the light fell on the film at an oblique angle. Similarly, pictures in this system provide only rough approximations to views. When we look at an object we turn our eyes so that the principal line of sight is directed toward it; and if the object is at a considerable distance away, so that the light rays are nearly parallel, they will intersect the frontal plane at an angle which is close to a right angle. If we are looking at a rectangular object such as a cube, we will see either the front face only as a true shape (as in orthogonal projection), or, if the object is turned through 45°, we will see foreshortened views of both the side and front faces—subject to the effects of shape constancy, however.

Pictures in true horizontal oblique projection are thus more naturally defined in terms of secondary geometry. One way of doing this is to say that horizontal directions in the picture are used to represent both side-to-side

Fig. 2.7. Paul Cézanne, *Still Life with a Commode,* c. 1887–1888. Oil on canvas, 65.1 × 80.8 cm. Bequest—Collection of Maurice Wertheim, Class of 1906. Courtesy of the Fogg Art Museum, Harvard University Art Museums.

and front-to-back directions in the scene. A simpler definition, which only works for strictly rectangular objects, is to say that both the front and side faces of objects are represented as true shapes. Consequently, the mapping rule for this system, applied to object-centered descriptions of rectangular objects, is: "Add a front face to a side face." Horizontal oblique projections are common in folk art (fig. 8.12), icon paintings (fig. 8.13), and Byzantine art (fig. 14.9); occasional examples of the use of horizontal oblique projection can also be found in Egyptian painting (Dubery and Willats, 1983), Chinese painting (fig. 10.6), and early Italian paintings (Willats, 1990). In Cézanne's *Still Life with a Commode* (fig. 2.7), the commode appears to be in horizontal oblique projection, with both the side and front faces drawn as true shapes. A close inspection of the painting, however, shows that the bottom edges of the side of the commode slant upwards: as is so often the case in Cézanne's paintings, one drawing system is disguised as another.

Horizontal oblique projection is common in naive landscape paintings and children's drawings of houses. Fig. 2.8 shows an American folk painting in which each building individually could be described as being in horizontal oblique projection; however, it could equally well be argued that these

Residence of Mr E. R. Jones. Town Dodgeville. Wis. 1881.

FIG. 2.8. Paul A. Seifert, *Residence of Mr. E. R. Jones,* 1881. Watercolor, 54.6 × 69.9 cm. New York State Historical Association, Cooperstown, New York.

FIG. 2.9. Child's drawing of a house in horizontal oblique projection. Courtesy of Claire Golomb (1992) *The Child's Creation of a Pictorial World* and the Regents of the University of California.

buildings are not in true horizontal oblique projection, but are simply shown as foreshortened views. It is worth comparing this painting with fig. 6.1a, which shows a *photograph* of a foreshortened view of a house.

Drawing the front and side faces as true shapes and adding them together only works properly for objects that are strictly rectangular. The child's drawing of a house shown in fig. 2.9 contains a characteristic error which suggests that the roof has, as far as possible, been drawn as a true shape; as a result, the side edge of the roof at the right has been drawn using a vertical line. The same kind of error also appears in the folk art painting of a house shown in fig. 8.12.

Vertical Oblique Projection

In vertical oblique projection, defined in terms of primary geometry, the projection rays are parallel and intersect the picture plane at an oblique angle in the vertical plane. The object to be drawn is positioned so that its front face is parallel to the picture plane. If the angle between the picture plane

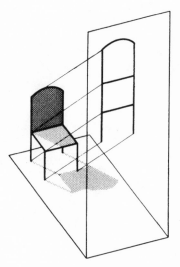

FIG. 2.10. Vertical oblique projection: primary geometry. Copyright Fred Dubery and John Willats 1972.

and the projection rays is 45°, both the front and top faces will be projected as true shapes (fig. 2.10).

In pictures based on the primary geometry of horizontal oblique projection, the forms appear to be drawn out sideways. In pictures in vertical oblique projection, the forms appear to be drawn out in a vertical direction: fig. 2.11 shows this effect in a drawing of a cup in vertical oblique projection,

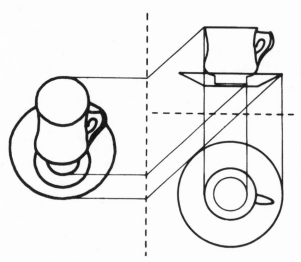

Fig. 2.11. Drawing of a cup in vertical oblique projection. Copyright Fred Dubery and John Willats 1972.

produced as an auxiliary view from drawings in orthogonal projection. In this drawing the projection lines on the surface intersect the picture plane (represented by dotted lines) at an angle of 45°. The top of the cup is drawn as a true shape, and the body of the cup appears to be elongated in a vertical direction. This drawing may be compared with the images of the glass, the cups, and other cylindrical objects which appear in Juan Gris's *Breakfast*, 1914 (color plate 6 and fig. 12.2).

In terms of secondary geometry, drawings of rectangular objects such as tables may be produced by applying the rule: "Draw the top face and the front face as true shapes and add them together." Drawings of tables in vertical oblique projection are common in Cubist still lifes, and in paintings of this type the table top is drawn as a true shape. The table shown in Cézanne's *Still Life with a Commode* (fig. 2.7) may perhaps be regarded as a precursor of such paintings; here the orthogonals converge slightly, so that the drawing of the table approximates more closely to a possible view, albeit a view from a considerable distance.

Paintings in approximations to vertical oblique projection are also fairly common in Indian art: in the Indian miniature painting shown in fig. 2.12,

FIG. 2.12. *Raj Dip Chand of Bilaspur Listening to a Group of Musicians,* c. 1660. Victoria and Albert Museum, London.

Fɪɢ. 2.13. Claude Rogers, *The Hornby Train,* 1951–1953. Oil on canvas, 142.2 × 177.8 cm. Fischer Fine Art, London.

the carpet—which of course lies in the ground plane—is drawn as a true shape. However, although the upper parts of the figures are drawn as if from the side, the lower parts are partially foreshortened. Similarly, the hookah in the middle of the painting is shown in a foreshortened view rather than as a true vertical oblique projection, while the cup below it is drawn more or less as a side view. This painting may be compared with the modern English painting shown in fig. 2.13. Again, the carpet is shown as a true shape, but the picture as a whole approximates to a possible view taken from a considerable distance, and a comparison between the size of the woman and the sizes of the children in the painting shows that there is a slight change of scale with distance.

Oblique Projection

Fig. 2.14 shows the primary geometry of oblique projection. In this system the projection rays are parallel and intersect the picture plane at an oblique angle in both the horizontal and vertical directions. The front face of the object is parallel to the picture plane, as it is with all the other systems discussed so far, and is projected as a true shape.

Pictures of rectangular objects in oblique projection may be produced by applying the rule: "Draw the front face as a true shape and represent the orthogonals by oblique lines." As before, this rule must be understood as applying to an object-centered description: the front face is drawn as a true shape defined relative to its own coordinate system, and the oblique lines represent edges at right angles to the front face.

Oblique projection has the advantage that it gives a strong impression of three-dimensional shape, and yet is easier to draw than true perspective, partly because all the oblique lines are parallel and run in the same direction, and partly because all objects are drawn to the same scale, irrespective of their distance from the viewer. Fig. 8.14 shows the kind of muddle that painters were liable to get into during the transition from the earlier, medieval use of oblique projection to the use of perspective. Perhaps the relative simplicity of the rules of secondary geometry for producing pictures in oblique projection, compared with the rules for perspective, is the reason why this system is found in the art of so many periods and cultures. The system has also often been used for more prosaic purposes, like the illustrations which the nineteenth-century American craftsman Henry Lapp used to show his furniture designs (fig. 2.15).

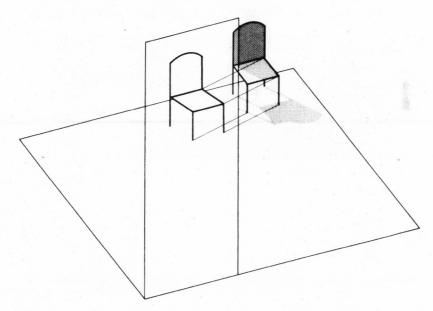

FIG. 2.14. Oblique projection: primary geometry. Copyright Fred Dubery and John Willats 1972.

Fig. 2.15. Henry Lapp, *A Desk and a Table*, Pennsylvania German, nineteenth century. Watercolor and ink, 11.4 × 20.3 cm. The Titus C. Geesey Collection, Philadelphia Museum of Art.

In Chinese painting, oblique projection became the standard way of depicting objects such as houses or tables and chairs, and fig. 1.2 shows a detail from a twelfth-century scroll painting in which a group of buildings is shown in a strict version of this system. The use of oblique projection for whole scenes is unusual in Chinese painting, however. More often, isolated houses or small groups of houses in oblique projection are set in rural landscapes in perspective. Many of the Japanese woodcuts of the seventeenth and eighteenth centuries (*ukiyo-e* art) are drawn in oblique projection, although an informal version of isometric projection is probably almost as common, for both whole scenes and individual objects.

Oblique projection can appear in various guises. The front face is always drawn as a true shape, and the angle between the oblique orthogonals is usually about 45°, although this can vary (compare the directions of the orthogonals in the two drawings of furniture shown in fig. 2.15). The scale of the orthogonals can also vary, and two varieties of oblique projection are recognized in engineering drawing. In *cavalier oblique projection* the oblique lines representing edges in the third dimension are drawn (to scale) as true lengths. This has the advantage that the lengths of edges in the third dimension can be measured directly from the drawing. Subjectively, however, these edges then look too long. *Cabinet oblique projection* is similar to cavalier oblique projection, but the receding edges are drawn to half scale, giving a more natural appearance. In artists' pictures the scale used for the orthogonals is usually somewhere between these two extremes.

Isometric and Axonometric Projections

There are a number of other parallel projection systems, but for our purposes the two most important are *isometric projection* and *axonometric projection*. Pictures of objects in these two systems look very much alike, and the rules of secondary geometry by which they can be produced are very similar; but in terms of their primary geometry the two systems are quite different.

Fig. 2.16 compares the primary geometry of axonometric projection with that of isometric projection. In terms of its primary geometry, isometric projection (fig. 2.16a) is a variety of orthogonal projection: the projection rays are parallel and intersect the picture plane at right angles. It differs from orthogonal projection only in that the object is shown in a foreshortened position relative to both the horizontal and vertical axes. This is equivalent to viewing a cube along the length of one of its longest diagonals. With the object in this position, all the edges appear equally foreshortened, and in

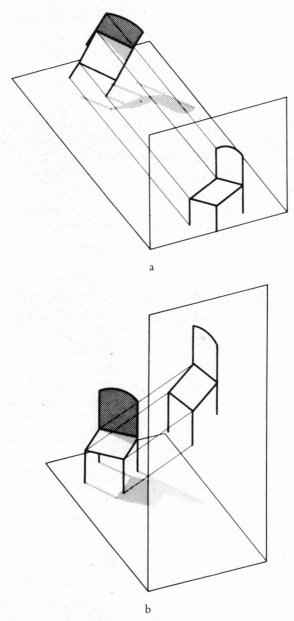

a

b

FIG. 2.16. Comparison of the primary geometry of (a) isometric projection and (b) axonometric projection. Copyright Fred Dubery and John Willats 1972.

engineering working drawings the scale is arranged so that all the edges are drawn as true (scale) lengths.

In contrast, axonometric projection (fig. 2.16b) is, in terms of its primary geometry, a variety of vertical oblique projection. The projection rays are parallel and intersect the picture plane at an angle of 45° in the vertical plane, as they do in vertical oblique projection. In axonometric projection, however, the object is turned through an angle of 45° about a vertical axis. With the object in this position, the top face is projected as a true shape, and the vertical edges are projected as true lengths.

Defined in terms of their secondary geometry, however, both these systems may be regarded as alternative forms of oblique projection. The rule for drawing rectangular objects in isometric projection is: "Represent the side and front edges by oblique lines at an angle of 30° to the horizontal, and draw all the edges as true lengths." The corresponding rule for axonometric projection is: "Represent the side and front edges by oblique lines at an angle of 45° to the horizontal, and draw all the edges as true lengths." Defined in this way, the two systems differ only in the angle between the oblique lines and the horizontal. Another way of defining axonometric projection is to say: "Draw the top face (or the plan) as a true shape at an oblique angle to the picture surface, and add the verticals as true lengths."

Isometric projection as a formal system was introduced in the nineteenth century by a Cambridge engineer and mathematician, the Rev. William Farish, in an attempt to make the complex engineering drawings of the industrial revolution, like the drawing of a steam boat engine shown in fig. 2.17, more understandable: that is, more effective as representations in the sense defined in Chapter 1 (Booker, 1963). The advantage of isometric projection for this purpose, which it shares with oblique projection and axonometric projection, is that it provides a more general, and therefore more pictorial, view than drawings in orthogonal projection, and yet all the rectangular edges can still be drawn as true lengths. An additional advantage of isometric projection is that objects drawn in this system, particularly cylindrical objects, look more natural and less distorted than they would in either oblique projection or axonometric projection.

Axonometric projection has been widely used for architectural drawings, particularly in the latter half of the twentieth century (fig. 2.18). When the system is used for this purpose, the plan of the building is first drawn as a true shape. The paper is then taken off the drawing board and replaced at an oblique angle, usually, but not necessarily, 45°. Vertical edges are then drawn as true lengths. Just as drawings in cavalier oblique projection appear to exaggerate the apparent lengths of the side edges of rectangular objects, so drawings in axonometric projection appear to exaggerate their vertical dimensions.

The use of axonometric projection for architectural drawings was popularized by the engineer and historian Auguste Choisy at the end of the nineteenth century (Blau and Kaufman, 1989). In the 1920s the system was taken up by Le Corbusier (1923/1981) and Theo van Doesburg along with other members of the De Stijl group (Blau and Kaufman, 1989), and it seems likely that Mondrian took his diamond-shaped canvases from the same source. Axonometric projection was probably the most commonly used system in Cubist paintings: Juan Gris's *Breakfast* (color plate 6) provides a particularly good example, and the way in which the cups, glasses, and other

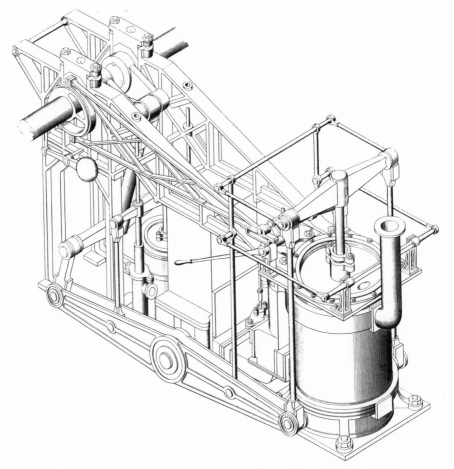

FIG. 2.17. *Steam Boat Engine,* nineteenth century. From Tredgold (1838).

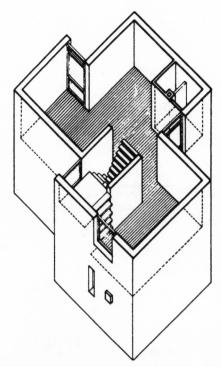

F_IG_. 2.18. James Stirling, *House in North London*, 1953. Courtesy of Michael Wilford and Partners.

cylindrical objects are drawn illustrates the close relationship between this system and vertical oblique projection.

Perspective

Perspective is so well known as a system, and so many books have been written on the subject, that it is hardly necessary to provide many examples. The main point I wish to make here is that perspective—like all the other projection systems that provide possible views—can be defined in two different ways: that is, in terms of both primary and secondary geometry.

The primary geometry of perspective is most naturally defined in terms of the intersection between rays of light from the scene and a picture plane, and this picture plane can be thought of as corresponding to the ground glass screen in a *camera obscura,* or the plane of the film in a modern camera. Fig. 2.19 shows Vermeer's *The Music Lesson,* a painting which, in common with many of Vermeer's paintings, may have been produced with the help of a *camera obscura,* the forerunner of the modern camera. *Camera obscura* means, literally, a darkened room, and Kemp (1992) suggests that the room itself in which the paintings were made may have been used as a *camera obscura.* An image of the scene to be painted would have been thrown onto a paper screen at the end of the darkened room using a convex lens, and the outlines of this projected image would then have been traced on the paper. These outlines would then have been transferred onto the painting surface by one of the standard methods, such as pricking through the paper. Alternatively,

FIG. 2.19. Johannes Vermeer, *The Music Lesson (A Lady at the Virginals),* c. 1665–1670. Oil on canvas, 73.7 × 64.0 cm. The Royal Collection, Her Majesty Queen Elizabeth II.

Vermeer may have either laid some of the preliminary colors directly over an image projected onto the surface of the canvas, or traced over the outlines of this image using white lead paint (Anfam, Beal, Bowes, et al., 1987).

Perspective can also be defined in terms of rules mapping the locations of primitives in an object-centered description into the coordinate system of the picture surface. The first description of a construction resulting in a picture in true linear perspective—sometimes called "artificial" or "scientific" perspective (White, 1967)—was given by Alberti in his *Della pittura,* written in 1436 (Spencer, 1966). Alberti called his construction the *costruzione legittima.* Fig. 2.20 illustrates a perspective construction similar to the *costruzione legittima* taken from the famous book on perspective by Jan Vredeman de Vries. All the tiles on the floor, ceiling, and walls are representations derived from squares in an object-centered description. De Vries gives few explicit instructions for producing the types of perspective displayed in his illustrations, but the basic principles which he used seem quite clear. The scale dimensions of the tiles would have been marked out on the base line, and then the horizon line, corresponding to the eye level of the artist and the figures in the composition, would have been drawn in at an appropriate scale distance above the base line. The central vanishing point, and the distance points to either side of it, would then have been established on the horizon line. The distances between these distance points and the

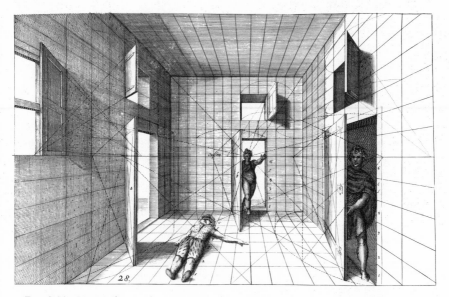

FIG. 2.20. Jan Vredeman de Vries, *Perspective,* 1604 (plate 28 in Vredeman de Vries, 1604–1605/1968).

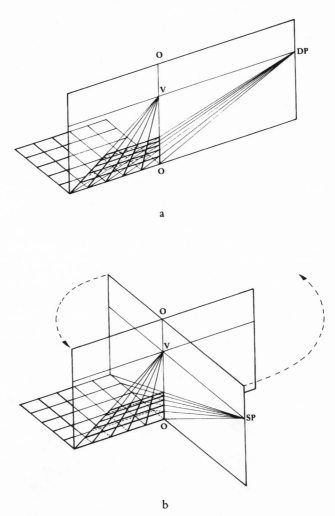

a

b

Fig. 2.21. (a) A construction similar to Alberti's *costruzione legittima* showing the relation between the vanishing point V and the distance point DP. (b) A diagram showing how the secondary geometry of the *costruzione legittima* is related to the primary geometry of perspective. The spectator point SP, corresponding to the position of the eye of the artist or viewer, becomes the distance point DP when the plane containing SP and V is folded back into the picture surface; consequently, the distance between the distance point and the vanishing point corresponds to the distance between the eye of the artist or viewer and the picture plane. Copyright Fred Dubery and John Willats 1972.

central vanishing point correspond to the distance between the artist or viewer and the picture plane. The central vanishing point then provides the point to which the orthogonals (in this case the side edges of the tiles) converge, and the distance points provide the vanishing points for the diagonals of the squares. These construction lines are obvious in the drawing shown in fig. 2.20. Fig. 2.21 shows why this construction leads to a drawing in true perspective: the lines from the distance points on the surface of the paper in fig. 2.21a correspond to light rays projected from the edges of the tiles to the spectator point in the three-dimensional scene shown in fig. 2.21b, and their intersections establish the positions of the transverse edges of the tiles in the plane of the picture.

Naive Perspective

Alberti's *costruzione legittima* was intended to replace earlier and cruder workshop rules which did not result in pictures in true perspective: the rule that the depth of each successive tile in a representation of a tiled pavement should be reduced by one-third, for example.

An example of an even cruder rule is Cennino Cennini's famous advice on how to paint pictures in perspective:

> And put in the buildings by this uniform system: that the moldings which you make at the top of the building should slant downward from the edge next to the roof; the molding in the middle of the building, halfway up the face, must be quite level and even; the molding at the base of the building underneath must slope upward, in the opposite sense to the upper molding, which slants downward. (Cennino d'Andrea Cennini, fifteenth century/1954, p. 57)

Applying this rule will result in a painting like Giotto's painting of a building shown in fig. 2.22a. The directions of the main orthogonals are shown in fig. 2.22b, and, in accordance with Cennini's rule, the moldings at the top of the building slope downwards and those at the bottom slope upwards, while the moldings in the middle are level. Cennini regarded himself as a direct heir of the Giotto tradition (Kemp, 1992). Applying this rule results in a picture in which the orthogonals converge, but not to a single coherent vanishing point.

It seems natural to think of Cennini's rule as being applied to an object-centered description, especially if the building is an imaginary one rather than a real one. The front faces of the building are drawn first as true shapes, and then the orthogonals, representing the "moldings" of the building in the third dimension in an object-centered description, are drawn according to the dictates of the rule. Such a rule is only a step away from the rule for drawing objects in oblique projection: in Giotto's painting, as in many similar early Renaissance paintings, the top of the building is, in effect, drawn in oblique projection with the orthogonals sloping downwards, and the bottom of the building is drawn in oblique projection with the orthogonals sloping upwards. It is, however, possible to think of a similar rule as being applied to a *view* of a building: instead of the directions of edges in the visual field being mapped accurately, those edges above eye level which appear to slope downwards in the visual field are simply mapped into parallel lines sloping downwards, and those edges which appear to slope upwards in the visual field are mapped into parallel lines sloping upwards.

Fig. 2.23 shows an eighteenth-century British painting which seems to have been based on a similar rule, although here the orthogonals on the left slope inwards to the right, and the orthogonals on the right slope inwards toward the left. The flower bed on the right is in almost pure oblique projection, and this, coupled with the fact that the artist would have been

FIG. 2.22. (a) Giotto, *Painting of a Building* (detail of *The Dream of the Palace and Arms*), c. 1297–1300. Assisi, Upper Church of San Francesco. (b) The heavy lines show the directions of the orthogonals.

FIG. 2.23. *Ladymead House, Walcot, Bath.* British, oil on panel, early eighteenth century, 68.2 × 98.1 cm. Victoria Art Gallery, Bath. Courtesy of Bath City Council.

unable to view the scene from such a height, suggests that the rule was applied to an object-centered description.

In the experiment which I described in Chapter 1, children were asked to draw a real table from a fixed viewpoint. Thus the drawing system in the child's drawing in fig. 1.9f, which was assigned to the class of drawings in naive perspective, can be described in one of two ways. The left half of the table, including the box, can be thought of as being in oblique projection, but with the orthogonals sloping to the upper right, while the right half can also be thought of as being in oblique projection, but with the orthogonals sloping toward the upper left. Described in this way, the drawing has been derived from an object-centered description. Alternatively, however, the drawing can be thought of as a mapping from viewer-centered description, with the apparent shape of the table top modified by the effects of shape and size constancy. Without some additional evidence it is difficult, if not impossible, to know which is the more appropriate way of defining the projection system in this drawing.

Inverted Perspective

In theory at least it would be possible to provide a definition of *inverted perspective* given in terms of primary geometry. In normal perspective the picture plane lies between the object or scene and the eye of the viewer, and the projection rays correspond to rays of light which pass through the picture plane as they would through a window. If the eye is kept fixed, a line traced round the outlines of the object as it appears through this window will correspond to a picture of the object in perspective. If this relation is reversed, so that the object lies between the point of projection and the picture plane on one side of the picture plane, and the eye of the viewer is on the other side of the picture plane, the projection rays will throw an image in inverted perspective onto the picture plane. However, such a definition is not of much practical consequence, because the point of convergence of the projection rays does not correspond to the position of a possible viewer.

Inverted perspective makes an occasional appearance in Cubist paintings (fig. 1.10) and Chinese and Japanese art, but it is very frequently found in Byzantine art and Orthodox icon paintings (color plate 1). The Byzantine manuscript illustrations of the Gospels shown in figs. 2.24 and 2.25 display several varieties of inverted perspective. In fig. 2.24 the seat on which St. Luke is sitting, the footstool, and the desk are all drawn in variants of oblique projection: in the seat and the footstool the orthogonals diverge, whereas in the desk the orthogonals of the top converge while those of the side diverge. In addition, the orthogonals of the seat and the footstool run off to the left, whereas those of the desk run off to the right, so that the orthogonals of the scene as a whole diverge.

The illustration of St. Mark's Gospel shown in fig. 2.25, painted perhaps some fifty years later, clearly draws on a similar iconography, but here the seat and the desk have been combined to make a table in which the top, front, and two sides are shown together. The footstool shows yet another variant of divergent perspective: an alternative form of isometric projection with the orthogonals diverging.

Western children around the age of 10 years very often produce drawings of cubes whose geometry corresponds to that of inverted perspective (fig. 8.3, class 5), and Court (1990) in a study of rural Kenyan children found that inverted perspective was one of the most commonly used systems for drawings of tables by older children in that group (fig. 2.26).

In spite of its name, the most natural way of defining inverted perspective would seem to be as a variant of oblique projection. Instead of the orthogonals being parallel, however, as they are in oblique projection, there is a tendency for the orthogonals to diverge, either within individual objects or in the picture as a whole. It is difficult to think of pictures in inverted perspective as being derived from views, especially in cases like the drawing

FIG. 2.24. *The Four Gospels, Luke,* 1380. Byzantine, Selymbria(?), manuscript, black and red ink on paper, 28.5 × 20.0 cm. The Art Museum, Princeton University, Museum purchase, Caroline G. Mather Fund.

Fɪɢ. 2.25. *Bifolio from a Gospel Book: Mark,* first quarter of the fifteenth century. Byzantine, vellum manuscript, 20.7 × 15.0 cm. The Art Museum, Princeton University, Bequest of Professor Albert Mathias Friend, Jr., Class of 1915.

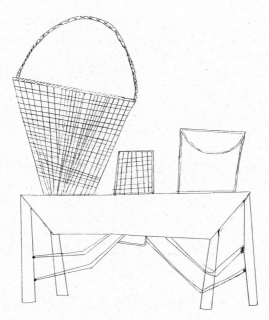

FIG. 2.26. Yerpene Lekerpeet (15-year-old girl), *Drawing of a Table*. Samburu, Kenya.
Courtesy of Elsbeth Court.

of the desk in fig. 2.25 or the child's drawing of a table shown in fig. 2.26,
where more than three principal faces of an object are represented. Instead,
it seems most natural to define this system in terms of a rule of secondary
geometry applied to an object-centered description: in most examples the
front face is drawn as a true shape, and edges in the third dimension are
represented by diverging lines.

CHAPTER THREE

Topology and Extendedness

Topological Transformations

In addition to defining the spatial relations in pictures in terms of projective geometry, the other main way of defining the drawing systems is in terms of topological transformations. Topology is often described as "rubber sheet" geometry. If a figure is printed on a rubber sheet and the sheet is stretched or twisted, basic spatial relations such as proximity and enclosure will remain unchanged, although the distances between the marks may change and straight lines may not remain straight. These very basic spatial relations form the subject of topological geometry.

Figures or shapes are said to be topologically equivalent ("homeo-morphs") if they share the same topological properties. For example, a circle and a square are topologically equivalent because in both figures the outline is closed and separates the inside of the figure from the outside in two-dimensional space. Similarly, a closed box and a hollow rubber ball are topologically equivalent because the surface of each separates the inside of the shape from the outside in three-dimensional space.

There is an extensive literature on projective geometry as a basis for depiction, but although some pictures, such as the map of the London Underground (fig. 1.11), clearly preserve topological properties rather than projective properties, I know of no *formal* account of topology as applied to pictorial representation.[1] In pictures of this kind, spatial relations in the scene such as spatial order, proximity, and connectedness are preserved in the picture, but not true shapes or true lengths. Piaget and Inhelder (1956) suggested that the spatial relations in drawings by young children are based on topological rather than projective geometry, and I shall suggest that the spatial relations in some artists' pictures, such as some of Klee's drawings, as well as many cartoons and caricatures, can also be described in terms of topological geometry.

In pictures, topological relationships in the scene are represented by topologically equivalent relations on the picture surface. Route maps provide what are perhaps some of the commonest examples of pictures based on topological rather than projective geometry. What the traveler wants to know from bus or railroad maps are the connections between stations and the spatial order in which they occur, and these are the relations which are represented. The exact shapes of the lines and the stations and the distances between stations, on the other hand, are not represented. Similarly, in electrical circuit diagrams it is usually the connections between components that are important rather than the shapes of the components, or the shapes of the wires in three-dimensional space.

Fig. 3.1 shows an example of one of the forerunners of modern route maps, the so-called Gyogi-type maps. This map comes from the *Shugaisho,* a thirteenth-century Japanese gazetteer. According to Cortazzi,

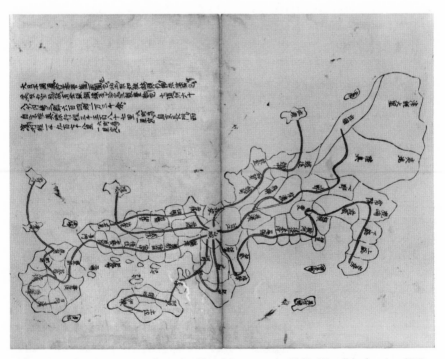

FIG. 3.1. Gyogi-type map from the *Shugaisho* gazetteer, 1291. Woodblock print, 27.5 × 17.5 cm. Nara, Japan, Tenri Central Library.

The term "Gyogi-type maps" came to be used in Japan for diagrams or primitive drawings which showed the interrelationship of the provinces with the capital as well as the seven regions and five special provinces nearest the capital. . . . their most notable feature was the way in which they depicted the provinces in balloon shapes (round or oval) clustered round Kyoto, the capital. The main purpose of Gyogi-type maps seems to have been to show the relationship of the provinces with one another and with the capital. (Cortazzi, 1983, p. 5)

As with modern route maps, the spatial relations represented in the Gyogi-type maps are connectedness, proximity, and spatial order, and we can imagine a Japanese mapmaker starting with a representation of Kyoto at the center and then working outward, connecting the regions representing provinces to each other according to the connections between the provinces in a two-dimensional scene (the earth's surface), without being concerned to represent the true shapes of these provinces. In formal terms, we can think of maps like this as mapping a two-dimensional object-centered description of the ground plane of the scene into a two-dimensional representation in the picture. In the course of this mapping, however, it is only topological properties such as spatial order, proximity, and connectedness that are preserved. These properties are also preserved in projective transformations, but in projective transformations additional properties such as straightness are also preserved.

Pictures that preserve only topological relations can also be derived from *views:* that is, projections from three-dimensional scenes into the frontal plane. The geographer William Bunge pointed out that topological transformations derived from views can be described in terms of topology, provided that the projection rays remain neighbors over short distances. Imagine a view projected onto a glass window, or the ground glass screen of a *camera obscura,* and then assume that "The glass plate is heated until it becomes viscous and infinitely stretchable. Remove the glass from the frame and stretch the glass most outrageously. Any such transformation belongs to the geometry of topology. There are, perhaps surprisingly, many invariances remaining in this geometry" (Bunge, 1966, p. 221).

An example of a picture derived from a view in which only topological relations are preserved is Klee's drawing of a camel (fig. 3.2). We can think of this drawing, and many other caricatures and cartoons, such as the cartoon by Calman shown in fig. 4.2b, as line drawings representing views which have been stretched "outrageously." In Klee's drawing the shapes of the lines in the drawing representing the contours of the camel's body have been grossly distorted, but Klee has been very careful to preserve the topological properties of these lines, and in particular the connections between the line junctions: in this case, the connections between the T-junctions representing points where one form overlaps another in a view of the scene, and end-junctions where the contour fades away in the interior of the form. As a result, the object depicted is still surprisingly recognizable.

The Gyogi-type map and Paul Klee's drawing represent two clear cases: the Gyogi map represents the topological properties of the spatial relations between objects in an object-centered description of the scene, while Klee's drawing represents the topological properties of the relations between features in a *view* of a scene. In the previous chapter I showed how pictures based on projective relations can be derived from both object-centered and viewer-centered descriptions, and the same approach can be applied to pictures based on topological relations. In some cases, however, it may not be immediately obvious whether the picture represents the spatial relations in an object-centered description or a view. The purpose of the map of the London Underground (fig. 1.11) is to show the actual connections between stations in an object-centered description of the scene; the traveler is not interested in the map as providing a view. Nevertheless, because the system as a whole is so complex and occupies three-dimensional space rather than

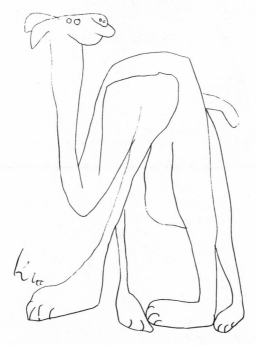

FIG. 3.2. Paul Klee, *Und noch ein Kamuff* (*Another Camel!*), 1939. Pen drawing, 29.2 × 21.0 cm. F. C. Schang Collection, New York. Copyright Design and Artists Copyright Society 1997.

a two-dimensional surface, the mapmaker has been forced to present the map in the form of a view (albeit a distorted one) in which some of the lines representing the tracks pass behind each other with respect to the viewer, much as some of the lines representing contours pass behind surfaces in the drawing by Klee. Complications like this arise because of the difficulty of mapping topological relations in a three-dimensional scene onto a two-dimensional surface. As a result, it can sometimes be difficult—as it is with pictures based on projective geometry—to decide whether a particular picture has been derived from an object-centered description or from a view.

The first spatial relations to be represented in children's early drawings seem to be those of proximity and spatial order. Even 2-year-olds, who rarely create recognizable drawings spontaneously, can show body parts in spatial relations corresponding to their order and proximity in an object-centered description when someone dictates a list of features. Winner (1986) illustrated a drawing produced by a 2-year-old in response to a list of dictated features such as "head," "tummy," "arms," and "legs" (fig. 3.3). She

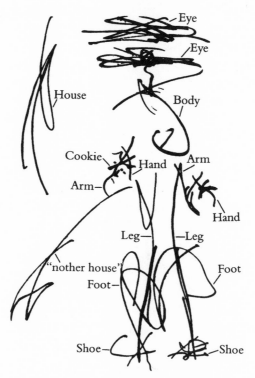

FIG. 3.3. Drawing of a man by a 2-year-old, with dictated features. From Winner (1986), courtesy of Ellen Winner.

commented that children who produced drawings of this kind had no way of representing recognizable features, since they lacked the idea of using a line to stand for an occluding contour: instead, each body part was represented by a patch of scribble. Nevertheless, these children clearly understood that marks on a surface can be used to represent features in the scene, and that these marks can be used to show the relative spatial locations of features.

It seems likely that the relations between the marks in these drawings are intended to represent the relations between features in an object-centered description, but we cannot be certain of this because the relations of proximity and spatial order represented in the drawing shown in fig. 3.3 also correspond to those which would be represented in a possible view of a figure, standing upright with the arms extended to either side.

The topological relations of connectedness, separation, and enclosure seem to emerge somewhat later in children's drawings. In spite of its simplicity, the drawing by a 5-year-old boy shown in fig. 1.12 is much more advanced than the drawing shown in fig. 3.3. The ears and legs are shown connected to the head/body, while the eyes, nose, and mouth are shown separated from each other and from the outline of the figure. Moreover, the eyes, nose, and mouth are correctly shown enclosed within the outline of the face, considered as a two-dimensional surface.

Enclosure within three dimensions is also often represented in children's early drawings. As Piaget and Inhelder pointed out: "On a surface, one element may be perceived as surrounded by others; such as the nose framed by the rest of the face. In three dimensions enclosure takes the form of the relation of 'insideness,' as in the case of an object in a closed box" (Piaget and Inhelder, 1956, p. 8). The rule for representing three-dimensional enclosure seems to be: "When one object is enclosed by another, represent the enclosed object within the outline representing the surface of the enclosing object." The application of this rule leads to the so-called "transparencies" which are so common in children's early drawings. A clear distinction must, however, be made between drawings in which transparencies arise as a result of the child's attempts to show one object *behind* another with respect to the viewer, and transparencies apparently showing one object *enclosed* by another.[2]

Examples of transparencies were reported very early in the history of the study of children's drawings. Corrado Ricci (1887) noticed transparencies in children's spontaneous drawings of a boat and a man on horseback: these drawings show the legs and bodies of the men through the sides of the boat, and both legs of the rider on horseback. Such transparencies may have arisen as the result of planning problems, or they may result from attempts to show

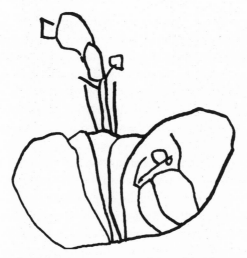

Fig. 3.4. Ben Matthews (aged 3 years 3 months), *Father Christmas Coming down the Chimney.* From Matthews (1994), courtesy of John Matthews and Hodder and Stoughton Educational.

one object behind another. Children's drawings which seemed to represent three-dimensional *enclosure* were first reported by Clark (1897). Clark asked children aged between 6 and 16 to draw an apple with a hatpin stuck horizontally through it, and found that the younger children drew the pin "clear across the apple." Clark commented: "The six-year-old does not notice that part of the pin is out of sight, or does not draw it so if he does; because he is trying to show not appearances but facts. The pin goes through the apple, and he draws it so" (p. 287).

Fig. 3.4 shows a drawing by Ben, a gifted 3-year-old, representing Father Christmas coming down the chimney (Matthews, 1994). In terms of the topology of the scene, Ben is shown, as he said himself, "in his little bed" inside the house, while Father Christmas is penetrating this space, from outside to inside, by coming down the chimney. The line representing the house in the picture thus serves to separate inside from outside in the topological space of the picture surface, providing a topological equivalent for the surface of the real house, which separates inside from outside in three-dimensional space.

Extendedness

In drawings like the map of the London Underground shown in fig. 1.11, the Gyogi-type map shown in fig. 3.1, and the child's drawing of a man shown in fig. 1.12, the spatial relations between the features are topological in character rather than projective. But topology by itself is not adequate to explain the ways in which the *shapes* of these features are represented. Why are the stations in the map of the London Underground represented by small circles or rectangles and the tracks by lines, and not the other way round? And why, in their early drawings of people, do most children use lines or long regions to represent the arms and legs, and round regions to represent the head or head/body? The obvious answer is because the roundness of a circle or a round region reflects the relative roundness of shapes like an eye or a head, or a station on the Underground, and the longness of a line or a long region reflects the longness of shapes like arms and legs, or the longness of the track compared with a station. In Chapter 1, I used the term *extendedness* in order to specify the relative extensions of scene or picture primitives in different directions in space. Informally, the words "round," "flat," and "long" can be used to refer to extendedness: that is, saliency of extension in one, two, or three dimensions. Again, however, I must emphasize that extendedness does not only apply to smooth regular shapes. A round object such as a ball can be described as about equally extended in all three directions in space, but so can cubic objects such as dice or houses, or irregular objects such as potatoes or clouds.

Extendedness is perhaps the most basic of all shape properties. The term originated in linguistics, and in this field three-dimensional objects are described as "nonextended" if they are about equally extended in all three directions in space, and "extended" if they are more extended in one or two directions than they are in a third. However, the use of the term *nonextended* to describe an object which is about equally extended in all three dimensions, or a region in a picture which is about equally extended in two dimensions, could be misleading. Instead, I shall, wherever possible, use the informal terms "round," "flat," or "long" to describe the extendedness of three-dimensional shapes, and "round" or "long" to describe the extendedness of two-dimensional shapes. Where it is necessary to be more precise, I shall use the notational scheme described in Willats (1985, 1992a).

In this scheme the numbers 0, 1, 2, and 3 are used to stand for the dimensional index of a shape primitive: that is, the number of dimensions within which a primitive can potentially be extended. In addition, the subscripts "1" and "0" are used to denote relative extension or lack of extension within a particular dimension. What is important is not the absolute lengths of these extensions, but the ratios between the lengths of the extensions in different directions. When the relative extension of a shape in a given direction is significantly greater than it is in other directions, I shall refer to this as *saliency* of extension. Volumetric shapes may thus be described as about equally extended in all three dimensions (3_{111} volumes or *lumps*), saliently extended in two dimensions but not the third (3_{110} volumes or *slabs*), or saliently extended in one dimension only (3_{100} volumes or *sticks*). Similarly, regions in pictures may be described as about equally extended in two dimensions (2_{11} regions or *round regions*), or saliently extended in one dimension (2_{10} regions or *long regions*).

In natural languages, extendedness is represented by the use of noun classifiers: words or morphemes which classify objects according to their relative extensions in two- or three-dimensional space. The representation of extendedness in natural language is, according to Denny, "a widespread and perhaps universal principle of noun classification" (Denny, 1979a, p. 101), and both Clark (1976) and Denny (1979a) cite a survey of thirty-seven Asian languages made by Adams and Conklin (1973) in which they speak of "round," "flat," and "long" as basic semantic primes. English has a relatively impoverished system of noun classifiers, although words like "lump," "slab," and "stick" act rather like classifiers. In English, we cannot speak just of "a wax," but rather of "a lump of wax," "a slab of wax," or "a stick of wax."

Extendedness also plays an important part in children's early speech and is a common source of overextensions.[3] Young children will often use words like *baw* (ball) to mean anything round, like an apple or a bell clapper, and words like *tee* (stick) to mean anything long, like an umbrella or a ruler (Clark, 1976).

Extendedness thus appears to be a natural category, rather than an artificial or invented one. Natural categories, according to Rosch (1973), are highly structured internally and do not have well-defined boundaries. Such categories are composed of core meanings consisting of the clearest cases,[4] surrounded by other cases decreasing in similarity to the core meaning. Rosch gives examples from experiments with color perception which show that there are "natural prototypes" such as pure blue, which shades off into green on one side and purple on the other. In the same way, "slab" as a shape category does not have well-defined boundaries, but shades off into "lump" on one hand and "stick" on the other. Rosch argues that the core meaning of such categories "is not arbitrary but is 'given' by the human perceptual system; thus, the basic content as well as structure of such categories is universal across languages" (p. 112).

In pictures, the extendedness of objects in the scene is represented, far more directly than it is in language, by the extendedness of corresponding shapes on the picture surface. In the map of the London Underground, the longness of the track is represented by lines or long regions, while the relative roundness of the stations is represented by round regions. In the Gyogi-type map shown in fig. 3.1, the round or oval "balloon shapes" clustered round Kyoto represent the provinces, while lines are used to represent the routes. Finally, the representation of extendedness seems to play an important role in children's early drawings. In the tadpole figure shown in fig. 1.12, the head or head/body, the mouth, and the ears are all represented by round regions, the eyes are represented by small round regions or dots, while the legs and the nose are represented by lines. Stern (1930) called these marks "natural symbols" because the roundness of a circle or a round region reflects the roundness of a lump like a head, or the roundness of a round surface like the mouth; while the longness of a line, or a long region, reflects the longness of a stick like an arm or a leg. However, representing the extendedness of a *flat* three-dimensional shape by the corresponding extendedness of a mark or picture primitive on the picture surface is not quite as straightforward as might at first appear.

What does the roundness of the region standing for the head in the child's drawing shown in fig. 1.12 actually represent: the roundness of the head in a three-dimensional object-centered description, or the roundness of a *view* of the head? The question is problematic, because a round volume or lump like a head is not only round in itself, but will appear round from whichever direction it is viewed. Using Marr's terminology, a lump can be described as "round" in both object-centered and viewer-centered descriptions. That is, a lump like a head can be described as about equally extended in all three directions in three-dimensional space relative to its own natural axes, and at the same time its image in the viewer's frontal plane will be about equally extended in both directions, whatever the orientation of the lump may be relative to the viewer's line of sight. It is thus easy to see why a round region might be a natural symbol for a lump.

On the other hand, although a long volume or stick such as an arm or a leg is both long in itself and long in appearance from most directions of view, there are two special directions (the two end views) from which it will appear round—at least in monocular vision, or where the object is seen from some distance away. Fig. 3.5a shows the silhouettes of a stick resulting from forty-one viewing directions spaced at roughly equal intervals over the viewing hemisphere. Only one of these silhouettes is round; the rest are long. Thus, although a round region provides a *possible* view of a stick, the view it provides is an unlikely one, and it is easy to see why a long region might be a much more natural symbol for a stick than a round region. A long region in a picture reflects the fact that a stick is long in three-dimensional space, and in addition corresponds to the most probable view of a stick. In contrast, a round region used as a representation of a stick would fail to reflect the extendedness of a stick in three-dimensional space and would correspond only to a most improbable view. Stern's suggestion that "a long stroke is a natural symbol for an arm or a leg" seems to be justified.

However, there do not seem to be any corresponding natural symbols for *flat* shapes like slabs and discs. If a round region is a natural symbol for a lump because lumps are round in three-dimensional space, and a long region is a natural symbol for a stick because sticks are long in three-dimensional space, it is not obvious whether a disc ought to be represented in a picture by a long region or a round region: a long region would disguise the fact that a disc is round, whereas a round region would disguise the fact that it is flat. If, on the other hand, a long region is a natural symbol for a stick because it provides the most probable *view,* it is not immediately obvious whether the most probable view of a disc is a round region or a long region. Fig. 3.5b shows the silhouettes of a flat disc corresponding to the same forty-one viewing directions, and in this picture there are about equal numbers of long and round regions. Consequently, we cannot be confident in saying that either a long region or a round region is more likely as a view of a disc.

The evidence from children's drawings suggests that children do not have natural symbols for discs or slabs as they do for lumps and sticks. In their spontaneous drawings, some children will use round regions to stand for flat shapes like the palm of the hand, as in the drawing shown in fig. 3.6a, while others will use a line for the same purpose, as in fig. 3.6b. In pictures by adults, it can be hard to recognize discs or slabs in silhouettes (pictures made

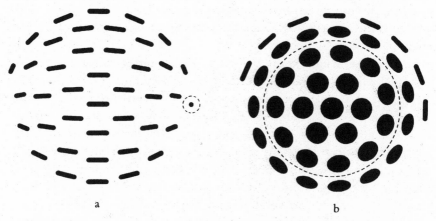

a   b

Fɪɢ. 3.5. Forty-one views of (a) sticks and (b) discs spaced at roughly equal intervals over the viewing hemisphere. The dotted lines separate long regions from round regions. From Willats (1992a, figs. 4 and 5). Courtesy of Pion Ltd., London.

up of regions only, without any internal details), although it is easy to recognize lumps and sticks, such as the head, body, arms, and legs of men or animals. Fig. 3.7 shows drawings representing gladiators in combat carved into rock faces in Camonica Valley in northern Italy. In the first, earlier drawing (fig. 3.7a), it is easy to recognize the various body parts: the heads are represented by round regions and the bodies, arms, and legs by long regions. The figures seem to be fighting with clubs or swords, and the right-hand figure perhaps holds a weapon represented by a long, bent region. But it is difficult to tell whether the figures are also holding shields, seen edge-on and represented by long regions, or whether both figures are holding swords or clubs only. In the second, later drawing (fig. 3.7b), it is obvious, because of the shapes of the outlines of the regions, that both figures are holding shields as well as lances.

In Picasso's *Rites of Spring* (fig. 3.8), the silhouette of the central dancing figure is very similar to that of the dancing figure in Nicholas Poussin's *The Triumph of Pan* (London, National Gallery), which is shown playing two tambourines. Thus it seems likely that the two regions at the ends of the arms of the dancing figure in Picasso's painting are also intended to represent tambourines: flat, drumlike discs with a length/width ratio of about 5:1. In this painting, one tambourine is represented by a region that is almost round, and the other by a region that is more elongated. Even with prior knowledge of what these regions are intended to represent, however, it seems quite hard to see them as discs. The round region looks more like a slightly flattened lump, and the more elongated region looks like a thick stick.

By counting the long and round regions in figs. 3.5a and 3.5b, and making certain assumptions, it is possible to estimate the relative probabilities of

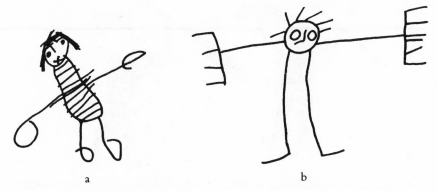

a   b

FIG. 3.6. Children's drawings of figures showing the alternative use of (a) regions and (b) lines to denote flat volumes. From Willats (1987), courtesy of *Archives de psychologie*, Geneva. Drawing (b) courtesy of Dennie Wolf, Harvard Graduate School of Education.

seeing lumps, sticks, and discs in silhouettes. The first assumption is that all directions of view are equally probable. Of course, this assumption is not always justified in the real world: we usually see small flat objects from on top because they are lying on surfaces, whereas people are rarely seen either from the top or from the bottom. The second assumption is that the universe contains equal numbers of lumps, discs, and sticks; again this assumption is not necessarily justified in the real world. In picture perception, however, these two assumptions taken together are equivalent to saying that we have no prior expectations or preconceptions of what the image is likely to represent. Given these two assumptions, it can be shown (Willats, 1992a) that the probability of a long region as a view of a stick having a length/width

a

b

FIG. 3.7. Rock drawings from Camonica Valley. (a) *Gladiators in Combat,* c. 1000 B.C. (b) *Ithyphallic Warriors,* c. 700–600 B.C. From Anati (1964). Copyright 1994 by WARA, Centro Camuno di Studi Preistorici, 25044, Capo di Ponte, Italy.

ratio of 5:1 is about 3 in 5, whereas the probability of a round region as a view of the same stick is about 1 in 60. That is, a long region in a picture is quite probable as a representation of a view of a stick, whereas a round region is highly improbable. These values seem to agree with our intuitions: a line or a long region seems "natural" as a representation of a stick, whereas a round region would seem highly unnatural. In terms of picture perception, this means that, other things being equal, we are likely to interpret a long region in a picture as a representation of a stick, like the long regions representing swords or clubs in the drawing of the gladiators shown in fig. 3.7a, and the long regions representing the arms, the legs, and the pipes in the drawing by Picasso shown in fig. 3.8.

Similarly, it can be shown that, given the same assumptions, the probability of a round region as a view of a disc having a length/width ratio of 5:1 is about 1 in 3 and the probability of a long region as a view of a disc is also about 1 in 3. These values suggest that round regions and long regions are about equally good as representations of discs; but because the probabilities are less

FIG. 3.8. Pablo Picasso, *Rites of Spring*, 1959. Copyright Design and Artists Copyright Society 1997.

than evens in each case, both interpretations ought to be somewhat improbable. Again, this seems to agree with our intuitions: in the absence of prior knowledge, the long regions at the ends of the arms of the gladiators in fig. 3.7a are more likely to be interpreted as swords or clubs than as shields. Similarly, the regions at the ends of the arms of the dancing figure in fig. 3.8 look more like flattened lumps or fat sticks than discs, even though they are almost certainly intended to represent tambourines.

Thus it is easy to recognize lumps and sticks, but not discs or slabs, in silhouettes. There seem to be no "natural symbols" for slabs or discs: both long regions and round regions provide possible views of discs or slabs, but both are mildly improbable. Other things being equal, we are more likely to see a round region as a representation of a lump and a long region as a representation of a stick. Consequently, it can be difficult to represent slabs and discs in silhouettes.

Secondary Shape Properties and Shape Modifiers

Extendedness does not just provide a way of describing smooth regular shapes. A round object such as a ball can be classed as a 3_{111} volume—that is, as a lump—but so can cubic objects such as houses, or irregular objects such as clouds or the tops of trees. Thus, at the most basic level, all objects in the physical universe which have fixed shapes can be described in terms of their extendedness.

Similarly, noun classifiers which define extendedness in language do not just apply to regular shapes: ko, which is used to define 3_{111} shapes (lumps) in Japanese does not simply mean "round" since it is also applied to square-shaped objects such as children's blocks (Denny, 1979b). There is also a good deal of evidence to suggest that the round regions in children's early drawings are not just intended to represent smooth round shapes in the scene. Instead, these round regions are used to represent all kinds of objects which are about equally extended in all three directions of space, irrespective of other secondary shape properties which they might have, such as "having an irregular surface" or "having flat faces." In the drawing of *Father Christmas Coming down the Chimney* (fig. 3.4), the house is simply represented by a smooth closed curve, even though children know that houses have flat faces, and that the walls of houses have straight edges and square corners. Similarly, in a well-known drawing of *A Man with a Saw* illustrated by Arnheim (1954), the only marks in the drawing are lines, long regions, round regions, and areas of scribble: even the triangular teeth of the saw are represented by round regions (Willats, 1985).

There is some evidence to suggest that some children may represent the primary property of extendedness and secondary properties such as "having flat sides" or "having corners" as separate shape properties. When Piaget and Inhelder (1956) asked children aged between 3 and 5 years to copy drawings of circles, squares, and diamonds, they found that some of the children represented the squares and diamonds by round regions having little ticks or hats added to represent the corners. Fig. 3.9 shows two successive attempts by a 3½-year-old girl to copy a square (Hayes, 1978). The first drawing (fig. 3.9a) was produced after the girl had watched the experimenter draw the model square using four discontinuous strokes. The second drawing was produced after the experimenter had drawn the model square in one continuous movement. Since the first drawing showed that the child possessed the necessary manual skills to draw straight lines and corners and had some conception of the idea of copying, she was asked to describe the marks in her drawing. When she was asked to identify the "side bits" and the "stiff things" in her drawing, she pointed to the horizontal lines and the corners in the experimenter's drawing. This suggests that this child was representing the extendedness of the square first, using a round shape, and then adding separate representations of the secondary properties "having straight sides" and "having corners."

Instances of this kind of drawing are, however, relatively rare. Normally, secondary shape properties can be represented very directly in drawing—much more directly than they are in language. In the drawing of a man by a 5-year-old boy shown in fig. 1.12, the primary shape property represented is extendedness, but two secondary shape properties are also represented:

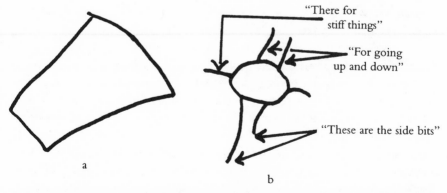

"There for
stiff things"

"For going
up and down"

"These are the side bits"

a

b

FIG. 3.9. Three-year-old's copies of a square. (a) Produced after the girl had watched the experimenter draw the model square using four discontinuous strokes. (b) Produced after the experimenter had drawn the model square in one continuous movement. From Hayes (1978), courtesy of *Cognitive Science*.

relative size, and a property which might be referred to as "being textured." A large round region is used to represent the head or head/body, medium-sized regions are used to represent the mouth and ears, and the eyes are represented by small regions or dots. Only one size of line is used: the legs and the nose are all represented by lines of the same length. In addition, forms that we might think of as being relatively smooth in the scene—the head or head/body, the legs, and the nose—are represented by smooth outlines in the picture, whereas forms that might be considered to be irregular or textured in the scene—the ears and the mouth—are represented by areas of scribble. Thus we can think of drawings like this in two different ways: we can think of them as crude approximations to projected images, or (as compared with earlier drawings) as attempts to capture successively richer and more complex shape properties in object-centered descriptions. The only spatial relations captured by the dictated drawing shown in fig. 3.3 are proximity and spatial order, and the only shape property represented is simply "being there"; even extendedness hardly seems to be represented. In contrast, the 5-year-old's drawing of a man captures the spatial relations of connectedness and enclosure within two dimensions, the primary shape property of extendedness, and the two secondary properties of relative size and being textured.

We can also think of adult pictures in the same way. We can think of Picasso's *Rites of Spring* (fig. 3.8) as a more or less crude reproduction of a projected image of a scene; but we can also think of it as capturing certain primary and secondary shape properties: extendedness, relative size, and the properties of "being pointed" and "being bent." Thus we can think of the regions representing the arms of the dancing figure as more or less crude approximations to views of arms, but we can also think of them as representing the primary property of "being saliently extended in one direction" together with the secondary shape property of "being bent." Similarly, we can think of the regions representing the horns of the goat as representing the three-dimensional properties of "being saliently extended in one direction," "being bent," and "being pointed." Following Hollerbach (1975), I shall refer to features of the picture that represent secondary shape properties in the scene as "shape modifiers."

Secondary shape properties like "being straight," "being pointed," "having flat faces," and so on have much in common with what are called "nonaccidental properties" in theories of scene perception (Biederman, 1987; Witkin and Tennebaum, 1983). The main idea behind Biederman's theory of "recognition-by-components" is that certain shape properties of lines in the two-dimensional image are taken by the visual system as good evidence that corresponding edges in the three-dimensional scene have the same properties. For example, a straight line in the image is likely to have been derived from a straight edge in the scene: the visual system ignores the possibility that the property in the image of "being straight" might be the highly unlikely result of accidentally viewing a curved edge from edge-on so that the line of sight lies in the plane of curvature.

Biederman describes five nonaccidental properties of this kind: collinearity of points or lines, curvilinearity, symmetry, parallel curves, and the termination of two or more vertices at a common point. Lowe (1987) adds "texture properties" to this list. In general, Biederman argues that the visual system assumes that the view it has of a scene is general or *generic* rather than special. Similarly, Nakayama and Shimojo (1992) argue that "when faced with more than one surface interpretation of an image, the visual system assumes that it is viewing the scene from a generic, not an accidental, viewpoint" (p. 1360). Such accidental alignments are unlikely to occur in the perception of real scenes: a slight change in position will reveal whether or not the viewpoint is accidental; if the image remains unchanged, the viewpoint is nonaccidental, or generic. In picture perception the image *cannot* change, and it seems likely that the assumption that shape modifiers like "being straight" or "being curved" represent similar properties in the viewed object may play an important part in our interpretation of pictures.

Conversely, this suggests that it will be desirable for an artist or draftsman who wishes to produce a picture that provides an effective shape representation to choose generic views which preserve these nonaccidental properties. If it is important for the viewer to be able to recognize a stick in a picture, it is better for the draftsman to choose a long region as a view of a stick rather than a round region. However, some shapes may not have unique generic views. As I have shown, there does not seem to be one single generic view of a disc or a slab which preserves the property of "being flat."

Nevertheless, picture production may not always involve choosing an appropriate view of an object. Drawings like the unusual or anomalous representation of a square illustrated in fig. 3.9b, and the similar drawings of squares and diamonds illustrated by Piaget and Inhelder (1956), seem to have been produced by children who represented the nonaccidental properties of squares by separate features in the picture: "being 2_{11} extended," "having straight sides," and "having corners" separately. As a result, such drawings do not provide possible views. More normal drawings of squares, like that shown in fig. 3.9a, may have been produced as direct copies of the visual image; but it seems possible that such drawings may also have been produced by children who wanted to represent the same nonaccidental properties, but managed to combine these properties more directly and, as a result, produced drawings which do correspond to possible views.

Such an argument may seem rather far-fetched when applied to drawings or copies of two-dimensional models, but it becomes more plausible when we look at children's early drawings of three-dimensional objects like houses, such as the drawing of a *House with a Huge Snowdrift* (fig. 3.10). It is possible that this drawing is intended to represent a view of a house, with a cross-section through a snowdrift. However, it seems more likely that the region representing the front of the house is intended to represent the house as a 3_{111} volume (like the house by a younger child shown in fig. 3.4), but with the addition of straight lines representing the property "having flat faces." This interpretation seems more plausible when we consider a feature that is very common in children's drawings of houses: the windows are often shown connected to the outline of the region representing the house as a whole. If this outline represents the topological surface separating the inside of the house from the outside—like the outline of the house shown in fig. 3.4—then it might have seemed natural to these children to represent the windows as connected to this surface. Finally, if this interpretation is

FIG. 3.10. Arfan Kahn (boy, 7.5 years), *House with a Huge Snowdrift*. From Willats (1990).

correct, the region representing the snowdrift which encloses the house in the two-dimensional topological space of the picture surface may be intended to represent a snowdrift enclosing the house in the three-dimensional scene.

Thus drawings such as this can be interpreted in two quite different ways: as approximations to possible views, or as representations of object-centered descriptions which capture topological relations like connectedness and enclosure, basic shape properties of the scene like extendedness, and secondary shape properties like "having flat faces." It can be difficult to determine, from single finished drawings, whether such drawings have been derived from views, or whether they represent a combination of topological relations and nonaccidental shape properties which, fortuitously, have resulted in an approximation to a possible view. However, this question can often be decided experimentally by asking children to draw the same object from more than one viewpoint or direction of view, and seeing if their drawings change in appropriate ways. The experiment described in Chapter 13, in which children of various ages were asked to draw sticks and discs in foreshortened and nonforeshortened positions, was based on this approach.

Finally, many accounts of nonaccidental shape properties, such as those described in Biederman's theory of recognition-by-components, are based on lines and edges as shape primitives: a straight line in the image is assumed to be a representation of a straight edge in the scene. However, a full account of the spatial relations in pictures ought to include an account of the relations between all kinds of primitives, not just one-dimensional primitives such as lines and edges. The relations between different kinds of scene and picture primitives form the subject of the next chapter.

Part Two

DENOTATION SYSTEMS

CHAPTER FOUR

Regions as Picture Primitives

There are three classes of denotation systems, based on regions, lines, and points as picture primitives. Regions in pictures can denote whole volumes, as they do in the tadpole figures (fig. 1.12); or the faces of objects, such as the faces in the fold-out drawing of a box standing on the table in fig. 1.9d; or regions projected into the frontal plane, such as the regions in Picasso's *Rites of Spring* (fig. 3.8).

Once again I must emphasize the distinction between drawing systems and denotation systems. Whereas the drawing systems map spatial relations in the scene into corresponding relations in the picture, the denotation systems, which form the subject of Part 2, map scene primitives into corresponding picture primitives. That is, the denotation systems say what the picture primitives refer to, or *denote*. This reminder is needed because it can be easy to confuse the drawing systems with the denotation systems; and also because it can be difficult to appreciate that there is any need to define the denotation systems at all. As Richard Gregory said, pictures have a "double reality": when we look at a picture we can see it as a pattern of marks on a flat surface, but also as something else, such as a house or a ship at sea (Gregory, 1970, p. 32). Moreover, as Wollheim pointed out, we often "use the same word to refer both to the lines in a drawing and to the edges of perceived objects"; and this is surely, Wollheim argues, no coincidence, because although the lines are not themselves edges, we see them as edges when we look at a drawing as a representation (Wollheim, 1973, p. 22).

However, it is precisely the seeming ease and naturalness of this double reality, and the double usage in language that it gives rise to, that makes it difficult to see that there are any problems at all in the analysis of the denotation systems in pictures. The fact that we are tempted to use the same word to describe both lines and edges disguises the complexity of the relation between scenes and pictures; and this relation can be explored only by distinguishing carefully between the words we use to describe features of scenes and the words we use to describe features of pictures. The purpose of this and the following two chapters is to make explicit the relations between picture primitives and the objects and shapes in the real world to which they refer. A fully explicit account of the denotation system in a picture involves a description of four kinds of entities. The picture as a physical object is made up of marks (dots, lines, or areas), and these marks represent picture primitives. Picture primitives denote corresponding scene primitives, such as edges or corners, or faces, or whole volumes. Finally, combinations of these scene primitives can represent objects like tables and people.

Different pictures use different kinds of shape primitives: zero-dimensional primitives or points, one-dimensional primitives or lines, and two-dimensional primitives or regions; and the first step in the analysis of a picture is to decide whether the primitives are zero-, one-, or two-dimensional. The goal of an early program in the field of artificial intelligence (Guzman, 1971) was to assign names of objects to the regions in line drawings, so it would seem that Guzman's intention was to treat the regions in the picture as picture primitives: that is, as the smallest units of shape information available in the picture. However, the shapes of these regions were initially defined in terms of the positions of a large number of points, while the pictures themselves were actually line drawings. The drawings used as input pictures to the program consisted of "ordinary" line drawings, like the drawing shown in fig. 4.1a; no caricatures or distortions were allowed. The input picture was stored in the machine as a collection of points closely spaced along each line, as in fig. 4.1b. The desired output was a description of the objects in the scene; that is, the goal of the program was to find names for each part of the scene, like those given in fig. 4.1d. "We could think of a person looking at the drawing and saying: there is a tree there, a big rock, and a boy, an armadillo behind that coconut tree" (Guzman, 1971, p. 328). Young children, as well as adults, can accomplish such feats of recognition easily and rapidly: so easily, in fact, that it is hard to see that there are any problems at all in recognizing objects in pictures. The question that Guzman asked was, how can machines be programmed to carry out the same operation automatically?

Guzman proposed that interpretation depends partly on the shapes of regions, but also on the context in which these shapes occur. Local analysis suggests that certain shapes can be interpreted as representing certain objects, but a particular shape can usually be interpreted in more than one way. On the basis of shape alone, the irregular region at the bottom right of fig. 4.1 could be a hand, but it could also be the tail of a fish, or perhaps a hank of hair. Similarly, the more or less rectangular region above it could be an arm, or it could be a stick, a box, a leg, or a handle.

Guzman argued that the global context in which these shapes appear narrows down their meaning, and in order to make this idea clear he drew on an analogy with language. To translate a sentence into a different language it is necessary to find the precise meaning of each word, but many words have more than one meaning, depending on the context. For example, the word "kick" in the sentence "The boys kick the ball" has a very different meaning in the sentence "The boys kick the habit." Similarly, the word "ball" in the sentence "The boys kick the ball" has a very different meaning in the sentence "The princess enjoyed the ball." Using this analogy, Guzman argued that the global contexts in which the regions appear in pictures like fig. 4.1 allow us to assign labels such as "hand," "brush," "bucket," and so on to these regions, in preference to other interpretations suggested by their local shapes alone.

FIG. 4.1. Analysis based on global information. From Guzman (1971).

In the event, this approach proved to be not very successful. Context may perhaps be important in the interpretation of silhouettes based on regions as primitives in which not very much information about three-dimensional shape is available. For example, the context in which the long regions in the picture of gladiators in combat shown in fig. 1.5 appear may contribute to their interpretation as arms, legs, or weapons. However, Guzman's approach would not explain how we can interpret cartoons, caricatures, and pictures like Klee's drawing of a camel (fig. 3.2) in which the shapes of the regions are grossly distorted. In general, context and global information seems not to be very important for object recognition. It now seems more likely that we interpret pictures like fig. 4.1 by recognizing the three-dimensional shapes of the parts of objects represented in the picture, and that the picture primitives we use in doing this are not regions, but lines and line junctions. In fact, the problem of object recognition in scenes and pictures turned out to be very much more difficult than early researchers in artificial intelligence had anticipated, and for scenes or pictures of scenes of the kind shown in fig. 4.1, the problem has still not been solved. Most current work in this field concentrates on the problem of the recognition of three-dimensional shapes, independently of the context in which they appear. Nevertheless, early work of this kind was important because it showed how crucial it was, in the analysis of pictures, to make a clear distinction between scenes and pictures, and scene primitives and picture primitives.

Scene Primitives

Scene primitives may be zero-, one-, two-, or three-dimensional. It is easy to see how a shape description of a table might be built up of zero-dimensional primitives such as corners, or one-dimensional primitives such as edges, or two-dimensional primitives such as surfaces; but it is more difficult to imagine what a description of a table composed of three-dimensional or *volumetric* shape primitives might be like. Marr (1982) argued that, for reasons of economy, shape descriptions in long-term memory must be built up of volumetric primitives; and the question of whether we do indeed use volumetric primitives for this purpose and, if we do, what form these primitives might take, is, according to Pinker (1986), one of the most important problems in current research on shape recognition. According to Marr and Nishihara (1978, p. 275): "The simplest volumetric primitive specifies just a location and an extent, and corresponds to a roughly spherical region in space." By adding a vector, a roughly cylindrical primitive can be specified, and this can be further modified by adding an additional vector specifying curvature in the axis of the cylindrical volume, to give a long, curved volume. This leads to the idea of generalized cones as volumetric scene primitives: Marr (1977, pp. 442–443) defined a generalized cone as "the surface swept out by moving a cross-section of fixed shape but smoothly varying size, along an axis." Biederman (1987) proposed a similar scheme based on what he called "geons" as volumetric scene primitives. Geons are generalized cones which are distinguished from each other by the possession of nonaccidental shape properties such as "being bent," "having straight edges," and so on.

Marr's proposal works quite well for living things like people and animals, but many objects such as faces, shoes, clouds, and trees cannot easily be described within this scheme. As Marr himself said: "It is important to remember that there exist surfaces that cannot conveniently be approximated by generalized cones, for example a cake that has been cut at its intersection with some arbitrary plane, or the surface formed by a crumpled newspaper" (1978, p. 73). As an alternative, I suggested in Willats (1992a) that volumetric shape primitives can be defined in terms of what I have previously referred to as "extendedness": the property of being saliently extended in one or more directions in space. Thus a volumetric description of a table might be given by saying that a table consists of a 3_{110} volume or slab supported on four 3_{100} volumes or sticks.

I shall refer to two-dimensional scene primitives in object-centered descriptions as *faces* or *surfaces,* and two-dimensional scene primitives in viewer-centered descriptions as *regions.* These regions correspond to the projections of objects in the frontal plane.

Edges, such as the edges of a table or a cube, are one-dimensional scene primitives, and may be specified independently of any particular direction of view. However, it is necessary to distinguish between two kinds of one-dimensional primitives in *views* of scenes: edges and occluding contours. *Edges* in viewer-centered descriptions correspond to the projections of edges in the visual field, while *occluding contours* correspond to the projections of the boundaries of smooth surfaces in the visual field. As Koenderink and van Doorn (1982) said, it is not possible to see the entire surface of an opaque smooth object from a single position because parts of the surface are necessarily occluded by itself. The curve on the surface of the body that divides the visible parts of the object from nonvisible parts is called the *rim,* and this rim is the locus of points on the surface where the visual direction, or line of sight, just grazes the surface of the object. The *contour,* or more precisely the *occluding contour,* of the object is the projection of the rim in the frontal plane.

There are three main types of zero-dimensional scene primitives. *Corners* like the corners of a table or a cube are tangible and belong to object-centered descriptions. *Points of occlusion* are not tangible: they are the points in the frontal plane where the projection of an edge or a contour passes behind a surface. Finally, in pictures based on optical denotation systems, like the newspaper photograph shown in fig. 1.8, the picture primitives denote one-dimensional scene primitives consisting of the *intercepts of small bundles of light rays*.

Picture Primitives

Some pictures such as maps, Chinese paintings, and children's early drawings may contain arbitrary signs such as letters or numbers: Ben's drawing of Father Christmas coming down the chimney (fig. 3.4) contains the letter "b" standing for "Ben lying in his little bed." In this case, fortuitously, the letter "b" looks rather like a boy. Some of the early Chinese pictograms also look rather like the objects to which they refer (Fazzioli, 1987), and I am told that a relation continues to exist between some of the forms of the 214 radicals of modern Chinese and the objects or concepts to which they refer. For example, the four-sided boxlike structure of Radical 31 represents "enclosure," which seems highly appropriate (Matthews, 1956).[1] In general, however, the shapes of the characters in a written language bear no obvious relation to the shapes of the objects they denote.

Picture primitives can be zero-, one-, or two-dimensional. Examples of zero-dimensional primitives are *line junctions,* like the junctions between two lines representing a corner or a point of occlusion; and *points,* which in a Pointillist painting are represented by small dots of paint. Pictures can also be made up of one-dimensional primitives or *lines:* one-dimensional because, in the abstract, lines are only extended in one dimension on the picture surface, although the actual marks representing these lines may have a substantial thickness. *Outlines* are the lines denoting the outer boundaries of the projection of an object, and correspond, in silhouettes, to the outlines of regions.

Two-dimensional picture primitives are referred to as *regions.* At the most basic shape level, there are two kinds of regions: round regions or 2_{11} regions, which are about equally extended in both directions on the picture surface; and long regions or 2_{10} regions, which are saliently extended in one direction only.

Marks and Picture Primitives

Picture primitives are represented in pictures by physical *marks:* lines of ink or pencil, areas or dots of paint, tufts of wool, phosphors on a TV screen, or lines of stitches in a sampler. In practice, particularly in the case of children's drawings, it may be difficult to decide whether some of the variations in the marks do or do not carry meaningful shape information: whether, for example, variations in the outline of an area are accidental, or whether they

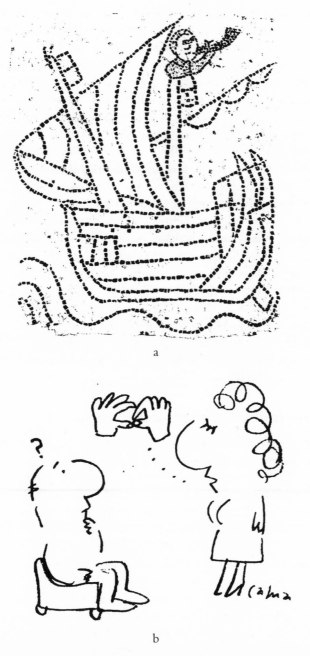

a

b

FIG. 4.2. The distinction between marks and picture primitives. (a) Floor mosaic on the left aisle of the basilica of St. John the Evangelist, Ravenna. From Bustacchini (undated). (b) Mel Calman, cartoon illustrating "Are the signs of language arbitrary?" From Deuchar (1990), courtesy of Cambridge University Press.

are intended to carry information about the occluding contours of the viewed surface. Moreover, physically different marks may carry similar information, or physically similar marks may carry different information. For example, the floor mosaics in the basilica of St. John the Evangelist in Ravenna (fig. 4.2a) are clearly intended as line drawings, although the actual marks are relatively small mosaic blocks. In contrast, most of the wall mosaics in Ravenna, such as the lunette in the basilica of San Vitale representing scenes from the life of Abraham (figs. 14.9 and 14.10), are based on an optical denotation system in which the individual tesserae represent point primitives denoting the intercepts of small bundles of light rays.

In some cases the picture primitives may be represented by marks which are not even physically present, but are only implied. In the cartoon by Mel Calman shown in fig. 4.2b, for example, lines denoting contours in the scene are represented by ink lines; but many of the line junctions, which are the smallest units of shape information and therefore crucial to the interpretation, are actually missing from the picture and are only implied by the directions of the lines. Similarly, the regions in children's drawings may be represented by blank areas enclosed by an outline.

Thus it is crucial to make a distinction between the *marks* in a picture and the more abstract notion of the *picture primitives* represented by the marks. This is akin to the distinction made in natural languages between *sounds* and *phonemes* (Willats, 1992b).

Formal Descriptions of Denotation Systems

In order to make the relations between the primitives in a picture and the scene primitives to which they refer completely explicit, it is sometimes necessary to resort to the formal descriptive system introduced by Willats (1981, 1985). In this system an arrow is used to represent the "denotes" relationship, and each scene and picture primitive is given a dimensional index. The dimensional index of a primitive is the number of dimensions into which the primitive can potentially be extended: a zero-dimensional primitive, for example, such as a point or a T-junction in a picture, or a point of occlusion or a corner in a scene, is given a dimensional index of zero ("0"). Lines, which can be extended only in one direction in pictures, or edges, which can be extended only in one direction in scenes, are given a dimensional index of one ("1"). Regions and surfaces are given a dimensional index of two ("2"), and these indices are given subscripts indicating the extendedness of the primitives to which they refer. The subscript "1" denotes a significant ("salient") extension of the primitive in a given direction, while the subscript "0" denotes a small or insignificant extension.

Fig. 4.3a shows views of a stick and a disc in foreshortened positions using a mark system consisting of small dots representing point primitives in an optical denotation system. In formal terms, this denotation system can be represented as follows:

Dimensional index	Picture primitives	Denotes	Scene primitives
0	0 dots	⟶	0 the intercepts of small bundles of light rays

Column headings are given in this diagram, but in general I shall use an abbreviated form of representation in which the headings "dimensional index," "picture primitives," "denotes," and "scene primitives" are omitted. In addition, the column representing the dimensional index will normally be included only if the dimensional index of a scene primitive is different from that of a corresponding picture primitive. In this abbreviated form, the denotation system in fig. 4.3a may be written as:

0 dots ⟶ 0 the intercepts of small bundles of light rays

Fig. 4.3b shows *line drawings* of the same foreshortened stick and disc. In this case the denotation system may be written as:

1 lines ⟶ 1 edges and occluding contours

Edges are sharp discontinuities in the scene: in this example, the edges of the ends of the stick and the faces of the disc. Occluding contours are the projections of rims of smooth objects in the frontal plane: in this example, the contours of the curved surfaces of the stick or disc.

Lines are sometimes used to denote only the outermost edges or contours of objects, as shown in fig. 4.3c. I shall refer to these lines as "outlines." Pictures in which the regions enclosed by outlines are filled in with areas of solid color or tone are commonly referred to as *silhouettes*. In his analysis of occluding contours, Marr (1977) argued that the outlines of silhouettes in pictures like Picasso's *Rites of Spring* (fig. 3.8) reflect real properties of the viewed surface: convex outlines are assumed to represent convex surfaces, and concave outlines are assumed to represent hyperbolic or saddle-shaped surfaces. Marr thus argues that silhouettes like the *Rites of Spring* are based on a denotation system in which outlines denote occluding contours:

1 outlines ⟶ 1 occluding contours

Fig. 4.3c is based on this system: there are no lines denoting internal edges or contours as there are in fig. 4.3b. In this figure I have left the regions enclosed by these lines blank in order to show that the smallest units of information in the picture (that is, the picture primitives) are lines rather than regions. The lines have been drawn carefully, and the objects can be recognized, though with some difficulty, as a foreshortened stick and a

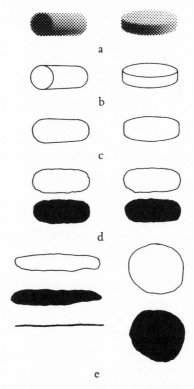

FIG. 4.3. Types of *denotation systems* and associated *marks* in pictures of partially foreshortened sticks and discs. (a) *Point primitives* denote *the intercepts of small bundles of light rays;* the *dots* carry information about light intensities. (b) *Lines* denote *occluding contours and interior edges;* the convexities and concavities of the *lines* carry information about the shape of the viewed surface, including surface discontinuities. (c) *Lines* denote *occluding contours* only; if the *outlines* are carefully drawn they can carry useful information about the viewed surface. (d) *Regions* denote *regions in the frontal plane;* the outlines are too irregular to carry information about the viewed surface, but the shapes of the *regions* carry information about the extendedness of the projection of the object in the frontal plane. (e) *Regions* denote *volumes;* the extendedness of the *regions* carries information about the extendedness of the object in three-dimensional space, and the *line,* as a mark, represents a narrow region as a picture primitive. Foreshortening cannot be represented within this denotation system. From Willats (1992b). Copyright the Society for Research in Child Development.

foreshortened disc. In the drawing of the disc, for example, the two relatively sharp discontinuities at each end carry important information about the shapes of the projections of the outer edges and contours of the object in the visual field: they represent points where the top planar surface meets the curved periphery. It is only details of this kind which enable the disc to be recognized.

In Picasso's *Rites of Spring,* in contrast, the outlines of the silhouette are irregular, so that small details in the outline cannot be used to convey information about details of the edges and contours of the viewed object as they can in fig. 4.3c. As a result, the two regions at the ends of the dancing figure, which we know from the context must represent tambourines, cannot be recognized as discs.

I therefore suggest that it might be better to regard pictures of this kind as being based on a different denotation system: one in which the regions stand for regions in a projection to the frontal plane. Fig. 4.3d shows drawings of the stick and disc based on this system:

$$2_{10} \text{ region} \longrightarrow 2_{10} \text{ region in the frontal plane (stick)}$$

$$2_{10} \text{ region} \longrightarrow 2_{10} \text{ region in the frontal plane (disc)}$$

Notice that the formal descriptions of the denotation systems in these two pictures are identical, and because the outlines of these drawings are irregular, it is not possible to say with any certainty what they represent: both look more like pictures of fat sticks than either foreshortened sticks or discs. It is not possible to represent foreshortening effectively using a denotation system of this kind.

In general, I shall regard drawings of the type shown in fig. 4.3c as *outline drawings,* irrespective of whether or not the marks used to represent the picture primitives are actually lines, or whether the areas enclosed by the outlines are filled in with solid colors or tones. In drawings of this kind, like the nineteenth-century silhouette shown in fig. 5.1, the details of the outline carry meaning, so that the smallest units of information are lines rather than regions. In contrast, in pictures of the type shown in fig. 4.3d, it is only the shapes of the regions that carry meaning. In practice, these regions may be represented by outlines only, or again they may be filled in, as they are here, with areas of solid tone or color.

The drawings shown in fig. 4.3e are based on a denotation system in which the regions denote whole *volumes:* long regions are used to stand for long volumes or sticks, and round regions are used to stand for round volumes or lumps. Discs are sometimes represented by long regions and sometimes by round regions. In practice, especially in children's drawings, the mark used to represent a long region may be a line. It is important to realize that in this case the line is not being used to represent either a contour or the outline of a long region: instead, the line represents the whole shape of a *region*. In fig. 4.3e, the stick is represented by a long region as a picture primitive, and this long region may in turn be represented by either a line or a long area as a mark. In the following diagram I have included a separate column showing the dimensional indices of the primitives, because the dimensional index of the picture primitive is different from that of the corresponding scene primitive:

In practice the long region may be represented by an outline, or again it may be filled in with a solid tone or color. Similarly, the disc is represented in fig. 4.3e by a round region. Once again this round region may be represented by an outline mark, or by an area of solid tone or color:

In drawings of the kind shown in fig. 4.3e, the extendedness of the picture primitives represents the extendedness of the scene primitives in an object-centered description: thus in fig. 4.3e, a line or a long region is used to represent a stick, and a round region is used to represent a disc. Because an object-centered description cannot contain a description of the orientation of an object relative to a particular point of view, foreshortening cannot be represented within this system.

Children's Figure Drawings Based on Regions as Picture Primitives

There is some evidence to suggest that drawings by children below the age of 6 or 7 years are based on denotation systems in which regions as picture primitives are used to stand for volumes in three-dimensional object-centered descriptions. An anecdote (for which I am indebted to Dennie Wolf of Project Zero) illustrates this possibility. A young girl was asked to draw a ball, and responded by producing a drawing similar to that shown in fig. 4.4a. This is in fact just what an adult would do, and without further evidence it would be natural to assume that the outline of this drawing is intended to stand for the occluding contour of a ball. However, this girl wanted to go on and add the mold mark on the ball, the thin web of rubber left on the surface of the ball by the meeting of the two halves of the mold when the ball was made. An adult would probably have produced a drawing similar to that shown in fig. 4.4b. In this case, however, the girl first drew a line outside the circle, saying as she did so, "I can't draw it here because it's not outside the ball" (fig. 4.4c). She then drew a line inside the circle, saying, "I can't draw it here because it's not inside the ball" (fig. 4.4d). Finally, she drew a line on top of the circle, saying, "And I can't draw it here because it won't show up. So I can't do it" (fig. 4.4e). It is hard to resist the conclusion that for this child the region enclosed by the circle was intended to stand for the whole volume of the ball, while the circle itself stood for the surface of the ball, dividing the inside of the ball from the outside in topological space. If this interpretation is correct, it makes perfect sense to draw the mold line where it belongs on the surface of the ball—except that a line drawn here "won't show up." This girl's drawing of a ball thus appears to be based on the denotation system

Fig. 4.5 shows an analysis of the drawing of a man by a 5-year-old originally shown in fig. 1.12, based on the assumption that the picture primitives are intended to denote scene primitives in an object-centered

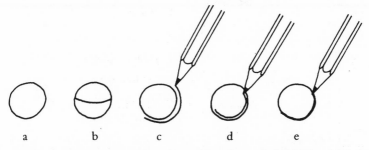

a   b   c   d   e

FIG. 4.4. A child's attempts to draw the mold mark on a ball. (a) The child's drawing of the ball. (b) An adult drawing, including the mold mark. (c) "I can't draw it here because it's not outside the ball." (d) "I can't draw it here because it's not inside the ball." (e) "And I can't draw it here because it won't show up. So I can't do it." From Willats (1985), courtesy of Cambridge University Press.

description. In this analysis I have suggested that the large round region stands for the head or head/body as a round volume or lump, and the smaller round regions stand for the ears as flat volumes or discs, and the mouth as a round surface. The lines, representing long regions, are shown as standing for the legs and nose as long volumes or sticks.

Various other interpretations are possible. It could be argued that all the primitives in the picture are intended to denote scene primitives in a viewer-centered description. In this kind of interpretation the large round region could denote the head as a large round region in the frontal plane, and the lines representing the legs would then denote long regions in the frontal plane.

It could also be argued that the picture primitives are lines rather than regions, and are intended to denote edges and contours in the visual field. This interpretation seems rather unlikely, however. In Joanne's *Self Portrait with Dogs* (fig. 1.7), the lines must denote edges and contours; we know that this must be the case because the T-junctions in the drawing clearly stand for points of occlusion: that is, points where an occluding contour passes behind

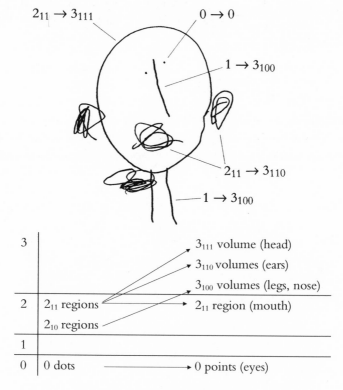

Fig. 4.5. Analysis of fig. 1.12, *Drawing of a Man* by 5-year-old boy.

a surface relative to the viewer's line of sight. In contrast, there are no overlapping forms in the drawing by the 5-year-old shown in fig. 4.5, and the two T-junctions at the bottom of the drawing clearly stand for points where the legs are *joined* to the head or head/body, rather than points of occlusion.

If the analysis given in fig. 4.5 is correct, however, the drawing is inconsistent, at least in terms of picture production. If the large round region is intended to stand for the volume of the head or head/body as a whole, the eyes, nose, and mouth ought not to be shown within it: in topological terms, this relation represents enclosure within a volume. However, there is nowhere else to draw these features in a drawing of a face if they are to "show up." Moreover, the drawing is consistent in terms of picture perception: adults, and perhaps children also, tend to interpret such drawings as providing views. In Chapter 13, I shall argue that it is inconsistencies of this kind that prompt children to acquire more effective denotation systems, and that it is the interaction between perception and production that provides the mechanism of development.

Finally, it is perhaps worth remarking that the problems raised by an analysis of this kind are different from those raised by the apparent lack of a separate body in so-called tadpole figures, of which the drawing shown in fig. 4.5 is an example. As Freeman (1975) pointed out, there has been a long-standing controversy as to whether the large round region in these drawings stands for the head alone, or the head and trunk. Golomb (1992) identified three kinds of explanations for the apparent lack of a trunk in tadpole figures: first, that the large round region stands for the head only, and that the lack of a trunk arises from the child's faulty knowledge of the figure, which she calls the "defect hypothesis"; second, Freeman's suggestion that the absence of a trunk arises as a result of performance problems, which she calls the "serial order hypothesis"; and third, Arnheim's suggestion (Arnheim, 1954) that the large circle stands for the head and body together, so that the tadpole figure provides a "structural equivalent" for the figure as a whole. Other explanations have been offered: for example, that the face is more important to the child than the trunk, perhaps for recognition purposes, and so the trunk is omitted. This long-standing controversy is concerned with what the large round region stands for at the *object* level: the head alone, or the head and trunk as a whole. In contrast, the question raised by an analysis of the type described above is what the marks or picture primitives stand for at the *shape* level: does the large round region stand for the whole volume of the head or head/trunk in an object-centered description, or a region in the visual field representing a view of the head or head/trunk? Or does the outline of this region represent an occluding contour?

Adult Pictures Based on Regions as Picture Primitives

Fig. 4.6 shows an analysis of the rock drawing of the gladiators in combat originally shown in fig. 1.5, based on the assumption that the picture primitives are intended to denote volumetric scene primitives in an object-centered description. In this analysis the round regions stand for the heads as round regions or lumps, and the long regions stand for the arms, legs, and swords or clubs as long volumes or sticks. Two of the long regions may also stand for shields as flat volumes or discs. As with the child's drawing shown in fig. 4.5, other interpretations are possible. For example, it could be argued that all the regions in this picture stand for regions in the frontal plane. I do not want to insist that the analyses given in figs. 4.5 and 4.6 represent the only possible ways of describing the denotation systems in these pictures, and I have suggested other possible interpretations. The point I want to make is that it is often possible to give a number of different accounts of the denotation systems in pictures, and that by using the formal scheme for representing denotation systems given above, these different accounts can be made completely explicit. In the case of children's drawings, it may be possible, by using the type of experimental design described in Chapter 13, in an experiment in which children were asked to make drawings of sticks and a disc in both foreshortened and nonforeshortened positions, to test between these different accounts.

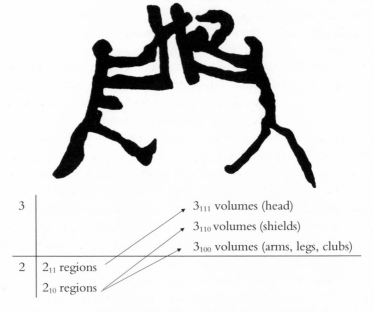

FIG. 4.6. Analysis of fig. 1.5, *Gladiators in Combat* (detail of fig. 3.7).

CHAPTER FIVE

Line Drawing

Outlines

Many of the shapes of the regions that go to make up the nineteenth-century silhouette shown in fig. 5.1 carry information about the extendedness of the shapes of the objects they represent. The leg of the table, the legs of the chair, and the spout of the teapot, all long volumes or sticks, are represented by long regions; and the head of the woman, the cups, and the body of the teapot, all of which may be regarded as round volumes or lumps, are represented by roughly round regions. The artist has had some difficulty in finding a satisfactory way of representing the disc which forms the circular table top, as one might expect from the analysis presented in Chapter 3, and has resorted to the not altogether successful device of representing this disc in a partially foreshortened position. The saucer in the woman's hand is represented by a long, bent region which is not, of course, possible as a projection of a saucer. Presumably this was done in an attempt to show the saucer as a disc which is concave on its upper surface.

The extendedness of the regions is not, however, the only source of shape information in this picture. Compared with the silhouettes shown in figs. 1.5 (*Gladiators in Combat*) and 3.8 (Picasso's *Rites of Spring*), the outlines of this silhouette are quite detailed and carry information about the shapes of the objects they depict which goes further than the mere extendedness of their volumes. For example, the table leg can be seen as a turned column made up of a number of curved convex surfaces, and the cup looks genuinely cup-shaped, with a curved cylindrical body and a sharp edge at the top. How do the outlines of the silhouette convey this kind of information?

Marr (1977) proposed that the convexities and concavities of the outlines of a silhouette reflect real properties of the viewed surface. He then went on to argue that this is equivalent to assuming that the viewed surface must be a generalized cone. The leg of the table represented in fig. 5.1 would be a good example of what Marr calls a generalized cone: the surface swept out by moving a cross-section of fixed shape but smoothly varying size along an axis, which may be straight or curved. In this example the cross-section is circular.

Marr assumed that the rim of an object always lies in a flat plane, and for the table leg shown in fig. 5.1 this would in fact be the case. However, Koenderink (1984) has shown that this assumption is not necessary, and that for most objects in most positions the rim is not planar. Koenderink then proved a general rule that holds for all objects and vantage points: convexities of the contour correspond to convex surface patches, and concavities correspond to saddle-shaped surface patches, that is, surfaces which are convex in one direction and concave in the other. Fully concave surfaces, like the top surface of the saucer shown in fig. 5.1, cannot be represented by occluding contours. In this particular silhouette, most, but not all, of the outlines are convex. Some of the convex outlines, like the outlines of the

Fig. 5.1. Charles (Karl) Christian Rosenberg, *Lady Taking Tea,* c. 1795. Painting on glass, 14.0 × 16.6 cm. Holborne Museum and Craft Study Centre, Bath.

table leg, the cup, and the teapot, represent contours that correspond to rims that *do* lie in a plane, and thus represent the contours of surfaces of generalized cones. Other convex outlines, like the outlines of the hand, represent contours that correspond to rims which do not lie in a plane, and represent the contours of more complex convex surfaces. The few concave outlines that appear in the silhouette, like the concave outline of the chair leg on the far right of the drawing, represent the contours of saddle-shaped surfaces.

Line drawings in which the outlines are actually drawn as lines rather than forming the boundaries of silhouettes are relatively uncommon. Fig. 5.2 shows examples taken from cave paintings: the outlines are skillfully drawn and provide information about the shapes of the animals which goes beyond that of mere extendedness, such as the saddle-shaped surfaces on the animals' backs; but there are no lines representing contours within the interior of the form.

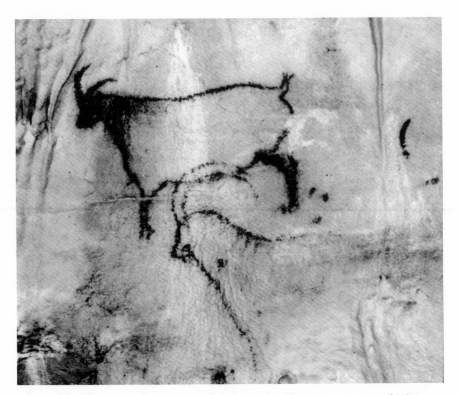

FIG. 5.2. Cave painting at Cougnac, France, *Le grand bouquetin,* courtesy of Edition Photo "Ged."

Line Drawings of Objects with Plane Faces

In line drawings of objects having plane faces, the lines denote *edges*. The denotation systems in line drawings of this kind were first described by Clowes (1971) in England and Huffman (1971) in the United States. Their accounts were subsequently extended by Waltz (1975) in order to describe line drawings of scenes with shadows. In each case the aim was to extract the meaning of a drawing automatically, without appealing to human intuitions. When we look at a line drawing like the drawing of the "tower" shown in fig. 1.15, its "meaning"—that is, the arrangement of three-dimensional shapes which the drawing is intended to represent—is immediately apparent, without our needing to make any conscious effort of interpretation. The hope was that if a computer program could be written that could mimic this process, this might provide an insight into the way in which we recognize objects in real scenes.

Writing in 1982, Marr was rather skeptical about the value of this kind of approach, although he conceded that constraints of the kind described by Waltz might be embedded in what he called the 2½-D sketch (an intermediate stage in the visual system) and so might play a part in our understanding of phenomena like the reversal of the Necker cube. However, Marr's theory of vision emphasized what is called a bottom-up approach and a reliance on the extraction of depth information using depth cues such as stereopsis and shape from motion. More recent writers such as Lowe (1987) and Nakayama and Shimojo (1992) have pointed out that human vision exhibits an excellent level of performance in recognizing images—such as simple line drawings—in which no such information is available. In spirit, this early work by Huffman, Clowes, and Waltz was closer than Marr's to more recent theories of shape recognition which make use of non-accidental shape properties; but it also links back to a much older tradition, exemplified by Helmholtz's "unconscious inference," which asserts that perception is inferential and that it can "cleverly determine the nature of the world with limited image data" (Nakayama and Shimojo, 1992, p. 1357).

What value this early work will ultimately prove to have in explaining our ability to recognize objects in real scenes is still uncertain; but what the work carried out by Clowes, Huffman, and Waltz did do was provide a powerful vocabulary for the analysis of *pictures*. In the following pages I shall describe some of the ideas behind their approach. The terms used by Clowes, Huffman, and Waltz differ somewhat from one writer to another, and in the following account I shall use those terms which seem to me to be the most easily understood, regardless of which paper they come from. For example, I shall use the term "line junction" used by Clowes and Waltz, rather than

Huffman's term "picture node." The structure of the argument which follows is, however, taken mainly from Huffman (1971).

Huffman begins by saying that our ability to recognize objects in line drawings depends on certain assumptions: that what appear to be straight edges represent edges that are actually straight; that edges which appear to be parallel actually are parallel, and so on. This is very similar to what writers such as Biederman (1987) have said about nonaccidental shape properties. One closely related assumption that Huffman makes is that all pictures are taken from a "general position"; that is, "that a slight change of the position from which the picture is taken would not change the number of lines in the picture or the configurations in which they come together" (Huffman, 1971, p. 298). This amounts to assuming that the picture does not represent views of scenes containing *accidental alignments* in which objects happen to line up unusually well. In pictures, accidental alignments are represented by what a painter would call *false attachments:* junctions that represent two unrelated corners, or lines which represent two unrelated edges. Examples of false attachments of this kind are shown in figs. 1.15 (Guzman's TOWER) and 1.16 (Klee's *Town with Watchtowers*).

Huffman says that the single most important insight which makes his analysis possible is that there are only four possible interpretations of a line in a picture of a scene containing objects with plane faces. A line can represent either a "convex" or a "concave" edge with the planes on both sides of the edge in view, or it can represent one or the other of two kinds of occluding edges. An occluding edge is an edge having a visible plane on one side only, and this plane can lie to one side of the edge or the other. This plane hides or "occludes" more distant parts of the scene. In pictures that provide possible views of scenes, "a given line segment cannot have two different 'meanings' in two different parts of the picture, and it is this constancy of interpretation of what a line must mean in a picture which is the key to the method of analysis presented here" (Huffman, 1971, p. 299).

The aim of the method of analysis which Huffman describes is to label the lines and line junctions in a drawing automatically, in a way that is consistent with their meaning. An edge that is convex to the viewer should, at the end of the analysis, be labeled with a plus sign (+), an edge that is concave to the viewer should be labeled with a minus sign (−), and an occluding edge should be labeled with an arrow. The direction of the arrow determines whether the plane that hides part of the background lies to one side of the edge or the other. The convention adopted by Huffman is that this plane lies to the right of the edge, moving along the edge in the direction of the arrow. Clowes describes a similar scheme for labeling line drawings of objects with plane faces, and Waltz describes a labeling scheme for line drawings with shadows in which some of the lines represent the boundaries of shadows. Once a drawing has been labeled correctly, its "meaning" as a viewer-centered shape description has been extracted.

Huffman begins by pointing out that there are four basic ways in which three plane surfaces can come together at a corner. These four types of corners are illustrated in fig. 5.3, and the edges flanking each corner are labeled in accordance with the conventions given above. Fig. 5.3a shows three views of the type of corner that is flanked by edges that are convex in

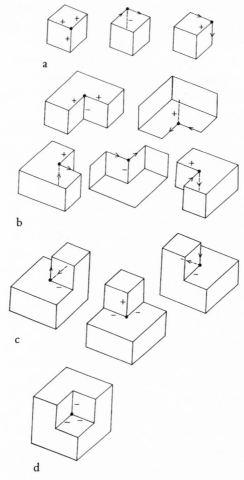

FIG. 5.3. Complete listing of possible pictures of corners in drawings of rectangular objects. From Huffman (1971), courtesy of Edinburgh University Press.

an object-centered description. Notice that the label assigned to a line depends on the direction from which the edge is *viewed*. For example, the hidden edge in the center drawing in fig. 5.3a is labeled with a minus sign because it is *concave to the viewer,* although in itself (that is, in an object-centered description) this edge would be convex. Thus the meaning extracted by an analysis of this type takes the form of a viewer-centered description: the meaning of a line is its meaning as an edge in the viewer's frontal plane. In order to extract an object-centered shape description of the objects or scenes represented in these drawings, a further level of analysis would have to be carried out.

Figs. 5.3b, 5.3c, and 5.3d show views of other possible types of corners. Fig. 5.3d, for example, shows a wholly concave corner flanked by three concave edges, and each of these corners is labeled with a minus sign.

Fig. 5.4 lists the types of line junctions that can stand for corners, extracted from the views of corners shown in fig. 5.3. I shall refer to this as a "look-up list." The first drawing in this list corresponds to the corner shown in the last drawing in fig. 5.3b (an arrow followed by a plus sign). The last drawing of a corner in the second line in fig. 5.4 corresponds to the corner shown in the first drawing in fig. 5.3a (three plus signs). Hidden edges are not shown in this list. I shall refer to the three types of junctions representing corners in the first two lines of this list as "L-junctions," "arrow-junctions," and "Y-junctions." Each of these junctions can appear in any orientation in a drawing. The third line in the list shows one other possible type of junction: a "T-junction" denoting the point where an edge

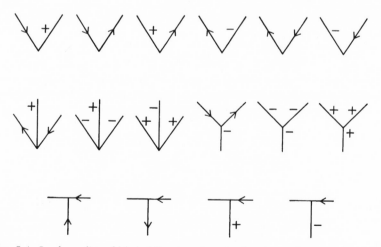

Fɪɢ. 5.4. Look-up list of labeled line junctions in drawings of rectangular objects. Adapted from Huffman (1971), courtesy of Edinburgh University Press.

just passes behind a face. Notice that this type of junction stands for a picture primitive which exists exclusively in the viewer's frontal plane, and has no correlate in an object-centered description. Because the line at the top of the "T" must be an occluding contour, the occluding plane must be above this line, so the "arrow" label must always run from right to left in the sense shown.

The following paragraphs illustrate in a simplified form the kind of process by which a line drawing like the one shown in fig. 5.5a can be analyzed. In Clowes's paper this process was embodied in a computer program. Carrying out this process depends on being able to relate a list of possible line junctions to a set of rules. The most important rule employed in the analysis is that a line must have the same meaning—that is, it must carry the same labeling—along its whole length. This rule is not conventional, but is based on what we expect of real objects. An edge of an object is not normally concave at one end and convex at the other, nor does an occluding edge normally change to a convex edge or a concave edge at

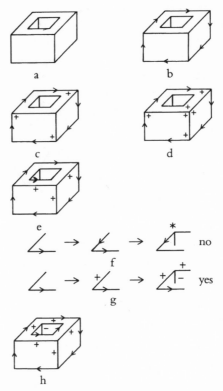

FIG. 5.5. Successive stages in the analysis of a rectangular object.

some point along its length, nor can the occluding plane change from one side to the other along a line.

At the beginning of the analysis it is necessary to decide whether the picture represents a solid or a hole. If the picture represents a solid, as it does in this case, the interior of the solid must lie to the right, going round the outline of the drawing in a clockwise direction. Thus this outline, which represents the outer edges of the object, can be labeled with arrows running all round it in a clockwise direction (fig. 5.5b).

We next go to the look-up list shown in fig. 5.4 to see whether there are any arrow-junctions with arrows running across the heads of the arrows in the appropriate directions. (There are no Y-junctions in the outline of this drawing, so there is no need to look in the list for Y-junctions.) In fact, there is only one junction which fulfills this requirement. The shaft of this arrow-junction is labeled with a plus sign, so all three lines in the drawing that correspond to the shafts of the arrows can now be labeled with a plus sign (fig. 5.5c).

We now apply the rule that says that lines must have the same meaning— that is, the same labeling—along their whole length. Applying this rule to the three lines labeled with a plus sign at one end results in a Y-junction in the middle of the drawing with all its arms labeled with a plus sign (fig. 5.5d). Checking this in the look-up list shows that such a junction is possible.

The next stage is to look at the single T-junction in the interior of the drawing. The look-up list shows that all T-junctions have an arrow running from right to left along the top of the T, so this line can be labeled with an arrow in the appropriate direction in the drawing (fig. 5.5e).

Now we have to find how the L-junction to the left of this arrow ought to be labeled. The look-up list provides two possible solutions: one with an arrow on the other arm of the L and the other with a plus sign on the other arm.

Try the L-junction with two arrows first (fig. 5.5f). If the arm of the L has an arrow at one end, it must have an arrow at the other end where it joins the arrow-junction. Look in the look-up list for an arrow-junction with an arrow running in this direction. There is no such junction in the list, so this is not a possible solution: this impossible junction is labeled with an asterisk.

Now go back and try the L-junction with an arrow and a plus sign (fig. 5.5g). If the arm of the L has a plus sign at one end, it must have a plus sign at the other end where it joins the arrow-junction. Look in the look-up list for an arrow-junction with a plus sign on this arm. There is only one junction in the list labeled in this way, and the other arm of the arrow head is labeled with a plus sign and the shaft with a minus sign. Apply this labeling to the drawing (fig. 5.5h).

All the visible edges and contours in the drawing have now been labeled. Although this labeling has been carried out without recourse to human intuitions, the result of the labeling process nevertheless agrees with our intuitions. For example, the labeling shows that there is a rectangular hole or depression in the top face, and this is the three-dimensional shape which we (intuitively) see in the drawing.

Both Clowes and Huffman explicitly compare this labeling process to parsing sentences in a language: that is, applying structural descriptions to sentences. Sentences that can be given a coherent structural description, like "The boy kicked the ball," intuitively *sound* "right" to a native English speaker; we say that such sentences are well formed or "grammatical." Similarly, drawings that can be labeled in a consistent way *look* "right," so that they appeal to our intuitions as drawings of possible objects.

The impression of three-dimensional shape given by such drawings is remarkably strong: normally much stronger than is given by silhouettes. Fig. 5.6 shows three rather similar drawings, all of which give a strong impression of three-dimensional shape. Intuitively, however, (a) is unambig-

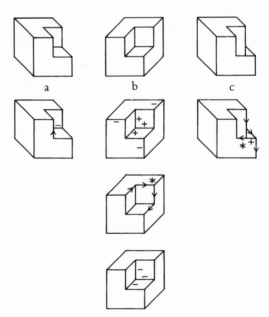

FIG. 5.6. Labelings for (a) unambiguous, (b) ambiguous, and (c) impossible drawings of rectangular objects. The "impossible" labeling is marked with an asterisk.

uous, (b) is ambiguous, and (c) represents an "impossible" object. In the drawings below, labeling reveals the structural features which provide the basis for these intuitions.[1]

Drawing (a) is unambiguous[2] because it can only be labeled in one way: the T-junction in the center of the drawing must represent the point at which an edge passes behind the L-shaped front face of the object.

Drawing (b) is ambiguous because it can be labeled in three different ways. The first drawing shows one possible labeling that represents a small cube stuck up into the corner of a ceiling. The drawing below shows a second possible labeling, representing a small cube sticking out of a larger cube at an odd angle. Notice, however, that this labeling involves a false attachment at the point marked with an asterisk. The drawing at the bottom represents a large cube with a smaller cube removed from one corner.

Finally, drawing (c) represents an impossible object because it cannot be labeled in any consistent way. The line at the top of the T-junction must be labeled with an arrow in the direction shown; but at the same time it must be labeled with a plus sign because that is the only possible way of labeling the corner to the extreme right of the drawing (cf. fig. 5.4). Because a line cannot have two different meanings at one and the same time, the drawing represents an impossible object.

In line drawings of rectangular objects, like the drawings analyzed above, the lines in the drawing stand for the visible parts of edges in the viewer's frontal plane. The smallest meaningful units of information in such drawings are the line junctions, and the analysis given above takes these units as primitives. Line junctions are zero-dimensional picture primitives which denote corners, or, in the case of T-junctions, the points at which an edge disappears behind a surface; and both corners and points of occlusion are zero-dimensional scene primitives. Consequently, the denotation system underlying drawings of this kind can be written as:

$$
\begin{array}{l}
\text{0 L-junctions,} \quad \longrightarrow \quad \text{0 corners} \\
\text{arrow-junctions,} \\
\text{and Y-junctions}
\end{array}
$$

$$
\text{T-junctions} \quad \longrightarrow \quad \text{0 points of occlusion}
$$

Line Drawings of Smooth Objects

Smooth objects are objects without edges, creases, or other surface discontinuities. Line drawings of smooth objects contain only two kinds of

FIG. 5.7. Look-up list of labeled line junctions in drawings of smooth objects.

junctions: T-junctions, where a contour passes behind a surface, and end-junctions, where the contour just fades away within the interior of a form. Fig. 5.7 provides a look-up list showing all possible labelings for these types of junctions. Contours are marked with an arrow, with the occluding surface to the right going in the direction of the arrow, as they are in drawings of objects having plane faces.[3] Consequently, the arrow must go from right to left across the top of a T-junction, as shown in the first two drawings in fig. 5.7. The parts of the contours that are hidden as they pass behind the top of the T are shown using hidden lines. The dotted line in the third drawing shows a hidden contour meeting a visible contour at the point where the visible contour ends.

Fig. 5.8 shows examples of unambiguous, ambiguous, and impossible drawings of smooth objects, together with possible labelings. Drawing (a) can be labeled in only one way, and thus can be interpreted in only one way, as a peanut shape. Drawing (b) can be labeled in two ways, as a peanut in

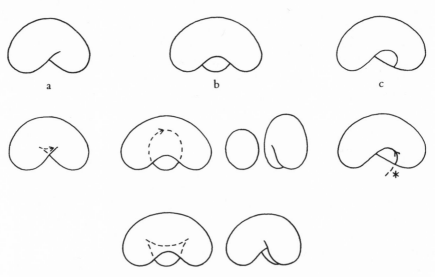

FIG. 5.8. Labelings for (a) unambiguous, (b) ambiguous, and (c) impossible drawings of smooth objects. The "impossible" labeling is marked with an asterisk.

front of a pebble, or as a three-lobed peanut. Finally, drawing (c) cannot be labeled in a consistent way, and consequently represents an impossible object.

Smooth surfaces can have one of three basic shapes at any given point: convex, concave, or saddle-shaped. The outside of an eggshell is a wholly convex surface, whereas the inside is a concave surface. Saddle-shaped surfaces are concave in one direction and convex in the other. There are also a number of intermediate types: cylindrical surfaces, for example, which are curved in one direction and straight in the other, and plane surfaces, which have no curvature. Apart from these degenerate cases, however, the surface of any smooth object can be divided into convex, concave, and saddle-shaped patches.

The contour of an object bounded by a single convex surface, such as an egg or a pebble, is a single, smooth, closed curve. In this case the contour has no end. In the general case, where an object is made up of a collection of convex, concave, and saddle-shaped patches of surface, the contour can end, and is represented in line drawings by an end-junction. Koenderink and van Doorn (1982) showed that visible contours always end in a simple, lawful manner: the visible contour must be concave at its ends, and the corresponding part of the rim must lie in a saddle-shaped patch.

Good examples of T-junctions and end-junctions can be seen in the drawing of Japanese sumo wrestlers shown in fig. 5.9. In this drawing, nearly all the lines representing contours obey the rule that the line must be concave to the occluding surface at an end-junction. For example, there are three end-junctions where the contours of the folds of the flesh under the chin of the wrestler on the right just fade away into the neck, and in each case the lines representing these contours are correctly drawn as concave at the end-junction. With a little imagination one can visualize the saddle-shaped surfaces at these points, as the surface of the neck turns under the outjutting chin. Similarly, the line representing the lower contour of the upper left arm of this wrestler is, correctly, concave at each end. As a result, this drawing has great authority, and the impression of three-dimensional shape which it gives is very strong.

It is worth comparing this drawing with one of similar quality: Picasso's drawing of Stravinsky (fig. 1.6). Compared with the drawing of the Sumo wrestlers, the folds of drapery in the right arm of Stravinsky's jacket look relatively flat. This effect is produced because few of the contours end correctly in concave end-junctions, and there are several incorrect T-junctions: for example, there is an incorrect T-junction close to the point where the lower arm rests on the arm of the chair. Several other incorrect T- and

Fɪɢ. 5.9. Katsukawa Shunsho, Japanese, 1726–1792, *Sumo Wrestlers of the Eastern Group: Nijigadake Somaemon from Ashu of Sekiwake Rank* [right] *and Fundenoumi Kin'emon from Kokura of Maegashira Rank* [left], c. 1782. Woodblock print, 26.0 × 38.2 cm. Frederick W. Gookin Collection, 1949.44. The Art Institute of Chicago. Photograph copyright 1944, Art Institute of Chicago, all rights reserved.

end-junctions appear in other parts of the drawing. It seems unlikely that these are simply "mistakes"; in Chapter 1, I suggested that this flattening was deliberate.

Fig. 1.7 (*Self-Portrait with Dogs*) shows a drawing by a talented 9-year-old girl. The configurations of T- and end-junctions in the drawing, particularly in the drawings of the dogs, are remarkably lawful, and as a result this drawing gives a strong impression of three-dimensional shape. There is only one obviously incorrect T-junction, at the point where the head of the dog at the bottom left of the drawing meets the body. It seems likely that this incorrect T-junction was unintentional: Joanne was probably thinking of the head and body of the dog as separate volumes.

Recognizing three-dimensional shapes in line drawings does not depend on our ability to recognize them as pictures of identifiable *objects*. Fig. 5.10 shows a painting by Paul Klee based on a very simple picture grammar of the type described above. Most of the paintings and drawings that Klee produced during 1939 and 1940 (the last two years of his life) are based on a picture grammar of this type (Willats, 1980). None of the shapes in the painting corresponds to recognizable objects, and yet the impression of three-dimensional shape is very strong. Nevertheless, our impulse to recognize identifiable objects in pictures is very powerful, and it is not difficult to interpret this as a painting of a classical urn with plants growing out of it: the title that Klee gave to this painting was *Der Park zu Abien (aus der Gemüse Abteilung)* (*The Park at Abien—from the Vegetable Department*). The overall composition consists of irregular, organic shapes at the top, a more regular shape in the middle, and a symmetrical pattern at the bottom with spiral loops which recall the scrolls in the capital of an Ionic column. This composition, together with the strong impression of three-dimensional shape, induces us to interpret the painting as a picture of plants in an urn: "As the figure grows little by little before our eyes an association of ideas may easily tempt us into objective interpretation. For with a bit of imagination every complex structure lends itself to a comparison with familiar forms in nature" (Klee, 1961, p. 89).

It is also apparent from this painting that, although recognition at the object level may depend on global information, shape recognition does not. An analysis of the shapes represented in this drawing may be compared with the account of Guzman's "Analysis of curved line drawings using context and global information," given in Chapter 4 (fig. 4.1). Provided a line drawing contains a few T- and end-junctions and obeys the rules for possible configurations of such junctions, it is easily and naturally interpreted as a picture of a possible smooth object, regardless of the context.

FIG. 5.10. Paul Klee, *Der Park zu Abien (aus der Gemüse Abteilung)* (*The Park at Abien—from the Vegetable Department*), 1939. Watercolor, 36.5 × 30.0 cm. Privatbesitz Schweiz. Kunstmuseum, Berne. Copyright Design and Artists Copyright Society 1997.

Features for Which Lines May and May Not Stand

The methods of analysis described above apply only to line drawings of objects in which the lines stand for edges or contours, but, as Kennedy (1974, 1983) has pointed out, there are a number of other uses of line which seem to be universally recognizable by human observers. Among the features that lines can stand for are:

1. edges, like the edges of objects having plane faces, and the edges of sheets, such as the edges of the shirt cuffs in Picasso's drawing of Stravinsky;

2. occluding contours, like the contours of the bodies of the wrestlers in fig. 5.9;

3. thin, wirelike forms like Stravinsky's hair, and the rims of his glasses;

4. cracks, like the crack between the lips of the wrestler on the left; and

5. creases, like the creases in the wrestler's stomach.

In addition, lines are often used to stand for:

6. the boundaries between areas which differ in local tone or color, like the lines used to depict the patterns on the wrestler's aprons or the spots on Stravinsky's tie.

However, this last use of line may not be universally recognizable. Kennedy and Ross (1975) showed a line drawing of a parrot in which lines were used to indicate areas of color change to the Songe, a people of Papua New Guinea whose culture includes no pictorial representation, and found that these observers did not interpret the lines correctly. Instead, they created an unexpected shape referent for them, suggesting that the parrot had been cut repeatedly in the places marked.

In addition, lines can be used to stand for:

7. surface contours.

Computer-generated drawings employing surface contours like those shown in fig. 8.2 show that such drawings can provide a good representation of three-dimensional shape. Drawings of this kind are especially useful in showing the shapes of concave patches, like the concave regions at the corners of the eyes and mouth. Lines denoting surface contours were often used in nineteenth-century engineering drawings, such as the drawing shown in fig. 6.3.

The Relation between Line Drawings and the Array of Light from a Scene

Lines are not, in general, acceptable when used to stand for the boundaries of shadows or highlights, that is, changes in tone that come about as the result of incidental lighting conditions, and it is difficult to account for the effectiveness of line drawings in terms of the traditional point projection theory of pictures. According to Gibson, "There is *no* point-to-point correspondence of brightness or color between the optic array from a line drawing and the optic array from the object represented" (Gibson, 1971, p. 28). Art students in life classes are very often tempted to use lines to stand for the boundaries of highlights and shadows: that is, the boundaries of regions in the frontal plane where the apparent intensity of the light changes abruptly. As a result, their drawing can look unconvincing. Pearson, Hanna, and Martinez (1990) referred to such changes as "luminance step edges." Fig. 5.11a shows a line drawing in which such edges have been extracted automatically, and it is apparent that this form of edge detection does not work very well. As Pearson et al. commented, "it tends to produce too many lines and at the same time to omit some key ones. Edge detected images of humans look vaguely human in outline but have poor facial features" (p. 48). They found, however, that what they called a "luminance valley," in which a column of darker elements in the image is seen against a lighter background, often corresponds to the array of light from an occluding contour of an object in which all the local surfaces have the same reflectance (for example, where the contour of a nose occludes a cheek). However, where the contour of a surface is seen against a background having a different reflectance (for example, a hand held up against a darker wall), the characteristic pattern in the image will be a luminance step. They therefore concluded that what is required is a feature detector with primary response to luminance valleys, but a secondary response to luminance edges.

Fig. 5.11b shows the result of applying a feature detector of this kind (which they called a "cartoon operator") to a photograph of a face. This operation, embodied in a computer program, resulted in quite acceptable line drawings, comparable to those produced by a human artist.[4] Thus it is not quite true to say that there is *no* point-to-point correspondence between the array of light from a line drawing and the array of light from the object represented; but the correspondence is not a very obvious one. It seems most unlikely that artists are able to detect a combination of luminance valleys and luminance edges in the light from a scene. What artists and draftsmen have to learn to do, if they want to produce drawings of smooth objects that are effective as shape representations, is look for the *contours* in views of scenes, and represent these contours by lines; and in particular they must look carefully for the points where contours end. They must also resist the temptation to use lines to represent the boundaries of highlights and shadows. Much of the authority of drawings such as Picasso's portrait of Stravinsky (fig. 1.6) and Katsukawa Shunsho's drawing of wrestlers (fig. 5.9)

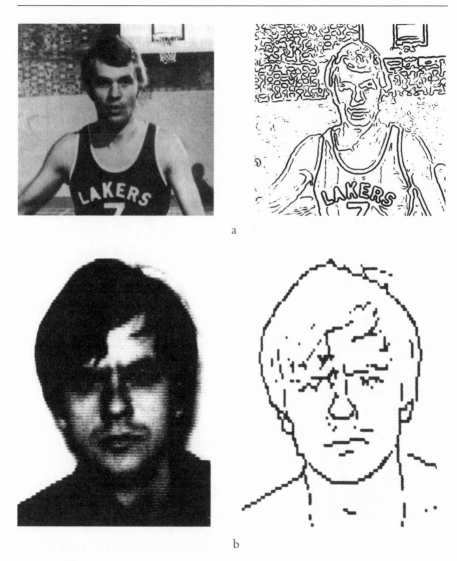

Fig. 5.11. Line drawings extracted from gray-scale images. (a) From Marr (1982), courtesy of BBC Horizon. (b) From Pearson et al. (1990), courtesy Don Pearson.

comes from the fact that these artists knew exactly what lines in line drawings may and may not stand for in drawings of smooth objects.

So far, in Part 2, I have described two kinds of denotation systems: line drawing, and systems based on regions as picture primitives. Both these systems can be related to the array of light coming from a scene, but not in any very easy or obvious way. Finally, in the next chapter, I describe systems that can be related much more directly to this array.

CHAPTER SIX

Optical Denotation Systems

In pictures based on optical denotation systems the picture primitives denote features of the array of light reaching the eye or the camera, rather than physical features of the scene such as edges and contours. The picture primitives in optical denotation systems are normally *points,* and these points denote corresponding points in the frontal plane or visual field: the colors and intensities of the intercepts of small bundles or sheafs of light rays. Pictures based on such systems include photographs, TV pictures, and Pointillist paintings. In the newspaper photograph of a hijacker shown in fig. 1.8 the marks are small dots of ink, and these dots represent point primitives in the picture. When the picture is viewed from a distance, these dots fuse in the viewer's eye, so that different sizes of marks provide different tones; and these tones represent the intensity of the light reaching the camera at each point. This denotation system can be written:

$$0 \text{ points (dots)} \longrightarrow 0 \text{ points (point intensities).}$$

The photograph of a house on a hillside shown in fig. 6.1a was taken from a considerable distance and then enlarged, so that the grain of the film shows up in the image. This image was subsequently fed into a computer, digitized, and printed in color using a bubble jet printer, and the marks in this image are a consequence of this process (fig. 6.1b). These marks represent, rather indirectly, the point primitives denoting the colors and intensities of the light as it reached the film in the camera. Although this image was processed by a computer, the information was derived from a viewer-centered description, in contrast to the drawings shown in fig. 8.2 which were derived from object-centered descriptions. Consequently, the marks in this image, and the picture primitives to which they refer, are not directly related to the

a

b

Fig. 6.1. (a) A foreshortened view of a house on a hillside near Bath. Photograph by Simon Ferguson. (b) Digitized version printed using a bubble jet printer. Photograph by Simon Ferguson; computer graphics by Lee Edwards.

three-dimensional shape features of the house, such as the edges of the building or the windows, but only to the light reflected from these features. All the work of feature detection has to be done by the viewer. Television pictures are also derived from views: here the marks (the phosphors on the screen) all have the same size, and the light they give off is related to the colors as well as the intensities of the light from the scene. In neither of these examples are the picture primitives directly related to or derived from distinct *objects* or the *shapes* of objects.

Line drawings like the *Sumo Wrestlers of the Eastern Group* (fig. 5.9) or Joanne's *Self-Portrait with Dogs* (fig. 1.7) and pictures based on optical denotation systems like the photographs shown in figs. 2.4 and 6.1a exemplify what Rosch (1973) called "clearest cases" of two distinct classes of pictures. But how should pictures like Raphael's *Study of the Three Graces* (fig. 6.2) or the drawing of a locomotive shown in fig. 6.3 be classified? Most of the marks in *The Three Graces* are lines, and some of these lines represent

Fig. 6.2. Raphael, *Study of the Three Graces,* before 1518. Red chalk over stylus underdrawing, 20.3 × 26.0 cm. The Royal Collection, Her Majesty Queen Elizabeth II.

occluding contours; but on the other hand, the tonal modeling and cast shadows in this picture give a strong impression of the effects of light.

Like many of Raphael's drawings, *The Three Graces* was intended as a study for a painting: in this case, for subsidiary figures in the frescoes in the vault of Angostino Chigi's *Logia di Psiche.* These frescoes were executed entirely by members of Raphael's workshop, Raphael's own involvement being limited to the design stages (Ames-Lewis, 1986). The colors and the background of the scene, missing from this drawing, would have been added in the finished fresco; and in the course of the painting the more overtly linear aspects of the drawing would have been suppressed, changing the mark system to one in which the tone and color varied from point to point across the surface. The resulting painting would then have provided a typical example of a realistic, "optical" Renaissance painting. On the other hand, there are numerous examples of drawings and engravings that have been derived from optically realistic paintings, but in which the original denota-

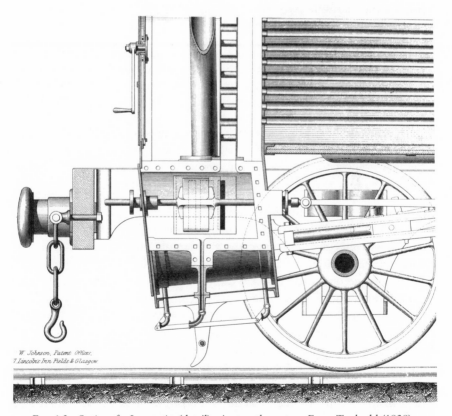

FIG. 6.3. *Section of a Locomotive* (detail), nineteenth century. From Tredgold (1838).

tion system has been replaced by line drawing. Marcantonio Raimondi's engraving of *The Judgement of Paris* (fig. 7.4a), after Raphael, is in effect a line drawing with the addition of tonal modeling and cast shadows.

Like Raphael's *The Three Graces,* the drawing of a locomotive shown in fig. 6.3 is basically a line drawing, and even contains examples of the (wholly conventional) use of dotted lines denoting hidden edges: a pictorial device that has no basis in optics. And yet, like *The Three Graces,* this drawing also contains convincing examples of the representation of the optical effects of tonal modeling and cast shadows. Is it possible to place such pictures, in terms of the denotation systems on which they are based, along a smooth continuum running from optically faithful pictures such as TV pictures at one end to pictures that are less optically faithful at the other?

Gibson (1954) suggested something of this kind in his original account of what he called the point-projection theory of pictures. According to this theory, a picture can represent a real object or scene insofar as the light rays from the picture are the same as the light rays from the original. Leonardo recommended a method for recording the changes in color resulting from atmospheric perspective which seems to fit this theory rather well:

> Take things positioned throughout the countryside at intervals of one hundred *braccia,* such as trees, houses, men and particular locations. Then in front of the first tree, with a well steadied plate of glass and a correspondingly fixed eyepoint, draw a tree on the said glass over the shape of the real one. Then move the glass far enough to one side so that the real one is aligned close to the side of the one you have drawn. Then colour your drawing in such a way that, with respect to colour and form, it is so alike the real one that both, if you close one eye, might seem to be painted on the aforementioned glass at one and the same distance. (Kemp, 1989, p.78)

This theory seems to provide a good account of pictures, like TV pictures, which capture and retransmit the light from real scenes, but there are clearly some pictures that do not replicate the light from real scenes in a completely faithful way. Even colored photographs, for example, cannot provide an array of light matching that from a real scene, if only because the light intensities from a real scene range over extremes that cannot possibly be matched by the light coming from a photograph or an artist's picture. Another difficulty is that an artist can judge the colors and tones in a scene only as they are perceived after the operation of the tone and color constancies; whereas a mechanical device like a TV camera captures the colors and intensities of light directly.

In his original essay, Gibson (1954) defined "the *fidelity* of a picture by analogy with the fidelity of a sound recording, assuming that it could go from a maximum to no fidelity at all" (Gibson, 1971, p. 28). It is tempting, in terms of this analogy, to imagine an artist setting out to copy or replicate the array of light from a scene, but failing to do so to a greater or lesser extent—rather like a sound recording instrument failing to record a sound with complete fidelity. In terms of this analogy, it could be argued that pictures like *The Three Graces* may not achieve complete fidelity, but they are more faithful than, say, pure line drawings. But quite apart from difficulties of actually producing "faithful" pictures, Gibson's analogy with the fidelity of a sound recording breaks down when it is applied to pictures like *The Three Graces* which are predominantly optical in character but nevertheless contain elements of other denotation systems: most obviously, line drawing. When a sound recording of a piece of music lacks fidelity, it is because it is contaminated by noise, not because it contains elements derived from some other musical system. In the event, one of the main reasons why Gibson abandoned the point-projection theory of pictures was that he was unable to accommodate line drawing within this theory.

Very few artists have, in fact, attempted to replicate the appearance of the optic array directly. Even the Impressionists, whose avowed aim was to paint their direct perceptions, were influenced by other paintings and current theories about painting: contemporary theories of perception and the pictorial devices used in other kinds of pictures, especially Japanese prints and early photographs. The use of areas of strongly contrasting light and dark at the expense of middle tones, which can be observed, for example, in Manet's *Déjeuner sur l'herbe,* 1863 (fig. 7.3), was derived from similar effects in contemporary photographs rather than from the direct observation of nature.

Thus even apparently realistic, optical paintings can be thought of not so much as direct facsimiles of the optic array as constructions on the picture surface made up of specific and largely independent pictorial devices: devices which, like line drawing, are related to features of the optic array but not necessarily derived directly from them. For example, artists and illustrators sometimes use thicker lines in the foreground of a drawing and thinner lines in the background in order to give an impression of depth (figs. 6.8 and 7.7a). This device is clearly related to the effects of atmospheric perspective, but it is equally clear that it is not derived directly from any identifiable feature in the array of light from a scene. I shall not attempt to give anything like a full account of these devices, but merely describe the more important of them in order to show their predominantly artificial character.

Tonal Modeling

As a matte surface turns away from a light source, the light reflected from it to the viewer will become less intense. This change in intensity can provide information about the shape of the viewed surface, an effect referred to in perception theory as "shape from shading" (Marr, 1982). The representation of this effect in pictures is called "tonal modeling."

Kemp (1992) describes a method given by Cennino Cennini for modeling form in light and shade which involved placing equal quantities of a given pigment in three bowls and mixing them with increasing quantities of white. These three grades of progressively lighter and less saturated pigment were then laid side by side over a green underdrawing, leaving the green showing through in the darkest areas. The most prominent parts of the form were then emphasized with an even lighter tone, while pure white was reserved for the highlights and pure black for the darkest shadows (fig. 6.4). The boundaries of the different tones were then blended into each other "like a puff of smoke."

This rough-and-ready way of producing an effect of tonal modeling is comparable to Cennini's workshop rule for producing pictures in perspective, quoted in Chapter 2: "And put in the buildings by this uniform system: that the moldings which you make at the top of the building should slant downward" (Cennini, fifteenth century/1954, p. 57). Following this rule gives a reasonably convincing effect of perspective, but it is not grounded, as Alberti's *costruzione legittima* was, in the primary geometry of the optic array. Similarly, Cennini's rule for producing an effect of tonal modeling results in a reasonably effective representation of the effects of light and shade, but its use is not dependent on the artist actually copying nature.

Marr (1982) described a method of representing shading taken from Horn (1975) based on a knowledge of surface orientation and surface reflectance, and shows that predicted appearance of a portion of the Swiss Alps computed by Horn's methods, and the actual appearance of the same

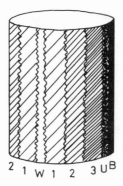

FIG. 6.4. Basic method for modeling form in light and shade, as described in Cennino Cennini's *Il libro del'arte*. From Kemp (1992), courtesy of Martin Kemp.

scene as represented in a satellite photograph, are remarkably similar. Here we have a rule-governed method for representing tonal modeling which may be compared with rule-governed methods of reproducing the geometry of perspective using techniques like Alberti's *costruzione legittima,* or the algebraic transformation rules used in a computer program.

The tones in a drawing are often produced using hatched lines. If the lines at a particular point are close together, they will appear to fuse, giving a darker tone at that point. By controlling the distance between the lines, or the thickness of the lines, or both, the artist can vary the tone of the drawing; and this technique can be used to produce an effect of tonal modeling. A simple form of tonal modeling can be produced using parallel hatched lines, as in the outstretched forearm of the figure of the woman on the extreme left of Raphael's *The Three Graces* (fig. 6.2).

Surface Contours

Lines can also be used to represent *surface contours,* and this provides another and quite distinct source of information about surface shape. These two techniques are often combined, and there are, in addition, at least two kinds of surface contours; so the functions served by the hatched lines in artists' drawings and engravings can be quite complex.

In the drawing shown in fig. 8.2a, produced by computer, the surface contours represent the edges of sections of the form, rather like the edges of a sliced loaf. The lines running from top to bottom in the picture represent the edges of vertical sections, and even where these lines are quite far apart they give a vivid impression of three-dimensional shape. In places where the lines are close together, however, as they are toward the contours of the eye and cheek, optical fusion takes place, so that the tone appears darker in this area, mimicking the effects of tonal modeling.

A related technique, which combines tonal modeling with surface contours in a rather similar way, is described by Rawson (1969), who refers to it as "bracelet shading." In this technique a series of curved, parallel lines are laid alongside the outlines of the form, giving an effect of tonal modeling but at the same time demonstrating the three-dimensional shape of the form through a series of sections. Rawson gives a number of examples of the use of this "bracelet shading" by Dürer and other German draftsmen and engravers, and according to Rawson, both Leonardo and Raphael adopted this technique from Dürer. Traces of this bracelet shading can be seen in Raphael's *The Three Graces*—for example, in the hatched shading on the breasts of the woman on the left—but the effect is much less pronounced here than it is in Dürer's engravings. A good example of bracelet shading can be seen in the leg of the seated figure shown in a detail of an engraving by Marcantonio Raimondi (fig. 7.4b). The lines running round the form correspond to the edges of cross-sections, and therefore to surface contours, but in addition the hatched lines have been thickened toward the outlines of the form, giving an effect of tonal modeling. The persistence of this device can be seen in the cover illustration for *Freak Comics* (fig. 7.7b): lines of bracelet shading run round the jeans of the figure on the right.

Lines can also be used to represent the directions of the *principal curvatures* of a surface: in fig. 6.5 the directions of the lines represent the directions of the principal curvatures on the surface of a torus, or doughnut. Lines of this kind can also be regarded as surface contours. Apart from special or degenerate cases (a plane surface, for example), there are always two principal curvatures associated with each point on a surface, and the directions of these principal curvatures are always at right angles. On wholly convex surfaces like the outer surface of the torus, both principal curvatures are convex and correspond to the greatest and least curvatures of the surface at that point. On wholly concave surfaces like the inside of an eggshell, both the principal curvatures are concave and again correspond to the greatest and least curvatures. On saddle-shaped surfaces, like the inner surfaces of the torus, one of the principal curvatures is convex and the other concave. At any point on the surface of a cylinder, one of the principal curvatures is convex, and the lines representing the direction of this curvature run round the form. The other principal curvature is zero, and lines representing the direction of this curvature run along the form.

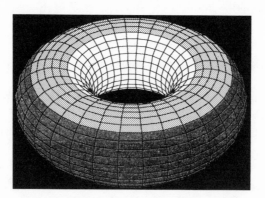

FIG. 6.5. Contour lines showing the directions of the principal curvatures on the surface of a torus. From Koenderink and van Doorn (1992), courtesy of Jan Koenderink and Andrea van Doorn.

Artists and draftsmen often seem to represent the directions of these principal curvatures by lines of shading. Koenderink (1984) illustrates an example by Dürer, taken from his *Samson Killing the Lion,* 1498, in which the lines representing the directions of the concave principal curvatures on the inside curve of the lion's tail are represented by lines running along the form, while the directions of the convex principal curvatures on the outside curve are represented by lines of bracelet shading running round the form. In the drawing of the locomotive shown in fig. 6.3, some of the smaller cylindrical forms have lines running along their length, and these directions correspond to those of one of the principal curvatures of the surface. This can be seen in lines running along the straight cylindrical portions of the coupling links at the front of the locomotive. These lines continue round the links, following the directions of the principal curvatures of the convex and saddle-shaped surfaces on the outer and inner parts of the curved ends of the links, like the lines representing the directions of the principal contours running round the torus shown in fig. 6.5. Similarly, the lines on the flares of the spokes as they join the rim and hub of the wheel follow the directions of one of the principal curvatures of these saddle-shaped surfaces. The representation of surface contours in this way gives a vivid impression of three-dimensional shape. However, these lines also mimic the effects of tonal modeling as they come closer together toward the outlines of the drawing. In the larger cylindrical forms in the drawing, such as the large exhaust pipe at the top center, a more deliberate attempt has been made to represent the effects of light falling across the surface: the lines are drawn closer together to produce lighter or darker tones in a way which could not represent equally spaced surface contours. In other places, for example, on the cushion-shaped buffer on the extreme left, the lines are not related to the representation of surface contours. Instead these lines are used merely as marks in order to give an effect of tonal modeling.

Compared with this drawing, Raphael made relatively little use of surface contours in *The Three Graces.* Only in a few places, like the area between the breasts and the junction between the neck and jaw of the woman on the left, do the lines seem to follow the directions of surface contours. In most places, most noticeably on the outstretched arm of the woman on the left, the directions of the lines are unrelated to surface shape, and it is only the thickness and tone of the line that is used to give an effect of tonal modeling. This makes good sense if the drawing was intended as a study for a finished painting in which these lines would be eliminated, and the tones and colors blended so that they varied smoothly from point to point.

Cast Shadow

Both these drawings contain examples of cast shadow, a pictorial device that is conceptually different from tonal modeling, although the two techniques very often appear together. In Waltz's illustrations to his paper "Understanding line drawing of scenes with shadows" (1975), diagonal lines are used to represent the tonal modeling, and horizontal lines are used to represent the shadows (fig. 6.6).

As Koenderink (1990, p. 27) says: "Possible optical interactions are . . . extremely diverse in their nature. Some of the interactions depend merely on the rectilinear propagation, that is on *perspective*. Others are of a photometrical nature. Still others depend on the wave character of the radiation." Representing shape through tonal modeling depends mainly on using variations of tone. Representing shape through shadows, on the other hand, depends mainly on the *shapes* of the shadows: representing shadows in a picture is a problem in perspective, using the term in a wide sense to include the parallel systems such as oblique projection.

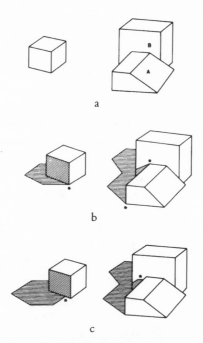

Fig. 6.6. Line drawings with shadows. (a) There is no evidence to relate the objects to each other or the table. (b) The junctions marked with asterisks provide evidence that the two objects or the object and the table *touch*. (c) The junctions marked with asterisks provide evidence that the objects or the object and the table *do not touch*. From Waltz (1975), courtesy of McGraw-Hill, Inc.

Because the sun's rays are parallel, any shadow that the sun throws on a flat surface will be an oblique projection: the outline of the shadow of a rectangular portico thrown onto the facade of a building, for example, will correspond to a drawing of the portico in oblique projection (fig. 6.7). This provided architectural draftsmen in the eighteenth and nineteenth centuries with a way of making their drawings look more three-dimensional: in effect, an outline drawing of a feature in oblique projection is superimposed on a drawing in orthogonal projection. For simple rectangular objects, the shapes of these silhouettes can be obtained using rules based on secondary geometry—that is, rules about the directions of lines representing the boundaries of shadows on the picture surface—similar to those used for producing drawings in oblique projection. Conventionally, the boundaries of the shadows of horizontal edges in the third dimension in these drawings run at 45° across the drawing surface, enabling the draftsman to represent the shapes of projections such as windows or moldings and providing the viewer with information about the extent of the projection of one surface in front of another. A similar technique was used in engineering drawings. In fig. 6.3 the shapes of some of the cylindrical forms in the drawing are revealed by throwing a shadow across them. In these cases the edges of the shadows correspond to the curve of the intersection between two surfaces. For example, the outline of the shadow on the buffer stock on the extreme left of the drawing corresponds to the curve of intersection between the real cylindrical surface of the stock itself and the elliptical prism of shadow cast by the cushion-shaped buffer. In effect, the boundary of this shadow acts as a special kind of surface contour.

An illustration in Waltz (1975) demonstrates the way in which shadows can be used to show whether objects are touching or not touching in the scene. As he points out, the drawing of the cube in fig. 6.6a is, by itself,

FIG. 6.7. Cast shadows as oblique projections: detail of an architectural drawing by Colen Campbell. From Dubery and Willats (1972).

ambiguous: it could be floating in midair, resting on a table, or even cantilevered out from a wall. In addition, it is not clear from the drawing whether object A is or is not touching object B. In drawings b and c, these ambiguities are removed by the addition of cast shadows. In drawing b, one of the points on the outline of the shadow representing a corner of the cube, marked with an asterisk, coincides with the junction representing this corner; consequently we infer that the cube is resting on a horizontal surface. A similar coincidence between a corner and its shadow, also marked with an asterisk, shows that the wedge-shaped block must be touching the rectangular block. In drawing c, however, the points representing corners in the outlines of the shadows, again marked with asterisks, do not coincide with junctions representing those corners. We thus infer that the cube is floating in midair, and that, although the two other objects are not touching, the wedge-shaped block is resting on a surface. This suggests a simple rule of secondary geometry: if a junction representing a corner coincides with the point on the outline of a shadow representing that corner, the corner must be in contact with the surface at that point. A similar rule applies to occluding contours and the shadows of contours, and this provides artists

Fig. 6.8. R. Earlom, *Pastoral Scene,* 1774. False mezzotint, after an original drawing by Claude Lorraine, 20.9 × 25.8 cm. Collection of the author. Photograph by Anne Shallis.

and draftsmen with a way of showing whether or not two objects are touching: something which would not be possible using line drawing alone. In the false mezzotint by R. Earlom shown in fig. 6.8, for example, the shepherd's foot is clearly resting on the ground because the outline of the little toe is attached to its own shadow. In addition, the outline of the shadow of the leg as a whole functions as a surface contour, like the shadow on the buffer stock of the locomotive, revealing the shape of the bank on which the shepherd is sitting.

Atmospheric Perspective

The representation of atmospheric perspective (or aerial perspective as it is sometimes called) has at least four components, each of which may be used separately or in combination. As with other optical devices, it is important to make a distinction between the actual effects of distance and the atmosphere on the optic array, and the pictorial devices used to represent these effects: in practice, these may be only loosely connected.

Diminution of Clarity of Form with Distance

In their passage through the atmosphere, the rays of light from an object will be scattered and the contours of distant objects will appear more or less blurred. It seems rare, however, in either Western or Chinese painting, to find this blurring represented directly. In fig. 6.8 the lines representing the contours of distant hills are drawn just as sharply as the lines in the foreground, but the lines show fewer details of the contours. In both cases, shape information is lost, but in the light from real scenes it is lost through blurring, whereas in drawings it is lost because the shapes of the lines are less detailed.

Diminution of Tonal Contrast with Distance

The apparent tonal contrast between light and dark objects tends to diminish with distance. In a foggy or misty landscape, the light from the sun is scattered by the atmosphere, giving a diffuse overall illumination, so that objects in the foreground are seen silhouetted against a uniformly pale background. In a brightly lit landscape, the foreground will contain strong contrasts of light and shade, but the scattering of the light from more distant parts of the scene will reduce the apparent tonal contrasts. Western academic landscape painting referred to, but did not directly represent, these light effects in nature.

Western academic drawings and prints also exploited the apparent diminution of tonal contrast with distance in real scenes by using thicker and darker *lines* in the foreground of the picture, and thinner and lighter lines in the background, in order to give an impression of depth. For example, the lines representing the contours of the tree in the foreground of fig. 6.8 are much stronger than the lines representing the contours of the hills in the background. Because there are no lines as such in nature, this device is quite unrealistic; but it is clearly related to the optical effects of atmospheric perspective in the light from real scenes. The use of this device is not confined to academic drawings and prints, however: the outlines of the seated girl in the foreground of the cover of *Freak Comics* (fig. 7.7a) are much thicker than the outlines of the figures in the background.

Chinese landscape painting also exploited atmospheric effects in order to represent depth, but in a different way. A typical Northern Sung landscape, like the detail from a twelfth-century scroll shown in fig. 10.8, is made up of a series of overlapping silhouettes of trees and mountain peaks with the mist swirling through the valleys between them. There is some diminution of tonal contrast with distance, but the depth in the painting is achieved mainly by exploiting the figure-and-ground effect. Each plane is dark at the top and fades away into a lighter base (suggesting mist in the valleys), which provides the ground for the dark top of the next nearest plane. Again, this alternation of light and dark regions is an artificial pictorial device, referring to real atmospheric effects rather than reproducing them directly.

Change of Hue with Distance

Blue light, which has a shorter wavelength than red light, is more readily scattered by the atmosphere: consequently the sky appears blue, and more distant objects appear bluer than nearer objects. This effect was also exploited in Western landscape painting in order to give an effect of depth. In Leonardo's *The Virgin of the Rocks,* c. 1508 (National Gallery, London), for example, the colors in the foreground of the painting are mostly warm reds, browns, and oranges, while the distant mountains are painted in cool blues and greens. According to Leonardo, "You know that in such air the furthest things seen in it—as in the case of mountains, when great quantities of air are found between your eye and the mountains—appear blue, almost the colour of the air when the sun is in the east" (Kemp, 1989, p. 80).

Change of Saturation with Distance

Colors in the distance appear less saturated than colors that are closer to the viewer. ("Saturation" refers to the purity of a given hue; a fully saturated red is "redder" than one that has been adulterated with an admixture of black or white pigment.) This was another effect of atmospheric perspective which was exploited in Renaissance painting: in Piero della Francesca's *The Baptism of Christ*, c. 1442 (National Gallery, London), the fully saturated reds and blues of the angel's clothing appear in the foreground, while the reds and blues of the clothes of the figures in the distance are more muted.

The color effects in these two paintings, both loosely related to atmospheric perspective, are, however, quite different. Although in Piero's painting the reds are more fully saturated in the foreground, the change of saturation with distance seems only to apply to these colors: the greens of the trees and hills in the background are just as saturated, and no bluer, than the greens of the grass and foliage in the foreground. In *The Virgin of the Rocks,* the greens in the background are colder than the greens of the foliage in the foreground, but no less saturated; and the warm colors in the foreground seem no more saturated than the cold colors in the background.

Color Modeling

The Impressionists' friend and patron Theodore Duret remarked in an essay written in 1878: "Before Japan it was impossible; the painter always lied. Nature with its frank colors was in plain sight, yet no one ever saw anything on canvas but attenuated colors, drowning in a general half-tone" (Anfam et al., 1987, p. 158). As a result of color constancy, we tend to see the true colors and color saturations of surfaces whatever the lighting conditions. However, it seems impossible to reconcile our perceptions of color in real scenes with the representation of color in paintings in which the shapes of forms are represented using academic tonal modeling, because in order to use tonal modeling, light and dark pigments have to be added to the basic color pigments, reducing their saturation. As Kemp pointed out, Cennini's method is essentially an artificial one, because it ties tonal modeling to the inherent tonal values of different areas of local color: "According to Cennino's system, the shadow of a blue garment will be a deeply intense blue, while the adjacent shadow of a yellow cloth will be a radiantly saturated yellow which is relatively light in tone. Most unsettlingly, a fully lit area of blue will tend to be darker in tone than the shaded area of yellow" (Kemp, 1992, p. 265). In Japanese prints, this problem was avoided by separating the representation of shape from the representation of color. All the work of shape representation was carried out using line drawing, leaving the areas of color in the print free to represent the pure local colors of surfaces. The Impressionists were influenced by the use of pure color in Japanese prints, and they tried to avoid the use of tonal modeling, which was associated with academic painting; but instead of using small patches of color to represent the local colors of surfaces, they attempted to use them to represent color *sensations*—something very different.

Another way of tackling the problem was to exploit the natural tones that are associated with different fully saturated colors. For example, fully saturated blue has a naturally dark tone, while fully saturated yellow has a naturally light tone. Thus an effect of tonal modeling can be obtained by using blue for areas of shadow, or surfaces that turn away from the light or from the viewer, and oranges, pinks, and yellows for surfaces that would face the light or the viewer. This technique was much exploited by Cézanne: in the *Grandes baigneuses* paintings, for example, the surfaces of the figures that face the viewer are painted in oranges, pinks, and yellows, while the surfaces that turn away from the viewer are painted in fully saturated blues. A similar technique was used by Fauve painters such as Matisse and Derain.

Another technique, used by the Pointillist painter Georges Seurat, and Neo-Impressionists influenced by Seurat such as Paul Signac, was to use small dots of pure color placed side by side, rather than adulterating areas of color with white or dark pigments. The different tones naturally associated with different colors were then exploited to give an effect of tonal modeling. For example, the areas of color close to the line of the woman's cheek in Seurat's *Young Woman Powdering Herself* (color plate 2), and the area of color beneath her chin, are made up of red and blue dots, giving an effect of tonal modeling at these points, but still enabling the artist to use almost fully saturated colors.

Seurat, like many of his contemporaries, claimed that this technique was intended to produce an optical mixture of color, but this is not actually what takes place, because the dots in Pointillist paintings, unlike the dots in newspaper photographs, are not small enough to fuse. It has been suggested instead that because the dots are still clearly visible as dots when the canvas is viewed from a normal distance, and the varied colors can still be identified separately, the dots seem to shimmer and vibrate, recreating in the eye of the viewer something of the effects of sunlight. Ogden Rood's *Modern Chromatics,* which Seurat had studied carefully, noted this phenomenon, and it seems likely that Seurat was deliberately seeking this effect (Farr and House, 1987). If this is the case, it provides yet another example of an artificial pictorial technique that refers to the effects of light but does not replicate them directly.

Yet another technique, used by Cézanne in *Le lac d'Annecy*, 1896 (Courtauld Institute Galleries, London [color plate 8]), was to exploit the fact that warm colors appear to come forward, and cool colors recede. This may be partly due to the effects of atmospheric perspective, but is also due to the fact that the human eye is not corrected for chromatic aberration: as a result of differences in the wavelengths of different colors, not all the patches of color from a given surface can be brought into focus on the retina at the same time. As a result, patches of red light can appear distinctly in front of patches of blue light; this effect can often be observed in stained glass windows, or when viewing a colored slide in a slide viewer. In *Le lac d'Annecy* (color plate 8), the turret of the building in the center of the painting is colored pale blue on one side and a pinkish yellow on the other, both patches of color having similar tones. This gives an effect of three-dimensional shape without recourse to either conventional tonal modeling or the inherent tonal differences in fully saturated colors (Anfam et al., 1987).

I have given brief descriptions of some of the pictorial devices used in what appear, at first glance, to be more or less realistic, "faithful" pictures in order to emphasize their artificial character. The pictorial devices employed in most artists' pictures, as distinct from photographs, are just that: pictorial devices, rather than direct facsimiles of the array of light from a scene. The effect of light and shade in a drawing like Raphael's *The Three Graces* is so convincing that it is all too easy to suppose that it has been produced by merely copying or replicating the appearance of the tonal gradations as they appear in the artist's visual field; but this would not in fact have been the case. Drawings like this are drawn from life, but they are not *merely* drawn from life. By the eighteenth century, when the classical techniques had become formalized, students were not allowed to draw from life, let alone use color, until the basic drawing techniques had already been mastered. The first stage involved copying drawings or engravings, first in line alone and then with the addition of hatched shading. In the next stage, students drew from plaster casts in shallow relief, and the fall of light and shade had to be translated into strictly conventionalized shading techniques. The next step was to draw from sculpture in the round. Only when all these stages had been mastered were students allowed to draw from life; and by this time their drawing style—that is, their mastery of specific drawing techniques—had already been formed (Anfam et al., 1987).

In the previous chapter I showed that line drawing can be described in terms of rules mapping lines into features like edges and contours. These rules are not, however, arbitrary like the rules of language. Line drawings are effective as representations because the human visual system is designed to pick up features in the light from the scene, such as the "luminance valleys" described in Chapter 5, that correspond to physical features, such as edges and contours; and line drawings provide effective pictorial equivalents for these structures. Similarly, "optical" pictorial devices like tonal modeling and atmospheric perspective can also be described in terms of rules: rules like Cennini's method for representing light and shade, and the rule that warmer and more intense colors ought to be placed in the foreground of a picture. Again, these devices provide effective equivalents for corresponding features in the optic array from real scenes: the visual system is designed to pick up shape from shading and, perhaps, depth from atmospheric perspective. Their use does not, however, depend on the artist imitating nature, and artists' pictures can never literally deliver an array of light to the eye which is the same as that which could be obtained from a real scene.

Part Three

PICTURE PRODUCTION

CHAPTER SEVEN

Separate Systems?

So far the various drawing systems and denotation systems have been defined separately. However, certain combinations of systems seem very common while others are much rarer, and this raises the question of the extent to which the drawing systems and the denotation systems are independent of each other. This question is important for two reasons. On a purely formal level, it could be argued that if some drawing and denotation systems always occur together, it might be possible to construct one simple classification scheme for the formal structures in pictures, rather than the two schemes required when the drawing and denotation systems are defined separately. In addition, the adoption of one single classification scheme could have wide-ranging psychological implications. As Gibson (1971) pointed out, what he called the point-projection theory of pictures is usually associated with the idea that pictures are derived more or less directly from the retinal image, and he quoted Newton's assertion that:

> The Light which comes from the several points of the Object is so refracted as to . . . paint the Picture of the object upon that skin called the *Retina*. . . . And these Pictures, propagated by motion along the Fibres of the Optick Nerves into the Brain, are the causes of Vision. For according as these Pictures are perfect or imperfect, the Object is seen perfectly or imperfectly. (Gibson, 1971, p. 28)

What could be more natural than to suppose that actual, physical pictures are replicas of these internal pictures painted "upon that skin called the *Retina*"? Gibson himself pointed out many of the shortcomings of the theory, and eventually abandoned it. But might it not be possible to "save the appearances" of the point-projection theory and avoid some of its shortcomings by supposing that different classes of pictures are related more or less directly to other internal images or descriptions that are formed at later stages in the visual system?

Natural Allies

Some drawing and denotation systems seem to belong naturally together. Photographs and TV pictures, for example, are of necessity in perspective, and are based on a denotation system in which dots of tone or color denote the intercepts of small bundles of light rays in the visual field (figs. 1.8 and 6.1). At the other end of the spectrum of drawing systems, pictures like the map of the London Underground (fig. 1.11) represent topological relations between objects (in this case, the track and stations) that are represented by primitives derived from object-centered descriptions. Thus, although for the purposes of exposition it might be useful to identify the drawing systems separately from the denotation systems, might it not be possible to build up a classification scheme for pictures that places them along a spectrum from more visually realistic to less visually realistic?

The distinction between the drawing systems and denotation systems is such a recent one that in the past the question of whether they ought to be defined separately has hardly arisen. The classification schemes for pictures described by psychologists and art historians are nearly always based only on the ways in which *spatial relations* are represented in pictures: that is, on classes defined in terms of the various drawing systems. The fact that pictures are also based on different denotation systems is nearly always ignored. For example, Hagen (1986) assigned pictures to classes based wholly on the different projection systems, and White's (1967) scheme, though less formal than Hagen's, was similar in that it grouped pictures according to the geometry of the views that they provided. Neither of these schemes takes account of the different denotation systems on which pictures are based.

Classification schemes for children's drawings are also usually based exclusively on the ways in which these drawings represent spatial relations.[1] The best-known scheme is probably that of Luquet (1913, 1927). In its original form, Luquet's scheme contained four stages: fortuitous realism, failed realism, intellectual realism, and visual realism. In practice, though, Luquet's scheme is usually simplified into two stages—intellectual realism and visual realism—leading to the well-known aphorism: "The young child draws what he knows and the older child draws what he sees." The examples used to illustrate these stages are nearly always based on different drawing systems: psychologists usually take it for granted that pictures by children of all ages will be line drawings. Drawings in oblique projection or perspective, for example, are usually described as being "visually realistic," and drawings in orthogonal projection—a square as a drawing of a cube, for example—are usually described as being "intellectually realistic." Again, neither Luquet's scheme, nor subsequent adaptations of Luquet's scheme such as Piaget's, take any account of the changes in the denotation systems that take place during children's drawing development.

In recent years a number of writers on children's drawings (Cox, 1985; Crook, 1985; Freeman, 1987; Light, 1985; Nicholls and Kennedy, 1992; Willats, 1981, 1987) have suggested that it might be possible to reinterpret Luquet's theory of intellectual and visual realism in terms of Marr's theory of vision (Marr, 1982; Marr and Nishihara, 1978), and in particular in terms of Marr's distinction between object-centered and viewer-centered descriptions. Cox, for example, associated intellectual realism with "array-specific" or object-centered responses, and visual realism with "view-specific" responses. However, Marr (1978) emphasized that any representational system must have at least two components. The first is the coordinate system on which it is based, which may be either object-centered or viewer-centered, and this is the aspect of Marr's theory that many writers have seized on as a way of describing the systems for representing spatial relations in children's drawings. But the second component is the nature of the shape primitives used by the representation: that is, the elements whose positions the coordinate system (whether object-centered or viewer-centered) is used to define. Thus any account of pictures as representational systems must include accounts of both these components—accounts, that is, of what I have called the drawing systems and the denotation systems. The question now arises, how are these two components related? And how are the drawing and denotation systems in pictures related to internal, mental representations of shape and space?

Marr's theory is based on the proposition that the purpose of the visual process is to translate the transitory, viewer-centered descriptions available at the retina into more permanent object-centered descriptions, which can be stored in long-term memory and used to recognize objects when we see them again from a different point of view or under new lighting conditions. These object-centered descriptions consist of descriptions of the shapes of objects which are independent of any particular point of view: the faces of a cube in an object-centered description, for example, would be described as squares (which is how young children would draw them) rather than as distortions of squares (as they would appear in drawings by older children in oblique projection or perspective).

According to Marr, object-centered shape descriptions cannot be derived from the retinal image in one single step. Instead, Marr divided the process of deriving object-centered descriptions from the image into three main stages. The image itself contains a viewer-centered description of the intensity values at each point. The first representational stage to be derived from the image, which Marr called the *primal sketch,* consists of a description of the intensity changes and local geometry of the image. The second stage, which Marr called the *2½-D sketch,* consists of representations of the shape properties of the visible surfaces of objects given relative to the viewer. These include properties such as the orientations of surfaces and their distances from the viewer, and surface discontinuities such as contours and projections of edges. The final stage, which Marr called the *3-D model,* consists of an object-centered description of the three-dimensional structure and organization of the viewed shape, given in terms of volumetric primitives.

The image, the primal sketch, and the 2½-D sketch are all viewer-centered, but they differ in terms of the primitives of which they are composed. The image is built up of zero-dimensional primitives representing the intensity values at each point in the optic array. The primal sketch is built up of one-dimensional primitives such as edge segments. Finally, the 2½-D sketch contains information about two-dimensional surfaces such as their local orientation relative to the viewer, and information about discontinuities in these surfaces such as edges and occluding contours. Thus, according to Marr, three kinds of viewer-centered representations are present as stages in the visual system, composed, respectively, of point, line, and surface primitives. The final stage, in contrast, that of the 3-D model, is object-centered and is composed of volumetric primitives.

It is tempting to associate the initial stages of the visual system with different kinds of "visually realistic" pictures. Pictures in perspective composed of zero-dimensional primitives, such as photographs and Pointillist paintings, would correspond to the image stage; and line drawings in perspective, with or without shadows and tonal modeling, would correspond to the 2½-D sketch. The 3-D model stage would then correspond to children's drawings at the stage of intellectual realism, as well as to pictures such as Cubist paintings that attempt to capture the object or scene as a whole rather than some particular view. Indeed, Marr himself suggested something of the sort:

> *If the overall scheme you describe is correct, would we be able to say anything about painting and drawing using this knowledge of what the visual system does with its input? Might it help to teach these skills, for example?* Perhaps, although I would hate to commit myself to a definite view yet. Nevertheless, it is interesting to think about which representations the different artists concentrate on and sometimes disrupt. The pointillists, for example, are tampering primarily with the image; the rest of the

scheme is left intact, and the picture has a conventional appearance otherwise. Picasso, on the other hand, clearly disrupts most at the 3-D model level. The three-dimensionality of his figures is not realistic. An example of someone who operates primarily at the surface representation stage is a little harder—Cézanne perhaps? (Marr, 1982, p. 356)

Acting on this hint, it looks as if it might be possible to build up a classification system for pictures corresponding to Marr's account of the main stages of the visual system. Notice, however, that this would still involve considering the drawing and denotation systems separately, because the image and the 2½-D sketch both provide viewer-centered descriptions (that is, representations whose geometry would correspond to a picture in perspective) but are based on different kinds of primitives. One class, corresponding to the image stage, might contain photographs, TV pictures, Impressionist paintings, and Pointillist paintings. A second class, corresponding to the 2½-D sketch, would contain pure line drawings, such as Picasso's drawing of Stravinsky (fig. 1.6) and drawings by older children such as Joanne's *Self-Portrait with Dogs* (fig. 1.7), line drawings with shading, such as Raphael's *Study of the Three Graces* (fig. 6.2), and paintings in which patches of tone or color represent local surface orientation, like Cézanne's *Le lac d'Annecy* (color plate 8) and his late watercolors. Finally, a third class, corresponding to the 3-D model stage, would contain Cubist paintings (fig. 1.10 and color plate 6) and children's drawings belonging to the stage of intellectual realism such as the tadpole figures (fig. 1.12).

A scheme of this kind has two great attractions. The first is its simplicity. There would in general be no need to describe the drawing and denotation systems in pictures separately, except when deciding whether a picture in perspective should be assigned to a class corresponding to the image or the 2½-D sketch. A photograph of St. Mark's Square, Venice, for example, or a painting of the same scene by Canaletto would be assigned to the "image" class, while a Canaletto line drawing of the same scene, also in perspective (fig. 1.1), would be assigned to the "2½-D sketch" class. If it were to be objected that a classification scheme which assigns line drawings by older children, Raphael's drawings, and Cézanne's late watercolors to the same class is too simple to be taken seriously, then perhaps subclasses could be added, again based on different kinds of primitives: one subclass for pure line drawings, another for line drawings with shading, and a third for pictures like Cézanne's that represent surface orientation alone without representing surface discontinuities such as edges and contours. Once this extra complication is introduced, however, the scheme would lose much of its simplicity;

one might as well classify the drawing and denotation systems separately from the start.

The second attraction of this scheme would be its apparent psychological plausibility: different kinds of pictures would simply correspond to different kinds of internal representation. Nevertheless, once we begin to look at this suggestion in detail, it begins to unravel.

Unusual Combinations

One way of testing this suggestion is to look for pictures that do not fit this scheme because they contain unusual combinations of drawing and denotation systems: unusual, that is, because they contain primitives derived from object-centered descriptions in combination with spatial relations derived from viewer-centered descriptions, or vice versa.

Fig. 7.1, which shows Van Gogh's *Jardin de fleurs,* 1888, is an example of the first kind of unusual combination: the picture as a whole is in perspective, but the primitives are silhouettes that appear to refer to object-centered rather than viewer-centered descriptions. At first glance this looks like a straightforward Impressionist drawing in perspective with the primitives standing for features of the array of light coming from the scene. Closer inspection, however, shows that there is very little attempt to represent the play of light. Instead, each mark stands for an object or a discrete part of an object in the scene: the leaves of the plants, the gravel in the path, and the palings in the fence. Moreover, the extendedness of the primitives represents the extendedness of the objects they denote, rather like the marks in early Chinese characters or children's early drawings. There seems little attempt to represent the foreshortening of these objects. The denotation system in this picture is thus one in which the picture primitives denote the extendedness of volumes: long lines or regions stand for long volumes, like the leaves of the plants in the foreground and the stems of the plants on the left of the picture, small round regions or dots stand for small lumps like the gravel on the path, and round regions stand for round volumes like the flower heads in the middle of the picture. Only in a very few cases do the lines stand for edges or contours such as the edge of the house or the roof tiles. In this drawing, then, a coordinate system based on a viewer-centered description is combined with primitives that represent objects or the volumes of objects. It is hard to see how this could fit into a classification scheme based on Marr's stages in the visual system.

Paintings and drawings of this kind are unusual in the West, but the combination of marks based on silhouettes with perspective is common in

Chinese landscape painting. Chinese painting is closely related to calligraphy: the early pictograms from which the later written characters were developed were silhouettes representing the extendedness of shapes of parts of objects. Manuals like the seventeenth-century *Mustard Seed Manual* give detailed instructions about the ways in which features like rocks and plum blossoms are to be represented using calligraphic marks, which are, in effect,

Fig. 7.1. Vincent van Gogh, *Jardin de fleurs,* 1888. Ink over pencil on paper, 61.0 × 49.0 cm. Collection of Mrs. E. Sigrist-Nathan. Courtesy of Christie's London.

silhouettes. Nevertheless, these marks are very often combined within an overall composition in perspective, like the Northern Sung landscape shown in fig. 10.8.

> By Northern Sung times, different kinds of rock surfaces were described by clearly defined systems of texture strokes or dots; and the trees were shown as a mixture of deciduous hardwoods and coniferous evergreens, with the leaves represented by a variety of foliage formulas—outlined patterns of circular and pointed leaves contrasting with ink-dotted or needle patterns. A Northern Sung landscape, conceived part by part, is read rather than experienced; it has a great intellectual sense of scale but lacks physically described space and recession. The result is a conceptual landscape that represents no mere retinal image of nature but a vision of the macrocosm. (Fong and Hearn, 1982, p. 10)

Thus although pictures of this kind look, superficially, like pictures in which an optical denotation system based on point primitives is combined with perspective, they are in fact nothing of the kind. It is very hard to see how pictures of this kind could be fitted into a "natural" classification scheme derived directly from different kinds of internal descriptions similar to Marr's stages in the visual system.

Fig. 7.2, in contrast, shows Severini's *Donna alla finestra,* 1914. The marks in the picture are dots of paint, resembling the marks in Pointillist paintings that represent point primitives standing for features of the optic array. The drawing system in this picture is, however, certainly not perspective.[2] To some extent Severini may have intended the spatial fragmentation in this picture to represent movement: Severini was probably influenced, like other Futurist painters such as Balla and Boccione, by Marey's photographs of men and animals in motion (Scharf, 1979). The major influence on Severini's work, however, was probably Analytical Cubism (Anfam et al., 1987), and one of the main aims of Analytical Cubism was to represent objects as they really are, rather than as they seem: something very close to what Marr would call an object-centered description. In 1912, two years before Severini painted the *Donna alla finestra,* the critic Jacques Rivière wrote:

> Perspective is as accidental a thing as lighting. . . . It indicates not the situation of the objects but the situation of a spectator . . . in the final analysis, perspective is also the sign of an instant, of the instant when a certain man is at a certain point. . . . The plastic image does not move; it must be complete at first sight; therefore it must renounce perspective. (Rivière, 1912, pp. 384–406)

In the *Donna alla finestra,* then, an optical denotation system in which the primitives denote features of the optic array is combined with a drawing

FIG. 7.2. Gino Severini, *Donna alla finestra,* 1914. Pastel on cardboard, 65 × 50 cm. Provenance: Fundación Colección Thyssen-Bornemiza, Madrid. Copyright ADAGP, Paris, and Design and Artists Copyright Society, London, 1997.

system whose geometry does not correspond to that of a possible cross-section of the optic array. The spatial relations are probably intended partly to suggest movement, and partly to suggest the shapes of objects in an object-centered description, independently of any particular viewpoint or lighting conditions.

Severini's Futurist paintings are admittedly exceptional, but they nevertheless show that it is possible to find examples of pictures that exploit a combination of drawing systems that is just the reverse of that found in Van Gogh's drawings and Chinese landscape painting. What such pictures demonstrate is that artists are able to use particular drawing and denotation systems *independently:* the combinations of systems that they use are deliberately chosen, rather than "natural" in the sense of reflecting internal images or descriptions in any direct way.

Transcriptions

Another way of judging the extent to which the drawing systems and denotation systems can be manipulated independently is to look at artists' transcriptions. Transcriptions in painting correspond to translations in language: the subject matter remains the same, but the language in which this subject matter is expressed is altered.[3] In transcriptions, either the drawing system or the denotation system of the original painting, or sometimes both, may be changed. For our purposes the most interesting transcriptions are those in which either the drawing system or the denotation system remains the same, because these examples show the extent to which the drawing and denotation systems in a picture can be manipulated independently.

Fig. 7.3 shows Manet's *Le déjeuner sur l'herbe,* a picture that has probably been the subject of more transcriptions than any other painting. Moreover, *Déjeuner sur l'herbe* is itself a transcription of a detail of a black-and-white engraving by Marcantonio Raimondi, which was in turn a transcription of a lost painting by Raphael called *The Judgement of Paris.*

The drawing system in *Déjeuner sur l'herbe* is straightforward perspective, and in most transcriptions of this painting, with the notable exception of those by Picasso, this drawing system remains unchanged. The denotation system in this painting is Manet's version of Impressionism, and the Impressionists' avowed aim was to perceive and record direct optical sense data—"visual sensations"—without the intervention of the intellect. It has been suggested, however, that the tonal system in Manet's painting was also influenced by nineteenth-century photography. As a result of technical limitations in the chemistry of the plates, nineteenth-century photographs emphasized the dark and light tones in the subject at the expense of the middle tones. Scharf (1979) gives several examples of this effect in Manet's work, and in *Déjeuner sur l'herbe* the intermediate tones in the female nude have been almost eliminated. It could be argued, then, that in the denotation system employed in *Déjeuner sur l'herbe,* the primitives stand for the intensities of the optic array which would have been received from an early black-and-white *photograph,* rather than the colors and intensities that would have been available in the array from a real scene.

Fig. 7.4a shows a detail of Marcantonio Raimondi's *Judgement of Paris,* the engraving after Raphael on which Manet's painting was based. The denotation system here is, in effect, the classical combination of line drawing with tonal modeling and shadows. The tonal modeling is carried out using the bracelet shading described by Rawson (1969): the lines running round the form and defining the shapes of the cross-sections are particularly obvious

Fig. 7.3. Edouard Manet, *Le déjeuner sur l'herbe,* 1863. Oil on canvas, 208 × 264 cm. Musée d'Orsay, Cliché des Musées Nationaux, Paris.

a

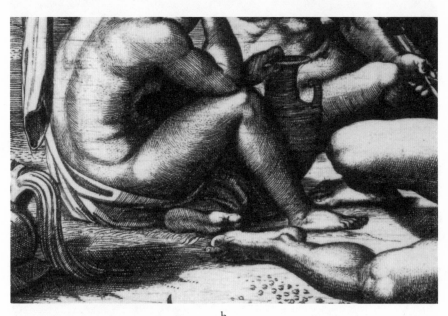

b

FIG. 7.4. (a) Marcantonio Raimondi, *The Judgement of Paris* (detail), c. 1517–1520. Engraving. Print Collection, Miriam and Ira D. Wallach Division of Art, Prints and Photographs, the New York Public Library, Astor, Lenox and Tilden Foundations. (b) Detail of (a) showing bracelet shading.

FIG. 7.5. (a) Pablo Picasso, *Le déjeuner sur l'herbe* (detail), 1959. Line drawing, 32.2 × 41.9 cm. Copyright Design and Artists Copyright Society 1997. (b) Detail of (a).

a

b

FIG. 7.6. (a) Radio Times, *Le déjeuner* (*Esther and Her Manet Men*). (b) Detail of (a). Courtesy of Radio Times.

a

b

FIG. 7.7. (a) Gilbert Sheldon, Hassle Free Press, *Freak Comics, Le déjeuner* (detail of cover), 1976. (b) Detail of (a) showing bracelet shading.

on the legs of the woman on the left (fig. 7.4b). Thus, although the modeling looks optically naturalistic, it is in fact highly contrived.

Fig. 7.5a shows one of many versions of *Déjeuner sur l'herbe* by Picasso. The overall composition of the Picasso transcription corresponds roughly to Manet's painting, although the way in which the shapes of the individual objects are represented in Picasso's version is different. Perhaps the nearest we can come to describing the denotation system in Picasso's version is to say that regions represent whole volumes. For example, the woman's body is shown using two related silhouettes, depicted in outline, with round regions representing the breasts and buttocks and a long region representing the trunk. Similarly, round regions are used to represent her head and the fruit on the tablecloth, and long regions represent her arms and legs (fig.7.5b). A similar system is used in the rest of the picture.

Fig. 7.6a shows a photograph based on *Déjeuner sur l'herbe,* and fig. 7.6b shows an enlarged detail. The photograph is, of course, in perspective, and the denotation system is straightforward: the marks are small dots, whose tone and color reflect the tones and colors of the optic array.

Finally, fig. 7.7a shows a detail taken from the cover of a copy of *Freak Comics.* This transcription is remarkably faithful to Manet's version so far as the composition is concerned, but the denotation system is typical of that used in comic books, and is in fact closer to that used in Marcantonio Raimondi's engraving than it is to the denotation system used in Manet's painting. The basic system is line drawing filled in with flat areas of color, rather like that of a Japanese print, but the mark system makes use of a combination of flat areas of color and colored dots, in the manner parodied by Roy Lichtenstein in his Pop Art paintings. Relatively little use is made of tonal modeling, but there is some bracelet shading on the jeans of the figure on the right, and the lines running round the jeans act as surface contours.

Apart from the Picasso, all these transcriptions are in perspective; but the denotation systems on which they are based are all very different. It is hard to see how all these different versions could correspond in any simple way to internal representations of a real scene at different stages in the visual system. Clearly, the artists involved have been experimenting with different stylistic techniques, and have felt free to alter the denotation systems in their versions while keeping fairly faithful to the original perspective drawing system used by Manet and Raphael.

Systems in Conflict: Anomalous Combinations of Drawing and Denotation Systems

So far I have emphasized the independent nature of the drawing and denotation systems, but there are circumstances in which the attempt to combine certain systems results in characteristic anomalies: contradictions are set up within the picture when an attempt is made to combine drawing and denotation systems that are formally irreconcilable. This is especially evident in children's drawings of rectangular objects that are based on a denotation system in which regions as picture primitives are used to stand for faces as scene primitives. If the regions are genuine primitives, carrying information about the shapes of the faces they denote, then their shapes cannot be changed; but this means that a denotation system of this kind cannot be combined with drawing systems like perspective and oblique projection that inevitably change the shapes of faces.

Fig. 7.8 shows the results of a well-known experiment carried out by Phillips, Hobbs, and Pratt (1978) in which children aged between 7 and 9 years were asked to copy flat, two-dimensional patterns along with pictures of three-dimensional cubes and dice. This experiment was important because it tested the extent to which errors in children's drawings could be attributed to mistakes in copying arising from poor motor skills or poor short-term memory, compared with errors arising from other, cognitive factors. That is, this experiment tested the extent to which the errors in children's drawings were competence errors rather than performance errors.

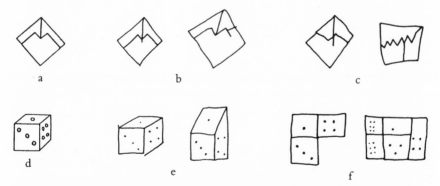

Fig. 7.8. Children's copies of a pattern and a picture of a cube: (a) stimulus pattern; (b) examples of drawings classified as correct; (c) examples of drawings classified as incorrect; (d) stimulus picture of a die; (e) examples of drawings classified as correct; (f) examples of drawings classified as incorrect. Adapted from Phillips et al. (1978), courtesy of Elsevier Science.

The drawing shown in fig. 7.8a shows the pattern that the children were asked to copy, fig. 7.8b shows two of the children's copies that the experimenters classified as "correct," and fig. 7.8c shows two drawings classified as "incorrect." It seems fairly evident that the errors in the incorrect drawings of patterns arose as the result of performance errors such as poor motor control: the spatial relationships in these drawings are incorrect compared with those in the test drawing, but they are at least of the same general type.

Fig. 7.8d shows a picture of a die that the children were asked to copy. Fig. 7.8e shows two children's copies of the drawing of the die classified as "correct," and fig. 7.8f shows two copies of the drawing classified as "incorrect."

The first of the two "correct" drawings of a die looks like a straightforward copy of the original: like the original, it is a line drawing in oblique projection. The second correct drawing is similar, except that the bottom of the drawing, depicting the base of the die, is a straight line. This error is very common in children's drawings, and has been given the name of the "flat bottom error." Because the base of the drawing is flat, the orthogonals of the side face diverge, so the drawing may be said to be in inverted perspective.

The drawings of the die classified as "incorrect" are of a different type. Like the test drawing, they are drawn in line, but they cannot be classified in terms of any of the drawing systems I have described so far. However, drawings of this general type, in which the faces are represented by squares and rectangles, are very common in children's drawings of cubes: Nicholls and Kennedy (1992) called them "fold-out" drawings. Similar drawings have been described by Cox (1992), Hayes (1978), Lewis (1963), Minsky and Papert (undated), and Willats (1981, 1984).

The main finding of the experiment described by Phillips et al. was "that drawings seen as objects are copied much less accurately than those not seen as objects. It is astonishing to see a child copy drawings of cubes using only squares and rectangles but copy similar designs not seen as cubes quite accurately" (p. 27). How did this result come about? The explanation seems to be that when these children were asked to copy a pattern, they simply copied it, so that the errors they made in their drawings were the result of performance factors like poor memory and poor motor control. However, when the children were asked to copy a picture of a cube, they recognized a cube in the picture and redrew it in terms of their own ways of drawing a real cube: that is, they produced a *transcription* of the original picture. Because the way most 7- and 9-year-olds draw cubes is different from the way the adult experimenters drew the cube, the geometry of their drawings was markedly different from the stimulus drawings, and a majority of their drawings were therefore classified as incorrect.

Moreover, these drawings were not only incorrect because they were based on different drawing systems from those in the test drawings. Drawings like those shown in fig. 7.8f are "incorrect" in the sense that they do not provide possible views; that is, they cannot be described in terms of any of the systems of projective geometry. I shall suggest in the following chapter that the anomalies they contain come about because children are attempting to combine drawing and denotation systems which are irreconcilable. Because the test drawings showed a general *view* of a die—that is, a view showing three faces—the children were prompted to attempt to produce a drawing that contained at least three faces. But a view of this kind cannot be reconciled with a denotation system in which regions are used to stand for the true shapes of faces: the regions simply will not join up properly.

Drawings of this kind provide yet another piece of evidence showing that the drawing and denotation systems have to be described separately. In addition, I shall show in the next chapter that drawings containing errors like the "flat bottom error" can provide valuable evidence for the drawing rules which children use at different stages of development.

CHAPTER EIGHT

Picture Production as a Process

In terms of actual mental processes, are pictures derived from views, or from object-centered internal descriptions? I showed in Chapter 2 that the spatial systems in pictures in nearly all the common drawing systems—perspective, oblique projection, orthogonal projection, and so on—can be described in terms of the projection of light through space, and by doing a certain amount of manipulation with a camera, it is possible to produce photographs whose geometry approximates to that of pictures in all these systems.[1] Clearly, humans do not possess any mechanism for fixing images directly, as does a modern camera. Nevertheless, it is possible to produce quite plausible pictures in perspective by judging the positions and orientations of edges or contours as they appear from a particular point of view, and representing these positions and orientations by corresponding lines on the picture surface. In practice, the difficulty of producing pictures in correct perspective by this means—pictures that correspond to true projections—lies in overcoming the effects of size and shape constancy: our tendency to see objects as nearer to their true sizes and shapes than to their projected sizes and shapes. Over the years, artists have developed various techniques for overcoming this difficulty. For example, the apparent size of an object or the orientation of its edges can be judged by holding up a brush or a thumb at arm's length and lining it up with the feature to be drawn: a technique parodied by Ralph Steadman in his drawing of Leonardo using a drawing machine (fig. 8.1).

However, I also showed in Chapter 2 that it is possible to describe the geometry of all the common drawing systems in terms of the rules of secondary geometry, and these rules are normally applied to features of object-centered descriptions, such as the true shapes of the faces of objects or the directions of their edges in the third dimension. In order to produce a drawing in single point perspective, for example, the rule would be: "Represent the front face of the object as a true shape, and represent edges in the third dimension by lines converging to a vanishing point." There is no reference in this rule to a *view* of the object. Similarly, drawings in oblique projection can be produced by applying the rule: "Represent the front face of the object as a true shape, and represent edges in the third dimension by parallel oblique lines." Although applying these rules will result in drawings that correspond to possible views, the rules themselves are not applied to views, and make no reference to views.

Because the geometry of the drawing systems can be defined in these two quite different ways, it can sometimes be difficult to determine, simply by inspection, whether pictures or groups of pictures—drawings by children at a particular age or developmental stage, or artists' pictures from a particular period or culture—have been derived from views or from object-centered descriptions. The question of how such pictures have been derived is an important one, however, because the way we answer it leads to very different accounts of the actual mental processes involved in picture production, and to different accounts of drawing development and art history. In this chapter I shall suggest that the characteristic anomalies that occur in both artists'

FIG. 8.1. Ralph Steadman, *Leonardo da Vinci Using a Drawing Machine.* From Steadman (1983), courtesy of Ralph Steadman.

pictures and children's drawings can provide valuable evidence about the nature of the mental processes involved in picture production, and in particular provide us with some clues as to whether these pictures have been derived from object-centered or viewer-centered internal descriptions.

Picture Production as a Process

In his account of visual perception, Marr (1982) pointed out that any complex information-processing system—such as the human visual system—can be understood at three quite distinct levels. The first level defines what Marr called the "computational theory" of the device: what the system is doing and why it is doing it. Marr illustrated this by reference to what happens at the checkout counter of a supermarket. *What* a cash register does is to add up the cost of the customer's purchases; *why* the process involves adding up and not, for example, multiplication has to do with the nature of the transactions involved in buying things. At this level, a mechanical or electronic cash register or a human shopkeeper would both do the same thing: the "computational theory" of the process is the same in each case.

The second of Marr's levels describes how the process is actually carried out: the nature of the representations for the input to the system and its output, and the rules that map the input into the output. The first level thus specifies what and why, but the second level specifies *how.* For example, numbers can be represented in terms of either Arabic or Roman numerals. At the first level of analysis, this would make no difference to a description of the processes involved in buying things, but at the second level it would make a great deal of difference. Finally, the third level describes the actual physical support for the process. In this respect a human shopkeeper and a cash register will operate quite differently. The physical support for the process in a human shopkeeper will be biological; in a cash register it will be mechanical or electronic.

Cameras, computers, and humans are all devices that can produce pictures, and the ways in which they do this can be analyzed in terms of these three levels. At the first level of analysis, a camera takes in the light that falls on the lens and maps it onto the surface of the film. Thus, at the first and most abstract level of description, the input to the system takes the form of a *view,* and the output also takes the form of a view: or, rather, a representation of a view in the form of a picture in perspective. At the second level, we would need to say something about the way in which the array of light from the scene is collected and inverted by the lens system, and at the third level

COLOR PLATE 3. John Nash, *Canal Bridge, Sydney Gardens, Bath,* twentieth century (undated). Oil on canvas, 71.0 × 76.2 cm. Victoria Art Gallery, Bath. Courtesy of John Nash Trust. Photograph Witt Library, Courtauld Institute of Art, London.

Color Plate 4. Master of the Lehman Crucifixion (perhaps Don Silvestro dei Gherarducci) (active second half of the fourteenth century), *Noli me Tangere*. Wood, 55.5 × 38.0 cm. National Gallery, London.

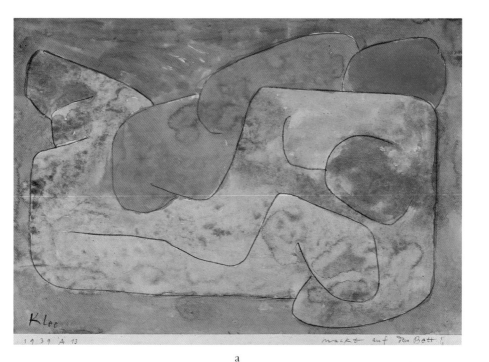

a

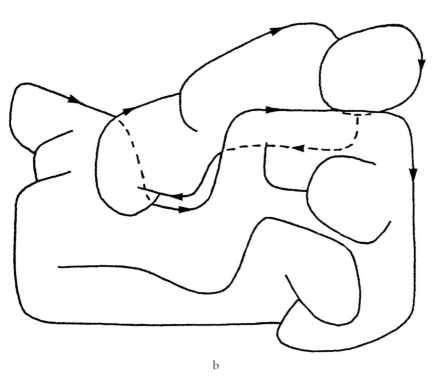

b

COLOR PLATE 5. (a) Paul Klee, *Nackt auf dem Bett* (*Naked on the Bed*), 1939. Watercolor and pencil on paper, 20.7 × 29.5 cm. Privatbesitz Schweiz, Kunstmuseum, Berne. Copyright Design and Artists Copyright Society 1997. (b) The overlapping forms are shown separately.

COLOR PLATE 6. Juan Gris (Jose Victoriano Gonzalez), *Breakfast,* 1914. Cut and pasted paper, crayon, and oil over canvas, 80.9 × 59.7 cm. Museum of Modern Art, New York. Acquired through the Lillie P. Bliss Bequest. Photograph copyright the Museum of Modern Art, New York. Copyright Design and Artists Copyright Society 1997.

Color Plate 7. David Hockney, *Play within a Play,* 1963. Oil on canvas and plexiglas, 182.8 × 198.1 cm. London, collection of Mr. and Mrs. Paul Cornwall-Jones. Courtesy of David Hockney.

COLOR PLATE 8. Paul Cézanne, *Le lac d'Annecy,* 1896. Oil on canvas, 165.1 × 205.7 cm. Courtauld Institute Galleries, London.

COLOR PLATE 9. Paul Nash, *Pillar and Moon,* 1932(?)–1940. Oil on canvas, 50.8 × 76.2 cm. Tate Gallery, London. Courtesy of Paul Nash Trust.

something about the physical properties of the lens and the chemistry of the film.

The input to a computer system used to produce pictures, however, normally takes the form of an *object-centered description:* typically, a list of coordinates that describes the shape of an object independently of any particular point of view. This algebraic description is subjected to transformation equations corresponding to the various drawing systems, and the output is then displayed on a screen or plotted onto paper. Fig. 8.2 shows two drawings, one in orthogonal projection and the other in perspective, obtained from a plaster cast of a Greek stone carving. A surveyor's digitalizer was used to establish the positions in Cartesian coordinates of about eight hundred points spaced at 5-mm intervals in the vertical and horizontal directions on the surface of the cast (Willats, 1974). These coordinates were then subjected to various transformation equations to produce drawings of the stone carving in a variety of projection systems. The equations used to produce the drawing in orthogonal projection were extremely simple: the dimensions in the second, horizontal direction were simply dropped from the shape description, and the remaining coordinate positions in the first and third dimensions were joined up, using a graph plotter, to produce the

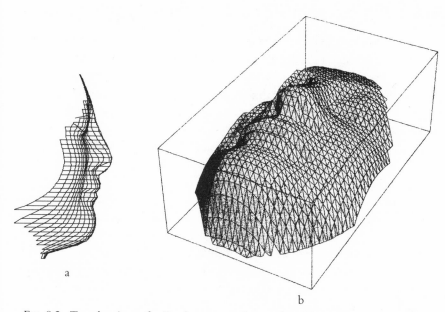

a

b

FIG. 8.2. Two drawings of a Greek stone carving produced by applying a computer program to an object-centered description. (a) Orthogonal projection. Program: the author. (b) Three-point perspective. Program: J. J. Koenderink. Courtesy of Jan Koenderink.

drawing. The equations used to produce the drawing in three-point perspective were, of course, more complex.

At the first level of analysis, the input to this system takes the form of an object-centered description and the output takes the form of a view: a view in perspective, or a drawing in orthogonal projection corresponding to a notional view, with the observer at an infinite distance away. In order to describe the process at Marr's second level of analysis, it would be necessary to describe the actual transformation equations and the details of the program; and at the third level to say something about the physical construction of the computer and the plotter.

Thus, at the first and most abstract level of description, the only level with which I am concerned in this chapter, cameras are devices whose input is a view and whose output takes the form of a picture of a view; whereas computers are devices that are capable of transforming an object-centered description into a picture of a view.

When artists or children are drawing or painting from life, the input to the production process takes the form of a view; but as Gibson (1978) pointed out, such views cannot be projected directly onto the picture surface by human subjects, as they can by cameras. Moreover, as Gibson (1950) had earlier pointed out, introspection yields an experience of two rather different kinds of views, and both these experiences can, under certain circumstances, be used as the basis for pictures. Gibson described these two different kinds of experience in terms of the distinction between what he called the "visual world" and the "visual field." According to Gibson, both correspond to possible ways of seeing, and different observers, who report these different ways of seeing, may be correct; but they are using the verb "to see" with different meanings. Moreover, there are, according to Gibson, transitional ways of seeing between these two extremes: stages that depend on the conditions of observation as well as on the attitude of the observer.

What Gibson called the "visual world" contains three-dimensional objects, and its primitives are surfaces, edges, and contours. It is colored, shadowed, illuminated, and textured. It is extended in depth, is stable, and without boundaries. It is subject to constancy effects, so that we tend to see objects in the visual world in terms of their true sizes and shapes. Nevertheless, the visual world is still seen as a view: objects are seen one behind another, and objects that are near to the observer occlude or partially occlude objects that are further away.

The "visual field," in contrast, is essentially flat, and consists of patches of color and tone. To the extent that it can be said to contain objects, such objects are seen to decrease in scale size as they become more distant. Their shapes and sizes thus correspond to possible projections from the scene, and in fact Gibson (1950) frequently compared our experience of the visual field with our experience of pictures: "The attitude you should take is that of the perspective draughtsman. It may help if you close one eye. If you persist, the scene comes to approximate to a picture" (p. 27).

It seems reasonable to suppose that pictures can be derived from both kinds of view. At one extreme, pictures by amateur and naive artists tend to contain pictures of *objects,* rather than consisting of flat patches of color or tone. Amateur and naive artists are usually much influenced by constancy effects, and tend to depict objects in their true sizes and shapes. Such pictures may be said to be derived from views of the visual world. On the other hand, professional artists working in the Renaissance tradition were trained to see the projected shapes and sizes of objects as a basis for their pictures. Because it can be so difficult to overcome the influence of size and shape constancy effects, however, they very often used mechanical devices like the *camera obscura* or the drawing machines illustrated by Dürer (Dubery and Willats, 1972, 1983) to help them see and depict the world in these terms. Pictures of this kind may be said to be derived from experiences of the visual field.

Thus pictures that provide possible views can be derived from views of scenes, or perhaps from our memories of views of scenes. According to whether we see views in terms of what Gibson called the visual world or the visual field, such views may be more or less subject to constancy effects; and the extent to which these constancy effects influence the final outcome may vary greatly from one observer to another and according to the conditions of observation. It seems that it ought to be possible to account, in this way, for a great variety of types of pictures. Moreover, the views we have of the world are very vivid; and the apparent similarity between the images thrown on the retina by the lens of the eye and the images thrown on a film by the lens of a camera, or on a screen by the lens of a *camera obscura,* together with photography as an obvious model for picture production, all tempt us to suppose that human artists and draftsmen operate in some similar way.

But is this account sufficient to explain the mental processes involved in the production of *all* kinds of pictures? An extreme position on this question was taken by Hagen (1986), who claimed that "*all* representational pictures from any culture or period in history, exploit the fact of *natural perspective,* the geometry of the light that strikes the eye" (p. 8).[2] The weakness of this position is that there still stubbornly remain some common types of children's drawings and artists' pictures that cannot be derived directly from views, but are quite easily and naturally explained as having been derived from object-centered descriptions: internal descriptions of the shapes of objects that are quite independent of any particular point or direction of view. Mental representations of this kind are probably, for most of us, much less vivid to introspection than are views. We can conjure up an image in the form of a view of an object, but it seems less easy to bring into consciousness a representation that is completely independent of any point of view.

Nevertheless, Marr's account of visual perception, which takes the construction of an object-centered shape description as the end point of the visual system, is probably now the most influential model of three-dimensional shape recognition (Pinker, 1986). Moreover, although not all researchers in this field would agree that the construction of an object-centered shape description is necessary for shape recognition,[3] "all parties agree that much of image processing, whatever it is, is inaccessible to consciousness, that experimental data and computational and neurological feasibility are the proper constraints on imagery theories, and that introspective reports are psychological phenomena to be accounted for, not accurate descriptions of psychological mechanisms" (Pinker, 1986, p. 38).

Finally, picture production by computer now provides a model for human picture production that is just as or more persuasive than photography; and most computer systems can take both object-centered and viewer-centered descriptions as the input to the production process. Such descriptions can be used to produce pictures in all the common projection systems, but they can also be used to produce pictures that do not provide possible views.

We ought, therefore, to be very cautious about jumping to conclusions about the mental processes that underlie picture production by artists and children, and in particular we ought to be very wary about assuming that pictures that provide possible views have necessarily been *derived* from views. How, then, can we come to know anything about these processes? In this chapter I shall argue that one important source of evidence about the nature of these processes, at the first or computational level, is provided by what I shall call "anomalous" pictures.

Anomalous Pictures

"Anomalous" pictures are pictures that purport to provide views of scenes, but are not in fact possible as projections of scenes. Intuitively, such pictures look "wrong," like the pictures in fig. 1.14. Clowes (1971) called such pictures "anomalous," while Huffman (1971) described them as being pictures of "impossible objects." Both Clowes and Huffman used pictures of this kind as a way of understanding line drawings, and both derived this technique from a similar technique used in the study of language. As Clowes pointed out, "there are three main vehicles which Chomsky employs to *expose* our intuitions: paraphrase, anomaly, and ambiguity" (p. 80). All native speakers of English know, intuitively, that the sentence "John the a dog breakfast" sounds wrong, and that "The police were ordered to stop drinking after midnight" is ambiguous. Trying to find out *why* such sentences sound wrong or ambiguous can provide valuable insights into the rules of language. Similarly, Clowes and Huffman used pictures like those shown in fig. 1.14 as a way of investigating the rules underlying line drawings.

Sentences like "John the a dog breakfast" are invented: we would not expect to find them in normal speech. However, children's early speech regularly contains words or sentences that are anomalous, judged against the standard of adult speech, and these "errors" can provide insights into the language rules that children use at different stages of development (Moskowitz, 1978; Pinker, 1994). For example, 2-year-olds regularly produce sentences like "No singing song" or "No the sun shining" by using the rule: "Attach *no* to the beginning of a sentence to make a negative." Similarly, older children use words like "bringed," "bringded," and "broughted" as the past tense of "bring," which suggests that at this stage they have learned a general rule for the past tense (put a "t" or "d" sound at the end of the word for the present tense) without learning the exceptions to the rule.[4] "Errors" of this kind provide valuable evidence for the kinds of rules that children use at different stages of development. Moreover, as Moskowitz pointed out:

> If a child says, "Nobody likes me," there is no way of knowing whether she has memorized the sentence intact or has figured out the rules for constructing the sentence. On the other hand, a sentence such as "Nobody don't like me" is clearly not a memorized form, but one that reflects an intermediate stage of a developing grammar. (Moskowitz, 1978, p. 89)

The same kind of argument can be applied to children's drawings. If children produce correct (that is, projectively possible) drawings of a cube, in systems such as orthogonal projection, oblique projection, or perspective, there is no way of telling whether they have produced these drawings by reproducing the directions of the edges of the cube as they appear in a view of a cube or by applying rules to an object-centered description; or, perhaps, by reproducing a learned graphic stereotype for a cube. On the other hand, when children produce anomalous drawings of a cube containing systematic anomalies, such drawings can provide not only good evidence for the drawing rules that children are using at different developmental stages, but evidence that they are using rules at all, rather than simply reproducing known stereotypes.

Children's Drawings: Anomalous Drawings of Cubes and Other Rectangular Objects

Children's anomalous drawings of cubes and other rectangular objects are of three main types. Examples of all three types appear in the classification scheme devised by Nicholls and Kennedy (1992) shown in fig. 8.3. Drawings by children below the age of 4 or 5 years often consist of single regions enclosed by a curved outline; Nicholls and Kennedy called these "enclosure" drawings (class 1). I shall argue that the majority of these drawings arise from the child's attempts to represent the three-dimensional extendedness of a cube in a volumetric object-centered description. The second type

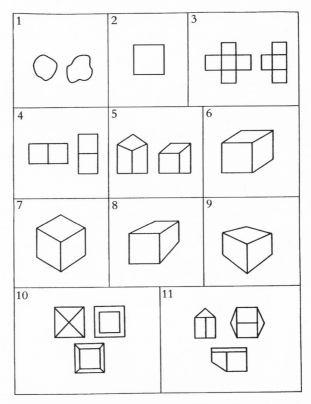

FIG. 8.3. Drawing classification categories. Top row, left to right: enclosure (category 1), one-square (2), fold-out (3); second row: two-squares (4), drawings with a frontal vertex shown by a Y-junction, and a vertex at the base shown by a T-junction (5), square with obliques (6); third row: edge with obliques (7), convergent square with obliques (8), convergent edge with obliques (9); bottom row: dissection (10), and other (11). From Nicholls and Kennedy (1992). Copyright the Society for Research in Child Development.

of anomalous drawing, produced by children at the age of about 8 years for cubes, consisted of three or more squares or rectangles joined together. Nicholls and Kennedy call these "fold-out" drawings, and a number of writers have suggested that these drawings arise as a result of the child's attempts to represent the true shapes of three or more faces in an object-centered description (class 3). Finally, the third type consisted of drawings based mainly on squares or rectangles, but containing at least one oblique

Class		Mean age	Drawing system	Denotation system
1	(circle shape)	4.0	Enclosure	(a) Region ⟶ Volume (o-c)
				(b) Region ⟶ Face (o-c)
				(c) Region ⟶ Face (v-c)
				(d) Region ⟶ Region (v-c)
2	(square shape)	6.7	Orthogonal	(a) Region ⟶ Volume (o-c)
				(b) Region ⟶ Face (o-c)
				(c) Region ⟶ Face (v-c)
3	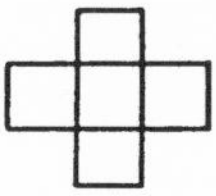 (cross shape)	8.2	Fold-out	(a) Regions ⟶ Faces (o-c)
4	(shapes)	8.6	Horizontal or vertical oblique	(a) Regions ⟶ Faces (o-c)
				(b) Regions ⟶ Faces (v-c)
5+11	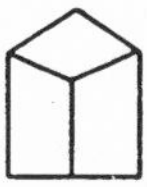 (house shape)	9.9	Near-oblique	(a) Regions★ ⟶ Faces (o-c)
6+8	(cube shape)	12.2	Oblique	(a) Lines ⟶ Edges (o-c)
				(b) Lines ⟶ Edges and contours (v-c)

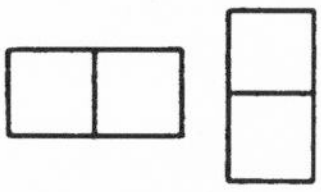

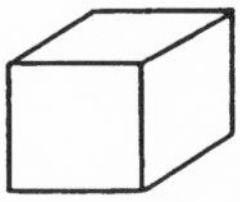

FIG. 8.4. Analyses of the drawing and denotation systems in children's drawings of cubes, and their possible derivations in terms of actual mental processes. o-c = derived from object-centered internal descriptions; v-c = derived from viewer-centered internal descriptions. The asterisk indicates that the regions in class 5+11 have been distorted. Based on drawings of cubes taken from Nicholls and Kennedy (1992).

line (classes 5 and 11). Drawings of this kind are similar to oblique projections, but contain anomalous T-junctions. Nicholls and Kennedy call these "drawings with a frontal vertex shown by a Y-junction, and a vertex at the base shown by a T-junction" (class 5) and "other" (class 11). I shall refer to both these types of drawings as "near-oblique" drawings, and suggest that these drawings, like the fold-out drawings, are based on regions as picture primitives. The difference is that in the near-oblique drawings some of the regions representing faces have been distorted in order to get them to represent the true connections between faces. The nature of the anomalies in all these three types of drawings suggests that they have been derived, at least in part, from object-centered rather than viewer-centered descriptions.

Fig. 8.3 shows the classification scheme used by Nicholls and Kennedy (1992) in a study in which 1,734 adults and children were asked to draw a cube. Fig. 8.4 shows typical examples of each class, together with my suggestions for possible analyses of these drawings at the first or computational level, given in terms of the drawing and denotation systems on which they might have been based.

Intuitively, some of these drawings look "right," while others look "wrong." In fig. 8.3 the drawings that look right belong to classes 2, 4, 6, 7, 8, and 9. Drawings in these classes correspond to possible projections of a cube and, consequently, approximate to the appearance of a cube as seen from a single viewpoint. Drawings in classes 1, 3, 5, 10, and 11 do not correspond to possible projections of a cube, and look "wrong." Adding up the percentage frequencies given by Nicholls and Kennedy shows that about one-third of all the children's drawings were anomalous, while the remaining two-thirds corresponded to possible projections. The anomalous drawings found by Nicholls and Kennedy consequently represented a significant proportion of all the children's drawings.

Enclosure Drawings

The drawings in Nicholls and Kennedy's class 1 consisted of regions enclosed by a curved outline. The only shape feature represented in these drawings is extendedness, but it is not possible to tell, simply by inspection, whether such drawings represent the extendedness of the whole cube or the extendedness of a single face. Moreover, it is also not possible to tell by inspection whether these drawings represent the extendedness of a face or a volume in an object-centered description, or the extendedness of a view of one face in a frontal view of the cube, or the extendedness of a view of a cube, regardless of its orientation. (Remember that the projection of a cube, like the projection of a ball, or any other 3_{111} shape that is about equally extended in all three dimensions, will always be a round or 2_{11} region rather than a long region.) There are thus no less than four possible interpretations of the enclosure drawings in Nicholls and Kennedy's class 1, and fig. 8.4 lists these interpretations for drawings in this class. The first (the "a" entries in fig. 8.4) is that the single region stands for the extendedness of the whole volume of the cube in an object-centered description. The second (the "b" entries) is that the region stands for the extendedness of one face of the cube in an object-centered description. A third (the "c" entries) is that the region stands for the extendedness of a single face in a frontal view of a cube; and the fourth (the "d" entries) is that the region stands for the extendedness of a view of a cube, whatever its orientation.

One-Square Drawings (Orthogonal Projection)

The one-square drawings in class 2 correspond to possible projections and are subject to the first three of these possible interpretations (the "a"–"c" entries in fig. 8.4).[5] The fourth, that a single square represents the extendedness of a view of a cube with the addition of the property "having straight edges in the outline of the silhouette," is possible but seems rather unlikely, because the four straight lines in the outline of the drawing can correspond to the four edges in the outline of the silhouette only in a *frontal* view: any other view of a cube would show six edges. Which of these interpretations is correct? The results of two experiments (Moore, 1986a; Willats, 1981) suggest that, at least for many younger children who produce drawings of this type, the first interpretation (that the single region stands for the whole volume of the cube) is perhaps the most likely.

   The aim of Moore's study was to investigate the extent to which children base their drawings on object-centered or viewer-centered descriptions (or "visual world relations" compared with "visual field relations," as she put it). She pointed out, as I have done, that "inspection of finished drawings provides a weak basis on which to distinguish between these alternatives, and evidence is lacking concerning the *child's* intention in making a particular drawing" (Moore, 1986a, p. 335).

   Moore's way of approaching this problem was to ask thirty 7-year-olds and thirty 9-year-olds to make pencil drawings of a cube having different colors on each face, and then to color in the finished drawings. Because only three faces could actually be seen when the cube was positioned in front of the child, a correct response would involve the use of three, or fewer than three, colors. An incorrect response would involve the use of more than three colors. She found, as expected, that drawings by the younger children included more "invisible" faces than drawings by the older children, consistent with the suggestion that younger children begin by deriving their drawings from object-centered descriptions that would include descriptions of all the faces of a cube, not just the faces that could be seen from a single viewpoint. Perhaps the most interesting result, however, concerned the way in which the children colored in the drawings that consisted of a single square. The two 9-year-olds who produced this type of drawing used just one color, showing that their drawings were intended to represent only one face of the cube (fig. 8.5a). In contrast, all six of the 7-year-olds used all six colors, in vertical or horizontal stripes (fig. 8.5b). This seems to show conclusively that these children intended their drawings to represent the cube as a whole. Moore commented:

> Thus, although the drawings of a 7-year-old and a 9-year-old may look identical in outline, it is clear that the individual child intended something quite different in making them. By extension, it is possible that orthogonal projections of other solid objects (e.g. a house) may be *intended* by young children to represent the whole object and not just the front face. (Moore, 1986a, p. 339)

Similarly, in an experiment described by Willats (1981, 1987), sixty-four children aged 6 to 12 years were asked to draw a large wooden die from four different fixed viewpoints showing one, two, and three faces of the die. All the children in all the age groups produced a drawing consisting of a single square for the condition in which they could see only one face of the cube. All the children, except six of the 6-year-olds, changed their drawings (by adding more regions representing faces) in the conditions in which they were shown more faces. Of these six children, three drew a square containing only three dots, whatever view they had of the die (fig. 8.6a). This

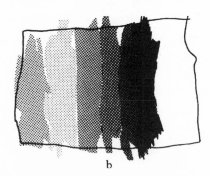

a   b

FIG. 8.5. Children's drawings of a colored cube. (a) A drawing of one face of the cube. (b) A drawing of the whole volume of the cube, filled in with colors from all six faces. Courtesy of Vanessa Moore.

suggests (because these children did not change their drawings in response to a change in viewpoint) that these children were representing the die by a single face in an object-centered description. However, two of the remaining children produced drawings in the form of a square containing large numbers of dots (fig. 8.6b), and one child drew a square containing dots representing all the faces in turn (fig. 8.6c)! This suggests that these children were representing the shape of the cube as a whole, as a 3_{111} volume or lump having plane faces.

The number of young children who produced drawings consisting of a single square in these two experiments is too small to allow firm conclusions to be drawn from them. However, the results do suggest that a substantial proportion of children under the age of 6 or 7 may intend their drawings of cubes to represent the object as a whole, in an object-centered description.

In Nicholls and Kennedy's experiment, only two children produced enclosure drawings, and both children were under 4 years old. It seems likely that these very young children intended their drawings to represent the extendedness of the whole volume of the cube in an object-centered description: that is, that they used a round region to stand for a 3_{111} volume or lump. Of the 182 children who produced one-square drawings, more than half were aged 6 years or under, and it seems likely that many of these children may also have been using a single square to represent the volume of the cube as a whole, with the straight sides of the square representing the secondary shape property "having flat faces." Older children and adults were probably either using a single square to stand for a single face in an object-centered description, or a view of a face, viewed orthogonally.

It must be emphasized, however, that these interpretations are likely rather than certain. It is possible that even the 4-year-olds were using a single round region to denote the extendedness of the cube in a viewer-centered description. Without some definite evidence, such as the evidence provided by the results of the experiments described by Moore (1986a) and Willats (1981, 1987), speculations about the actual processes involved in the produc-

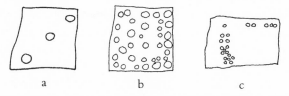

a   b   c

FIG. 8.6. Children's drawings of a die. (a) A drawing of one face of the die. (b) A drawing of the whole volume of the die. (c) A drawing of the whole volume of the die, including dots from all six faces.

tion of single finished drawings of this kind remain just that: speculations rather than certainties.

Fold-Out Drawings

Fold-out drawings of the type shown in Nicholls and Kennedy's class 3, fig. 8.3 are typically made up of three or more regions which are either square or rectangular. This strongly suggests that the shapes of these regions are intended to represent the shapes of faces in object-centered descriptions (Minsky and Papert, undated). This interpretation is shown in class 3, fig. 8.4. However, where such drawings consisted of only three faces—a very common type—they were probably intended to represent the *number* of faces, though not the shapes of faces, which can be seen from a particular point of view.

Two-Squares Drawings (Horizontal or Vertical Oblique)

Two-squares drawings (class 4, fig. 8.3) can be given at least two possible interpretations. One (the "a" entries in fig. 8.4) is that these squares are intended to represent the shapes of faces in an object-centered description. According to this interpretation, two-squares drawings are simply variants of fold-out drawings that happen, fortuitously, to correspond to possible views. Another possible interpretation (the "b" entries) is that they represent the shapes of faces, subject to the effects of shape constancy, as they appear in a view of a cube. Without some additional evidence it is not possible to say, in the case of individual drawings, which interpretation is correct.

Near-Oblique Drawings

Nicholls and Kennedy refer to drawings in class 5, fig. 8.3 as "drawings with a frontal vertex shown by a Y-junction, and a vertex at the base shown by a T-junction," and drawings in class 11 as "other." I see no good reason to distinguish between these two classes, except that drawings of the type shown in class 5 would, if they appeared in adult pictures, be described as being in inverted perspective. The distinguishing features of drawings in both these classes is that they contain one or more anomalous T-junctions: that is, T-junctions denoting a corner rather than the point in the visual field where an edge disappears behind a face. How do these anomalous T-junctions come about? The most obvious explanation is that these drawings are variants of fold-out drawings, but that the shapes of some of the faces have been distorted in order to get them to join up properly (the "a" entries in fig. 8.4).

Very often a child will begin by drawing a single square representing the top or front face of the cube. Previous experience has suggested to the child that adding further squares will result in fold-out drawings in which the faces, edges, and corners do not join up as they should. A child at this stage will look ahead a little and distort the regions representing the additional faces. However, since these regions are intended to represent square faces, the child will try to retain as many right angles in them as possible, and as a result the drawing is likely to contain anomalous T-junctions. For example, children who produce drawings similar to that shown on the left in class 5, fig. 8.3 probably begin by using a square or near square to represent the top face of the cube. The two other regions are then added, using right angles wherever possible. As a result, an anomalous T-junction appears at the bottom of the drawing. Similarly, the front face of the cube in the drawing on the right in class 5 was probably drawn first as a square. The region on the right would then be added, with right angles at the bottom, and an oblique line at the top ready to accommodate the third and final face. Again, as a result, the drawing contains an anomalous T-junction at the bottom. Drawings in class 11 have simply arisen as variants of this process.

In drawings of this kind, the bottom is very often drawn as a single horizontal line, an effect that has been called "the flat bottom error." It has been suggested (Deregowski, 1977) that this flat bottom is intended to represent the cube standing on a flat supporting surface: as Waltz (1975) pointed out, line drawings of cubes without shadows like the drawing shown in fig. 6.6a could represent a cube floating in midair. Alternatively, Phillips et al. (1978) suggested that this flat bottom might be intended to represent the inherent stability of a cube. Both these suggestions may have some validity as *post hoc* rationalizations on the part of the child, and if so this might account for the frequency and persistence of this kind of error. However, as Freeman put it:

> The oblique may not be generated to represent depth. It may be generated as an entirely local solution to the problem of getting two discrete faces to join at an edge. It might help to imagine the child planning to draw three squares, three distinct *regions,* and realizing that something will have to give if two of the regions are to join up to preserve the integrality of the object. . . . The "flat bottom error" is simply because those lines do not need to join on to any other region in the picture so there is no need to render them as oblique. (Freeman, 1986, p. 320)

Square-with-Obliques Drawings (Oblique Projection)

Finally, it is impossible to tell by inspection whether the drawings in oblique projection (square-with-obliques, class 6) have been produced by applying rules to an object-centered description ("Draw the front face as a square, and represent edges in the third dimension by parallel oblique lines") (the "a" entries in fig. 8.4) or by "Matching directions [in a view] from a vantage point," as Nicholls and Kennedy suggest (p. 240) (the "b" entries). A similar argument applies to the drawings in isometric projection and perspective shown in classes 7, 8, and 9 of fig. 8.3. However, the mean ages for children who produced drawings in these classes were all about 12 years, and the frequency of another kind of anomaly, produced by children of this age, suggests that a substantial proportion of these children may still have been basing their drawings, at least in part, on object-centered rather than viewer-centered descriptions.

Fig. 8.7 shows typical drawings taken from an experiment in which sixty-four children aged 6 to 12 years were asked to draw a die which was presented to them edge-on at eye level, so that they could see only two faces (Willats, 1981, 1987). Fig. 8.7a shows a drawing by a 6-year-old, of the type already discussed. All the spots are shown within a single region, suggesting that the region stands for the whole volume of the die.

Two of the 6-year-olds and two of the 8-year-olds produced drawings in which the two visible faces were represented by separate squares or rectangles. In the drawing illustrated (fig. 8.7b), these two faces were joined by a vee-shaped tick: presumably this child realized that the faces of the die were joined but was unable to use a line to depict the common edge. This suggests that these children were using regions rather than lines as picture primitives.

Six of the 10-year-olds produced drawings in which the top face of the die was represented, even though it was not visible from the child's viewpoint. In four of these drawings the spot on top of the die was not represented (fig. 8.7c), presumably because, although these children knew

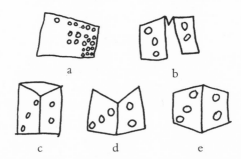

FIG. 8.7. Children's drawings of a die, presented at eye level. All the drawings except (e) show characteristic errors. From Willats (1987), courtesy of *Archives de Psychologie*, Geneva.

that another face must be there, they could not see how many spots it had on it. (The other children jumped up to see how many spots there were, thus changing their viewpoint.) These children had probably reached a stage in which they were able to use a rule which told them to represent edges in the third dimension by oblique lines sloping upwards, but were unable to coordinate this with a judgment about the number of faces in a view.

Six of the 12-year-olds produced a drawing of the type shown in fig. 8.7d. Children producing these drawings were able to assess and depict the number of *faces* in a view of a cube but were still unable to represent the orientation of edges in the visual field. This suggests that these children were using a rule like "use lines running obliquely upwards to represent edges in the third dimension" applied to an object-centered description. From the expressions on the faces of children who produced drawings of this type, it was clear that they knew that something was wrong with them; but they were unable to correct their drawings. Only four of the 12-year-olds produced a drawing, based on a full viewer-centered description, in which the lines correctly converged (fig. 8.7e).

Traditional wisdom says that young children draw what they know, and older children draw what they see, with a rather abrupt transition between the two at the age of about 8 years. In the light of Marr's (1982) account of visual perception, this is now often interpreted to mean that young children base their drawings on object-centered descriptions, and older children base their drawings on viewer-centered descriptions. Nicholls and Kennedy found two well-defined stages in children's drawings of a cube: single-square (mean age 6.7 years) and square-with-obliques (mean age about 12 years), and looking at these two classes of drawings only, it is very tempting to assume that these results confirm both the traditional, two-stage account of children's drawing development and its more modern counterpart.

However, it is impossible to tell, simply by inspection, whether "correct" finished drawings of this type have been derived from viewer-centered or object-centered descriptions, and the characteristic anomalies that appear in children's drawings suggest that this two-stage account is far too simplistic. Perhaps the most we can say is that there is a general tendency for younger children to base their drawing on object-centered descriptions, and for older children to base their drawings on viewer-centered descriptions; but a full account of children's drawings, including anomalous drawings, must specify the drawing and denotation rules they are using, as well as the nature of the internal descriptions to which these rules are applied.

Anomalous Drawings by Naive Adults

Freeman, Evans, and Willats (1988) carried out an experiment with first-year honors degree psychology students using a design rather similar to that used in the experiment, described in Chapter 7, which Phillips et al. (1978) carried out with 7- and 9-year-old children. The results of this experiment show that a substantial proportion of the young adults who took part in this experiment were unable to match the apparent directions of the edges of objects in a perspective picture of a scene, even in a simple copying task. The question is whether this is because these students were unable to overcome the influence of size constancy effects in copying a picture of a view of a scene, or whether they were basing their drawings on object-centered descriptions *derived* from this view.

Sixty-four students were asked to copy the salient features (the roof ridge, the stringcourse, and the curb line) of the picture of a street scene shown in fig. 8.8a. In this picture the stringcourse in each row of houses is horizontal, the ridge lines slope downwards at an angle of 39° to the horizontal, and the curb lines slope upwards at an angle of 42° to the horizontal. The overall angle of convergence between the roof and curb lines was thus 81°. This picture was projected onto a large screen and was in full view of the students during the whole course of the experiment.

The same students were also asked to copy the salient features (the horizontal and oblique spokes) in a picture of a broken wheel: effectively, a flat pattern with an angle of 30° between the oblique spokes and the horizontal (fig. 8.8b). The mean errors made by the students in copying this pattern were just over 2° for the horizontal lines, and just over 5° for the oblique lines. However, when the students copied the drawing of the street scene, the overall mean error made in copying the direction of the horizontal stringcourse was an astonishing 32°!

Eleven of the students drew lines representing the stringcourses correctly, as horizontal lines, with a mean error of 1°. A typical drawing of this type is shown in fig. 8.9a. The remaining fifty-three students all produced drawings in which the stringcourses sloped upwards, and the mean error made by these students in drawing these lines was 38.° Of these fifty-three students, twenty-six produced a drawing similar to that shown in fig. 8.9b in which the stringcourses and the curb lines sloped upwards, and twenty-six produced a drawing in which the ridge lines, the stringcourses, and the curb lines *all* sloped upwards (fig. 8.9c). The remaining subject produced a drawing in which all three lines sloped upwards and were parallel: that is, a drawing in oblique projection.

Our experience watching these students was similar to that reported by Phillips et al. It was astonishing to see the students make such gross errors in copying the picture even though it was in full view. On the other hand, when the same students were asked to copy the salient features of a wheel, the mean error in copying the horizontal lines was just over 2° and the mean error in copying the oblique lines was just over 5°, so it was clear that the mean error of 32° that the students made in copying the picture incorrectly could not be explained in terms of performance errors alone.

One possible explanation which might be suggested for these results is that the errors the students made in reproducing the apparent directions of edges in the depicted scene were due to the effects of size constancy. However, this explanation does not seem very plausible. It is true that the angle of convergence between the edges of the roof lines and the curb lines in most of the students' drawings was less than that in the original picture. That is, the roof and curb lines were more nearly parallel in their drawings than they were in the original, so that the change of scale with distance was rather less than that represented in the original picture. Fig. 8.9 shows typical examples of drawings showing this effect. However, this explanation cannot account for the gross errors that most of the students made in representing the direction of the horizontal stringcourse. If the results obtained were due only to constancy effects, one would expect the curb and roof lines to be more nearly parallel than they were in the original drawing, but the stringcourse to remain horizontal.

A more plausible explanation seems to be that the students who made gross errors in reproducing the directions of these horizontal lines did so because they interpreted the picture in terms of an object-centered description of the depicted scene, and then redrew this scene using simpler rules than those used to draw the original picture—rather like the children who produced fold-out drawings when they copied the picture of the die in oblique projection, in the experiment described by Phillips et al. (1978). These rules can be formulated in terms of the orthogonals representing the ridges, the stringcourses, and the curb lines.

The single student who drew the picture in oblique projection was using the simplest rule of all: "Use parallel oblique lines sloping upwards to represent edges in the third dimension." The twenty-six students who produced drawings similar to that shown in fig. 8.9c were using a slightly more complex rule: "Use *converging* oblique lines sloping upwards to represent edges in the third dimension."

The twenty-six students who produced drawings similar to that shown in fig. 8.9b added an extra feature to this rule: "Use converging oblique lines to represent edges in the third dimension. Let the edges above eye level slope downwards, and the edges at eye level and below eye level slope upwards."

None of these rules, however, captures the complexity of the rule used to produce the original drawing, which was: "Use converging oblique lines to represent edges in the third dimension. Let the edges above eye level slope downwards, the edges below eye level slope upwards, and the edges at eye level be horizontal." This is similar to the rule recommended by Cennino Cennini for drawing buildings in perspective, and similar to the rules used by Giotto, as described by Kemp (1992).

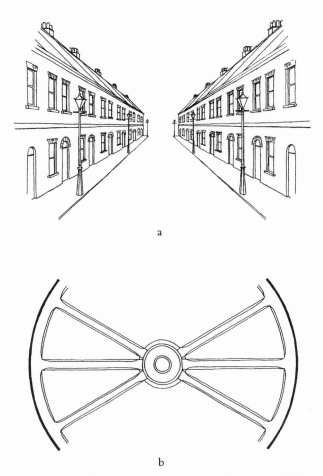

a

b

Fig. 8.8. (a) A drawing of a street scene, used as a stimulus picture. (b) A pattern in the form of a broken wheel. From Freeman et al. (1988).

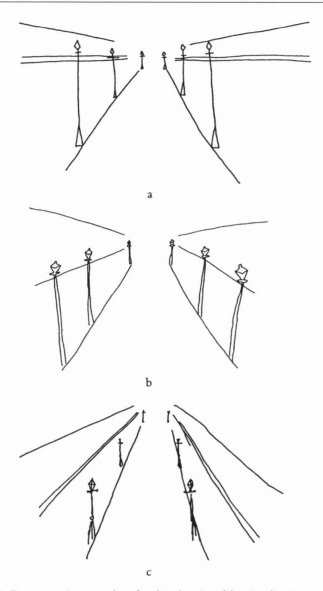

a

b

c

FIG. 8.9. Representative examples of students' copies of the stimulus picture shown in fig. 8.8. (a) The horizontal and convergence errors in this drawing are 1° and 15°, compared with group mean errors of 1° and 12°. Eleven subjects out of sixty-four produced drawings of this type. (b) The horizontal and convergence errors in this drawing are 27° and 12°, compared with group mean errors of 28° and 9°. Twenty-six subjects out of sixty-four produced drawings of this type. (c) The horizontal and convergence errors in this drawing are 51° and 43°, compared with group mean errors of 47° and 44°. Twenty-six subjects out of sixty-four produced drawings of this type.

The students who produced a correct copy, like the children who produced a correct copy of the cube in the experiment reported by Phillips et
al., may have done so by one of two routes. Some students may have simply
taken the picture as a pattern corresponding to a view of the scene and
copied this pattern correctly, noticing as they did so that the stringcourses
were represented by horizontal lines. Other students may have applied the
rule given above to an object-centered description of the scene. As both
routes would lead to the same result, it is impossible to decide in individual
cases which route was used.

The results of this experiment suggest that the majority of untrained
adults in the West will attempt to draw a scene containing rectangular
objects by applying rules to an object-centered description of the shapes of
the objects, rather than attempting to match the apparent directions of edges
in a view, even when the task is one of direct copying.

Anomalies in Artists' Pictures

In many cases we know whether pictures have been derived from object-
centered descriptions or from views. Drawings by engineers and architects
are derived from object-centered descriptions by the application of implicit
drawing rules, and in modern computer programs these rules are formalized
and take the form of algebraic equations. Photographs and TV pictures, on
the other hand, are, of course, derived from projections of scenes.

In other cases, art-historical evidence about artists' working methods is
sometimes available. Producing pictures by the application of drawing rules
to object-centered descriptions has a long history in painting, and painters
in the early Renaissance used workshop rules in order to produce pictures
in perspective. Kemp (1992), for example, described some of the "systematic
techniques based on rules" used by *trecento* painters before the discovery of
artificial perspective, beginning with the spatial system underlying Giotto's
Confirmation of the Rule of St. Francis, c. 1325. The spatial systems in early
Italian paintings such as Masaccio's *Trinity,* c. 1426, or Piero della Francesca's
Flagellation of Christ, c. 1460, are clearly constructed from object-centered
descriptions, using methods related to Alberti's *costruzione legittima,* rather
than being derived from views of real scenes.[6] Jan van Eyck's *The Arnolfini
Marriage,* 1434, on the other hand, was probably painted from life. Alpers
(1983) argued, if I understand her thesis correctly, that the spatial systems in
Italian Renaissance paintings were typically produced using rules similar to
the *costruzione legittima,* whereas seventeenth-century Flemish paintings
were more usually derived from views.

Fig. 8.10 shows a painting by the Dutch artist Pieter Saenredam, his *Interior of St. Bavo's Looking West,* painted in 1648. The strict rectangular frontal setting of the church interior, together with the precision of the geometry in the painting, might suggest that this geometry has been constructed from a knowledge of the true dimensions of the building, using a construction method similar to that recommended by Jan Vredeman de

FIG. 8.10. Pieter Saenredam, *Interior of St. Bavo's Looking West,* 1648. Edinburgh, National Galleries of Scotland.

Vries in his book on perspective published in 1604–1605 (fig. 2.20). On the other hand, this precision, together with what Kemp (1992) calls "his marvellously subtle use of light," could equally well suggest that Saenredam might have made use of a *camera obscura*. It seems impossible to tell, simply by looking at the finished painting, which of these methods might have been used.

In fact, art-historical evidence is available that provides us with a detailed knowledge of Saenredam's working methods. Kemp illustrates a study drawing of the interior of St. Bavo's (fig. 8.11a), the right and left halves of the more highly finished construction drawing that grew out of this study, and a tracing of the more readily visible lines in the graphite underdrawing in the right portion of the construction drawing (fig. 8.11b). These drawings were made in 1635, but the painting itself was not finished until 1648. Saenredam's method was thus to begin with an on-the-spot study from life. The construction drawing that grew out of this study contains the central vanishing point (marked with an E in fig. 8.11b) as well as one of the distance points. In the painting, this point lies almost directly under the cross on the shield which hangs on the column on the left; Saenredam noted its

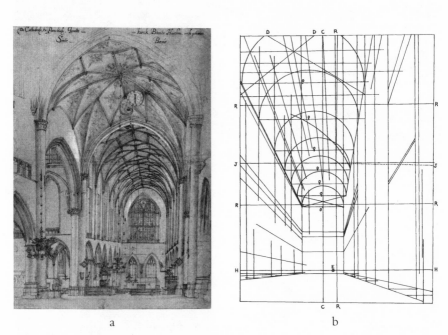

a   b

FIG. 8.11. (a) Pieter Saenredam, *Study of the Interior of St. Bavo's Looking West,* 1635. Municipal Archives, Haarlem. (b) Transcription of the more readily visible lines in the graphite underdrawing in the construction drawing for Saenredam's *Interior of St. Bavo's.* From Kemp (1992), courtesy of Martin Kemp.

distance from the central axis, which was 30 Dutch feet. From these two points all the construction lines in the drawing could be obtained. Thus Saenredam's working procedure was to begin with a sketch on the spot, drawn from life, and then to correct it using a construction based on secondary geometry. For example, in the original sketch (fig. 8.11a) the line above the arches in the chancel on the left of the picture is almost horizontal, an error which no doubt appeared as a result of constancy effects. In the construction drawing (fig. 8.11b), this error has been corrected so as to bring the line to a vanishing point, and this correction appears in the finished picture.

However, art-historical knowledge of this kind is not available in most cases. For example, Vermeer was a contemporary of Saenredam's, but there are no contemporary accounts of Vermeer's working methods and no known preliminary drawings by Vermeer; nor does infrared photography reveal the existence of any underdrawing in Vermeer's paintings. Vermeer's paintings, like Saenredam's, are remarkable for their clarity and subtle use of light, and this might suggest that their working methods were similar; but was this the case?

In the absence of art-historical evidence, anomalies in artists' pictures may provide the only evidence we can have of the processes of picture production. The pattern of the tiled floor in Vermeer's *The Music Lesson* (fig. 2.19), with the diagonals of the tiles leading to distance points on either side of the painting, might suggest that Vermeer used a construction method similar to those suggested by Jan Vredeman de Vries. Since the late 1920s, however, there have been a number of suggestions that Vermeer made use of a *camera obscura,* and this is now generally accepted, although the actual details of the method which Vermeer adopted are still in doubt. There are two main sources of evidence, both relating to characteristic anomalies in Vermeer's paintings. The first is the apparently unnatural enlargement of foreground objects in his paintings noted by R. H. Willenski in the late 1920s (Seymour, 1964). A painter working directly from life will normally depict objects in the foreground as smaller than their true projected images, as a result of the effects of size constancy. These size constancy effects do not seem to operate in the case of many of Vermeer's paintings, however: the soldier in the foreground of his *Soldier and a Laughing Girl,* 1660, for example, is painted larger than one would expect, as though the picture had been copied from a photograph.

A more persuasive piece of evidence is the presence in many of Vermeer's paintings of what are called "circles of confusion." This effect is produced when the light rays from a point on an object in the scene pass through a lens and are not fully resolved, or brought into focus, on the plate or film. It seems likely that this effect may have been present in early *camera obscura* images as a result of imperfections in the lens system, and it can be replicated in modern unfocused camera images (Seymour, 1964). The effect cannot be seen in ordinary vision, and it is now generally accepted that Vermeer must have made some use of a *camera obscura* (Kemp, 1992). Thus the presence of characteristic anomalies in Vermeer's painting suggests that he was working from the projections available in *camera obscura* images, rather than constructing or correcting his pictures according to the rules of secondary geometry applied to object-centered descriptions.

This is rather an exceptional example, however. The foreground details in Vermeer's paintings appear exaggerated because, paradoxically, they are in true perspective and not subject to the normal size constancy effects; and the circles of confusion arise as a result of imperfections in the lens system of an early *camera obscura*. In contrast, the errors that occur in pictures derived from object-centered descriptions normally arise as the result of artists using drawing rules that do not result in possible views. I have not found any examples of artists' pictures of rectangular objects corresponding to the anomalous drawings of cubes and dies found by Moore (1986a) and Willats (1981, 1987) illustrated in figs. 8.5 and 8.6, but there are many examples of artists' pictures having a surface geometry similar to the fold-out and near-oblique drawings shown in Nicholls and Kennedy's classes 3 and 5.

Fold-Out Pictures

Fold-out pictures are very common in Byzantine mosaics and Orthodox icon paintings, fairly common in eighteenth- and nineteenth-century naive paintings, and sometimes occur in Egyptian wall paintings. Both Cox (1992) and Hagen (1986) illustrate Egyptian fold-out drawings, and Cox draws attention to the similarity between the painting of a pond from Thebes, which she illustrates, and a child's fold-out drawing of a pond. Cox also shows an example of a fold-out drawing in the form of a map of a Shaker village drawn in 1845. The individual houses and barns are drawn in horizontal oblique projection, rather like the child's drawing of a house shown in fig. 2.9, but in addition the trees and buildings are folded out from the road that runs through the village. Similar examples of fold-out constructions in Shaker paintings can be found in Sprigg and Larkin (1987). Fig. 8.12 shows a detail from an eighteenth-century English naive painting in which the house and garden take the form of a fold-out drawing; the outbuilding has been added in oblique projection. Notice that the gable end to the right of the house is vertical, like the gable end in the child's drawing shown in fig. 2.9, suggesting that the artist has tried to draw the roof of the house as a true shape. Pictures like this are rather similar to engineers' drawings showing plan, front, and side elevations, but with all the faces joined together.

The commonest examples of fold-out pictures are probably those found in icon paintings: fig. 8.13 shows a typical example. The buildings on either side are drawn in horizontal oblique projection, so that the fronts and sides are drawn as true shapes, and the ground plane is folded down, like the garden in fig. 8.12. There must be thousands of examples of paintings of this type illustrating scenes from the Gospels or the lives of the saints to be found in the borders of Greek and Russian Orthodox icon paintings. As with children's drawings, it seems likely that the geometry of these fold-out pictures has been derived from object-centered descriptions rather than directly from views.

FIG. 8.12. M.S.L., *South View of Fen End Farm* (detail), 1790. Watercolor on paper, 25.5 × 40.5 cm. British Folk Art Collection, Bath. Photograph by Anne Shallis.

FIG. 8.13. Icon painting from a catafalque, Island Museum, Symi, Greece. Photograph by the author.

Near-Oblique Pictures

Anomalies similar or related to those shown in Nicholls and Kennedy's classes 5 and 11 are common in icon paintings, in Byzantine paintings and mosaics, in Persian and Indian miniature paintings, and in medieval and early Renaissance paintings and drawings. In some pictures of this type, the directions of the orthogonals are more or less incoherent, as they are in the drawings shown in class 11. In other examples the orthogonals diverge, as in the drawings shown in class 5, giving an effect of inverted perspective.

The drawing system in the detail of the painting by Giotto shown in fig. 2.22 is anomalous because it does not provide a coherent view. The orthogonals of the upper part of the building are parallel and run downwards, the orthogonals of the lower part of the building are parallel and run upwards, and the moldings in the middle of the building are level. It is just conceivable that the geometry of this picture might have been produced by replicating, incorrectly, the apparent directions of the edges of a view of a real building. However, it is more plausible to see in this picture the influence of an early Renaissance workshop rule, similar to Cennino Cennini's famous rule for producing pictures in perspective, which is implicitly intended to apply to an object-centered description.

The directions of the orthogonals in a predella panel from an altarpiece painted perhaps a hundred years later—Giovanni de Paolo's *Birth of St. John the Baptist*, fig. 8.14—are even more incoherent. The edges of the floor tiles and the moldings of the fireplace converge toward a rough vanishing point, but the bed may be regarded as being in an incoherent version of oblique projection. Again, it is tempting to suspect the influence of Cennini's advice. The top of the bed slopes downwards toward the background, while the bottom of the bed slopes up—although this is not quite what Cennini meant. Again, it seems likely that the surface geometry of this picture has

FIG. 8.14. Giovanni de Paolo (active 1420, died 1482), *The Birth of St. John the Baptist*. Oil on wood (predella panel from an altarpiece), 30.5 × 36.5 cm. National Gallery, London.

been derived from the application of a rule to an object-centered description rather than directly from a view of a scene.

Similar arguments apply to the very large number of paintings and mosaics in inverted perspective found in Byzantine art and Greek and Russian icons, like the mosaics in San Vitale, Ravenna, and St. Saviour in Chora, Istanbul, illustrated in figs. 14.9 and 14.11. It is not just that the orthogonals in these pictures diverge; the spatial systems in these pictures are incoherent. If pictures in inverted perspective are derived from possible views, as Parker and Deregowski (1990) have argued, we might surely expect the spatial systems in them to be no less coherent than in pictures in normal Renaissance perspective; but this is never the case.

Because so many pictures provide possible views, or at least approximations to possible views, it is very tempting to assume that most representational pictures, or even, as Margaret Hagen has argued, *all* representational pictures, have been derived from views. However, this makes it very difficult to account for the many anomalous constructions which are common in both children's drawings and artists' pictures. Pictures containing characteristic anomalies of the types I have described seem to provide clear cases of pictures that have been derived from object-centered descriptions by the application of mapping rules, rather than being derived directly from views. There are in addition a vast number of pictures which do not contain anomalies, like the twelfth-century Chinese painting in oblique projection, *Lady Wenji's Return to China* (fig. 1.2), which do provide possible views, and yet I suspect have not been derived from views, if only because of the practical difficulties involved in the artist getting into a position from which such a view could be seen. This does not mean that views are not involved in the process of picture production; but the views in question are views *in the emerging picture,* not views of a real scene. I suspect that what happens in cases like this is that the artist or draftsman begins by drawing, say, the front view of a building as a true shape, derived from an object-centered description. The next stage is to add one or more orthogonals, using a rule like: "Represent edges in the third dimension by parallel oblique lines across the picture." Again, this is a rule applied to an object-centered description. Once this has been done, however, a view of a scene begins to emerge, and the artist or draftsman can then continue the picture by adding further details in accordance with the coordinate system set up *within this pictorial view.*

A similar process, but involving in this case an interplay between an object-centered description of a scene, a viewer-centered description of a scene, and the view emerging in the developing picture, may take place even in the case of pictures drawn directly from life. This could, for example, explain why it is that the points of occlusion (indicated by asterisks) represented in the child's drawing of a table shown in oblique projection in fig. 1.9e are correct *within the context of the drawing,* even though they do not correspond to the points of occlusion (shown in fig. 1.9a) in the child's view of the real scene. It seems likely that this child began the drawing in a mixture of oblique projection for the table and orthogonal projection for the box and radio, and then dealt with the problem of representing points of occlusion *within the context of the depicted view* which began to emerge during the course of the drawing process.

If these accounts are correct, it suggests that the analogies between picture production by either photography or computer graphics and human picture production which I drew at the beginning of this chapter are grossly oversimplified. The processes involved in both photography and computer graphics are unidirectional, whereas in human picture production I suspect that in all cases (except perhaps in the case of pictures by very young children) there is a constant interplay between an internal representation of the scene, whether object- or viewer-centered, and a view of the depicted scene as it emerges during the depiction process. Very little research has, however, been carried out in this area.[7] Such research would be concerned with the question of the actual details of the drawing process—that is, it would be concerned with describing the drawing process at the second of Marr's three levels of analysis—and so would in any case be beyond the scope of this chapter. The main point I want to make here is that at the most abstract level of analysis—Marr's level one—pictures can be derived from either object-centered descriptions or viewer-centered descriptions; and we ought to be very cautious about jumping to conclusions about which is which in individual cases. In the absence of experimental evidence— evidence that is necessarily unavailable in the case of most artists' pictures— the presence of characteristic anomalies of the type I have described may provide the only available evidence about the nature of the production process.

Part Four

THE FUNCTIONS OF REPRESENTATIONAL SYSTEMS

CHAPTER NINE

Representing Shape

In the nineteenth century it was taken for granted that perspective was the best of all representational systems; not only because it seemed to agree with what was known about perception but because it was the system that had been adopted by the most civilized—that is, Western European—people. Few people would now hold this opinion, which seems hopelessly tainted with racial prejudice.[1] Nevertheless, as Gombrich said, "evolutionism is dead, but the facts which gave rise to its myth are still stubbornly there to be accounted for" (Gombrich, 1960/1988, p. 18). One of these facts is that there are periods in art history that seem to present us with a systematic pattern of development directed toward some definite goal: most obviously, the period covering the development of Greek vase painting, and, perhaps, rather less obviously, the period from the beginning of the Renaissance to the late nineteenth century.

But if the nineteenth-century account of perspective as the best of all possible systems is simply a "Western ethnic myth," as Margaret Hagen called it (Hagen, 1985, p. 60), what is the alternative? Hagen's own explanation was that the unique status of perspective, as normally understood, is itself an illusion. Because all the common projection systems can be defined in terms of primary geometry, all these systems—orthogonal projection, oblique projection, and perspective itself—are, properly understood, simply variants of what she called "natural perspective," the geometry of the light projected from the scene to the retina (Hagen, 1986, p. 8). It follows from this that all the representational systems employed by artists, except "arbitrary and completely idiosyncratic representations" (Hagen 1986, p. 4), can, in effect, be regarded as versions of perspective. That is, artists have always used perspective but have simply chosen to represent scenes from different directions of view. Hagen called these choices "cultural canons." Thus artists during the Renaissance chose to represent scenes from a relatively close viewpoint at eye level, like the Canaletto drawing shown in fig. 1.1. Oriental artists generally chose an oblique bird's-eye view at a very considerable distance from the scene, like the Chinese painting shown in fig. 1.2, so that the projection rays were virtually parallel. And the Greek vase painters, for the most part (fig. 1.3), chose a viewpoint situated at a considerable distance from the scene but at eye level, so that again the projection rays were virtually parallel. Hagen therefore concluded that, because artists have always used "natural perspective," there can be no systematic changes in art history and, in particular, no development in art directed toward the discovery or invention of perspective: "I cannot find evidence that the art styles of different cultures have developed systematically in an Orthogonal to Affine to Projective progression. Even in Western art (including Egypt), one can make this case only by choosing stylistic ancestors with great care and by ignoring diversions such as Cubism" (Hagen, 1985, p. 69). Thus all these different drawing systems are just different, rather as languages are different: artists in different periods and cultures have simply elected to adopt different viewpoints in relation to the scene.

The fallacy in this argument is that Hagen's classification scheme was based on definitions given only in terms of primary geometry: what she failed to appreciate was that the drawing systems, and especially the projection systems, can also be defined in terms of secondary geometry. One consequence of this was that she was unable to admit the existence of inverted perspective, except as an occasional aberration.[2] But an even more important consequence was that she failed to realize that the various projection systems, at least when they are applied to the representation of rectangular objects, *are* distinctly different in terms of the geometry of the picture surface. And the result of this difference in secondary geometry is that different systems are best suited to serve different functions.

As soon as we step outside the confines of art history, it is obvious that different disciplines have adopted those representational systems that are *best suited to the functions they have to perform.* I gave three examples of this in Chapter 1, but it is worth repeating them here. The first and perhaps most obvious example is the use of topological geometry for route maps and electrical circuit diagrams. Topological geometry is used for route maps like the map of the London Underground (fig. 1.11) because only those spatial relations with which the traveler is concerned—connectivity and spatial order—are preserved in topological transformations. Other properties, especially the appearance of the system from a particular point of view, which would be preserved in a perspective projection and with which the traveler is not concerned, are not represented. In addition, the traveler is not as a rule concerned with the true, architectural shapes of the stations, and so the only shape property represented is their extendedness—simply as a way of distinguishing stations from track in the picture. In the map of the London Underground, secondary shape properties—relative size, and the difference between square and round shapes—are used only conventionally, to indicate the difference between ordinary and interconnecting stations.

The second example I gave in Chapter 1 was the use of orthogonal projection in engineering working drawings. As I pointed out, engineers use this system because they need to provide accurate shape information. The fact that this system shows objects from a distant viewpoint, and in a frontal view, is a disadvantage in engineering drawing because it can make such drawings difficult to interpret: the drawing shown in fig. 1.13a provides an extreme example. Nevertheless, engineers have to put up with this disadvantage because this is the only system in which the true shapes of faces can be represented.

The third example I gave was the use of silhouettes in road signs. Here it is the choice of an appropriate denotation system that is important rather than the choice of an appropriate drawing system. And here again the reason for this choice is fairly obvious. If the objects depicted in road signs are to be recognized from a considerable distance, or in poor lighting conditions, or in rain or fog, then it is the shapes of the regions that are important rather than the shapes of lines; and these regions must reflect the extendedness of the shapes of the objects or parts of the objects they represent, together with other secondary shape properties like "being bent" or "being pointed," if the object portrayed in the sign is to be recognized.

Perspective, too, has its advantages, and so have the optical denotation systems. One advantage of perspective is that it allows the artist to portray objects of very different sizes. Thus it would hardly be possible to introduce an object as large as the Campanile shown in Canaletto's drawing of Venice (fig. 1.1) if the drawing had been carried out in oblique projection, like the street scene shown in the Chinese painting of *Lady Wenji's Return to China* (fig. 1.2), without reducing the figures of people to an absurdly small scale. By using perspective, Canaletto could draw his figures of people to a large scale by putting them in the foreground, and large objects such as the Campanile and St. Mark's could be drawn to a smaller scale in the background.

Another advantage of perspective is that it can provide the basis for an illusion in the way that other systems cannot. Hoogstraeten's perspective *View down a Corridor* painted on a wall at Dyhram Park, near Bath, provides a very convincing illusion of a real corridor extending into space, and it would hardly do so if it had been painted in, say, oblique projection. On the other hand, Peto's *Old Scraps,* which Gombrich (1960/1988) gives as an example of a convincing *trompe l'oeil* painting, shows various objects such as letters and a ribbon pinned to a board, and the depicted space is so shallow that the question of the representation of depth in space hardly arises. The basis of the illusion here, if it is an illusion, is the use of a highly optical denotation system: the same picture would hardly work as a line drawing. The whole question of illusion in painting is, however, a tricky subject. By "illusion," do we mean a mistaken belief about the existence of objects, or an overwhelmingly persuasive impression of three-dimensional shape such as one can obtain from a stereogram or autostereogram? Virtual reality, perhaps as close as we can get to achieving Gibson's definition of a faithful picture, which I quoted in Chapter 1, would seem to require a combination of perspective with an optical denotation system; but a very convincing stereogram can be produced using line drawing.

But I am not writing a treatise on illusion. I am using these examples only to suggest that different systems and combinations of systems are best suited to serve particular functions, and I shall argue that the reason why artists in different periods and cultures have represented the visible world in such different ways is that they have used those representational systems that best suited the different functions they were intended to serve. In artists' pictures these functions are generally much more complex than they are in route maps or engineering drawings, and three out of the four chapters in this part of the book describe applications of functions that go far beyond the mere representation of shape and space. Nevertheless, because the representation of shape is such a basic function of pictures, I want to begin, in this chapter, by describing the constraints that apply to the choice of particular drawing and denotation systems if they are to serve the purpose of providing effective representations of three-dimensional shape. In particular, I shall describe differences in the constraints that apply to pictures of smooth objects and objects having plane faces, and how these constraints apply differently to pictures based on line drawing and silhouettes.

Wollheim defined representation in terms of *seeing in:* "a necessary condition of R representing x is that R is a configuration in which something or other can be seen and furthermore one in which x can be seen" (Wollheim, 1977, p. 182). As Wollheim pointed out, this gives necessity rather than sufficiency because this definition would include as representations such cases as a cloud that looks very like a whale, or a photograph of Charlie Chaplin that anyone might mistake for a photograph of Hitler.

Wollheim therefore goes on to add the further conditions that the representation must be *intended* by whoever made it to be a configuration in which
something specific can be seen, and also that whoever made the representation must have the necessary competence to form and act on this intention.

Our subjective experience of "seeing in" as Wollheim describes it seems
to be a crucial factor in any definition we might want to give of representation: the drawings shown in figs. 1.13a and 1.13b both provide the same
shape *information,* but only in the case of fig. 1.13b is it possible to see the
three-dimensional shape the draftsman intended to represent *in* the drawing.
However, Wollheim's account seems to include two rather different kinds of
"seeing in": object recognition and shape recognition: we might see a whale
in a cloud, but only because the shape of the cloud resembles the shape of a
whale. Research in scene perception suggests that we recognize *objects* in
scenes because we recognize their *shapes,*[3] and in picture perception it is
important to distinguish between these two kinds of experience. For example,
it is possible to recognize a number of objects in Picasso's *Rites of Spring*
(fig. 3.8)—a goat, a bird, and two human figures—even though our perceptions of the three-dimensional shapes of these objects is very weak; but our
perception of the three-dimensional shapes of the bodies portrayed in Klee's
The Park at Abien (fig. 5.10) is quite vivid, even though this painting does not
depict a recognizable *object* in the normal sense of the word.

However, I am not concerned here with developing or defending any
general theory of representation. What I am concerned with is describing the
constraints that operate on representational systems if they are to provide
effective representations of three-dimensional shape, and I have used the
word "effective" rather than "good" because I want to avoid any judg-
mental, racial, aesthetic, or evolutionary connotations. Thus I shall define an
effective shape representation as a representation in which it is possible to
see, clearly and unambiguously, the three-dimensional shapes of the objects
that the artist or draftsman intended to portray. Which drawing and denotation systems are best suited to provide effective shape representations in this
sense?

Line Drawings of Objects Having Plane Faces

I have already suggested that if a picture is to provide an effective shape
representation, it must provide a possible *view:* that is, its geometry must
approximate to that of a possible projection. However, this is not the only
constraint that must be satisfied. Consider, for example, the drawings shown
in fig. 9.1, all of which, with the exception of drawings j and k, are possible

projections of the same object. Of all these drawings, only fig. 9.1a satisfies my definition of an effective representation. We can immediately, and without any conscious effort, see that this drawing is intended to represent a cube with a smaller cube removed from one corner, and we can see the three-dimensional shape of this object clearly and unambiguously in the drawing. Although in theory any picture is capable of an infinite number of possible interpretations, it is in practice very difficult to see this drawing in any other way. Presumably this is because the visual system tends to adopt the simplest and most likely interpretation of a picture. Thus it is possible, by an effort of will, to impose the interpretation that this is a drawing of part of the corner of a ceiling with a small, oddly shaped, folded plane attached to it, but this is such an unlikely interpretation that the visual system will normally reject it. In addition, the hidden faces of the object could be curved or irregular, but in the absence of any information to the contrary, the visual system makes the simpler assumption that these faces are flat.

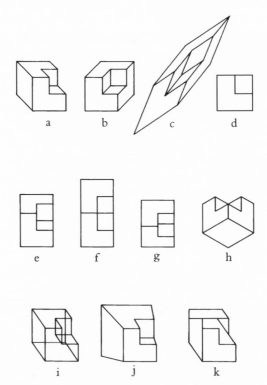

FIG. 9.1. Effective, ineffective, and impossible shape representations of a rectangular object.

The drawing shown in fig. 9.1b gives a strong impression of three-dimensional shape, but is ambiguous; with a conscious effort of will, we can change the interpretation. Presumably this is because all three possible interpretations are about equally likely. One possible interpretation of the drawing is that it represents a cube with a smaller cube removed from one corner, another is that it represents a cube with a smaller cube sticking out of it at an odd angle, and yet another that it represents a corner of a ceiling with a cube stuck into the corner. Fig. 5.6 shows labeled versions of this drawing which make these interpretations explicit.

Drawing c corresponds, despite appearances to the contrary, to a possible projection of the object: if this drawing is viewed at an oblique angle along the axis of symmetry of the drawing, it will appear similar to the drawing shown at b. If a "view" is defined simply as a possible projection of an object onto a plane surface, then drawing c corresponds to a possible view. The view it shows is, however, too oblique to provide an effective representation.

Perkins (1972) showed that adult subjects judged line drawings of a cube that corresponded to normal views as possible drawings of a rectangular box, but rejected drawings like fig. 9.1c in which the angle between the picture plane and the projection rays was too small. This condition can occur at the edges of pictures in perspective if the station point is too close to the picture plane; Leonardo recommended that this distance should not be less than three times the length of the object or scene to be depicted.

Drawings in oblique projection correspond to an oblique direction of view, and if this direction is too oblique, the orthogonals look too long and the drawing will be unacceptable. In drawings in cavalier oblique projection, in which the front and side edges are drawn to the same scale, the side edges look rather too long, whereas in drawings in cabinet oblique projection, in which the side edges are drawn to half scale, these side edges look rather too short. The best compromise is to use a scale of about 0.7 for the side edges. This is the proportion used in drawings a and b.

Fig. 9.1d corresponds to a plan or elevation in orthogonal projection. Although this drawing corresponds to a possible view, it does not provide an effective representation because the three-dimensional shape of the object cannot be seen in the drawing. Although with an effort of will one can perhaps impose a three-dimensional interpretation on it, the drawing is essentially flat. Engineers' and architects' working drawings are invariably in orthogonal projection, and two related drawings in orthogonal projection are normally sufficient to define the three-dimensional shape of any object. The penalty for using this system is that drawings in orthogonal projection are not as a rule effective as representations. Although such drawings define the shapes of objects, it can be difficult to see the shapes of objects in them, and we often speak of *reading* engineering drawings. Attempts are often made to improve engineering drawings as representations, and this can be achieved in two ways. One is to use one of the parallel oblique systems such as oblique projection or isometric projection instead of orthogonal projection. Oblique projections show the front faces of objects as true shapes, and in cavalier oblique projection the side edges are shown as true (scale) lengths. In isometric projection (figs. 2.16 and 2.17), all the edges are shown as true (scale) lengths, although none of the faces is shown as a true shape. Another approach, popular in the nineteenth century but less often used today, is to add tonal modeling and/or shadows (fig. 6.3).

Figs. 9.1e and f are both representations of the object in vertical oblique projection. In fig. 9.1e the angle between the projection rays and the picture plane is greater than 45°, and as a result the top faces are shown foreshortened. Fig. 9.1e is more effective as a representation than the drawing in orthogonal projection shown at fig. 9.1d, but the drawing still appears relatively flat, and it requires something of an effort of will to impose a three-dimensional interpretation. In fig. 9.1f the angle between the projection rays and the picture plane is 45°, and all the faces are shown as true shapes. As a result, a false attachment has been introduced in the center of the drawing, and this has the effect of flattening the image and reducing the effectiveness of the drawing as a representation.

Fig. 9.1g shows the object in orthogonal projection but in a foreshortened position, so that both the top and side faces are foreshortened. Drawing g perhaps looks slightly more natural than drawing e, which is in vertical oblique projection, but it could be argued that because drawing e shows the front face of the object as a true shape, it actually corresponds more closely than drawing g to the appearance of the object, allowing for the influence of constancy effects.

Fig. 9.1h is in isometric projection, and like drawing f contains a false attachment, which tends to reduce the picture to a flat pattern. In addition, the drawing is symmetrical, and this also tends to reduce its effectiveness as a representation.

Fig. 9.1i is difficult to interpret because lines representing all the edges of the object, including hidden edges, have been included in the drawing. Like a Necker cube drawing, in which all the edges of a cube are represented, this drawing is reversible, although alternative interpretations are more difficult to impose than they are with the Necker cube (try to imagine the front face as a large square).

Fig. 9.1j is similar to fig. 9.1a but is in inverted perspective rather than oblique projection. Like fig. 9.1a, it gives a strong impression of three-dimensional shape, but a distorted shape rather than the shape it is intended to represent.

Finally, fig. 9.1k is neither effective nor acceptable as a shape representation. It does not show a view of a possible object, and the configurations of lines and line junctions do not obey the rules for line drawings described in Chapter 5.

Our intuitions about these drawings seem to be very strong, and we can deduce from them a number of constraints with which a line drawing of an object having plane faces must comply if it is to provide an effective shape representation:

A1. The drawing should show a possible view (failure to meet this constraint eliminates drawings j and k).

A2. This view must not be taken from too oblique an angle (eliminates drawing c).

A3. The view must be taken from a general position, in order to avoid false attachments arising from accidental alignments in the scene (eliminates drawings d, e, f, g, and h).

A4. The drawing should show only those faces, edges, and corners that can be seen from a single viewpoint (eliminates drawing i).

A5. The drawing should contain, if possible, at least one T-junction (eliminates drawing b, which is ambiguous).

All these constraints seem understandable in terms of normal scene perception. The geometry of drawings in any of the projection systems described in Chapter 2 (with the exception of naive perspective and inverted perspective) will correspond to the geometry of projections of real objects in the frontal plane, provided the angle of projection is not too oblique: normally we direct our eyes toward objects, rather than viewing them obliquely. In addition, the visual system seems to work on the assumption that we view things from a general direction of view so that accidental alignments are avoided. If there is a straight line in the image, the visual system infers that the edge producing that image is also straight, and ignores the possibility that the property "being straight" in the image might be the result of a highly unlikely alignment between the direction of view and the plane of curvature of a curved edge. Finally, the presence of T-junctions which show one feature behind another provides a highly effective substitute in pictures for the absence of other sources of information about depth such as stereopsis and motion parallax.

Line Drawings of Smooth Objects

Somewhat similar constraints apply to line drawings of smooth objects if they are to be effective as representations, but there are important differences of detail. Richards, Koenderink, and Hoffman (1987) examined these constraints in relation to outline drawings of smooth objects and began by examining three simple outline drawings. Two of these were similar to those shown in fig. 9.2, which they called the "ellipse" (drawing a) and the "peanut" (drawing b). The third drawing, which is not shown here, they called the "dumbbell." The simplest of these outlines is the ellipse which, as Richards et al. say, we "naturally" interpret as the silhouette of an ellipsoid or egg. Alternatively, this drawing *could* represent the outline of a peanut viewed from above, but in this view the concave part of the outline representing the saddle-shaped surface forming the lower part of the peanut would not be visible. As a result, we would not normally interpret fig. 9.2a as the top view of a peanut, and Richards et al. proposed that this is because we normally assume that all the undulations necessary to infer a plausible three-dimensional shape from a picture are visible in the silhouette. This, as they point out, is an extension of the "general position" restriction, defined by Huffman (1971), which requires that the view of an object is not a special one. Richards et al. thus defined what they called a "canonical" (p. 1169) (or "prototypic," p. 1170) view of a smooth object as one whose silhouette reveals all the undulations in its surface. A slight change in the viewpoint, for such a view, should not suddenly reveal any new "bumps" or "dents"[4] (p. 1169) in the surface that were previously hidden by occlusion.

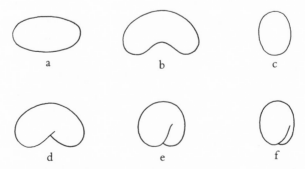

FIG. 9.2. Effective and ineffective shape representations of a smooth object.

Special views may not just be misleading as to surface undulations, however. Fig. 9.2c shows the end view of the peanut, and this view is not only misleading because it disguises the surface undulations but also because it disguises the extendedness of the peanut, suggesting that its volumetric shape is round rather than long. A top view, in contrast, similar to the view shown in fig. 9.2a, would disguise the surface undulations but correctly represent the extendedness of the peanut. Thus, if a line drawing of a smooth object is to be effective as a representation, it should not only show a *canonical* view which reveals all the surface undulations, but must also show a *representative* view: that is, a view that reflects the extendedness of the viewed object (Willats, 1992a, p. 488).

As with rectangular shapes, the presence of one or more T-junctions in a drawing of a smooth object very much enhances its effectiveness as a representation. End-junctions are also valuable because they show that the drawing is intended to represent a smooth object (Koenderink, 1990). Thus drawing d is more effective as a representation of a peanut than drawing b, which might equally well represent the edges of a flat cutout or a closed wire frame.

Fig. 9.2e must also represent a smooth solid object, and provides about as effective a representation as drawing d. Although the extendedness of its silhouette does not reveal the extendedness of the peanut, the concavity of the line close to the end-junction gives a vivid impression of the three-dimensional (saddle-shaped) surface at this point, so that we can recognize drawing e as a *partially foreshortened view* of the peanut. Fig. 9.2f is perhaps rather less effective as a representation of a peanut, however. Not only does the extendedness of its silhouette disguise the extendedness of the peanut, but the lines representing contours almost merge at the T-junction, rather than intersecting at right angles. The representation would become even less effective if the peanut were to be turned a little further. Koenderink (1990) says: "Tangencies of contours and curves should only occur if they indicate an actual tangency of the spatial configuration. This holds equally true for T-junctions. You must substitute—almost—orthogonality for mere trans-versality because otherwise it is quite likely that your intention will not clearly register" (p. 623).

Thus, as with rectangular objects, it is possible to infer a number of constraints on line drawings of smooth objects if they are to be effective as shape representations:

B1.   The drawing must show a possible view (same as A1 above).

B2.   This view should normally be *representative* (that is, it should reflect the extendedness of the viewed object). This constraint eliminates drawings c and f. However, it may sometimes be possible to override this constraint by showing a view including T- and end-junctions, so that the object can be shown in a foreshortened position, as in drawing e.

B3. The view shown must be *canonical* (that is, it should reveal all the surface undulations). This eliminates drawing a.

B4. The drawing should, if possible, contain T- and end-junctions (similar to A5).

Silhouettes

Fig. 9.3 shows silhouettes corresponding to some of the drawings in figs. 9.1 and 9.2, and it is intuitively obvious that the impression of three-dimensional shape given by these silhouettes is greatly inferior to that given by most line drawings. In addition, the effectiveness of a silhouette as a shape representation depends in the case of rectangular objects on the sharpness of the outline. In figs. 9.2e to h and l to n, the outlines of the silhouettes have been artificially blurred to simulate the appearance of these shapes as they would appear when seen from a considerable distance or in conditions of poor visibility. In the case of drawings e to h, these blurred silhouettes are much less effective as representations of rectangular objects than the silhouettes with sharp outlines. In the case of drawings l to n, however, the effectiveness of the blurred silhouettes as representations is not much less than it would be in the case of the silhouettes with sharp outlines.

The "general position" restriction, which was originally intended to apply to line drawings of objects having plane faces, also seems to hold true for silhouettes of objects having plane faces. Koenderink (1984) illustrates a figure taken from a book on drawing (Hogarth, 1981) which suggests that, for rectangular figures such as the cube, the pyramid, and the cylinder (a "mixed" figure which contains both plane and smooth faces), the strongest spatial impression is given by generic (that is, general) views. Figs. 9.3a to d show silhouettes of the cube with a smaller cube removed from one corner, the object shown in line in fig. 9.1a, and it is obvious that the silhouettes shown in figs. 9.3a and b, which show general views, are better as representations than the silhouette shown at d which shows a special (front) view. In addition, fig. 9.3a is more effective as a representation than fig. 9.3b: not, as in the corresponding drawing shown in fig. 9.1a, because fig. 9.3a contains a T-junction, but because the concavity in the outline of this figure reveals the concavity in the volumetric shape of the object, which fig. 9.3b does not. Thus the restriction previously suggested for smooth objects by Richards et al. (1987), that the outline of the silhouette ought to reveal all the surface undulations (that is, that it should be canonical), seems also to hold good for silhouettes of rectangular objects. It also seems to hold good for the outlines of line drawings of rectangular objects, like the line drawing shown in fig. 9.1a, and for the outlines of line drawings combined with silhouettes, like Greek black-figure and red-figure vase paintings. This restriction thus appears to be a particularly important one.

Another restriction which also holds good for silhouettes is that the picture should not show a projection that is too oblique. Fig. 9.3c is clearly misleading as a representation, although it shows a possible projection from a general position. Perkins (1972) discusses this restriction in line drawings of similar figures in terms of the relations between the angles between lines

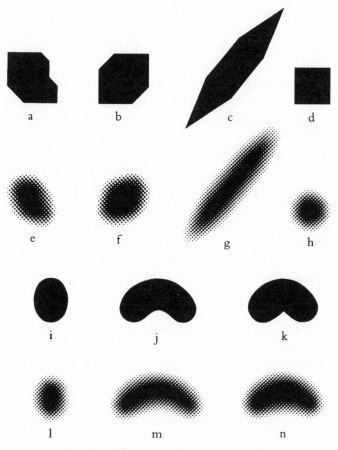

Fig. 9.3. Silhouettes as shape representations.

representing internal edges. In silhouettes these lines are not, of course, present; nevertheless, fig. 9.3c is still not acceptable as a representation. Presumably this is because the extendedness of the silhouette does not reflect the extendedness of the object it is intended to represent. Again, this restriction also seems to apply to line drawings, and line drawings combined with silhouettes; and again this restriction is a particularly important one.

Fig. 9.3i shows an end view of the peanut shown in fig. 9.2 and is not effective as a representation because it represents neither the extendedness nor the surface undulations of the viewed object. Fig. 9.3j shows a silhouette of a profile view of the peanut and, like the outline drawing shown in fig. 9.2b, provides a reasonably good representation. The silhouette shown in fig. 9.3k corresponds to the outline of the line drawing shown in fig. 9.2d, but whereas fig. 9.2d is more effective as a representation than the outline drawing shown in fig. 9.2b because it contains both T- and end-junctions, the silhouette corresponding to this slightly foreshortened view is rather less effective as a representation than the silhouette shown in fig. 9.3j. This is because fig. 9.3k contains a cusp—that is, an L-shaped discontinuity in the outline—which gives the misleading impression that the silhouette represents a smooth surface with a *crease*. In this respect, the constraints that apply to silhouettes of smooth objects, if they are to be effective as representations, appear to be different from those that apply to line drawings: silhouettes of smooth objects are not more effective as representations if they show such objects in general positions. As a result, it is usually difficult or impossible to use silhouettes to show smooth objects in foreshortened positions: a constraint that has important implications for the patterns of development exhibited in both children's drawings (Chapter 13) and Greek vase painting (Chapter 14).

Where the outlines of a silhouette of a rectangular object are sharply defined, the details of the outline are usually crucially important, because the outlines can show the shapes of features like edges and corners. Where the outlines are blurred, it is only the shapes of the regions that are informative, and these regions can show only the simplest and most basic three-dimensional shape features such as extendedness, together with some secondary shape properties such as "having a dent." Fig. 9.3e represents the cube with a cube removed from one corner as a lump with a dent in it: the property "having flat faces" has virtually disappeared. Figs. f and h merely represent the object as a lump, and the "general position" restriction has become largely irrelevant. Fig. 9.3g totally misrepresents the object because it misrepresents its extendedness. Similarly, fig. 9.3l misrepresents the extendedness of the peanut. Figs. 9.3m and n both represent the peanut, reasonably effectively, as a long bent volume; because the outline is blurred, the presence or absence of a cusp in the contour becomes irrelevant.

It is thus possible to infer the constraints on silhouettes of objects of this kind if they are to be effective as representations:

C1. The silhouette should show a *representative* view (it should reflect the extendedness of the viewed object).

C2. The silhouette should show a *canonical* view (it should reveal all the surface undulations).

By comparing line drawings with silhouettes, it is possible to draw some general conclusions from these pictures. To begin with, it seems immediately obvious that line drawings provide far more effective representations of objects than silhouettes: the drawings shown in figs. 9.1a and 9.2d provide us with far more vivid impressions of three-dimensional shape than the corresponding drawings shown in figs. 9.3a and 9.3k. Second, it seems hardly possible to produce silhouettes showing impossible objects, like the drawing of an impossible object shown in fig. 9.1k. *Any* silhouette, of whatever shape, can be interpreted as a picture of a possible object. Third, foreshortening cannot be shown effectively in silhouettes of smooth objects. Whereas the line drawings shown in figs. 9.2d and 9.2e provide effective representations of peanuts in foreshortened positions, fig. 9.3k does not. Notice that this is a consequence of using different denotation systems; it hardly matters whether we think of these drawings as being in orthogonal projection or perspective.

Finally, there are differences in the effectiveness of silhouettes as representations of smooth objects, and objects having plane faces. First, the most effective representation in silhouette of the cube with a smaller cube removed from one corner is fig. 9.3a, which shows a three-quarter view, whereas the most effective silhouette of the peanut is fig. 9.3j, which shows a profile view. Second, blurring the outline makes a very considerable difference to the silhouettes of objects having plane faces, but little difference to the silhouettes of smooth objects. Compare, for example, figs. 9.3b and f, and figs. 9.3j and m.

The examples given in figs. 9.1, 9.2, and 9.3 depict objects with relatively simple shapes. It seems likely, however, that the constraints that they suggest can be generalized to more complex objects, and if this is so, these constraints have important consequences for artists and draftsmen. This is especially important in the case of objects with complex smooth surfaces such as the human figure. For example, the head of the figure shown in silhouette in *Lady Taking Tea* (fig. 5.1) is shown in profile, and this view, like the profile view of the peanut shown in fig. 9.3j, provides the best possible representation of a head in silhouette because it shows the maximum number of surface undulations without cusps. On the other hand, in the line drawing of Stravinsky shown in fig. 1.6, the drawings of the wrestlers shown in fig. 5.9, and the red-figure painting of Phoenix and Achilles shown in fig. 14.8, the heads are shown in three-quarter views. In line drawings, three-quarter views of this kind often provide the most effective representations because they maximize the number of informative T- and end-junctions in the drawing. In silhouettes, however, such views would be ineffective. Fig. 14.8 provides an example of silhouette combined with line drawing, and the element of silhouette in this painting detracts from the effectiveness of the line drawing, so that the representation of shape seems rather weak—and would seem weaker still if the vase were to be viewed from a considerable distance.

I have suggested that a picture provides an effective shape representation if it is possible to see in the picture, clearly and unambiguously, the three-dimensional shape of the object that the artist or draftsman intended to depict. If the shape of the object can be seen in the picture, then the object can be recognized.

Under normal viewing conditions, line drawings will be more effective as representations than silhouettes. Under exceptional viewing conditions, such as when a picture is seen from far away, or in mist or driving rain, or under poor lighting conditions such as the interior of a dimly lit church, silhouettes may be more effective as representations: hence the use of silhouettes in banners, road signs, and icon paintings.

Pictures based on optical denotation systems may provide more effective representations than silhouettes, but this will depend very much on the way the subject is lit and the size of the marks in relation to the subject. The detail of a newspaper photograph shown in fig. 1.8, for example, provides only a rather poor representation of a figure: the representation of shape in this photograph is little better than in the rock engravings of gladiators in combat shown in fig. 1.5 or the Greek vase painting of the geometric period shown in fig. 14.1.

Line drawings with shadows may sometimes be better as representations than plain line drawings: as Waltz (1975) has shown, the presence of shadows may be helpful in removing ambiguities. Tonal modeling and/or surface contours may be helpful in showing surface undulations in drawings of smooth objects—like the figures of women shown in Raphael's *Study of the Three Graces* (fig. 6.2)—in cases where these undulations would not be revealed by the outline alone.

Thus I shall argue in this part of the book that particular representational systems are best suited to serve particular functions. In this respect, pictorial representation appears to be very different from natural language. All natural languages seem to be about equally good for the same things, and any thought can be expressed with almost equal ease in any language. Contrary to popular belief, it does not appear to be true that some languages are better than others for discussing certain topics: that the Inuit (Eskimo) languages have hundreds of words for snow, for example, while English has only one or two.[5]

Finally, the constraints on pictures if they are to provide effective shape representations are all constraints imposed by the design features of the human visual system. It seems highly unlikely that these constraints are conventional. In this respect also, pictures are very different from natural languages.

CHAPTER TEN

Flattening the Picture Surface

As a number of writers have pointed out, pictures provide us with a view of an apparently real world but are at the same time merely blobs or dots of paint or pigment. Gibson (1978) refers to this property as *duality:* "a picture is both a surface in its own right, and a display of information about something else" (p. 231). But it is not *merely* a display of information, like a list of words or numbers. As Wollheim says, a representation is a configuration in which something or other can be seen, and this "seeing in" is central to our experience of pictures.

In the language of artificial intelligence, pictures represent scenes. Scenes are three-dimensional and are made up of scene primitives such as corners, edges, and surfaces. Pictures, on the other hand, are two-dimensional and are made up of picture primitives such as regions, lines, and line junctions. These are the two domains with which we are mainly concerned in the analysis of pictures. In addition, it is necessary to distinguish between marks and picture primitives: actual drawings and paintings are made up of physical marks such as lines of ink or areas of paint, and in real pictures marks of this kind represent the picture primitives. Moreover, the depicted world is made up of objects, like people and chairs, and the scene primitives represent the abstract shape attributes of such objects.

It is only in exceptional circumstances that we have the experience of seeing any of these domains in isolation when we look at a picture. At one extreme we may, when we look at a picture, have a mistaken belief that we are looking at a real scene. As I pointed out in the previous chapter, we may actually believe when looking at a *trompe l'oeil* painting that what we are seeing is a collection of old letters, ribbons, and other objects stuck on a board. Or, looking at Hoogstraeten's *View down a Corridor,* we may believe that we are looking down a real corridor. This experience may not necessarily be accompanied by any very strong sensation of depth, although it sometimes may be: what we think we see is the *object* domain. In contrast, the impression of depth and three-dimensional shape given by some special kinds of pictures such as stereograms may be almost as strong as that obtained from a real scene, but this experience is not necessarily accompanied by an erroneous belief that we are looking at real objects. When we look at an Impressionist painting, on the other hand, we may, if we are sufficiently close, see nothing but *marks:* blobs of paint on a flat surface.

These are exceptional cases, however. Most paintings and drawings do not provide complete illusions because, although we may see objects in them, we do not experience them as fully real. Nor do we experience the same sensation of depth and three-dimensional shape in the painting as we would in a real scene, although we do see depth and shape in the painting. Nor do we normally experience a painting simply as a configuration of picture primitives, or marks on a surface. To a greater or lesser extent, we may be aware of some or all of these domains, and the strength with which they impress themselves on our awareness may vary greatly from one picture to another. Looking at Picasso's drawing of Stravinsky (fig. 1.6), we will probably not be very aware of the pencil lines as marks on the surface, unless we choose to pay special attention to them, but we probably will be aware of the lines in the drawing as configurations of picture primitives. Looking at a Pointillist painting or an Impressionist painting, especially at close hand, we will probably be more aware of the marks on the surface; whereas looking at Vermeer's *The Music Lesson* (fig. 2.19), we may be more aware of the objects in the depicted scene. Thus, although Gibson speaks of the "duality" of pictures, up to four domains may be involved in normal picture perception. Moreover, by choosing appropriate pictorial devices, the artist can tilt the balance of our awareness of these different domains one way or the other. In the twentieth century, many painters have tilted the balance away from illusion toward an awareness of the picture surface: that is, toward "flatness."

In the first part of this chapter I shall describe the various pictorial devices that an artist might use in order to tilt the balance toward flatness, and in the second part I shall try to say something about the reasons why artists in different periods and cultures might want to tilt the balance in this direction.

Techniques for Flattening the Picture Based on the Mark Systems

Obtrusive Marks

The surfaces of pictures intended to provide an illusion are invariably smooth, and the marks blend into each other imperceptibly: "like a puff of smoke," as Cennino Cennini said. The eye is not tempted to linger on the surface of the picture, but looks through it to the depicted scene. If, on the other hand, the surface marks are obtrusive, they draw attention to the picture surface. This is the case with mosaics, tapestries, and many Impressionist and Cubist paintings.

In Roman mosaic pavements the spaces between the marble tesserae are filled in with mortar so that the surface is relatively smooth, but in Byzantine wall mosaics the interstices are left empty so that the tesserae are strongly present as individual units, and the surface as a whole appears rough and irregular. Moreover, the surfaces on which these mosaics are set are not completely flat. Both these factors draw attention to the picture as a physical surface. Very much the same factors operate in the case of tapestries. Many Impressionist paintings have rough-textured surfaces, and the Cubists sometimes added sand to their paint to make a rough texture.

The Size of the Marks

In normal book or newspaper photographs the dots of pigment are too small to be resolved as separate units. If these illustrations are enlarged, however, like the newspaper photograph of a hijacker shown in fig. 1.8, the dots become too large to fuse on the retina and this draws attention to the picture surface. Roy Lichtenstein exploited this effect in his paintings: the mark system is an enlarged version of that used in printing cheap comics (fig. 7.7). A similar effect can be observed in Pointillist paintings such as those of Seurat (color plate 2), and large-scale marks that force themselves on the viewer's attention are also found in most Impressionist and Post-Impressionist paintings: they are particularly noticeable in Van Gogh's paintings and drawings, for example (fig. 7.1). In Matisse's Neo-Impressionist paintings the individual marks are huge in relation to the overall size of the canvas.

Uniformity of Texture

Gibson (1950) suggested that surface texture, such as the texture provided by pebbles on a beach, can provide important information about the shape and orientation of surfaces. It is not essential that all the pebbles should be the same size, but merely that the texture should be composed of elements that are more or less uniformly distributed. If the textured surface lies at an angle to the viewer, the units of texture that are further away will project a smaller image. Texture gradients, as they are called (that is, the change in the size of the units of texture with distance), are simply a form of linear perspective, and like linear perspective provide a cue to distance (Marr, 1982).

Conversely, a uniformly distributed pattern of marks on the surface of a picture (whether or not they are all the same size or shape) will tend to emphasize the flatness of the picture: because there is no texture gradient in the pattern of these marks, we read the picture as a flat, vertical surface. The flattening effect of a uniformly distributed pattern of marks can be seen very clearly when fig. 6.1a is compared with fig. 6.1b. In the photograph shown in fig. 6.1a the grain of the film, though perceptible, is not very obtrusive, and consequently the foreshortening of the house relative to the plane of the picture can be seen quite clearly. In contrast, the image shown in fig. 6.1b appears completely flat.

In earlier Impressionist paintings the brushwork was descriptive: that is, the directions of the brushstrokes followed the directions of the principal curvatures of the surfaces of the depicted forms. These brushstrokes acted as surface contours and enhanced the representation of three-dimensional shape produced by the tonal modeling. During the latter half of the 1870s, however, the brushwork became more independent of the depicted form and took on a different role: "The size of brushstroke was kept relatively uniform over the entire canvas, and so it no longer aided an illusion of recession, but emphasized the physical surface of the picture. Thus, the artist forced the spectator to remember that the picture confronted was a *painting,* which had its own reality, and was not simply an extension of the spectator's world" (Anfam et al., 1987, p. 213). This device is very evident in Cézanne's later paintings.

Facture

Facture is the term used by art historians to describe the manner in which a painting has been executed, especially as it testifies to the work of human hands. In some cases the manner of workmanship may not be immediately evident, but in other cases we may be made aware of the physical reality of the picture because of this element of facture. In the Chinese painting by Chu Ta shown in fig. 10.9, for example, the ink has obviously been brushed, blobbed, and flooded on the surface of the paper under the operation of human control. In *trompe l'oeil* and ultrarealistic paintings, in contrast, traces of the operations of the human hand are, as far as possible, suppressed: nothing must interfere with the illusion provided by the pictorial image. Facture is, however, a tricky business, and the effort involved in eliminating the element of facture can itself draw attention to the physicality of the picture:

> Between 1908 and 1910 I made my first attempts to transcend inherited art forms, inherited prejudices. . . . All accident was excluded. No spots, tears, fibres, imprecisions, should disturb the clarity of our work. For our paper pictures we even discarded the scissors with which we had first cut them out, since they too readily betrayed the art of the hand. From this time on we used a paper cutting machine. (Arp, 1948, p. 76)

In spite of all this effort, and perhaps because of it, the paintings and collages of this period are readily identifiable as the work of a particular person at a particular time, and this in itself seems to draw attention to their physical reality.

These pictorial devices may all be present together, or they may be used separately or combined in various ways. In the mosaics at Ravenna (fig. 14.10), the marks (the tesserae) are strongly physical, roughly uniform in size, and more or less uniformly distributed across the picture surface; but there is little or no element of facture. In Chinese painting there is often a strong element of facture, but the surface is usually relatively smooth, and the marks may be varied in both shape and distribution.

Techniques for Flattening the Picture Based on the Drawing Systems

The Geometry of the Different Drawing Systems

One of the most important cues to depth in pictures is linear perspective. In the perception of real scenes the image of an object projected onto the retina will be smaller as the object is further away, and the representation of this effect in pictures gives a strong impression of depth. If this cue is not present, the picture will appear relatively flat, so, although Hagen (1986) has argued that systems like orthogonal projection and oblique projection may be regarded as versions of what she called "natural perspective," pictures in these systems do not provide the same depth cues.

I showed in Chapter 9 that if a picture is to provide a good representation of three-dimensional shape, it should show rectangular objects from a general position. In practice this means using either perspective or one of the parallel oblique systems such as oblique projection or isometric projection or their variants. Conversely, pictures in orthogonal projection or horizontal or vertical oblique projection provide only poor representations, and pictures based on these systems look relatively flat. In addition, false attachments in the picture ought to be avoided if the picture is to provide an effective representation of three-dimensional shape.

Pictures in orthogonal projection and horizontal or vertical oblique projection thus look relatively flat compared with pictures in oblique projection or perspective, partly because they do not contain the depth cues provided by linear perspective and partly because they do not show rectangular objects from a general direction of view, and are therefore more likely to contain false attachments representing accidental alignments within the scene. However, an additional factor seems to be involved. In pictures in horizontal or vertical oblique projection, all the edges of rectangular objects are represented by horizontal or vertical lines, and the grid which this sets up on the picture surface will be aligned with the edges of the picture itself, or with the picture frame. That is, all three axes of the coordinate system of the pictorial image will be aligned with the axes of the coordinate system of the picture. In real life this would be very unlikely to happen: if we were looking at a real scene through a window, it would be very unlikely that the directions of the projected edges of objects in the third dimension would coincide with the horizontal and vertical edges of the window frame. This coincidence can be regarded as a special case of false attachment; and this tends to draw attention to the picture as a flat surface. For example, Bonnard's *Nude in a Bathtub* (fig. 10.1), in which the projected edges of the bath mat and the bathtub in the third dimension are both (nearly) aligned with the vertical axis of the picture surface, looks relatively flat. Similarly, in Cézanne's *Still Life with a Commode* (fig. 2.7), the horizontal edges of the side of the commode are aligned with the horizontal axes of the picture surface, and again this tends to flatten the picture.

Pictures in oblique projection show objects from a general direction of view, and thus normally give a relatively strong impression of three-dimensional shape. There is, however, no perspective cue to depth. Moreover, the orthogonals are parallel and run obliquely across the picture surface, so that in pictures like *Lady Wenji's Return to China* (fig. 1.2), the orthogonals form a regular grid which sits comfortably with the geometry of the picture. This tends to pull the third axis of the perceived scene back to the picture surface. The same argument applies, though with somewhat less force, to pictures in isometric projection or axonometric projection. For example, the dominant geometry of the picture in Gris's *Breakfast* (color plate 6) is that of axono-

FIG. 10.1. Pierre Bonnard, *Nude in a Bathtub,* 1935(?). Oil on canvas, 103 × 64 cm. Copyright ADAGP/SPADEM, Paris, and Design and Artists Copyright Society, London, 1997.

metric projection, so that the perceived scene looks flatter than it would be if the picture had been in perspective. In Gris's painting, however, many other pictorial devices are used to flatten the image still further.

In pictures in perspective the correspondence between the directions of the projected edges in the picture and the principal axes of the picture itself is broken, and the orthogonals running toward a central vanishing point tend to "punch a hole in the canvas." This is most obviously true in pictures in three-point perspective in which none of the projected edges is represented by a horizontal or vertical line. In pictures in two-point perspective it ought to be less true, as the vertical axis of the image is represented as vertical; but as we normally experience vertical edges in the scene as vertical, the coincidence between the vertical axes of the image and the picture is not experienced as a coincidence. Presumably a similar factor operates with pictures in single-point perspective: we are so used to seeing paintings, and even photographs, in which objects are shown frontally (Costall, 1993) that we do not experience this as a coincidence and hence as a special case of false attachment.

In pictures in inverted perspective the diminution of size with distance represented in pictures in normal perspective is reversed, and this destroys the illusion of depth. In Rublev's *The Holy Trinity* (color plate 1) and in the manuscript illustrations shown in figs. 2.24 and 2.25, the diverging orthogonals flatten the depicted scene back onto the picture surface. However, insofar as it is possible to speak of a direction of view in connection with pictures in inverted perspective, this system, like linear perspective and the oblique systems, shows objects from a general position. For example, a step to one side would not change the topology of the table on which the saint is sitting in fig. 2.25, or the altar at which Abraham is sacrificing Isaac in fig. 14.9. As a result, pictures in inverted perspective, unlike pictures in horizontal or vertical oblique projection, give a strong *local* impression of three-dimensional shape. There is thus a conflict in pictures in this system between the impression of depth provided locally by the shapes of the objects and the denial of depth overall provided by the divergence of the orthogonals. Moreover, the spatial systems in pictures in inverted perspective are rarely, if ever, coherent: although the orthogonals of the chairs and footstools in Rublev's *Trinity* diverge, they do not diverge from what would be, in linear perspective, a single vanishing point; and the building in the background is represented to a much smaller scale. Finally, because the orthogonals in pictures of this kind run in a variety of directions, they do not form a simple pattern on the picture surface, like the orthogonals in *Lady Wenji's Return to China*. As a result, pictures in inverted perspective do not simply look flat, but have a restless, dynamic quality: the conflict between the three-dimensional qualities of the perceived scene and the picture as a flat surface is left unresolved.

Mixed Drawing Systems

One of the most characteristic features of Persian miniature painting is the use of mixtures of drawing systems. In *Laila and Majnum at School* (fig. 10.2), the fountain at the bottom left and the little hexagonal building to the right of the raised terrace are both in vertical oblique projection; but the terrace itself, the steps up to the terrace, and the main building at the top of the painting are all in oblique projection. Moreover, the directions of the orthogonals in the terrace and the main building are not consistent with each other. The orthogonals of the main building slope, impossibly, downwards to the right, while the orthogonals of the terrace slope upwards to the right.

Thus, although individual parts of the scene look strongly three-dimensional, the eye cannot make sense of the space of the scene as a whole, and this destroys the illusion of a real three-dimensional scene and flattens the picture.

Cutting-Off

In Bonnard's *Nude in a Bathtub* (fig. 10.1), parts of the figure on the left and the nude figure in the bathtub are cut off by the frame of the painting. Scharf (1979) refers to this compositional device, in which figures or objects in the foreground are truncated by the frame, as "cutting-off." This device is fairly common in Impressionist painting. Degas in particular makes considerable use of it, and he seems to have been influenced in his use of this device by its presence in both Japanese woodblock prints and photography. In the photographic views published in large numbers from about 1860 onwards, such peculiarities frequently occur, and Degas would certainly have been aware of them. In addition, according to Scharf, "the association between Degas's compositions and those of Japanese artists was made at least as early as 1880 when Huysmans described the way figures in the paintings were cut off by the frame, 'as in some Japanese prints'" (1979, p. 196). Scharf points out that the use of this technique appears in a particularly exaggerated form in Hiroshige's prints of *One Hundred Views of Yedo* (fig. 10.3) and suggests that in these later prints Hiroshige may also have been influenced by photography.

FIG. 10.2. Kamsa of Nizami, *Laila and Majnum at School,* painted by Bihzad, Herat, 1494. 21.9 × 14.0 cm, OR6810, folio, 10b verso. By permission of the British Library, London.

FIG. 10.3. Hiroshige, *The Haneda Ferry and Benten Shrine,* 1858. Woodblock print, from *One Hundred Views of Yedo.*

One might have thought that a technique so closely associated with photography would have enhanced the illusionistic qualities of a picture, but this does not seem to be the case. The images in pictures are inherently flat because motion parallax cannot occur within them: object boundaries do not move relative to each other in response to a movement to one side on the part of the spectator, nor do the boundaries of depicted objects change their positions relative to the frame. This effect is not so noticeable when objects are set back in the picture and wholly in view within the frame, as they are, for example, in Hoogstraeten's *trompe l'oeil* wall painting of a *View down a Corridor*. But if an object in the real world is set close to a window frame and cut off by it, the slightest movement on the part of the spectator changes the visible boundaries of the object. The fact that this does not happen in a picture when the boundaries of depicted objects are partially cut off by the picture frame emphasizes the flatness of the picture.

The Effects of False Attachment

A false attachment in a painting or drawing represents an accidental alignment between two or more parts of a scene and the position of the viewer. Because a false attachment in a picture does not disappear with the movement of the viewer, as it would in a view of a real scene, instances of false attachment tend to draw attention to the flatness of the picture surface. Paul Klee's *Town with Watchtowers* (fig. 1.16) contains numerous instances of false attachments between the lines representing the edges and corners of the buildings, and this tends to flatten the drawing into a pattern on the picture surface. Rather surprisingly, perhaps, Monet also made fairly frequent use of false attachments or near false attachments in his paintings. In his *Rocks at Port Coton, with the Lion Rock,* 1886 (fig. 10.4), the use of false attachment is very obvious: the top of the cliff is falsely attached to the horizon. The flattening effect of the false attachment is, however, contradicted by the pattern of the brush marks: the marks at the bottom of the picture are larger and rougher than those at the top, giving an effect of depth.

Symmetry

The use of symmetry as a device to flatten the image is fairly rare. Monet's painting of *The Seine at Giverny, Morning Mist* (fig. 10.5) is, however, almost completely symmetrical about a central horizontal axis, and a number of his paintings of the *Waterlily Pond (Japanese Bridge)* are nearly symmetrical about

FIG. 10.4. Claude Monet, *Rocks at Port Coton, with the Lion Rock,* 1886. Private Collection, on loan to the Fitzwilliam Museum, University of Cambridge, courtesy of the owner.

a central vertical axis. The use of symmetry in these pictures can be thought of as yet another special case of false attachment: in this case, a false attachment between the axis of symmetry of the pictorial image and the axis of symmetry of the picture.

The Avoidance of Atmospheric Perspective

In real scenes the tonal differences between objects are reduced with distance, colors become cooler (that is, they tend toward the blue end of the spectrum), colors become less saturated, and the contours of objects become less sharp. All or any of these effects may be represented in pictures and are referred to under the general heading of atmospheric perspective. To the extent that these factors are present in pictures, they operate as depth cues. In the false mezzotint *Pastoral Scene* shown in fig. 6.8, for example, the contrasts between the darkest and lightest tones are in the immediate

FIG. 10.5. Claude Monet, *The Seine at Giverny, Morning Mist,* 1897. Oil on canvas, 88.9 × 91.4 cm. North Carolina Museum of Art, Raleigh. Purchased with funds from the Sarah Graham Kenan Foundation and the North Carolina Art Society (Robert F. Phifer Bequest).

foreground of the picture, and the lines representing the contours of objects are lighter in tone and less distinct toward the background of the scene. Pictures in which these factors are *not* present generally appear relatively flat: in Orthodox icon paintings and many early Italian paintings, for example, objects in the background are painted just as distinctly as objects in the foreground, the hills in the distance are not given a bluish tint, and there is no change of tonal contrast with distance.

Atmospheric perspective was employed in Chinese painting from an early date. Cahill (1985) says of *A Buddhist Temple in the Mountains,* attributed to Li Ch'eng (tenth century, but probably painted in the eleventh century): "In

FIG. 10.6. Huang Kung-wang, *The Orchard Pavilion*, 1342. Whereabouts unknown.

the stillness of a mountain gorge, bare trees stand against thin mists. Those in the foreground are dark and distinct; further back they fade to pale silhouettes" (p. 32). Later Chinese painters, however, often seem to have avoided the use of atmospheric perspective even where the subject matter would seem to demand it. Fig. 10.6 shows *The Orchard Pavilion* by the fourteenth-century painter Huang Kung-wang; Loehr (1980) quotes Osvald Sirén's comment that this is "among the noblest of all the Chinese ink-paintings that have been preserved." As Loehr points out: "There are no tone values to speak of, and hence no atmosphere. The trees are constructed of horizontal and vertical strokes, lacking individuality. Yet all these unpromising forms vibrate with life" (pp. 241–242).

The flatness of this painting produced by the absence of atmospheric perspective is reinforced by three other factors: the almost uniform distribution of the marks, the predominantly horizontal and vertical emphasis of the brushstrokes used to represent the trees, and the use of horizontal oblique projection for the houses. In addition, any suggestion of illusion is destroyed by the presence of a written inscription and a number of seals.

The Reversal of Normal Atmospheric Perspective

Some modern artists have gone a step further and *reversed* the normal rules for atmospheric perspective. In John Nash's *Canal Bridge, Sydney Gardens,*

Bath (color plate 3), the tonal contrasts in the foreground of the painting are relatively muted. The area of greatest tonal contrast occurs at the top of the painting between the trees in the middle ground and the sky; and the areas of next greatest contrast lie in the sunlit building and the strip of canal beyond the bridge, and in the bridge itself. There are no strong tonal contrasts in the immediate foreground of the painting. As a result, the middle and background areas are pulled forward into the surface of the picture.

The normal rules governing the use of *color* in atmospheric perspective are also reversed in this painting. The warmest tones in the painting are in the background: the windows of the building at the back are painted in Indian red, and the chimneys are orange. In contrast, there are no warm tones in the foreground, except for a few strokes of orange-brown in the tree on the right.

This reversal of the normal rules of atmospheric perspective as they apply to color is even more evident in some of the landscape paintings by Paul Nash (John Nash's better-known brother). In many of his later paintings, such as in *Monster Field,* 1939 and *Landscape of the Moon's Last Phase,* 1944, the warmest and most fully saturated colors are in the background at the top of the painting in the form of a red sky or red clumps of trees, while the colors in the foreground are cooler and more muted. In *Pillar and Moon,* 1932 (color plate 9), most of the painting is in dull greens, blues, browns, and ochers, and the strong perspective effect of a receding line of trees is countered by the warm pink of the clouds in the distance. This painting also includes a particularly subtle device for flattening the picture: the ball on the top of the pillar in the foreground and the moon in the background are exactly the same size and shape, implying that they lie at the same depth. A somewhat similar device, but in a rather less obvious form, appears in Monet's *Rocks at Port Coton* (fig. 10.4). Here the silhouette of the rocks and the cliff in the background is echoed by the similar silhouette of the rocks in the foreground.

Finally, in Gris's *Breakfast* (color plate 6 and fig. 12.2), the normal rules governing atmospheric perspective are again reversed by placing the warmest and most fully saturated areas of color at the top of the painting. Most of the picture is in dull browns, grays, and blues (all recessive colors), but the parcel and the coffeepot lid are in red, bringing the top of the picture, where one would expect to find the greatest depth, toward the spectator. In this painting the reversal of the normal rules for atmospheric perspective is combined with the use of a form of inverted linear perspective, implied by the diverging edges of the rectangular forms imposed on the underlying composition in axonometric projection.

Techniques for Flattening the Picture
Based on the Denotation Systems

Silhouettes and Line Drawings

Silhouettes by themselves give very little impression of three-dimensional depth, so the images in pictures based on silhouettes, like Picasso's *Rites of Spring* (fig. 3.8), are already inherently flat. Line drawings and fully optical pictures can both give a strong impression of depth, but only fully optical pictures which give off rays of light with, in Brook Taylor's words, "All the same Circumstances of Direction, Strength of Light and Shadow, and Colour, as they would do so from the corresponding Parts of the real Objects seen in their proper Places" can provide a convincing illusion. Line drawings can never give a complete illusion of depth because the lines are always so patently on the picture surface. Thus the contrast between the apparent depth in the pictorial image, and the flatness of the picture as a configuration of picture primitives represented by marks, will normally be greater in a line drawing than it will be in a silhouette or a fully optical picture: in a silhouette the balance will always tip toward flatness, whereas in a fully optical picture it will tip toward an illusion of depth.

In a pure line drawing in which the lines are all more or less of the same thickness, and there is little or no facture, there is little distinction to be made between the picture primitives and the marks that represent these primitives. The lines that constitute these primitives form configurations on the picture surface, and the geometry of these configurations is of course identical with the geometry of the projections of the edges, contours, and other scene primitives that these lines represent. We see these edges and contours as existing in three-dimensional space; but the lines which represent them, and lie directly over them, belong to the picture surface. Thus these edges and contours draw the lines back into the scene, while the lines in turn draw the edges and contours forward into the picture surface, flattening the pictorial image.

As I have suggested above, a variety of factors can draw attention to the marks that represent picture primitives, such as the physical nature of the marks or the quality of execution. In Chu Ta's *Magnolia* (fig. 10.9), the manner of execution is very apparent:

> Its most captivating quality is a combination of energy and elegance in the flowers, realized in their shapes, their spacing, and their brushwork. Contrasting with the stately forms of the flowers are the brittle flicks describing small boughs. *The Magnolia* is the work of a mature artist conscious of his powers, which he is not loath to display. (Loehr, 1980, p. 302)

These qualities draw our attention to the brushstrokes as physical entities on the picture surface; and of course the geometry of these brushstrokes also coincides with the geometry of the picture primitives they represent. We can thus speak of a tension between the three-dimensional primitives of the pictorial image on one hand, and the two-dimensional picture primitives and the physicality of the marks representing these primitives on the other.

Mixed Denotation Systems

In Western illusionistic painting, in photographs, and in TV pictures, every point on the picture surface represents some part of the array of light from the real scene. In contrast, in Chinese paintings, Japanese woodcuts, Persian miniature paintings, Byzantine mosaics, and Cubist paintings, it is common to find text sharing the picture surface with the pictorial image. Such inscriptions draw attention to the picture surface. The surface on which they are printed or written is essentially two-dimensional and has, in relation to the characters themselves, no denotational function. But at the same time, this surface stands for part of the depicted scene: in the *Orchard Pavilion* (fig. 10.6), the characters share this surface with the foreground, the sky, and the mountaintop. As a result, these parts of the image are brought forward onto the picture surface.

Similarly, the Persian miniature *Laila and Majnum at School* (fig. 10.2) contains numerous inscriptions within the frame, both on the depicted surface of the building and on the real surface of the painting. The names of Jeremiah and Moses are inscribed above the lunette showing *Scenes from the Life of Abraham* in the mosaics at Ravenna (fig. 14.9); three seals appear within the frame of the Hiroshige print shown in fig. 10.3; and Gris's *Breakfast* (color plate 6 and fig. 12.2) includes part of a printed newspaper *en collage*. In all these cases, the inclusion of printed or written characters within the frame draws attention to the surface of the picture and flattens the pictorial image onto this surface.

Laila and Majnum at School also contains a pictorial device that looks strange to Western eyes but is common in Persian miniature painting: parts of the depicted scene leak out past the frame into the surrounding surface of the page. Within the frame, the denotation system is similar to what it would be in a Western painting, where every part of the surface depicts some part of a view of a scene. But the surface on which that part of the tree that lies outside the frame is painted either has no denotational function or stands for surrounding space. Like the confusion of drawing systems in this painting, the confusion of denotation systems is another device that draws attention to the picture as a surface.

Ben Nicholson's *Girl in a Mirror* (fig. 10.7) provides a final example of a picture containing a mixture of denotation systems. In this drawing the reflection of the face in the mirror looks more real than the face itself: the

FIG. 10.7. Ben Nicholson, *Girl in a Mirror*, 1932. Pencil on paper, 36.8 × 30.5 cm. Private collection. Copyright Angela Verren-Taunt 1997. All rights reserved Design and Artists Copyright Society.

face is drawn in silhouette, in outline only; but the reflection is a true line drawing, with the addition of local tone. Notice, too, that the "transparency" of the drawing of the window stay, the girl's finger against her arm, and her ring against her hand are yet other devices that draw our attention to the lines as lines on the paper, rather than as parts of an apparently three-dimensional image.

If a picture is to work convincingly as an illusion, the denotation system within the frame must be consistent. Any inconsistency—the inclusion of text, allowing parts of the picture to leak out past the frame, the inclusion of real objects as in Cubist painting, or the use of inconsistent mixtures of systems —destroys the illusion, flattens the pictorial image, and draws attention to the picture as a collection of marks on the surface rather than a glimpse of the real world.

It is not difficult to see the practical, social functions of pictures that provide useful technical information, a good representation, or an illusion. We need to know the true shapes of objects in engineering drawings and X-ray photographs; we need to be able to recognize objects in road signs at a distance or under poor weather conditions; we need to be able to see the three-dimensional shapes of objects in pictures in order to recognize the objects in them; and a story is all the more exciting if we have the illusion that we are taking part in it ourselves. But what purpose could there be in seeking to *destroy* the elements of three-dimensionality or illusion in a picture? There seem to have been at least four reasons why artists might have wanted to do this, and these motives, or mixtures of them, are to be found in the art of a number of different periods and cultures.

The Avoidance of Idolatry

Both Christianity and Islam have prohibitions against idolatry, the sin of worshiping God's creatures rather than God himself. In Christianity this prohibition is expressed in the second commandment. Nevertheless, many religions have felt the need to tell the stories of that religion and to teach its beliefs in the form of pictures. The way to do this, and at the same time to avoid idolatry, was to prevent the worshiper from mistaking the images of God for God himself by setting them within a spatial system that was clearly different from the everyday corporeal world. In Byzantine mosaics, this was achieved by using quite specific pictorial devices: obtrusively physical marks, a uniform surface texture, inverted perspective combined with an inconsistent mixture of other drawing systems, and the inclusion of text within the frame.

Persian miniature painting characteristically contains mixtures of drawing systems and mixtures of denotation systems. The origin of these inconsistencies probably lies in the mixture of Eastern and Western influences to which Persian artists were subject: fifteenth-century Persian painting was influenced by both Chinese and Byzantine painting (Robinson, 1967, p. 32). For example, in *Laila and Majnum at School* (fig. 10.2), the use of oblique projection and the way in which the foliage of the tree is set against a plain ground on the right of the painting seem typically Chinese; but the incongruous mixture of drawing systems (versions of oblique projection and vertical oblique projection), and the way in which the whole surface within the frame is used to represent features of the scene, are more typically Byzantine. These mixtures of systems also play a part in flattening the picture surface, a function that seems very appropriate to their role in manuscript illustrations. However, this mixture of drawing and denotation systems, destroying the illusion of real space, is so characteristic of Persian miniature painting that it is tempting to wonder whether its continued use in secular illustrations may not have been influenced by the Islamic prohibition of figural representation in religious art.[1]

Composition

Greek vase painting had its origin in the abstract painted decoration of the geometric period, but during the eighth and seventh centuries B.C. representations of figures of men and animals began to appear, originally in pure silhouette (fig. 14.1). Because the outlines of these figures are irregular, and silhouettes give, in any case, very little impression of depth, such figures can be represented without apparent distortion on a curved surface. Problems arise, however, in representing rectangular objects on a curved surface like the surface of a vase, because from most directions of view the lines representing straight edges in the scene will appear curved, and the edges of the rectangular objects they represent will therefore appear distorted. Although this problem will occur with all the projection systems, it is minimized in orthogonal projection, which, of all the drawing systems, gives the least illusion of depth. For example, the ground plane in pictures in orthogonal projection is represented by a horizontal line, and this can fit without much distortion onto the curved surface of a vase because it corresponds to the edge of a horizontal cross-section and will appear straight when viewed at eye level. This may explain why the Greek vase painters persisted in using orthogonal projection until a relatively late period, rather than developing the use of systems such as oblique projection which provide better representations of rectangular objects.

The compositional problems involved in representing rectangular objects on a curved surface are different from those which arise with a flat surface. In vertical oblique projection the lines representing edges in the third dimension are vertical, and these lines can sit comfortably on the surface of a flat, rectangular picture because their directions coincide with the vertical axis of the picture surface. But on a convex surface such as the surface of a vase the lines representing these edges will appear to curve inwards or outwards, distorting the shapes of horizontal surfaces such as the top of a table. Perhaps this is the reason why vertical oblique projection was not used in Greek vase painting for representing rectangular objects, even when the subject matter, such as that of the famous painting by Exekias of Ajax and Odysseus playing dice (Rawson, 1969, p. 152), would suggest that its use would be highly appropriate. In horizontal oblique projection the orthogonals are horizontal and so can fit more naturally on the belly of a vase; and in fact there are a number of instances of the use of horizontal oblique projection in Greek vase painting from the fifth century onwards, although these are mainly confined to representations of chariots.

Similar problems arise with oblique projection. Oblique projection is a perfectly appropriate system to use on the surface of a scroll painting like *Lady Wenji's Return to China;* far more appropriate, in fact, than using perspective because pictures in oblique projection can be extended indefinitely in any direction without distortion, whereas in pictures in perspective, objects at the edge of the picture begin to appear distorted once the angle of view begins to exceed about 25° (Dubery and Willats, 1983). However, it is difficult to imagine a painting in oblique projection like *Lady Wenji's Return to China* fitting satisfactorily onto the curved surface of a Greek vase, because rectangular objects would appear distorted. Oblique projection does not appear in Greek vase painting until the late stages of development, and even then it is used only intermittently. Many of the later masterpieces of Greek vase painting such as *Leave-taking* (fig. 11.3a) still employed orthogonal projection, with some foreshortening in a horizontal direction.

Philosophical and Aesthetic Balance

If there is one philosophical idea that can be said to underlie Chinese art it is that of the balance between Yin and Yang qualities:

> Because the Chinese perceive the universe as consisting of contrasting and complementary Yin and Yang qualities and substances, brush and black ink—in their infinite line-and-surface, bone-and-flesh, thin-and-thick, and dry-and-wet relationships—can represent just about everything in a monochrome world. In fact, the remarkable qualities of the black inks—which, used in their purest state, produce a lustrous black and, diluted with water, a full range of translucent grays—have been a vital factor in determining the nature of Chinese painting. (Fong and Hearn, 1981/1982, p. 5)

This balance finds its purest form in calligraphy, in the contrast between black ink characters on white paper. However, as the passage above makes clear, this balance can take many forms in Chinese painting, and among them, I suggest, is the balance between the two dimensions of the surface of the picture and the three dimensions of depicted space. The scholar–painters of China would, I suspect, have found most Western paintings unbearably vulgar in their lack of aesthetic balance and their insistence on the representation of illusionistic depth at the expense of the picture surface.

By the end of the thirteenth century—that is, by the end of the Sung period—Chinese painters had solved all the problems involved in representing shape, and in particular the problem of creating illusionistic depth (Fong and Hearn, 1981/1982; Loehr, 1980). They did, however, solve these problems in their own way. In place of chiaroscuro, which they called "receding and protruding painting," the Chinese painters developed a technique of thickening and thinning the line and shading it away toward the interior of the form in order to represent the curvature of the surface at right angles to the contour as the form turns away (Rawson, 1969, pp. 109, 113). Instead of linear perspective, they adopted oblique projection for representing individual rectangular objects such as tables and houses. In the relatively rare instances in which a coherent ground plane exists in Chinese painting, it is merely implied by the presence of rectangular objects (fig. 1.2), whereas in Western Renaissance painting the scene is built up on the ground plane as a foundation: establishing this ground plane was the whole object of Alberti's *costruzione legittima*.

For representing depth in landscape the Chinese painters used a variety of techniques, including that aspect of perspective which entails the diminution of size with distance: a device almost impossible to avoid if objects of such disparate sizes as trees, huts, and mountains are to be shown in one and the same picture. The most common technique for representing depth in Chinese painting, however, exploited the simple device of using light and dark regions to represent the alternations of figure and ground. In this technique, depth is represented by a series of overlapping regions, dark at the top but gradually fading away at the bottom, rising up through the picture and suggesting a series of mountain peaks rising from misty valleys: a favorite subject in Chinese painting. In the Northern Sung landscape illustrated in fig. 10.8, the sharp outlines of the dark areas of tone at the top of a mountain peak bring the figure forward against the lighter tone of the ground. As this tone fades away toward the bottom of the region, it provides the ground for the next, darker area of tone representing a plane that is closer to the viewer: "The mountain forms of the Metropolitan's scroll are superimposed in overlapping silhouettes, a compositional device typical of the twelfth century. There is no receding ground plane to link or hold the major elements: only the mist that curls through the valleys unites them" (Fong and Hearn, 1981/1982, p. 15). An additional and quite separate device for representing depth, which had been fully mastered by the end of the Sung period, was the use of atmospheric perspective. In the landscape illustrated in fig. 10.8, these two techniques are combined, but this was not always the case. In some late Southern Sung landscapes, atmospheric perspective is the only device used to create depth, while in some landscapes of the Yuan period (1279–1367), it is absent altogether.

Painting in the Yuan period was decisively different from Sung painting. During this period, painting was no longer a matter of simply describing external reality. The scholar-painters of the Yuan period aimed at self-expression: *hsin-hsueh,* "the realization of what is already within oneself," rather than *li-hsueh,* "the objective study of things within the universe" (Fong and Hearn, 1981/1982, p. 7). As a result, painting during the Yuan period and the subsequent Ming (1368–1644) and Ch'ing (1644–1911) periods became increasingly abstract, with less emphasis on the representation of depth and more emphasis on finding pictorial equivalents for the external world, expressed within the two-dimensional space of the picture surface. Consequently, we find during these periods a considerable use of pictorial devices intended to flatten the image, rather than give it depth.

I have already drawn attention to some of these devices in *The Orchard Pavilion* (fig. 10.6). The use of horizontal oblique projection as the drawing system for the huts emphasizes the flatness of the image. There is almost no significant use of atmospheric perspective or the technique of overlapping planes. The trees are drawn as characters rather than as representations; and because the marks by which they are represented are all more or less the same size over the whole surface, there is little or no texture gradient, and (what amounts to the same thing) little or no change of scale with distance. Depth is represented in this picture, but it is balanced by the devices that draw attention to the picture surface.

FIG. 10.8. After Fan K'uan, *Mountain Landscape,* Chinese, Early Sung Style (probably Early Ming Dynasty). Ink on silk, 164.8 × 103.8 cm. Metropolitan Museum of Art, New York, Gift of Irene and Earl Morse.

In the Ch'ing period this emphasis on the picture surface was achieved by calligraphic abstractions, as in Chu Ta's *Magnolia* (fig. 10.9). In a painting by Tao-chi (a near contemporary of Chu Ta), the *Ten Thousand Ugly Ink Dots,* this technique is taken about as far as it can go, so that the painting becomes a statement about painting rather than a representation of a scene:

> In Richard Edward's felicitous characterization, "Ugly Ink-dots is above all an artist's statement about art." The painting, in other words, is not a picture representing a thicket, a homestead, a cliff, and a cavern, but an assemblage of forms reminiscent of such motifs, though primarily an exposition of boisterous brushwork. The scroll exemplifies nicely how far a Chinese painter will go in abstractions: here the technique as such becomes the subject-matter. (Loehr, 1980, pp. 306–307, fig. 169)

FIG. 10.9.   Chu Ta, *Magnolia,* late 1660s. Princeton University, The Art Museum.

The Response to Photographic Realism

The invention of photography in the 1840s marked the end of a long period in which depiction was based on physical optics, and the beginning of a new period in art. Artists reacted to the invention of photography in a number of ways. One was to emphasize the role of painting as a means of expression, primarily self-expression. A similar motive seems to have informed painting during the Yuan period in China, in contrast to the desire on the part of painters in the preceding Sung period to find ways of representing external reality. And of course, expression in painting does not necessarily involve creating an illusion of reality; in fact, creating an illusion may well interfere with expression. Consequently, just as expressive painting in the Yuan period tended to become flatter, so painting after the invention of photography also became flatter. It is hard to look at the *Ten Thousand Ugly Ink Dots* without thinking of the Abstract Expressionist paintings of Jackson Pollock.

Another motive behind the impulse to flatten painting may have been purely aesthetic. Gombrich quotes the German art critic Konrad Lange, writing at the beginning of this century, who believed that aesthetic pleasure was rooted in the tension and balance between art and illusion: "Following the over-emphasis of the idea of nature for a time, we now have the stressing of the idea of art. . . . after the illusion of depth, artists now strive with equal passion to emphasize the plane" (Gombrich, 1960/1988, p. 238).

Yet another reason why paintings tended to become flatter was the abandonment of perspective as the only possible basis for painting. A number of artists and critics argued that representing what we perceive is not just a matter of replicating the array of light from a scene, but of representing our experience of the world as we move through it: an argument that led to the renunciation of perspective and the rise of Cubism. "Perspective is as accidental a thing as lighting. . . . The plastic image does not move: it must be complete at first sight; therefore it must renounce perspective" (Rivière, 1912, pp. 384–406). And of course, once perspective had been abandoned, illusion was no longer possible.

However, there may have been an even more powerful psychological motive that led painters, after the invention of photography, to insist on paintings as symbol systems made up of pictorial devices that could be manipulated at will rather than as passive surfaces capturing the light from the scene. What modern painters wanted to be above all was creative and original, and this was clearly incompatible with carrying out a task that could be performed just as well or better by a machine.

The concept of originality was much debated among artists in the nineteenth century. Traditionalists associated originality with the idea of genius: a unique ability that set the individual apart from the common herd. A newer and more "democratic" definition of originality saw it as an innate characteristic of every human being (Anfam et al. 1987).[2] But in either case, photography presented artists with a very direct threat. On the simplest level it threatened their livelihood: social functions such as portraiture or the recording of events could be carried out much more quickly and cheaply by photography than they could by an artist. On a somewhat higher level, it challenged their technical skill, traditionally the artists' main stock-in-trade:

> The faculty of photographs to reproduce the most minute objects in view, rendered solely by light and shade, had seldom been approached in painting or drawing. The exquisite tonal delicacy and miraculous uniformity with which natural objects were simulated elicited the highest praise, but also the most profound despair, from artists who felt themselves incapable of matching the virtuosity of the picture-making machine. (Scharf, 1979, pp. 12–13)

But at the highest level of all, the invention of photography threatened the artist's status as a creative human being. Thus it became increasingly necessary for artists to insist on painting as a symbol system based on pictorial devices which were not under the control of external stimuli, but which could be manipulated at will like the symbols of language. When these devices were freed from their association with the optic array, however, the illusion of depth disappeared and pictures became increasingly flat.

CHAPTER ELEVEN

Anomaly in the Service of Expression

In the past, little distinction was made between pictures that merely con-
veyed technical information and pictures that performed some higher
function; in most past cultures the concept of "art" in the modern sense
hardly existed. In more recent times, however, we have come to think of
"artistic" pictures as a separate class, and there seems to be a consensus that
what separates artistic pictures from pictures in general is that they are
expressive. For Gowans (1979), for example, "Art nowadays is an activity
defined by, and a vehicle for, the self-expression of artists" (p. 248)—rather
an empty and depressing prospect. However, expression need not always be
self-expression: artists in many other cultures have used pictures in order to
express beliefs and emotions that were shared by religious groups or the
community as a whole.

Part of the expressive quality of a picture—a war photograph, for
example—is obviously derived from its subject matter, but it has often been
suggested that there may be a connection between the formal properties of
a picture and its expressive qualities. Kandinsky, the leading German Expressionist, and the first and probably the most important of the pioneers of
abstract art, began his painting career in Munich at the time when Theodore
Lipps was lecturing at the University of Munich on his theory of empathy:
the subjective identification of the viewer with abstract forms in painting
(Teuber, 1980). More recently, Goodman (1968) has suggested that certain
formal qualities are "symptomatic" of artistic pictures as compared with
pictures such as engineering drawings. One of these symptoms, Goodman
suggests, is "repleteness," a term he proposed in order to separate works of

art from pictures that merely provide factual information. In an electro-cardiograph reading, for example, only the shape of the graph is significant, whereas if the same shape were to be employed in a Japanese print as a representation of the outline of Mount Fujiyama, every variation in thick-ness, brightness, and tone would be potentially relevant to its interpretation. "Exemplification," another term suggested by Goodman, refers to the fact that works of art may exemplify certain ideas or feelings metaphorically, although they do not contain them literally. A painting or drawing may literally possess any number of properties such as tone and color, and a representational picture literally denotes the objects represented. "But to perceive what a painter expresses, it is necessary to go beyond the literal" (Blank, Massey, Gardner, and Winner, 1984, p. 127). Thus a simple stick figure of a tree is unlikely to be read as expressing any mood; but if the tree is shown devoid of leaves, and with its branches bowing close to the ground, it may be read as expressing sadness.

In practice, both means of expression—the nature of a painting's subject matter and the use of expressive formal properties—are usually employed together, and the way a picture is drawn or painted may be used to reinforce the expressive qualities of its subject; but the balance between the emotional charge carried by the overt subject of a painting and the formal means by which this subject has been expressed may vary a great deal. At one extreme we might put Abstract Expressionism: the attempt to produce a painting that is expressive, but freed from the need to represent the usual subject matter of painting. Painting of this kind is often compared with music, which can be highly expressive without making use of any overt subject matter. At the other extreme, Surrealist painting, which is normally highly representational, is generally considered to be very expressive; but there seem to be two kinds of Surrealist painters: painters like Salvador Dali who achieve their effects through the use of an emotive subject matter, and painters like Giorgio de Chirico or René Magritte who used unusual or incongruous structures in their paintings although their overt subject matter is often quite prosaic.

The majority of Dali's pictures are carried out in a meticulously realistic, almost photographic style, and some of them are actual photographs. Most of their emotional impact, therefore, comes from the outrageous and repul-sive nature of their subject matter rather than their formal qualities (Orwell, 1980). Compared with Dali's paintings the subject matter of Giorgio de Chirico's *Mystery and Melancholy of a Street* (fig. 11.1) is not especially remarkable, although the shadow of a hidden statue, thrown across the otherwise empty street, may perhaps convey a sense of menace. Otherwise, the picture shows only a street scene in bright sunlight with buildings with arcades on either side, an empty four-wheeled van, and a girl playing with a hoop.[1] The powerful suggestion of mystery and melancholy that this painting conveys thus seems to have little to do with its overt subject matter. Rather, the effect seems to be produced by the incongruous mixture of drawing systems on which the picture is based. The arcades to either side of

FIG. 11.1. Giorgio de Chirico, *Mystery and Melancholy of a Street,* 1914. Oil on canvas, 87.0 × 71.0 cm. Private collection. Copyright Design and Artists Copyright Society 1997.

the picture have different vanishing points, while the van is drawn in an approximation to oblique projection, so that the spatial system of the picture as a whole is incoherent.

Some linguists have suggested that a defining characteristic of poetic speech, as distinct from ordinary speech, is its use of unusual or ungrammatical structures for expressive purposes:

> The discussion centres around two observations. The first is that ungrammatical sentences tend to occur far more frequently in poetry than in prose. . . . The second is that although, inevitably, we recognize these deviant sentences as being deviant, it is sometimes also the case that they are felt not to be deviant within the context of the poem. (Thorne, 1972, p. 192)

Thorne illustrated this by analyzing John Donne's "A Nocturnall Upon S. Lucies Day." He points out that Donne's poem contains a number of ungrammatical constructions such as *(mee) who am their Epitaph,* and *I am every dead thing, I . . . am the grave of all,* and *Yea plants, yea stones detest and love,* and suggests that "It seems likely that these linguistic facts underlie the sense of chaos and breakdown of natural order which many literary critics have associated with the poem" (Thorne, 1972, p. 193).

Similarly, Soby (1966), describing the spatial systems in de Chirico's *Gare Montparnasse (The Melancholy of Departure),* 1914, painted in the same year as *The Mystery and Melancholy of the Street,* wrote that "geometry has been wilfully altered for purposes of poetic suggestion" (p. 71). Thus within the context of de Chirico's work these mixtures of systems are not "mistakes," but the means by which the artist obtained a particular expressive effect.[2]

The subject matter of Francis Bacon's *Three Studies of Lucian Freud* (fig. 11.2) is, again, not in itself remarkable, except perhaps for the inclusion of the abstract space frame and the tense, awkward pose of the seated figure. Instead, much of the sense of unease which this picture conveys comes from the tension between the rigid space frame drawn in distorted perspective and the painterly handling of the figure it encloses.

These examples suggest that just as some poets have used anomalous or ungrammatical constructions for expressive reasons, so some artists have used anomalous or "ungrammatical" pictorial structures to serve expressive ends. It would be a mistake, however, to suppose that when anomalies occur in artists' pictures they are always there to serve some expressive purpose. During periods of transition in art history, for example, mixtures of drawing systems may occur for reasons that have little to do with expression. To modern eyes, the mixture of drawing systems in Giovanni de Paolo's *Birth of St. John the Baptist* (fig. 8.14) may seem expressive; but this incongruous mixture of systems is more likely to have arisen as a result of the artist's

FIG. 11.2. Francis Bacon, *Three Studies of Lucian Freud,* 1969. Center panel of a triptych, oil on canvas, 198.0 × 147.5 cm. Private collection, courtesy of Estate of Francis Bacon. Photograph Marlborough Fine Art (London) Ltd.

struggle with perspective. Similarly, many of the scenes in the frescoes in the upper church of San Francesco at Assisi contain incongruous mixtures of drawing systems, or incorrect versions of perspective; but it is difficult to know if any of these anomalies were deliberately introduced to serve some expressive purpose, and how many resulted from the artist's or artists' inability to handle perspective. For example, White (1967) has suggested that the change in the spatial system from top to bottom in the *Vision of the Thrones* may have been intended to portray "a change from one reality to another, from a material to a visionary world." This idea is a very attractive one, and to a modern spectator the use of two spatially incompatible systems within the same painting does carry with it a strong suggestion of the supernatural; but how deliberate this choice of different systems was seems rather uncertain. Nearly all the frescoes in the upper church at Assisi contain mixtures of drawing systems of one kind or another, and by no means all of them deal with visions. On balance, it seems likely that the mixtures of systems in the "vision" frescoes, which to us look like the result of deliberate choice, may have been just happy accidents. A middle course of interpretation is also possible. It may be that these anomalies occurred because the artist was still struggling with the problems of perspective; but that he was content to leave them unresolved, rather than attempting to correct them, because he was at some level sensitive to their expressive effect.[3]

A similar problem of interpretation arises with children's drawings. Drawings by young children often seem especially expressive to adults, and it is just this expressiveness which seems to give them a status as works of art. But much of this expressive quality comes from the anomalies they contain, and as Gardner has pointed out, these anomalies, however charming they may seem to adults, may merely be the result of the child's inability to produce the correct form: "Even as a metaphor by the young child may be a simple overgeneralization, with a word merely carrying a broader meaning for him than it does for most adults, so, too, drawings by the young child may be uncontrolled forms which come forth simply because the youngster is unable to produce anything more faithful to the real world" (Gardner, 1980, p. 100). Winner (1982) makes much the same point.

Because of the difficulty of assessing children's expressive intentions I have not attempted to analyze any children's drawings in terms of their expressive qualities. The three artists' pictures which I have chosen all contain examples of pictorial anomalies used for expressive purposes. In the case of the first two examples the supposition that the use of these anomalies was in some sense deliberate—that is, that they are not merely accidental—can only be inferred from the aptness of these anomalies to their subject matter. With

Klee's *Naked on the Bed* the evidence is more direct, because Klee has given us some account of his intentions in his diaries and notebooks.

Leave-taking

Fig. 11.3a shows a Greek vase painting of the middle or third quarter of the fifth century B.C. The style of this painting is known as white-ground painting: the lines are drawn in relief in black glaze on a white ground. Originally the figures in these vase paintings were covered with a thin wash of color, but in most cases these colors have since either altered or disappeared. The vases (or "lekythoi") on which the painting was carried out were used only in connection with funeral rites, and were either buried with the dead or thrown on the funeral pyre.

Leave-taking is attributed to the Achilles painter, who also produced red-figure vase paintings: red silhouettes with black lines on a black ground. Red-figure painting, like the figure of Herakles on a vase by the Kleophrades painter (fig. 14.5), is often skillful and robust; but Greek vase painting is at its most expressive in the white-ground lekythoi.

The expressive quality of the *Leave-taking* is no doubt due in part to the nature of its subject matter: "In the wonderful picture of the young warrior and the seated woman the whole expression is given by the simple presence of one fair young creature with another: the picture says without words that the young man did not come home from the war" (Pfuhl, 1955, p. 68). In other similar paintings the subject matter is also directly related to mourning and the cult of the dead. In one painting an apparition of the dead youth stands by the grave while it is tended by a young woman. In another painting, Sleep and Death lay the young warrior in his grave, and in another a girl brings gifts to the grave while the spirit of the dead youth looks on. In yet another, a girl mourns while a servant brings wine for a libation to the dead. However, it cannot be only the overt subject matter of these paintings which carries this expression because many of them simply portray scenes from domestic life. There is no obvious way in which the painting shown in fig. 11.4, also attributed to the Achilles painter, commemorates the dead: it shows a lady handing a bundle of clothes to a young maid. And yet in its way this painting seems almost as expressive as the *Leave-taking,* or the scenes by the tomb.

The emotional content of these paintings can perhaps be summed up as a mixture of sadness and reverence, and these qualities are expressed in part by the way in which the participants fail to meet each others' gaze, and instead withdraw into their own thoughts. In the white-ground paintings of the

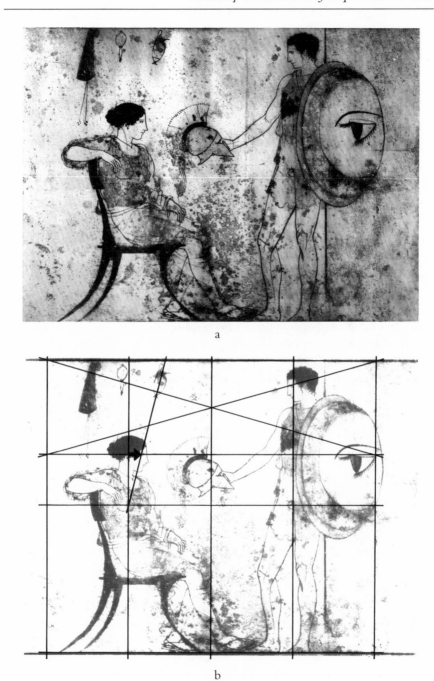

a

b

FIG. 11.3. (a) Achilles painter, *Leave-taking,* middle of the fifth century B.C. Athens, National Museum. From Pfuhl (1955, fig. 94). (b) The woman's eye is moved forward against the grid set up by the salient features of the picture.

funeral lekythoi this inner reflection is represented by eye direction. To quote Pfuhl again:

> Thus, in a vase which is not even very fine in drawing and is therefore not reproduced here, the dead youth returns the young woman's greeting shyly, as if the sight of life in its bloom made him hesitate. Another picture is no less touching: the girl with the basket of gifts looks at the youth muffled in his cloak, yet he does not return her gaze, but looks stilly and absently in front of him. The downward look, emphasised by the staff, and the dark muffling garment, speak death and mourning. (Pfuhl, 1955, p. 71)

This same kind of feeling—a combination of sadness, gravity, and reverence —seems to pervade the painting illustrated in fig. 11.4, although the subject of this painting is purely domestic. The lady gazes solemnly into the girl's eyes, while the girl's own eyes meet her gaze shyly, or even perhaps seem slightly downcast. Is it too fanciful to think that the artist intended us to realize that both figures are thinking about the dead? In the red-figure vases, in contrast, eye direction, where it is significant at all, seems merely to indicate what the person depicted is attending to. For example, in the vase by the Kleophrades painter to which I have already referred (fig. 14.5), Herakles is looking at the Delphic tripod, which he has stolen from Apollo. But in the funeral lekythoi, eye direction seems to signal something far more subtle, which can be characterized by saying that the persons depicted are attending to their own internal thoughts rather than to any external object.

Baron-Cohen, Campbell, Karmiloff-Smith, et al. (1995) have shown that eye direction can be a powerful indicator of mental states, and they list four pieces of knowledge about eyes that even quite young children normally possess. The first is that eyes are for seeing, and that for a person to see something their eyes need to be open. Most children know this from at least 30 months of age. The second is that the direction of someone's gaze indicates what they are interested in or attending to. The third is that people use their eyes to communicate what they are interested in to someone else. And finally, they found that by the age of 3 or 4 years most children know that if a person is looking up or away, this is a sign that that person is *thinking*. Presumably eye direction is interpreted in this way because in the absence of an external object to be looked at, the person is assumed to be attending to his or her own thoughts. Eye direction in the red-figure paintings, where it is significant at all, merely indicates what the person depicted is attending to, and corresponds to the second stage of awareness described by Baron-Cohen et al. In the white-ground paintings, in contrast, the eye directions of the figures represented in these paintings correspond to their final stage and show that these figures are absorbed in their own thoughts.

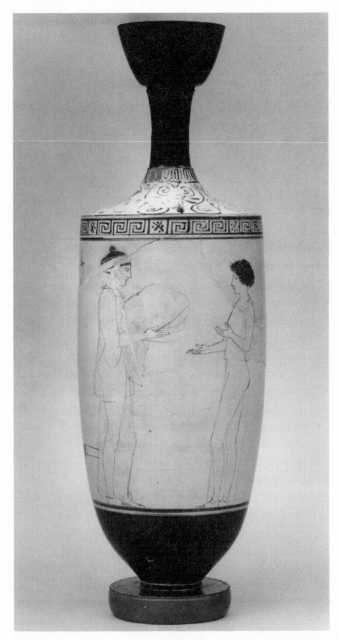

FIG. 11.4. Achilles painter, white-ground lekythos, *A Woman Handing a Garment to a Girl,* Attic, c. 440 B.C. Terra-cotta, ht. 38.6 cm. Metropolitan Museum of Art, New York, Dodge Fund, 1954.

In a cross-cultural and developmental study, Baron-Cohen, Riviere, Fukushima, et al. (1996) considered the question of whether emotion recognition is culture-specific or universal, and they cited Darwin (1872) who proposed that there were universal facial behaviors for each emotion. After reviewing the evidence currently available, they concluded that Darwin was right, and that there was "strong evidence for both the production and recognition of universal emotions being 'hard-wired' in the human brain" (p. 41). Of particular interest for this study was the finding by Elkman (1973, 1992) that six emotional facial expressions, including *sadness,* are universally recognizable.

The young woman in *Leave-taking* is not looking at any external object, nor is she looking into the eyes of her companion. Instead, her withdrawn gaze suggests that she is looking forward, metaphorically, to the outcome of the leave-taking, which may well be his death. Moreover, these inner thoughts seem to be represented figuratively by the eye on the young man's shield, and they are reflected back to her, as if in a mirror, by the curve of the shield itself. But in addition this "looking forward" has been represented by a formal device within the structure of the picture: the girl's eye has been moved forward against a frame of reference set up by the positions of the most important details in the picture.

Fig. 11.3b shows the positions of these details relative to a grid superimposed on the picture. These details are: the eyes of the man and the woman, the eye on the man's shield, the woman's breasts, especially the right breast, and the man's genitals. All these details, with the exception of the woman's eye, lie on a grid defined by horizontal and vertical lines. This grid divides the picture horizontally into halves and thirds: the woman's eye and the eye on the shield lie on a horizontal line two-thirds of the way up the picture, and the woman's breasts and the man's genitals lie on a line halfway up the picture. Vertically, the picture is divided into quarters, with the position of the center line marked by the boss on the helmet. The woman's right breast lies on the quarter line to the left of the painting, and the man's eye and his genitals lie on the quarter line to the right. The corner of the eye on the shield lies on the right-hand edge of the grid. Finally, the position of the man's eye, and the direction of his gaze, is fixed by one of the diagonals of the upper third of the painting.[4]

All these details lie on the grid with the exception of the woman's eye, which is *moved forward* relative to the grid along the direction of her gaze, toward the eye on the shield. Finally, the *amount* by which this eye is moved forward is fixed by a line that has been swung round with the woman's right breast as a center, and passes through the axis of the vase hanging on the wall.

Thus all but one of the most important elements in the scene—the woman's breast, the man's genitals, the man's eye, and the eye on the shield—are fixed relative to the verticals and horizontals of the composition. The exception is the eye of the woman, and she is *looking forward:* literally looking forward, relative to the structure of the grid. Metaphorically, she is looking forward to the outcome of the leave-taking: as Pfuhl says, "the picture says without words that the young man did not come home from the war."

Noli me Tangere

Figs. 11.5 and 11.6 and color plate 4 show three paintings whose subject is known as the *Noli me Tangere:* literally, "Do not touch me." The subject is taken from John 20:14–17: Mary Magdalene comes to the empty sepulcher, and Jesus appears to her but she does not recognize him. Then, in one of the

FIG. 11.5. *Noli me Tangere* (detail of an icon), Creto-Venetian, sixteenth century. Wood, 91.0 × 74.0 cm. Musée d'art et d'histoire, Geneva, gift of Mme. B. Mavromichalis.

FIG. 11.6. Giotto, *Noli me Tangere,* 1302–1305. Arena Chapel, Padua. Courtesy of the Italian State Tourist Office (ENIT), London.

most famous passages in the Bible, Jesus speaks to her; and as she recognizes him, he says: "Touch me not; for I am not yet ascended to my Father."

The subject was a common one in the later Middle Ages and was represented in two different ways. In one, Christ turns back toward the standing Magdalene who bends forward as he walks away; in the other, the Magdalene kneels as Christ turns back toward her (Offner, 1981). Three versions of this second type are shown here: the first by an unidentified icon painter (fig. 11.5) and the second by Giotto (fig. 11.6). The third version (color plate 4) is attributed to the Master of the Lehman Crucifixion, so called by Offner after a Crucifixion now in the Robert Lehman Collection in the Metropolitan Museum, New York (Davis, 1988). This painter[5] was working in Florence during the second half of the fourteenth century; Offner describes this version as "very similar" to a panel by the Master of the Fabriano Altarpiece (reproduced in Offner, 1981, sec. 3, vol. 5, pl. XLVI).

The subject depicted in these paintings is a highly dramatic and emotional one. According to Barasch (1990) the essence of this drama is the contrast between carnal and spiritual love. Mary's love is unambiguous:

> Her leaning to sensual love may perhaps explain her desire for physical touch, a desire emphasized in literary descriptions as well as in pictorial depictions. . . . The desire for physical touch is not usually characteristic of saints, and in no other saint, so far as we know, is it so overwhelming as in Mary Magdalen. This desire is, of course, an important feature in the background of *Noli me tangere.* (Barasch, 1990, p. 176)

Christ, however, withdraws from Mary's attempt to touch him.

In a number of examples, Barasch shows how this drama is expressed in terms of the gestures and stance of the participants. In an early example, Mary is kneeling and Christ extends his hand toward her, but the movement does not imply any rejection: it looks instead as if Christ were blessing her. In Giotto's version (fig. 11.6), Christ's gesture, Barasch argues, is much more ambiguous: it blesses, but it also rejects. In the predella panel by the Master of the Fabriano Altarpiece cited by Offner, Christ is moving away from the kneeling Magdalene but turns back to look at her and extends his arms toward her with outstretched fingers almost as if drawing her to him. In a later fresco in S. Trinita in Florence by the same painter, an almost similar gesture seems like one of rejection, and even perhaps horrified withdrawal. In Fra Angelico's fresco in S. Marco the mood is much quieter: Mary spreads her hands in submission while Christ appears to be both blessing and rebuking her. In a version by an imitator of Mantegna in the National Gallery, London, Christ blesses Mary but shrinks away from her. In a much later version by Titian, also in the National Gallery, a kneeling Mary supports herself with one hand and stretches out the other, while Christ withdraws his garment from her. Barasch gives numerous other examples.

In all these paintings the emotions of the participants are reflected in their gestures, and these gestures are represented figuratively in the picture. But in the versions by Giotto and the Master of the Lehman Crucifixion illustrated in fig. 11.6 and color plate 4 the theme of touching, and the rejection of touching, are represented in formal as well as figurative terms.

Barasch describes the way in which the drama of the scene is expressed by the gestures and stance of the participants in the version by Giotto, but also draws attention to a compositional element in the painting noted by Rintelen (1923): the composition is organized round two diagonal lines like a letter X, one arm of which follows the outline of the angel's wing and continues through the top edge of the rocks, while the other follows the line of Christ's outstretched arm and the direction of his gaze, and runs through Mary's body to her feet. Christ's outstretched hand is placed at the intersection of these two diagonal lines, and the purpose of this geometric construction seems to be to draw attention to Christ's hand, and in particular to the way in which the tip of his thumb is just touching the outline representing the upper edge of the rock. Above and to the left of the point of intersection, two of his fingers just penetrate this outline. This touching and penetration takes place within the two-dimensional space of the picture surface; clearly Christ's hand is in front of the rock in the three-dimensional scene. Technically, then, there is a false attachment at the center of the composition.

It is possible, of course, to argue that this may merely be an accident, and that Giotto may simply not have noticed this anomaly. But as a compositional device this false attachment seems so apt in the context of the subject of the painting that it is tempting to suppose that Giotto used it deliberately in order to express the meaning of the painting in formal terms, reinforcing and repeating the message carried by Christ's stance and gestures: "The *contrapposto* of Christ's body reveals the struggle of his impulses—the attraction to Mary Magdalen, and the desire to withdraw and avoid her touch. The outstretched hand of Christ is typical in its ambiguity: it is rejecting, but also has features of blessing" (Barasch, 1990, p. 180). On a formal level, the coincidences and near coincidences between Christ's fingers and the outline of the rock which forms the boundary of Mary's space repeat the same message. Christ's fingertips are just penetrating Mary's space to bless her, but at the same time they emphasize the boundary between them: "Thus far," he seems to be saying, "but no further." In contrast, in the icon painting reproduced here (fig. 11.5), in the version by Fra Angelico, and in the versions by Titian and an imitator of Mantegna, both in the National Gallery, London, it is only the gestures of the participants that carry the meaning of the painting.

Similar false attachments and near false attachments appear in the *Noli me Tangere* by the Master of the Lehman Crucifixion (color plate 4). Here the outline of the hillside, which represents the skyline in three-dimensional space, divides the picture surface into two regions. Mary inhabits the dark earthly region below the skyline: the tips of the fingers of her left hand just reach the boundary between the two regions, while those of her right hand just penetrate this boundary. The lower half of the figure of Christ also inhabits the dark, earthly region, but the upper half inhabits the golden region of the sky above. The tips of Christ's fingers almost, but not quite, reach the boundary between the earthly and heavenly regions.

In terms of a representation of a three-dimensional scene we would have to count the relations between the fingers of the participants and the outline of the hillside as examples of false attachment, near false attachment, and avoidance of false attachment. But in terms of the two-dimensional geometry of the picture surface they provide examples of touching, withdrawal, and penetration: just those physical relations that could provide a metaphor for the spiritual relations between the two figures.

As with the anomalies in *Leave-taking,* this metaphor is so apt that it seems unlikely that the anomalies present in these two paintings were mere coincidences. Moreover, there is some physical evidence in the version by the Master of the Lehman Crucifixion that suggests that the spatial relations between the fingers and the outline of the hillside were deliberately contrived. An examination of the picture surface[6] shows that the main outlines of the composition were drawn in first, using an incised line. Then the figure of Mary was painted in, with the hands in the present position. The landscape was painted in next; but at the point where the outline of the hill passed behind Mary's left hand the painter extended the contour of the hillside beyond the original incised line. This incised line, which is visible below the paint surface, touches the tip of the little finger of the right hand of the Magdalene, runs just below the thumb of her right hand, through the first joint of the little finger of the left hand, between the first and second joints of the first finger of the left hand, and then rejoins the existing outline. Originally, then, at the underdrawing stage, the fingers of both hands would have penetrated the golden, heavenly space. At a later stage, however, the outline of the hill was altered so that the left hand would touch the boundary between the two figures, rather than extending beyond it.

The projection of the right hand beyond this boundary seems always to have been intended, and the positions of the incised lines show that Christ's right hand was always intended to be in its present position.

These observations suggest that the painter originally planned the layout of the painting in such a way that *both* Mary Magdalene's hands penetrated into Christ's "heavenly" space. At some point during the painting process he evidently realized that the painting would be more effective if the fingers of her left hand just touched the boundary of this space instead of penetrating it; and the line of the hillside was changed so as to bring this about. What was the reason for this decision? It serves no representational purpose; but it does enrich the expressive quality of the picture by adding a third element of touching to the two original elements of penetration and withdrawal. It is hard not to believe that this change was deliberately effected in order to serve an expressive purpose.

Paul Klee: *Naked on the Bed*, 1939

Successive stages of Klee's career are characterized by the use of a number of different pictorial devices or motifs, and Marianne Teuber has shown that many of these are derived from or can be related to the psychological literature of the period. By 1905 Klee had read Mach's *Analysis of Sensations;* in July of that year he described Mach's first illustration and exclaimed, "The object is surely dead. The sensation of the object is of first importance. The old-master school is finished" (Teuber, 1980, p. 2). Some years later Klee began to make use of Mach's reversible figure of a folded card in his paintings and drawings: it appears in *Untitled, Like a Vignette,* 1915, for example (Teuber, 1976), in *Fantastic Architecture with the Rider,* 1918, and *The Tightrope Walker,* 1923.

Teuber (1980) goes on to trace the influence of other perceptual psychologists such as Schumann, Wertheimer, and Fuchs on Klee's work as a painter and teacher. During his first year of teaching at the Bauhaus in 1921/22, Klee showed his students how Schumann's checkerboard experiments demonstrated perceptual grouping, and he had already made use of Schumann's demonstrations in his own paintings: in 1915 he transformed a field of black and white diamonds from one of Schumann's illustrations into the watercolor *In the Garden of Franz Marc.* By the end of the 1920s, Gestalt psychologists had been invited to lecture at the Bauhaus, and in 1930 the Bauhaus offered an entire course in psychology, with the emphasis on Gestalt psychology, as a part of the regular curriculum. In his later works Klee also drew on Wertheimer's essay on the "Theory of Form" (1923), which established the Gestalt principles of proximity, similarity, and good continuation. Motifs from Wertheimer's illustrations appear transcribed into paintings like *Child in Red,* 1937, and *Blue Night,* 1937. Klee was thus well acquainted with the psychological literature on perception of the period, taught it to his students, and made use of it in his own paintings and drawings.

In 1935 Klee began to suffer from a serious illness, which ultimately led to his death in 1940. During 1936 he produced few paintings and drawings; when he resumed work in 1937 he began to paint in a new style: heavy black lines arranged in simple patterns, together with areas of brilliant color. In these paintings the patterns of lines are purely two-dimensional, and Teuber (1976) has shown how they were derived from Wertheimer's demonstrations of Gestalt principles. Klee continued to produce paintings in this style until his death, but in the last two years of his life he also produced a large number of paintings and drawings, some semi-abstract and some representational, in which the lines stand for the contours of smooth three-dimensional shapes. Fig. 5.10, *The Park at Abien—from the Vegetable Department,* shows a painting typical of this style and period.

In spite of the fact that none of the forms of which this picture is composed directly represents familiar objects, the way in which they are drawn strongly suggests a group of solid, three-dimensional shapes. With the exception of the sharp corner at the top, the drawing is composed of two kinds of junctions—T-junctions and end-junctions—and the configurations of lines and junctions obey Huffman's rule for drawings of smooth objects. As a result we interpret the lines in drawings of this kind as the occluding contours of smooth shapes.

Fig. 11.7a shows a drawing that Klee produced in the same year entitled *Little Baroque Basket.* Like *The Park at Abien,* the shapes represented do not correspond to those of familiar objects, but they nevertheless look convincingly three-dimensional. Again there is one sharp corner, and the small closed form at the top contains a junction which is incorrect within the language of smooth forms; but, with these exceptions, all the junctions within the main forms are either end-junctions, or T-junctions correctly representing points of occlusion. However, this drawing, unlike the drawing in *The Park at Abien,* contains a major inconsistency. If we trace the line in the middle of the drawing along its length, from the lower T-junction on the right to the upper T-junction on the left, it is apparent that the occluded surface lies to the right at the beginning of the line, but to the left at the end of the line. Fig. 11.7b makes this anomaly explicit. The directions of the arrows follow Huffman's convention that the occluding surface lies to the

a

b

c

FIG. 11.7. (a) Paul Klee, *Barockes Körbchen* (*Little Baroque Basket*), 1939. Pencil on paper, 20.9 × 29.7 cm. Paul Klee-Stiftung, Kunstmuseum, Berne. Copyright Design and Artists Copyright Society 1997. (b) The question mark indicates the point at which the forms overlap. (c) The overlapping forms are shown separately. (b) and (c) From Willats (1980), courtesy of MIT Press.

right going in the direction of the arrows, and these arrows must always run from right to left along the top of a T-junction because the lower arm of a T-junction represents a contour that disappears behind the contour of the occluding surface represented by the top of the T (fig. 5.7). The question mark shows that somewhere along this line the directions of the arrows must change. This means that somewhere along its length the line has changed its reference or "meaning," thus apparently disobeying Huffman's fundamental rule that a line must have the same meaning along its whole length. In drawings like those shown in fig. 1.14, disobeying this rule results in an "impossible object," but this is not the case in *Little Baroque Basket*. What has happened is that two correct T-junctions have been run together; if these two junctions are separated, as shown in fig. 11.7c, it becomes clear that the original drawing represents two overlapping forms in intimate contact. As these two forms are brought together, the two T-junctions lose their orthogonality and become more transverse, until eventually they merge. As Koenderink (1990) emphasized, accidents like this ought to be avoided "like the plague . . . except when you explicitly want to exploit their effect" (pp. 622–623).

In *Little Baroque Basket*, Klee seems merely to have been experimenting with this device: "I have carried out many experiments with laws and taken them as a foundation. But an artistic step is taken only when a complication arises" (Klee, 1961, p. 454). But exactly the same device appears in Klee's *Naked on the Bed* (color plate 5a), and here, I believe, Klee used this "complication" as a metaphor for the sexual act (Willats, 1980). Although the shapes in the drawing are only partially representational, they clearly represent a man and a woman, and the merging of the outlines of these shapes, representing contours that would normally be represented as separate (color plate 5b), provides a metaphor for the union between the two figures. The two forms overlap in the center of the painting, and Klee marked the point of contact between the man and the woman by a subtle change of hue from blue to ocher in the body of the woman.

This painting thus seems to illustrate Klee's contention that "a picture representing a naked person must not be created by the laws of human anatomy, but only by those of compositional anatomy" (Klee, 1965, entry 840, 1908). Early in his life Klee had used sexual intercourse as a metaphor for painting: "In the beginning the motif, insertion of energy, sperm" (Klee, 1965, entry 943, 1914). In *Naked on the Bed,* one of his last paintings, Klee used a complication in the formal structure as a metaphor for the sexual act.

CHAPTER TWELVE

Investigating the
Nature of Depiction

Perhaps one of the most profound changes to take place in painting between the nineteenth and twentieth centuries was that painters became increasingly aware that there was more than one way of painting a picture. This led to an increasing self-consciousness on the part of painters about the techniques of depiction and, eventually, to an investigation of these techniques within painting itself.

No doubt artists, or at least some artists, have always been highly conscious of the techniques of painting and drawing and the rules governing these techniques, as witness Leonardo's notes and his projected treatise "On Painting," and the many books by artists on perspective, including Piero della Francesca's *De prospectiva pingendi* and Dürer's account of perspective in his *Underweysung der Messung*. And no doubt there is a sense in which the act of painting is, in all but the most banal cases, in itself an experiment in the techniques of painting. But what seems to have been new in the twentieth century was the choice, by so many artists, of the techniques of painting, and painting itself, as the *subject matter of painting*. David Hockney made a distinction between what he called "technical paintings" in which the balance of interest is toward the form, and paintings in which the balance is toward the subject matter: "I use the word 'technical,' in the sense that they're about the techniques of painting, my painting, painting going on round me, as opposed to life. They're statements in a way about painting" (Hockney, 1976, p. 150). The three paintings analyzed in this chapter are all "technical" paintings, in Hockney's sense of the word, and the technique that all these three artists have used to deal with this subject matter is to break certain selected rules of depiction that had previously been taken for granted as self-evidently "true" or "natural," at least by the standards of Western realistic painting.

Far and away the commonest function of painting, prior to the twentieth century, had been to represent the *object* domain: the domain made up of objects like people and tables, whether real or imagined. When a symbol system is used to give an account of the object domain it is known as an *object language*. Just as the sentence "The grass is green" tells us something about the color of grass, so a portrait or a landscape can tell us something about the shapes and colors of objects in the scene. In these examples, English and painting are employed as object languages. However, a symbol system can also be used to comment on or investigate other symbol systems, and a symbol system employed for this purpose is described as a *metalanguage*. This book can itself be regarded as an extended metalinguistic essay: its subject matter is not objects—although of course paintings and drawings are objects—but painting and drawing as symbol systems.

Object languages and metalanguages differ in their functions, rather than in the sets of symbols they happen to use. Very often the symbols used in object languages differ from the symbols used in metalanguages. For example, in this book I am using English as a metalanguage to comment on systems like Pointillism and perspective that are not, in themselves, parts of English—although their *names* are parts of English. However, it can happen that the symbols used in a metalanguage are the same as the symbols used in the object language on which it is commenting; and then, unless certain precautions are taken, things can get very confusing.

For example, "Chicago is a populous city" is simply a sentence in an object language: it tells us something about Chicago, and there is little danger of confusion. The sentence "*Das Gras ist grün* is a grammatical sentence in German" is a sentence in a metalanguage—it tells us something about German as a symbol system—but again there is not too much likelihood of confusion, partly because the words "Das," "Gras," "ist," and "grün" are not words in English, and partly because I have used the normal convention of italicizing words in a foreign language.

The sentences "Chicago is trisyllabic" and "The grass is green is a grammatical sentence in English" could be confusing, however, because they mix English used as a metalanguage and English used as an object language. The normal precaution taken against this confusion is to separate the two by using single quotation marks, thus: "'Chicago' is trisyllabic" and "'The grass is green' is a grammatical sentence in English." Alternatively, I can avoid using two sets of quotation marks by saying:

1. "Chicago" is trisyllabic.

2. "The grass is green" is a grammatical sentence in English.

Sentence 2 appears to contain, within quotation marks, the sentence "The grass is green," which is a fragment of English used as an object language. I say *appears* to contain because it does not actually contain this sentence, but rather the *name* of the sentence—which happens, in this case, to be identical in its form to the sentence to which it refers. Just as normal English sentences cannot literally contain objects such as grass, so metalinguistic sentences cannot literally contain parts of an object language, but only their *names* (Nagel and Newman, 1964).

Even with the help of conventions like the use of single quotation marks, however, distinguishing between object languages and metalanguages can be difficult, and using symbol systems as metalanguages rather than as object languages can sometimes seem both obscure and perverse:

> "You are sad," said the Knight in an anxious tone: "let me sing you a song to comfort you. . . . The name of the song is called 'Haddocks' Eyes.'"
>
> "Oh, that's the name of the song, is it?" Alice said, trying to feel interested.
>
> "No, you don't understand," the Knight said, looking a little vexed. "That's what the name is *called*. The name really *is* 'The Aged Aged Man.'"
>
> "Then I ought to have said 'That's what the *song* is called'?" Alice corrected herself.
>
> "No, you oughtn't: that's quite another thing! The *song* is called 'Ways and Means': but that's only what it's *called,* you know!"
>
> "Well, what *is* the song then?" said Alice, who was by this time completely bewildered.
>
> "I was coming to that," the Knight said. "The song really *is* 'A-sitting on A Gate': and the tune's my own invention." (Carroll, 1962, pp. 184, 185)

It is easy to understand Alice's bewilderment. But in fact, metalanguages can serve important functions, and their employment within mathematics, verbal language, and artificial intelligence developed quite naturally in response to real problems. The attempt to discover, in the nineteenth century, whether ordinary Euclidean geometry was consistent, and the discovery of new geometries such as Riemannian geometry, raised crucial questions about which of these geometries, if any, best described the real world (Nagel and Newman, 1964). This led to the study of formal structures within mathematics, and then to the use of metamathematics to describe these structures: it is no coincidence that Lewis Carroll, the author of the *Alice* books, was a mathematician. Similarly, the investigation of archaic written languages, the rediscovery of Sanskrit, and attempts to describe and record the American Indian languages before they became extinct, led at the beginning of the twentieth century to the establishment of linguistics as an autonomous discipline: the use of language as a metalanguage, in order to study language itself.

It is probably not possible to point to any one moment at which painters first began to use painting to comment on the nature of depiction. During the nineteenth century the increasing accessibility through mechanical reproduction of paintings from other periods and cultures forced painters to compare pictures based on very different drawing and denotation systems. Japanese woodblock color prints, for example, became widely popular in France from the early 1860s, and their lack of tonal modeling and use of pure color offered a particularly intriguing alternative to the conventions of European painting and the use of chiaroscuro. In addition, the invention of photography in the nineteenth century confronted painters with a mode of depiction which shared some features with contemporary painting—the use of perspective, and a tonal system derived from the play of light—but which in other ways was very different. The impact of such alternative forms of depiction naturally raised questions in artists' minds about Gombrich's "riddle of style": "Why is it that different ages and different nations have represented the visible world in such different ways?" (Gombrich, 1960/ 1988, p. 3).

Two nineteenth-century discoveries seemed relevant to this question, but unfortunately they pointed in different directions. The first was the invention of photography. The mechanical nature of photography seemed at the time to guarantee its truth: what Fox Talbot called "the pencil of nature" must, it seemed, be more truthful than even the best of painting because it appeared to be free of subjective human interference.[1] And of course, capturing the light from the scene directly by photography fitted in perfectly with accounts of painting and visual perception that were based exclusively on physical optics. Thus the superiority of Western art, already established on cultural grounds, seemed to be confirmed by nature itself. The paintings of other cultures were simply stages in the evolution of photographic realism.

The discovery of photography was announced in 1839 (Scharf, 1979). But only a very few years later Hermann von Helmholtz, perhaps the greatest single figure in the experimental study of vision, suggested that what we actually experience in vision is not a series of single, static, photographlike retinal images. In his *Physiological Optics* he attempted to describe what happened *beyond* the retina in terms of the formation of what we would now call internal shape descriptions. And Helmholtz's theories, like the discovery of photography, also had a profound influence on painting. Teuber (1980) has argued that it was Helmholtz's writings that prompted Cézanne's famous advice to "treat nature in terms of the cylinder, the cone, and the sphere."

> It was Helmholtz who had shown in the third part of the *Physiological Optics* (French translation, 1867) that we see in each illusionistic or perspective transformation of an object more than the retinal image, that we "add to it," as his followers put it (nous ajoutons) the basic form or idea of the object. We see in all perspective renderings and even in the confusing shapes of nature the constant, non-illusionistic forms of cylinder, cube and sphere. Helmholtz elaborated on this in *L'Optique et la Peinture* which was included in the highly popular *Principes Scientifiques des Beaux-Arts* of 1878 (with three more editions to follow). In *Les Peintres Cubistes* (1913) Apollinaire distinguished in a similar manner between *la réalité de vision* (which is illusionistic) and *la réalité de connaissance*. And he went on: "All men have a sense of this interior reality. A man does not have to be cultivated to conceive of a round form, for instance. The geometrical aspect, which made such an impression on those who saw the first canvases of the scientific cubists, came from the fact that the essential form was rendered with great purity, while visual accident and anecdotes had been eliminated." (Teuber, 1980, pp. 3–4)

So just at the moment when it at last became possible to produce pictures that appeared to provide a perfect record of the light from a scene, the validity of such a record in relation to our actual experience of the visual world was being questioned.

Thus at the end of the nineteenth century painters were confronted with a number of circumstances that challenged current ideas about painting: the increasing availability of pictures from other periods and cultures, the discovery of photography, and the beginning of new theories of vision. These influences inevitably made painters more self-conscious about the techniques of depiction, and raised profound questions about the very nature of painting. In the early twentieth century this led many painters to turn away from painting as a way of depicting objects in the scene, and instead to begin to use their paintings as metapictures, as a way of investigating the nature of depiction itself.

The scientific study of picture languages, and with it the use of pictures as metapictures, began in the 1960s within artificial intelligence. Many of these studies were greatly influenced by Noam Chomsky's account of generative grammar (Chomsky, 1957/1972, 1965/1972), then at the height of its popularity. The main problem in analyzing pictures was seen to be the problem of finding "descriptive schemata" for pictures: explicit ways of describing the elements—lines, dots, blobs, and so on—of which a picture is composed, and the relationships between them: in other words, finding ways of describing what I have called the drawing systems and denotation systems.

> Kirsh showed that this problem was closely analogous to the problem of describing sentences in a natural language like English and proposed that the same technical means, namely a generative grammar, be adopted to solve it. Among attempts at putative "picture grammars" some have utilised a two-dimensional format for the grammatical rules thus making the syntax of the meta language mirror that of the object language—as it does in the traditional corpus of generative grammar. (Clowes, 1971, p. 81)

This is, so far as I know, the first reference to the possibility of using pictures to serve a metalinguistic function. By analogy, I shall refer to pictures used in this way as "metapictures."

As I emphasized in Chapter 1, one of the most important outcomes of these studies was the realization that it was necessary to make a careful distinction between words that describe picture primitives such as *lines* and *regions,* and words like *edges* and *surfaces* that describe corresponding scene primitives. In verbal language the problem of distinguishing between a word and its referent is not nearly so urgent: we are never likely to suppose that the sentence "Chicago is a populous city" actually contains the city itself. But pictures are often so persuasive that it is all too tempting to describe them, as we often do in everyday language, as containing features like edges and surfaces, or objects like tables and people. What they actually contain, of course, is lines of ink or patches of paint. Once we forget this distinction, and begin to think that pictures actually contain *objects,* it becomes impossible to talk about them in any useful way.

Because of this danger of confusing the picture domain with the object domain, frames serve a crucially important function in depiction: a function somewhat similar to that performed by quotation marks. In written English, quotation marks are used to separate direct speech or writing from the rest of the sentence: that is, to mark the boundary between the text and the words quoted, which come from a different domain: another written text, or the domain of the real world if we are quoting the words spoken by a real person, or the domain of an imagined world in a novel. However, because we are not usually in any danger of confusing a written text with a real or imagined world,[2] there is no need to put the whole of a novel within quotation marks. But with pictures there can be such a danger; so many pictures, at least in the Western tradition, are enclosed by a frame, just as in a traditional Western theater the audience is separated from the stage by a proscenium arch.[3] In fact, the one crucial defining feature of Western pictures is that they should have a frame. As Clowes put it, in the context of artificial intelligence: "Minimally a picture consists of a single region whose outer closure is a frame" (Clowes, 1971, p. 94).

Because frames play such a crucial role in marking the boundary between the picture domain and the object domain, it is possible to question the nature of depiction by employing anomalous relations between the frame and the picture: for example, by falsely attaching features of the picture to the frame, or by allowing features of the picture to leak out past the frame into the object domain, or by allowing features of the object domain to pass the frame into the picture domain, as in the typically Cubist device of using pieces of real wallpaper or newspaper as part of the picture. Moreover, pictures used as metapictures very often employ *two* frames, very much as sentences used for metalinguistic purposes employ two sets of quotation marks.[4] Magritte's famous painting *This Is Not a Pipe* (*Ceci n'est pas une pipe*) would be more or less trivial as an *object* painting of a pipe; what Magritte was doing was drawing attention to the fact that this painting, in spite of its realism, is not a pipe but a *picture* of a pipe. In a later version, *The Air and the Song* (*L'air et la chanson,* 1964), he made the same point more explicitly. The picture itself is not merely a picture, but a picture of a picture: in this case, a picture of a picture of a pipe. This picture of a pipe is contained within an elaborate frame, confirming its status as a picture; but to confound matters, the smoke from the pipe drifts out past the frame into the domain of the picture that contains this picture as a representation. Yet another version, *The Two Mysteries* (*Les deux mystères,* 1966) (fig. 12.1) depicts both a pipe and a picture of a pipe.[5] Of course, many paintings contain representations of pictures as part of the depicted scene, but here Magritte seems to be *quoting* his earlier painting: the frame within *The Two Mysteries* acts like the second set of quotation marks within a metalinguistic statement.

The paintings analyzed below illustrate three different styles of metalinguistic investigation. Gris's *Breakfast,* 1914, is highly complex, and employs a number of different anomalous pictorial devices. These include the reversal of the normal rules of occlusion; the extensive use of false attachment both within the picture and between the picture and the frame; and the importation of both parts of the real world, and a different, nonvisual symbol system, into the domain of the picture. All these devices, with the exception of the false attachments or near false attachments between features of the picture and the frame, were used by Picasso and Braque, and it could be argued that Gris's *Breakfast* is not a metapicture at all: perhaps Gris was simply displaying or experimenting with different pictorial devices. In contrast, Klee's *Oh, but oh!* (*Ach, aber ach,* 1937) could almost come from a paper on picture

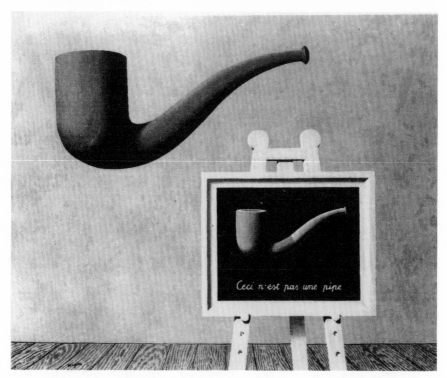

FIG. 12.1. René Magritte, *Les deux mystères,* 1966. Oil on canvas, 64.8 × 80.0 cm. Private collection. Copyright Design and Artists Copyright Society 1997.

languages in the field of artificial intelligence: it consists of a concise essay on one very simple proposition, that lines can stand for many different kinds of features in the real world. Finally, Hockney's *Play within a Play,* 1963, takes the possibility of using painting as a way of making statements about painting for granted. There are no anomalies within the painting; like Magritte's *The Two Mysteries,* it contains a picture within a picture, and only the relation between the picture and the domain of the viewer is anomalous, questioning the relation between representation and reality—or between "art and life," as Hockney himself put it.

Juan Gris, *Breakfast,* 1914

The structure of Gris's *Breakfast* (color plate 6) is based on the contrast between the use of a (fairly) straightforward drawing system and a number of complex and anomalous denotation systems (Willats, 1983). A tracing (fig. 12.2a) shows that the table is drawn in axonometric projection (a

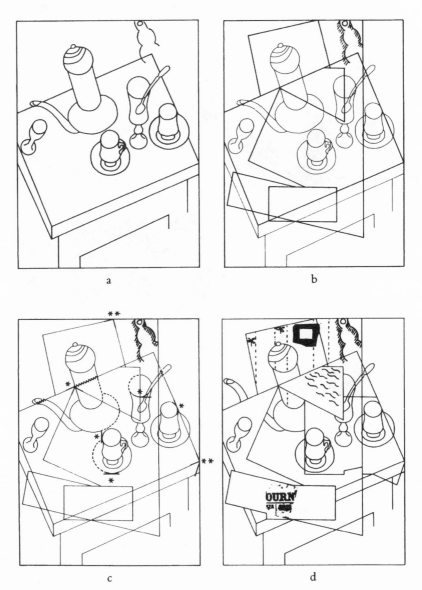

a   b

c   d

FIG. 12.2. Analysis of Juan Gris's *Breakfast*. (a) The table is in axonometric projection, and the cups and other objects are in vertical oblique projection. (b) The rectangular forms fan out from the lower half of the picture, giving an impression of inverted perspective. (c) The normal rules for the representation of occlusion are reversed: parts of the scene which should be omitted are included (zigzag lines), and parts of the scene which should be included are omitted (dotted lines). Single asterisks mark instances of false attachment within the picture; double asterisks mark instances of false attachment or near false attachment between the picture and the frame. (d) The normal rules of atmospheric perspective are reversed by placing the warmest and most fully saturated area of color at the top, in the background of the picture. The painter's name is signed *en collage*.

variety of vertical oblique projection with the object shown in a fore-shortened position), while the cups, the wineglass, the egg cup, part of a bottle, and the coffeepot are all drawn in vertical oblique projection. The cups and the glass look rather elongated, but analysis (fig. 2.11) shows that the cups are perfectly ordinary ones, and that their elongated appearance is a result of using this particular drawing system. Thus in terms of projective geometry the picture can be regarded as showing a view of a breakfast table from above, and from a considerable distance, with the table turned at an angle to the viewer. One anomalous feature of the way this drawing system is used here, however, is that the vertical axes of the bottle and the coffeepot are aligned with the side edges of the table, while the axes of the egg cup and part of a cup in the middle of the picture are tilted in the opposite direction. In addition, the spout of the coffeepot and part of the front edge of the table are displaced. The straightforward nature of this view is, moreover, some-what disguised by the more or less abstract rectangular forms imposed on the picture surface (fig. 12.2b). These forms fan out from the lower half of the picture rather like a hand of cards, giving an effect of inverted perspective that tends to disguise the underlying system of vertical oblique projection.

The basic denotation system of this picture is that of a line drawing with shading. The shading is used for two main purposes: to show the shapes of rounded objects through the representation of tonal modeling, and to bring edges or surfaces forward relative to their background. Both these effects can be seen in their simplest form in the bottle at the top of the picture. The right-hand contour of the bottle is shaded on its inner side, with the tone fading away toward the interior of the form (fig. 12.2b). This gives an effect of tonal modeling, and shows how the surface turns away from the spectator at the edge of the form. On the left-hand side of the bottle, however, the contour is shaded on its *outer* side, and this serves the purpose of bringing the bottle foward relative to the background. Similar effects can be seen along the contours of the coffeepot. The rounded forms of the table legs are shown using tonal modeling on both sides, while the flat surfaces of the table top and the frame of the table are brought forward by shading outside the contour. The shading on the cups and saucers is more closely related to the play of light: the tonal modeling is more elaborate, and there is some suggestion of highlights and cast shadow. Thus although Gris's use of shading in this picture varies from one part of the picture to another, it is fairly orthodox; more so than it is in a number of his other paintings and drawings carried out at this period.

Apart from some dislocation of the forms, then, Gris's representation of shape in *Breakfast,* both in his drawing and his use of tone, is fairly conventional. His use of axonometric projection is similar to that used in contemporary architectural drawings; and apart from the use of shading to bring objects forward relative to the background, the tonal system in *Breakfast* is similar to that used in the engineering drawing shown in fig. 6.3. The main anomaly in this painting is the way in which the normal rules for the representation of occlusion are reversed. In some places those parts of the scene that would normally be hidden, such as the far edge of the table where it would be hidden by the coffeepot, are included in the painting. In fig. 12.2c this edge is identified by a zigzag line. Conversely, some parts of the scene that would normally be seen in the painting, such as parts of the coffeepot, the wineglass, and the lowest cup, are left out. In fig. 12.2c these are shown using dotted lines. As Koenderink (1990) said, "occlusion is by far the most powerful depth cue that you can draw on" (p. 615), and reversing the normal rules for representing occlusion flattens the picture almost completely, in spite of the presence of a number of other powerful depth cues.

In addition, there are numerous instances of the use of false attachment, both within the picture and between objects depicted in the picture and the frame. Within the picture, these include false attachments between the rim of the right-hand cup and the edge of the table; between the rim of the lowest cup, and its saucer, and the edge of the tablecloth; and between the edge of the coffeepot, the far edge of the table, and the abstract rectangular form which occupies the middle of the painting. In fig. 12.2c these false attachments are indicated by single asterisks. In addition, there appear to be false attachments or near false attachments between the right-hand corner of the table and the frame, and between the abstract rectangle at the top of the picture and the frame; these are shown in fig. 12.2c by double asterisks. Finally, there is a false attachment or near false attachment between the frame and the spout of the coffeepot.

There are three other types of anomaly in the picture. Most of the picture is in dull browns, grays, and blues, all of which are recessive colors; but the parcel and the coffeepot lid are in red. This reverses the normal rule of atmospheric perspective, that the warmest colors should appear in the foreground (fig. 12.2d). Second, some of the regions in the painting are not painted, but are made up of real woodgrain paper, real wallpaper, and part of a real newspaper, so that these surfaces represent themselves, instead of being depicted. Finally, by using a newspaper, *Le Journal,* as part of the painting, Gris introduced an additional symbol system—verbal language—into the domain of the picture. Even this anomaly is given an additional twist: Gris used this fragment of newspaper to sign his name—Juan (OURN) Gris.

What was Gris's purpose in introducing these anomalies into what would be, otherwise, a fairly straightforward picture? According to Cooper and Tinterow (1983), "Gris's fundamental pictorial aim was to represent a three-dimensional experience of reality in two-dimensional terms on the surface of the canvas without recourse to illusion" (p. 136). To the extent that this aim is satisfied in a normal engineering drawing showing a pictorial view, Gris could have achieved that aim simply by combining a line drawing in axonometric projection with a conventional system of shading. The anomalies in the picture—the reversal of the normal rules for the represen-tation of occlusion, and so on—destroy any possible illusion, but they do not add to the spectator's experience of three-dimensional reality. The most obvious effect these anomalies have is to draw the spectator's attention to the painting as a *picture:* that is, as an artificial symbol system rather than a slice of real life. When confronted with pictures that are realistic in a photo-graphic way, such as TV pictures, we tend to pay attention to the depicted scene rather than the picture itself: we look through the picture, rather than at it. With Gris's *Breakfast* the anomalies in the painting make this impossible: we have to pay attention not only to what the artist is saying, but how he is saying it.

But in addition, anomaly provides a method of exploring the ways in which symbol systems work—a method that has now become standard practice in psychology. Chomsky used this method in his explorations of linguistic structures, and the same approach was adopted by Clowes and Huffman in their investigation of pictorial structures. As Clowes said, "There are three main vehicles which Chomsky deploys to *expose* our intuitions: paraphrase, anomaly and ambiguity" (1971, p. 80). The difference is that whereas Chomsky, Clowes, and Huffman were scientists, Gris was a working painter who was looking for a pictorial language. Gris said, "Cézanne turns a bottle into a cylinder, but I begin with a cylinder and create an individual of a special type: I made a bottle—a particular bottle—out of a cylinder." Whereas Cézanne started from observation, Gris started from theory: "The mathematics of picture-making lead me to the physics of representation" (Kahnweiler, 1969, p. 139). With hindsight it is tempting, though perhaps unjustified, to see Gris, the most intellectual and scientific of the Cubist painters, as the first painter to use painting as a metalanguage. No doubt, like the other Cubists, he used anomaly for compositional ends: destroying illusion and flattening the picture surface. But the way in which Gris deploys these anomalies in his painting seems so deliberate and so controlled that it is difficult to avoid feeling that he is, at least in this painting, using painting as a metalanguage in order to explore the nature of painting itself.

Paul Klee, *Ach, aber ach! (Oh! but oh!)*, 1937

In Gris's *Breakfast* the anomalies are extremely complex. In contrast, *Oh! but oh!* (fig. 12.3a) is a simple, elegant essay on the uses of line. The painting deftly combines two different kinds of anomaly. In previous chapters I have described two different kinds of denotation system, both using lines as picture primitives. The first is very familiar: it forms the basis for most adult drawing from both East and West, including Japanese prints, line drawings by Western draftsmen from Mantegna to Picasso, Disneylike cartoons, and engineering drawings. This is the denotation sytem analyzed by Clowes and Huffman. In it, lines can stand for edges, contours, thin, wirelike forms, and cracks. Children, however, produce line drawings based on a quite different denotation system, one in which the one-dimensional lines stand for volumes or surfaces. In the tadpole drawing by a 5-year-old boy shown in

a   b

FIG. 12.3. (a) Paul Klee, *Ach, aber ach! (Oh, but oh!)*, 1937. Crayon and watercolor on paper, 36.5 × 30.0 cm. Privatbesitz Schweiz, Kunstmuseum Berne. Copyright Design and Artists Copyright Society 1997. (b) A single line is used to denote, successively: the edges of a bow tie, the contour of a cheek, an eyebrow, the ridge of the nose, and the furrow in the upper lip.

figs. 1.12 and 4.5, for example, the single lines used to represent the legs appear to stand for the legs as whole volumes, while the single line used to represent the nose appears to stand for the nose as either a volume or a ridge, that is, as a convex surface.

In Klee's *Oh! but oh!* these two kinds of denotation systems are combined. Not only does the principal line in the picture change its reference along its length, but the denotation systems to which the line belongs also change. Klee's picture thus violates the two rules on which an adult line drawing is normally based: that lines normally stand for one-dimensional shape features such as edges and contours, and that a single line segment cannot have more than one meaning at different points along its length.

In the previous chapter, I showed how Klee violated the second of these two rules in *Naked on the Bed* in order to obtain an expressive effect, but in that painting the line stands for just one kind of shape feature: the contour of a smooth form. In *Oh! but oh!,* in contrast, the principal line in the picture changes the nature of its reference no less than five times along its length (fig. 12.3b). Beginning at the bottom right, the line starts by standing for the edge of a bow tie, with the surface of the tie to the right of the line. Then the reference of the line changes so that the surface of the other half of the tie lies to the left of the line. Continuing upwards, the line changes its reference again and becomes the contour of the head and cheek. At the top of the picture there is another change where the line stands for one of the eyebrows, an area of darker local tone on the surface of the head. Continuing down, the line now stands for the nose, either as a volume or as a ridge. Finally, between the nose and the mouth, it denotes the convex furrow in the middle of the upper lip.

Thus along its length one single line is used to stand for five different kinds of shape features: edge, contour, area of tone, ridge, and furrow. Klee does not seem to have any particular expressive intentions here. Apart from its playful title, this painting is probably about as close as one could come in painting to a scientific treatise, in the manner of Clowes and Huffman, on line reference.

David Hockney, *Play within a Play,* 1963

One thing that comes over very clearly from both his paintings and his autobiography (Hockney, 1976) is Hockney's preoccupation with style. Hockney's way of dealing with the problems raised by the existence of many different kinds of style in painting was to take style itself, rather than the world of objects, as his subject matter. From what Hockney says himself, it is clear that he was very conscious of the formal devices that he used in *Play within a Play* (color plate 7).

> Immediately after *The Hypnotist* I painted *Still Life with Figure and Curtain,* which was done in a very formal way. Soon after I began it, I went in the National Gallery one day and had a very rare experience of seeing. I thought I knew the National Gallery and all the pictures very well, but in 1963 they'd bought a group of paintings by the seventeenth-century artist Domenichino. I wandered in and found them in a room and they thrilled me, because they were things I could use. I suddenly saw what they were about. The moment these pictures revealed themselves, I realized my ideas were far from being new. It wasn't their subject matter from Greek mythology which interested me, but the fact that they really seemed like *trompe-l'oeil* painting. They were paintings made to look like tapestries made from paintings, already a double level of reality. All of them had borders round and tassels hanging at the bottom and perhaps an inch of floor showing, making the illusionistic depth of the picture one inch. In one of them, *Apollo Killing Cyclops* [fig. 12.4a], the tapestry was folded back a little, like the illusionistic device on a Kodak film box, and in front of this was a dwarf. I don't really know who he is or what it was meant to be about but the doubling back from the spectator interested me. *Play within a Play* is my version of *Apollo Killing Cyclops.* Instead of calling it "Picture within a Picture within a Picture," I thought I'd use the common literary version of it: *Play within a Play.* It uses Domenichino's idea of a very shallow space with a picture on a tapestry that has illusion and you don't know whether the illusion is real or not, because it has this border round it. You're playing so many games, and they are visual. The tapestry is invented, using images from previous work. The figure is a portrait of John Kasmin [fig. 12.4b]. Kas had always wanted me to paint him but I'd never got round to it as I couldn't really decide how to do it. Now it seemed appropriate to trap him in this small space between art and life (the sheet of glass is real, and where his hands or clothes touch they are painted on the surface of the glass). (Hockney, 1976, p. 90)

Both Gris's *Breakfast* and Klee's *Oh! but oh!* use anomaly as a way of exploring pictorial structures. Hockney's *Play within a Play* exploits a major anomaly, but it also uses transcription: a technique closely related to para- phrase, one of Chomsky's other ways of "exposing our intuitions." Like other metalinguistic techniques, transcription originally developed quite naturally in response to straightforward needs. Before the invention of photography, many pictures were copied by artists in order to provide patrons with a version of a picture that they admired but could not buy. Copying also provided an excellent way for artists to learn technique: the act of copying forces the copyist to study, and learn from, the techniques of another artist. Inevitably, the style of such copies differed to a greater or lesser extent from that of the original. In Rembrandt's copies of Persian miniature paintings, for example, the style is much closer to Rembrandt's normal style than it is to the style of Persian miniature painting, and pictures like this may be regarded as transcriptions rather than copies.

Toward the end of the nineteenth century, many artists began to make transcriptions as a conscious way of exploring style. One great advantage of transcription, from the artist's point of view, is that it allows him or her to explore pictorial structures without worrying too much about the subject matter. Paradoxically, this has led many modern artists to draw their themes from the past. As Steiner put it:

> The history of Picasso is marked by retrospection. The explicit variations on classical pastoral themes, the citations from and *pastiches* of Rembrandt, Goya, Velazquez, Manet, are external products of a constant revision, a "seeing again" in the light of technical and cultural shifts. Had we only Picasso's sculptures, graphics, and paintings, we could reconstruct a fair portion of the development of the arts from the Minoan to Cézanne. . . . The apparent iconoclasts have turned out to be more or less anguished custodians racing through the museum of civilization,

a   b

FIG. 12.4. (a) Domenichino and assistants, *Apollo Killing the Cyclops*, 1616–1618. Fresco transferred to canvas and mounted on board, 316.3 × 190.4 cm. National Gallery, London. (b) Photograph of John Kasmin, photograph by David Hockney.

seeking order and sanctuary for its treasures before closing time. In modernism *collage* has been the representative device. The new, even at its most scandalous, has been set against an informing background and framework of tradition. Stravinsky, Picasso, Braque, Eliot, Joyce, Pound—the "makers of the new"—have been neo-classics, often as observant of canonic precedent as their seventeenth century forebears. (Steiner, 1977, pp. 465–466)

Hockney's *Play within a Play* is a collage of transcriptions taken from at least three sources. The primary source was, as Hockney says, Domenichino's *Apollo Killing the Cyclops* (fig. 12.4a). What Hockney has taken from this picture, however, is not so much its composition as its formal structure. Like Magritte's *The Two Mysteries,* it questions the nature of pictures as symbol systems by showing two different levels of reality: the dwarf in the foreground is on a different plane of reality than the scene from the Greek myth being enacted behind. Like the picture of the pipe shown in Magritte's picture, this second scene is enclosed within a frame, which in this case is also the border of a tapestry.

The second source from which *Play within a Play* is taken was a photograph of the artist's dealer, John Kasmin (fig. 12.4b), who is seen pressing his face and hands against a sheet of glass. Finally, a third source is one of Hockney's own paintings, *The Hypnotist,* also painted in 1963. *The Hypnotist* shows two figures on a stage flanked by curtains: a rather evil-looking hypnotist and a helpless boy. This picture is itself a transcription: the source was a scene in a movie called *The Raven* where Vincent Price and Peter Lorre are magicians trying to impress each other with their magic. The two figures in the tapestry in *Play within a Play* are reminiscent of the two figures in *The Hypnotist.*

Play within a Play thus exploits two classic metalinguistic techniques: transcription and the representation of multiple levels of reality. In addition, it contains one major anomaly. Like the frame, the glass in a picture serves two functions: one practical and the other formal. The glass protects the picture from damage and at the same time marks the boundary between the picture domain and the object domain. If, in a Renaissance painting, the frame represents the frame of a window, then the glass represents the window glass, separating the domain of the picture from the domain of the real world.[6] Hockney makes this function explicit by allowing his figure to press his face and hands against the glass. This device can be thought of as a very special form of false attachment, like the false attachments between objects in the picture and the frame in Gris's *Breakfast.*

In terms of technique, subject matter, and surface composition, Magritte's *The Two Mysteries,* Gris's *Breakfast,* Klee's *Oh!, but oh!,* and Hockney's *Play within a Play* have almost nothing in common. What links them is that these are not object pictures, but metapictures.

Part Five

CHANGES IN
REPRESENTATIONAL
SYSTEMS
OVER TIME

CHAPTER THIRTEEN

Children's Drawing Development

Studies of children's drawing development go back as far as the end of the nineteenth century. Corrado Ricci's *L'arte dei bambini* (1887) is usually cited as the first work on children's drawings, and it was followed a year later by Bernard Perez's *L'art et la poésie chez l'enfant* (1888). James Sully's *Studies of Childhood* (1895) contained a comprehensive account of children's drawing development, and this provided a basis for subsequent studies such as those of Kerschensteiner (1905) and Luquet (1913, 1927). The literature on children's drawing development within the field of developmental psychology is now very extensive.

However, because most of these studies have been carried out by developmental psychologists, most writers have been concerned with giving an account of the *mental processes* underlying children's drawings, and the way these processes change as children get older. The problem with this approach is that these processes cannot be observed directly but can only be inferred from the drawings that children actually produce; and in default of any accurate, comprehensive formal scheme for describing the representational systems in children's drawings, the validity of any such inferences must remain doubtful. I shall therefore begin this chapter by showing how children's drawings can be classified in terms of the drawing and denotation systems I have described in previous chapters, and how their drawings change with increasing age, and only then turn to the question of how and why these changes take place.

What alternative classification schemes are currently available? The most widely known and, until recently, most generally accepted theory of children's drawing development has been Luquet's theory of intellectual and visual realism. This theory is usually summed up by saying that young children draw what they know and older children draw what they see. The change from intellectual to visual realism is supposed to occur between the ages of about 7 to 9 years. Luquet's account of drawing development (Freeman, 1972) was actually more complex than this, but the idea that young children draw things as they are known to be, rather than as they appear from a particular point of view, goes back at least as far as Clark (1897). A number of writers, myself among them, have suggested that Luquet's distinction between intellectual and visual realism can be reinterpreted in terms of Marr's distinction between object-centered and viewer-centered internal descriptions. That is, children's early drawings might be derived from internal object-centered descriptions, while drawings by older children might be derived from viewer-centered descriptions (Cox, 1985; Crook, 1985; Freeman, 1987; Light, 1985; Nicholls and Kennedy, 1992; Willats, 1981, 1987).

Luquet's account of drawing development does not in itself provide a formal scheme for classifying children's drawings: "what children know" and "what children see" are ways of describing mental states, not ways of describing the drawings themselves. However, Luquet's stage of intellectual realism is usually associated with certain characteristic features of children's drawings, especially the so-called "transparencies," the use of multiple viewpoints, and the "examplarity" of shapes, in which each detail is drawn as clearly as possible, regardless of considerations of perspective (Freeman, 1972). Thus Phillips et al. (1978) associated fold-out drawings of cubes, like those shown in fig. 7.8f, with the stage of intellectual realism, and drawings approximating to oblique projections or perspective with visual realism.

Piaget endorsed Luquet's theory of intellectual and visual realism, but grafted it onto his own account of child development, and in particular his account of the development of the child's conception of space (Piaget and Inhelder, 1956). Piaget was influenced by Jules-Henri Poincaré's account of invariant geometry, in which different kinds of spatial relations remain invariant over transformations from one coordinate system to another. The geometries governing such transformations form a hierarchy arranged in the following order, in which each geometry is a special case of the one above it:

1. Topology
2. Projective geometry (corresponding to perspective)
3. Affine geometry (corresponding to oblique projection)
4. Euclidian-metrical geometry (corresponding to orthogonal projection).

In topological transformations, only the most general spatial relations remain invariant over transformations: relations such as spatial order, connectivity, and enclosure. In projective transformations, lines remain straight, but regions do not retain their true shapes. In affine transformations, the property of "being parallel" remains invariant. Finally, in Euclidean-metrical transformations, the most special properties such as the true shapes of regions are preserved.

Piaget and Inhelder suggested that this hierarchy could provide a framework for an account of the development of the child's conception of space and, consequently, the development of drawing ability, and this led them to identify Luquet's period of intellectual realism with the use of topological geometry. According to this account, the reason for the appearance of so-called transparencies in children's drawings during this stage, like the transparency drawings described by Clark (1897)[1] and the drawing of Father Christmas coming down the chimney shown in fig. 3.4, is that children are representing the topological property of enclosure, rather than representing perspective views. This suggestion is, I think, correct.

However, the developmental sequence observed in children's drawings of rectangular objects such as tables and cubes does not support the developmental sequence predicted by Piaget's account based on invariant geometry. Piaget's account suggests that in the later stages of development this sequence ought to be: perspective, oblique projection, and finally orthogonal projection. In fact, the actual sequence, observed in numerous experiments, is just the reverse of this. For example, the developmental sequence observed in the experiment (Willats, 1977a) in which children were asked to draw a table from a fixed viewpoint was: orthogonal projection, vertical oblique projection, oblique projection, and, finally, some form of perspective (fig. 13.1). Thus Piaget's account represents an advance on Luquet's in that it identifies a number of different drawing systems with different developmental stages, and is also important because it identifies the earliest stage of development with the use of transformations based on topological geometry. However, the sequence it predicts thereafter is incorrect.[2]

Hagen's account of the projection systems was given exclusively in terms of primary geometry and the projection of light (Hagen, 1985, 1986). Her scheme consists, effectively, of the same classes of transformation systems as Piaget's, with the exception of topology: projective projection, affine projection, and metric projection. However, because she based her account exclusively on primary geometry, she regarded all these systems as being of equal status, rather than as forming a hierarchy of geometries. Her account thus predicts that there is *no* developmental sequence in children's drawing abilities. Again, this prediction is not supported by the evidence.[3]

There are very few accounts of the development of what I have called the denotation systems in the literature on children's drawings.[4] Luquet's stage of visual realism is often associated with "photographic" realism: Bühler (1949) fulminated against young children's outline drawings which he called "an abortion" (p. 114) and equated "the realistic picture" with "a photograph" (p. 119). Freeman and Janikoun (1972) contrasted Luquet's stage of intellectual realism in which the child draws from an "internal model" with the later stage of visual realism in which the child attempts to "reproduce the visually available stimulus configuration" (p. 1116). But we cannot directly see or reproduce the "visually available stimulus configuration" if this is taken to mean either the light falling on the retina or the retinal image itself. Nor do children normally draw anything like photographically realistic pictures (that is, they do not use an optical denotation system) until well beyond the ages of 7 to 9 when the change from intellectual realism to visual realism is supposed to take place.

Although the vast majority of marks in children's drawings are lines, I have argued in earlier chapters that it is crucial to distinguish between *marks* (the actual physical traces made by the drawing instrument) and *picture primitives*. Describing children's drawings in terms of the picture primitives on which they are based provides a classification scheme for the denotation systems in children's drawings consisting of three classes:

1. *Regions* as picture primitives
2. *Lines* as picture primitives
3. *Line junctions* as picture primitives

I have set the classes out in this way in order to emphasize their differences. Because children use lines as marks from the very beginning of drawing, it is all too easy to assume that there is no developmental sequence in their use of denotation systems. I shall argue, on the contrary, that the use of different denotation systems by children of different ages is at least as important, if not more important, than their use of different drawing systems.

Thus I shall begin this chapter by describing the results of three experiments in terms of the drawing and denotation systems I have described in previous chapters. In previous chapters I have discussed a number of drawings by children, but the analyses I have given have not been set within a developmental context. In this chapter I want to emphasize the correlations between the formal hierarchies of classes within the drawing and denotation systems defined in terms of secondary geometry, and the order of the appearance of these classes in the development of children's drawings. The drawing systems can be arranged in the following order in terms of the complexity of the rules of secondary geometry on which they are based:

Drawing systems

1. Topology and extendedness
2. Orthogonal projection
3. Horizontal and vertical oblique projections
4. Oblique projection
5. Perspective

Denotation systems

1. Regions as picture primitives
2. Lines as picture primitives
3. Line junctions as picture primitives

In terms of picture production, drawing systems based on topology deal only with the simplest and most basic spatial relations, and only the simplest and most basic shape properties can be described in terms of extendedness and shape modifiers. At the other end of the scale, the rules of secondary geometry governing representations in perspective are quite complex. Similarly, denotation systems based on regions as picture primitives can only enter into the simplest topological relations, while at the other end of this scale the rules governing the ways in which line junctions may and may not be connected so as to provide possible views (as described in Chapter 5) are again quite complex. In this chapter I shall show that there is a correlation between these orders of complexity and the developmental sequence.

Children's Drawings of Tables

Fig. 13.1 repeats the results of the experiment to which I referred in Chapter 1 in which 108 English children aged 5 to 17 were asked to draw a table, with various objects on it, from a fixed viewpoint (Willats, 1977a). The view which the children had of the table is shown in fig. 13.1a. The drawings of tables that the children produced were assigned to six classes, typical examples of which are shown in figs. b to g. These classes were defined in terms of five projection systems, and the results showed that there was a highly significant correlation between class membership and the mean age

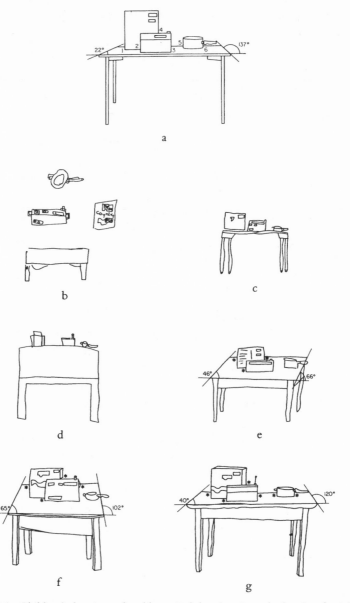

FIG. 13.1. Children's drawings of a table: typical drawings in each class (see fig. 1.9).

of children in each class.[5] These mean ages were as follows: no projection system, 7.4 years; orthogonal projection, 9.7 years; vertical oblique projection, 11.9 years; oblique projection, 13.6 years; naive perspective, 14.3 years; perspective, 13.7 years.

The projection systems were defined in terms of two measures: the *convergence* of the orthogonals and the *obliquity* of the orthogonals. The angles between the orthogonals and the line representing the front edge of the table were measured for each drawing, as shown in figs. e, f, and g, and the angles of convergence and obliquity were then calculated from these angles. The angle of convergence was defined as the *difference* between these two angles, and the angle of obliquity as the *mean* of the two angles. For example, the angle of convergence for the drawing shown in fig. e was 20° and the angle of obliquity was 56°, and the drawing was assigned to the class of oblique projections.[6] The angle of convergence for the drawing shown in fig. g was 80° and the angle of obliquity was 80°, so this drawing was judged to be in perspective. Drawings with no orthogonals, like the drawing shown in fig. c, were judged to be in orthogonal projection. A few of the youngest children produced drawings in which the depictions of the objects on the table were scattered across the page, or else arranged in a way that was roughly correct in terms of their spatial order but without their being connected. These drawings were assigned to class 1, no projection system.

The drawings were also classified in terms of the number of correct depictions of points of occlusion (or "overlap" as this was called in my original paper). In fig. 13.1 these points are marked with asterisks. The drawing shown in fig. e, for example, contains three such points compared with the six points of occlusion in the drawing shown in fig. a, and the overlap score for this drawing was thus 0.5. There was a highly significant correlation between the mean overlap score for each age group (from 6 to 17 years) and the mean group age.[7]

At the time that I reported this experiment I had not yet developed the concept of the denotation systems: thus the drawing systems were defined only in terms of the directions of the orthogonals, and the overlap scores were simply reported in terms of the child's ability to represent "overlap," as it was then called in the literature on children's drawings. With hindsight, however, it is possible to see the overlap scores as a measure of the child's developing ability to use T-junctions as picture primitives representing points of occlusion. In addition, it is also possible to interpret the drawings by the younger children in terms of the use of regions as picture primitives. There is no representation of occlusion in the drawings shown in figs. b, c, and d, and all the faces of the rectangular objects are drawn as true shapes. The only spatial relations represented in figs. c and d are touching and spatial order, while in fig. b objects are not even represented as touching. Moreover, fig. d includes a fold-out drawing of a box, which also suggests that this drawing is based on regions as picture primitives.

Thus the results of this experiment show a highly significant correlation between the sequence of drawing systems defined in terms of the rules of secondary geometry and the developmental sequence defined in terms of chronological age. In addition, a consideration of the types of drawings in each class, together with the highly significant correlation between the overlap scores and the mean ages for each age group, suggests a correlation between the sequence of denotation systems and the developmental sequence, although this correlation cannot now be quantified.

Children's Drawings of an Unfamiliar Rectangular Object

It is sometimes suggested that children learn to draw by drawing "what they know" in the sense of being able to reproduce a known graphic stereotype for a familiar object. That is, when children draw a familiar object they may produce a drawing derived not from the object itself, but from an internal representation consisting of a formalized way of drawing that object. Such stereotypes might be developed from the child's own early scribbles, in which he or she happened to see a fortuitous resemblance to a known object, as Luquet suggested in his account of what he called "fortuitous realism" (Freeman, 1972). Alternatively, a stereotype might be derived from drawings by adults or other children. Adults sometimes teach children how to draw a cube in the form of a Necker cube, for example (Hayes, 1978), and teenage children often copy drawings of figures such as Superman from comics (Wilson and Wilson, 1977). Wilson and Wilson (1981, 1984) have also shown that young children sometimes base their drawings of people on drawings by other children. Finally, Phillips et al. (1978) suggested that children might base their drawings of a familiar object such as a cube on what they called a "graphic motor schema."

> It is possible that there exist motor programs for drawing which are self-contained in the sense that they do not refer to any visual representation, but which, when executed, produce a picture of something. In other words, knowing how to draw something may mean knowing what movements to make to produce a picture of it. Such a motor program we will call a graphic motor schema. (Phillips et al., 1978, p. 29)

After carrying out the experiment described above, it occurred to me that it might be suggested that the results of this experiment could be explained by saying that, as tables are familiar objects which children often draw, children of different ages might have different, stereotyped ways of drawing them.[8] In order to test this possibility I carried out an experiment (Willats, 1981, 1984) in which 170 English children aged 4 to 13 years were asked to draw an unfamiliar object consisting of a wooden cube with a smaller cube removed from one corner. It seemed unlikely that children would have a graphic stereotype for such an object, and I wanted to see whether these children could use the projection systems previously found in children's drawings of tables in order to draw an object that they were unlikely to have seen or drawn before.

It was soon clear that the children could use these drawing systems to draw an unfamiliar object. Fig. 13.2 shows typical drawings produced by these children arranged into six classes. Most (though not all) of the drawings in class 2 were drawings in orthogonal projection (mean age 7.0 years), the drawings in class 4 were in vertical oblique projection (mean age 10.0 years), while the drawings in class 6 were in oblique projection (mean age 12.0 years). (No distinction was made between drawings in oblique projection and drawings in perspective; the object used was too small to allow this distinction to be reliable.) Given in terms of the projection systems, the developmental sequence was thus: orthogonal projection, vertical oblique projection, and oblique projection.

However, a puzzling feature of these results was the many anomalous drawings produced by the children, shown here in classes 1, 3, and 5 together with a few drawings of the type shown on the left in class 2. These drawings accounted for about one-third of all the drawings produced by the children in this experiment. It was the need to account for drawings of this type that originally prompted me to develop the concept of the denotation systems.

Nicholls and Kennedy (1992) found very similar types of drawings when they asked children and adults to draw cubes (fig. 8.3). Because some of the classes used by Nicholls and Kennedy to classify the children's drawings in their experiment were somewhat different from those used here, the results of the two experiments cannot be compared directly. However, the course of the developmental sequence, and the ages of children producing drawings of similar types, seem much the same in each case, suggesting that the children were applying the same kinds of drawing and denotation rules in order to draw this unfamiliar object as they would in drawing cubes. The main difference was that the children produced a higher proportion of anomalous drawings when drawing the unfamiliar object. Probably the reason for this difference was not only that the object was unfamiliar but also that its shape was more complex than that of a cube, and it was, in consequence, simply more difficult to draw, so that children were more likely to make mistakes.

Because I was still in the process of developing the concept of denotation systems when this experiment was first carried out in 1981, the classes to which the drawings were assigned were not so clearly defined as I would now like. However, they are quite clear enough to show the developmental sequence in the children's employment of denotation systems.

Fig. 13.3 shows an analysis of some of the drawings of this unfamiliar object. Nicholls and Kennedy's class 1, fig. 8.3 showed two examples of types of drawings of cubes that they referred to as "enclosure" drawings: both

Class	Mean age		
1	5.5		
2	7.0		
3	9.0		
4	10.0		
5	10.5		
6	12.0		

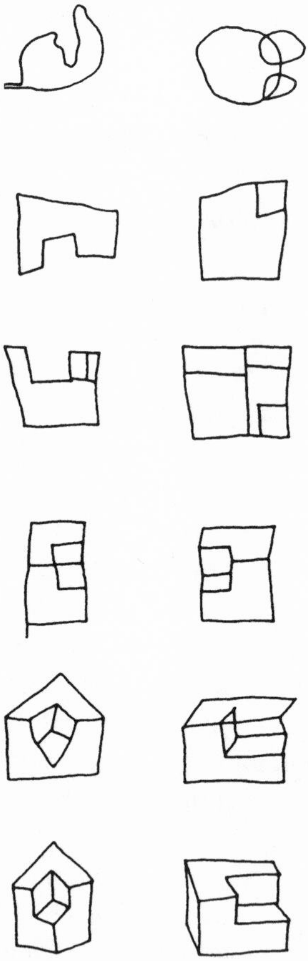

FIG. 13.2. Children's drawings of an unfamiliar object, showing the mean age for each class.

consisted of single roughly circular regions enclosed by a curved outline. Class 1, fig. 13.2, shows two types of drawings of the unfamiliar object, also involving curved lines, but these drawings appear to be based on two different denotation rules. The first type consists of a single region with a concavity in the outline, and it seems likely that this drawing is intended to represent the object as a round volume with a concavity: that is, the unfamiliar object was represented as "a lump with a dent in it." The second type, shown on the right in class 1, consisted of more than one round region,

Class		Drawing system	Denotation system		
2a		Topological	Region	⟶	Volume
2b		Orthogonal	Region	⟶	Face seen
3	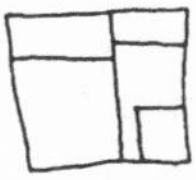	Fold-out	Regions	⟶	Faces
4	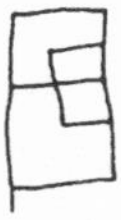	Vertical oblique	Regions	⟶	Faces seen
5		Near-oblique	Regions*	⟶	Faces seen
6		Oblique	L-, Y-, and arrow-junctions	⟶	Corners
			T-junction	⟶	Point of occlusion

FIG. 13.3. Analysis of children's drawings of an unfamiliar object, showing the associated projection and denotation systems. The asterisk denotes a transitional denotation system. Adapted from Willats (1984), courtesy of Elsevier Science.

and this suggests that in drawings of this type the regions were intended to represent individual *faces* of the object, rather than the volume of the object as a whole. If this is the case, these drawings may be regarded as examples of very early fold-out drawings.

Two types of drawings are shown in class 2. The first of these, on the left in fig. 13.2, also appears to represent the object as a lump with a dent, but the outline of the drawing is composed of straight lines apparently representing the shape property "having plane faces." Drawings of this type cannot be equated with views, because the individual line segments cannot be related to views of edges. The second type of drawing corresponds to an orthogonal projection, and thus to a possible view, and it seems likely that the regions in this drawing represent the faces that can be seen in an orthogonal view of the object. These two interpretations are shown in fig. 13.3, classes 2a and 2b.

The drawings shown in class 3, fig. 13.2, correspond to Nicholls and Kennedy's fold-out drawings of cubes; or perhaps, in the case of the drawing on the right in class 3, to what they call "dissection" drawings. In each case, the child has added extra rectangular regions in an attempt to represent additional faces. These drawings are clearly based on a denotation system in which regions are used to denote faces, and this interpretation is shown in fig. 13.3, class 3.

Drawings of the type shown in class 4, fig. 13.2, correspond to vertical oblique projections, and their geometry corresponds to what Nicholls and Kennedy called two-squares drawings of cubes. Nicholls and Kennedy emphasized that they found only relatively small numbers of drawings of this type, and as solutions to the problem of drawing rectangular objects these drawings represent something of a dead end in the developmental sequence because they do not show objects from a sufficiently general direction of view, and, consequently, do not provide effective shape representations. However, drawings of this type do have the advantage that they show the shapes of individual faces as true shapes, but also provide possible views. The denotation system on which these drawings are based is shown in fig. 13.3, class 4.

In order to produce drawings of objects in oblique projection, or one of the other oblique systems such as isometric projection or perspective, children have to abandon a denotation system in which regions stand for faces, and adopt one in which lines stand not only for edges, but the edges or parts of edges that can be seen from a particular point of view. The examples of drawings shown in fig. 13.2, class 5, contain oblique lines, but fail to meet these constraints completely. The drawing on the left is similar to the cube drawings containing the "flat bottom error" referred to in Chapter 8. Children who produce drawings of this type know that they must use oblique lines to represent edges in the third dimension, but are still trying, as far as possible, to represent the faces as true shapes; consequently, they include too many right angles in their drawings of individual faces. The drawing shown on the right in class 5 has been abandoned halfway through. This child was using a correct denotation rule—use lines to denote edges—and a correct drawing rule—use oblique lines to represent edges in the third dimension—but introduced a transparency, perhaps as the result of a planning error. Both these children were unsure about the use of lines, and these drawings can probably best be described as representing a transition stage between two denotation systems: a system in which regions denote faces, and a system in which lines denote edges. This transitional denotation system is shown marked with an asterisk in fig. 13.3, class 5.

The drawing shown on the left in fig. 13.2, class 6, is based securely on a denotation system in which lines stand for edges. The drawing on the right, however, is based on a rather more complex denotation system, in which the L-, Y-, and arrow-junctions denote corners, and the T-junction denotes a point of occlusion. This denotation system is shown in fig. 13.3, class 6.

The developmental order in which the drawing systems employed by the children in this experiment appeared was thus: topological; orthogonal projection; fold-out; vertical oblique projection; near-oblique; and oblique. The developmental order in which the denotation systems appeared was: regions denote volumes; regions denote faces; lines denote edges; and T-junctions denote points of occlusion.

The Representation of Foreshortening in Children's Drawings of Sticks and Discs

In the first experiment described in this chapter the children were confronted with a drawing problem which tested their ability to represent shape (the shape of the table) and spatial relations (the spatial relations between the table and the objects on it, including the representation of occlusion). The second experiment tested children's ability to represent shape only (the shape of an unfamiliar object). This third experiment (Willats, 1992b) tested children's ability to represent the *foreshortening* of objects, that is, their ability to represent the orientation of objects relative to a particular viewpoint. Foreshortening can be defined as the apparent change in the extendedness of the outline of the projection of an object as its orientation changes relative to the viewer.

In a classic experiment Piaget and Inhelder (1956) asked children of various ages to draw "sticks" and "discs" presented to them in foreshortened positions, that is, presented end-on in the case of the "stick" (a needle or a pencil, in their experiment), and edge-on in the case of the "disc." They found that the younger children (below the ages of 7 or 8 years) used a line or a long region to represent the stick and a round region to represent the disc, whether or not they were presented in foreshortened positions. However, the older children (8 or 9 years and above) used a dot or a small round region to represent the stick presented end-on and a line or a long region to represent the disc presented edge-on. This, they concluded, demonstrated the truth of Luquet's assertion that young children draw what they know (that a stick is long and a disc is round, in this case) rather than what they see (the projected shapes of the stick and the disc when they were presented in foreshortened positions).

Their explanation for the change from intellectual to visual realism (to use Luquet's terms) was not so much that young children see things differently from older children, although their claim that the child's conception of space changes from a system of spatial relations based on topological geometry to one based on projective geometry would seem to require this. Instead, they argued that young children draw what they know because they are not consciously aware of their own viewpoints. "In short, due to the lack of any conscious awareness or mental discrimination between different viewpoints, these children are unable to represent perspective and cling to the object in itself" (Piaget and Inhelder, 1956, p. 178). (It is not quite clear what Piaget and Inhelder meant by "the object in itself," but from the context in which it appears the phrase seems intended to express something like Marr's "object-centered description.") In this way, Piaget and Inhelder were able to bring the representation of foreshortening into the general framework of Luquet's theory. In their account, the representation of fore-shortening is just another aspect of perspective: older children are able to draw in perspective (that is, "what they see"), whereas younger children are not.

The results of the following experiment, however, showed that the representation of foreshortening is not quite as simple as Piaget and Inhelder suggested. Fig. 4.3 shows a number of drawings of a stick and a disc in foreshortened positions, and it is clear from this figure that only line drawings, and pictures based on an optical denotation system in which the primitives stand for features of the array of light, are able to provide effective representations of sticks and discs in partially foreshortened positions. Drawings based on the other denotation systems illustrated in this figure do not provide effective representations. Thus if children are to produce effective representations of sticks and discs in foreshortened positions, they not only have to learn to change the extendedness of the outlines of their drawings in response to a change in the orientation of the viewed object, but they also have to learn to use *lines*—rather than regions—as picture primitives.

In this experiment 128 English children aged 4, 7, and 12 years were asked to make two drawings of a wooden figure, shown in fig. 13.6a. The figure held a plate in its arms, and both the arms and the plate were movable, so that they could be presented in both foreshortened and nonforeshortened positions. The arms of the model figure thus played the role of "sticks" in this experiment (3_{100} volumes), while the plate played the role of a "disc" (a 3_{110} volume). In use, the model figure was placed on a table facing the child at a distance of 1.5 meters with the head of the figure at the child's eye level. The experimenter was careful to present the arms and the plate in either fully foreshortened positions (end-on for the arms and edge-on for the plate), or fully nonforeshortened positions (side-on for the arms and face-on for the plate). Each child made two drawings of the figure, with the arms and the plate presented in both foreshortened and nonforeshortened positions. Drawings of these features produced in the "foreshortened" conditions are highlighted in the figures.

Figs. 13.4, 13.5, and 13.6 show typical examples of pairs of drawings produced by children in each age group. These drawings were examined to see whether or not the children changed the extendedness of the outlines of their drawings of the arms and the plate in order to take account of changes in the orientations of these features, comparing the foreshortened and

FIG. 13.4. Children's drawings of arms and a plate. Girl aged 4 years 6 months. Changes of shape comparing foreshortened and nonforeshortened conditions: arms, *no* change of shape; plate, a *partial* change of shape. Marks used in the foreshortened condition: arms, *single lines;* plate, a *single region.* (Drawings of features produced in the foreshortened condition are highlighted.) Copyright The Society for Research in Child Development.

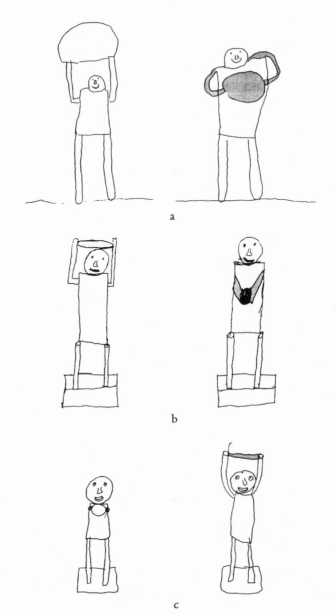

Fig. 13.5. (a) Boy aged 7 years 5 months. Changes of shape: arms, *no* change of shape; plate, *no* change of shape. Marks: arms, *single regions;* plate, a *single region.* (b) Girl aged 7 years 6 months. Changes of shape: arms, a *partial* change of shape; plate, a *full* change of shape. Marks: arms, *single regions;* plate, a region with *interior lines.* (c) Girl aged 7 years 7 months. Changes of shape: arms, a *full* change of shape; plate, a *full* change of shape. Marks: arms, *single regions;* plate, a *single region.* (After some hesitation this girl drew small circles for the arms and then, looking up at me, said, "Those are his arms!") Copyright The Society for Research in Child Development.

nonforeshortened conditions. The changes they made were assessed as no change of shape, a partial change of shape, or a full change of shape. For example, fig. 13.5a shows *no* changes in the extendedness of the shapes of the outlines representing the arms or the plate. Fig. 13.5b shows a *partial* change in the extendedness of the arms and a *full* change in the extendedness of the plate. Fig. 13.5c shows *full* changes in the extendedness of both the arms and the plate.

In addition, the drawings of the arms and the plate in the foreshortened condition were assessed in terms of the mark systems on which they were based. Fig. 13.4 shows the arms represented by *single lines,* and the plate by a

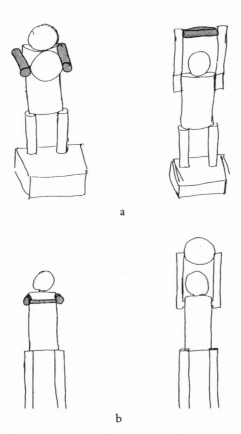

a

b

Fig. 13.6. (a) Boy aged 11 years 10 months. Changes of shape: arms, a *partial* chage of shape; plate, a *full* change of shape. Marks: arms, regions with *interior lines;* plate, a region with *interior lines.* (b) Boy aged 12 years 1 month. Changes of shape: arms, a *full* change of shape; plate, a *full* change of shape. Marks: arms, regions with *interior lines;* plate, a region with *interior lines.* From Willats (1992b). Copyright The Society for Research in Child Development.

single region. Fig. 13.5a shows both the arms and the plate represented by single regions. Fig. 13.6a shows both the arms and the plate represented by regions with *interior lines.*

The results showed age-related changes in both the drawing systems (the representation of extendedness) and the mark systems (and, by implication, the denotation systems) used by the children in this experiment.

The changes in the drawing systems used by the children were as follows. Very few of the 4-year-olds changed the extendedness of their drawings of either the arms or the plate in order to take account of foreshortening. In contrast, about two-thirds of the 7-year-olds and nearly all the 12-year-olds changed the extendedness of their drawings in one way or another from the nonforeshortened to the foreshortened conditions. This suggested that most of the 4-year-olds were basing their drawings on object-centered internal descriptions (which, by definition, cannot contain a description of the orientation of objects relative to a viewer), and that most of the 7- and 12-year-olds were basing their drawings on viewer-centered internal descriptions.

However, there were highly significant differences in the way the 7-year-olds and 12-year-olds represented the foreshortening of the arms and the foreshortening of the plate.[9] Whereas a majority of the 7- and 12-year-olds represented the foreshortening of the plate by a full change of shape, they represented the foreshortening of the arms by a *partial* change of shape (figs. 13.5b and 13.6a). The explanation for this difference seems to be that when it came to drawing the arms many of the children, especially the 7-year-olds, were faced with the almost insuperable problem of finding an effective way of representing a foreshortened stick within the constraints of a denotation system using regions as picture primitives. The problem is that although a dot or a small round region provides a true *view* of a fully foreshortened stick, it does not provide an *effective representation:* a dot or a small round region looks more like a small lump than a foreshortened stick. In the event, most of the children ended up by adopting a partial change of shape as a compromise solution. One of the few 7-year-olds who did use small round regions to represent the arms in the foreshortened position made her understanding of the problem quite clear (fig. 13.5c). This girl, after some hesitation, drew small circles for the arms and then, looking up at me and pointing to the circles, said, "Those are his arms!"

On the other hand, the problems involved in representing a foreshortened *disc* within the constraints of this denotation system are, as I have shown in Chapter 3, somewhat different. There are no natural symbols for discs: a long region disguises the fact that a disc is round, and a round region disguises the fact that it is flat. Consequently, it is difficult to represent discs in silhouettes, whatever their orientation; the tambourines at the ends of the arms of the dancing figure in Picasso's *Rites of Spring* (fig. 3.8) look more like fat sticks or flattened lumps than they look like discs, and it is difficult to tell whether the gladiators in the rock drawing shown in fig. 3.7 are carrying swords or shields.

Thus, although neither a long region nor a round region provides a very effective shape representation of a disc, one shape is no more or less effective than the other. Consequently, in the absence of any natural symbol for a disc, children who are old enough to be able to draw views will be just as willing to use a long region to represent a disc presented edge-on as they would be to use a round region to represent a disc presented face-on. This was borne out by the results of the experiment. More than half the 7–year-olds and nearly all the 12–year-olds represented the foreshortening of the plate by a *full* change of shape.

There were also age-related changes in the mark systems used by each age group, and these, taken in conjunction with changes in shape, can be used to infer the changes in the denotation systems used by the children. Most of the 4-year-olds used single lines to represent the arms and a round region to represent the plate, and made no changes in their drawings in order to represent foreshortening. These marks are probably best interpreted as representing long and round regions as picture primitives denoting long volumes and flat volumes as scene primitives (figs. 4.3e and 13.4). Similarly, about one-third of the 7-year-olds used long regions to represent the arms and round regions to represent the plate, and again made no changes in their drawings in order to represent foreshortening. Both these groups of children were thus effectively using the same denotation system: long regions standing for long volumes in an object-centered description, and round regions standing for flat volumes in an object-centered description. Foreshortening cannot be represented within this system.

Between half and two-thirds of the 7-year-olds, and a few of the 12-year-olds, used single regions to represent both the arms and the plate, and changed their drawings in one way or another in order to represent foreshortening. This suggests that these children were using a denotation system in which regions stand for regions in the frontal plane or visual field (figs. 4.3d and 13.5c). Although foreshortening can be represented within this system, it cannot be represented effectively: a round region as a view of a foreshortened stick looks more like a small lump than a stick, and a long region as a view of a foreshortened disc looks more like a stick than a disc.

Most of the 12-year-olds solved this problem by adopting a different denotation system: one in which lines stand for edges and contours. This system provides an effective way of representing the shapes and orientations of sticks and discs in both foreshortened and nonforeshortened positions (fig. 4.3b and 13.6a).

To sum up, most of the 4-year-olds used lines or regions to represent the extendedness of volumetric primtives in object-centered descriptions of the arms and the plate. Foreshortening cannot be represented in these systems. Most of the 7-year-olds used regions to represent the extendedness of views of the outlines of the arms and the plate. Foreshortening can be represented in this system, but it cannot be represented effectively. In order to solve this problem, the 12-year-olds adopted a new denotation system: one in which lines denote edges and contours. This system provides an effective way of representing the shapes and orientations of sticks and discs in both foreshortened and nonforeshortened positions.

These results show that the representation of foreshortening is primarily a *drawing* problem, rather than a problem in seeing or becoming consciously aware of one's own viewpoint. There is no reason to suppose that the children in this experiment saw the arms as partially foreshortened but the plate as fully foreshortened. Neither is there any reason to suppose that 12-year-olds "see" edges and contours any more clearly than 7-year-olds. It seems more plausible to say that 12-year-olds have learned to use lines rather than regions as picture primitives, and that they do this in order to be able to represent three-dimensional shapes, and the orientations of these shapes, more effectively.

Children's Drawings of People

In the experiments described above, children were asked to carry out three somewhat artificial drawing tasks. In the first experiment they were asked to draw a table from a fixed viewpoint; in the second they were asked to draw an unfamiliar object, one that they would be very unlikely to draw spontaneously; and in the third they were asked to draw sticks and a disc in foreshortened positions. To what extent can the methods of analysis I have described, and the conclusions I have drawn from these experiments, be applied to drawings produced by children under less contrived conditions?

Fig. 13.7 shows four drawings collected by Florence Goodenough in California during the first two decades of the twentieth century, in the course of what came to be known as the "Draw-A-Man" test (Goodenough, 1926; Harris, 1963). In this test the child was asked to draw a man, and was credited with points according to the number of body parts included in the drawing. These points were then converted to a standard score and used to give a measure of the child's intellectual maturity relative to other children of the same age. Goodenough chose the human figure as a basis for her test because a number of studies had shown that the human figure greatly exceeded all other subjects in popularity in children's spontaneous drawings.

Although some account was taken of the spatial relations between body parts in assessing the child's score, the "Draw-A-Man" test was based mainly on the number of body parts included in the drawing, rather like counting the number of words in a vocabulary test. Thus when Goodenough said of the young child "He draws what he knows, rather than what he sees," what she meant was that what the child knows is how to draw a symbol for a particular body part. But where do these symbols come from? Wilson and

FIG. 13.7. Children's drawings of a man. (a) Girl aged 4 years 4 months. (b) Girl aged 5 years 7 months. (c) Girl aged 8 years 6 months. (d) Boy aged 9 years 5 months. Florence L. Goodenough Collection, University Archives, Pennsylvania State University Libraries.

Wilson (1981, 1984) have argued that young children's figure drawings are primarily influenced by the drawings of other children. Certainly some of the drawings in the Florence Goodenough collection give the impression that they are based on graphic stereotypes shared by groups of children, and many of the drawings in the collection, including those given here, look rather different from the drawings one might expect to obtain from children at the end of the twentieth century. For example, Wilson and Wilson (1981) brought convincing evidence to show that what they called the "two-eyed profile," in which the head is drawn in profile with both eyes included, was very common in children's figure drawings during the last decades of the nineteenth century, but had virtually disappeared by the middle of the twentieth century. Moreover, they claimed that they could just as easily have studied the rise and fall of other features, such as "ladder mouths . . . the crossed arms transparency . . . the garden rake hands [as shown in fig. 3.6b] . . . and on and on" (p. 31).

However, although children's figure drawings may vary a good deal from one period and culture to another, and some children may well adopt solutions to drawing problems that they have observed in drawings by other children, the primary drawing problem that children have to solve is the problem of *shape* representation, and effective solutions to this problem are constrained by the design features of the human visual system. The drawings reproduced in fig. 13.7 (Willats, 1995) show just four examples out of a huge range of possible solutions adopted by children of different ages, but there are only a limited range of underlying principles, expressed in the form of drawing rules, that children can bring to bear in solving the problem of representing the shapes that make up the human figure.

Fig. 13.7a shows a tadpole figure produced by a 4-year-old. The considerations that I have advanced in this and earlier chapters suggest that the large round region is intended to represent the head or head/body as a round volume or lump, and the legs as long volumes or sticks. The eyebrows are represented by lines, and the eyes are represented by round regions. Thus only two shape features are represented in this drawing: extendedness (round or long) and relative size (large or small). In addition, the topological property of "being connected" in the scene is represented by the connections between the regions standing for the legs and the head or head/body. However, the eyes and eyebrows are shown *enclosed* within the region standing for the head or head/body. Thus even in this early drawing the region representing the head or head/body has to play a dual role: in production, as I have suggested, it is probably intended to stand for the head or head/body as a volume, but in order to put in the eyes and eyebrows the child has to see this region in the picture as representing the surface of the face.

The drawing shown in fig. 13.7b is probably based on similar drawing and denotation systems: that is, the spatial relations represented are topological rather than projective, and the round regions are intended to stand for round volumes and the lines and long regions for long volumes. In addition, the flat brim of the hat (a disc) is represented by a line. Notice that the drawing does not show a *view* of a hat, with the hat partially occluding the head; instead, it represents the topological relation of "touching" between the head and the brim of the hat.

The legs of this figure are represented by long regions that are bent at the end. In production it seems likely that these long regions are intended to represent the legs as long volumes, with the addition of the shape modifier "being bent," or "being bent at the end." Because "being bent" is a nonaccidental shape property, however, the resulting regions provide possible *views* of bent volumes. In terms of picture perception, therefore, we tend to see the outlines of these regions as representing the *contours* of the legs.

The drawing shown in fig. 13.7c includes features taken from both object-centered and viewer-centered descriptions. The regions representing the arms and the head are still probably intended to represent these features, in production, as long volumes and round volumes, and the arms are shown connected to the head, as they would be in a tadpole figure. On the other hand, the crown and brim of the hat are shown occluding the head, as they would in a view, and the complex outlines of the shoes are perhaps more plausibly interpreted as representing contours in a viewer-centered description than as the boundaries of regions denoting volumes.

Finally, fig. 13.7d shows a reasonably convincing view. The outlines of the drawing can be interpreted as contours, and the drawing contains two junctions that can be interpreted as T-junctions denoting points in the visual field where the lower contours of the left arm and the left leg disappear behind the contours of the body. However, this drawing still retains a number of features taken from object-centered descriptions: in particular there are no end-junctions denoting the points where contours end. In this respect, it is worth comparing this drawing with Joanne's *Self-Portrait with Dogs* shown in fig. 1.7. Joanne's drawing contains numerous examples of correct end-junctions, and as a result the drawing provides excellent representations of smooth shapes. In contrast, the outlines of the body in the drawing shown in fig. 13.7d merge into the outlines of the left arm and the left leg, instead of stopping short as they should if the drawing were to represent a correct view. This "merge" junction (Smith and Fucigna, 1988) can be regarded as a transitional stage between the representation of the topological property of "being connected" as shown in the drawings by the three younger children, and the correct projective relations between contours shown in the drawing by Joanne.

Summary of Developmental Changes

Most recent research has been directed toward describing age-related changes in the drawing systems, and in particular in the projection systems. As an irreducible minimum, many writers would now agree that two main stages can be identified in children's drawings of rectangular objects like tables, houses, and cubes: the use of orthogonal projection by younger children, and some kind of system involving the use of oblique lines, such as oblique projection or perspective, by older children. Some writers, including myself, would argue for the inclusion of horizontal and vertical oblique projection as intermediate stages. The actual ages at which children use these systems depend very much on the individual child, the nature and complexity of the task, and the object to be drawn.[10] However, these projection systems cannot readily be used to describe children's drawings of smooth objects like people. Nor can they be used to describe the characteristic anomalies that occur in children's drawings: tadpole figures, transparency drawings, fold-out drawings, and flat-bottom drawings that include false T-junctions.

Consequently, I have argued that drawing development, at the most fundamental level, can best be described in terms of changes in the denotation systems that children use. In the first stage, children use a system in which regions stand for whole volumes. The fundamental shape property represented at this stage is extendedness, and topological properties like touching and enclosure are used to represent the spatial relations between parts of objects. The application of rules governing such properties results in drawings like the tadpole figures, and drawings of cubes, houses, or other rectangular objects made up of curved lines. The addition of the shape modifier "having straight lines" to represent the nonaccidental property "having plane faces" may then result in drawings of rectangular objects that, fortuitously, resemble possible views in the form of orthogonal projections.

In the next main stage, children use regions to denote either the faces of objects or regions in the visual field. In the case of rectangular objects, this results in drawings that may be anomalous, like the fold-out drawings, or drawings that may, fortuitously, resemble possible views, such as, again, drawings in orthogonal projection, or drawings in horizontal or vertical oblique projection. In drawings of people or animals, regions are used to represent individual body parts like arms and legs, but as a result of the application of shape modifiers like "being bent" or "being pointed," the outlines of these regions begin to resemble possible contours.

Finally, children change to a system in which lines are used to denote edges and contours. This frees them from the obligation to draw faces as true shapes, and ultimately enables them to produce drawings of rectangular objects in systems like oblique projection or perspective, and to produce drawings of smooth objects that contain T- and end-junctions. It thus enables them to produce drawings that are highly effective in representing the shapes of objects, their spatial relations, and their orientations relative to each other and to the viewer. The characteristic drawing system associated with the final stage in drawings of rectangular objects is oblique projection; the use of variants such as perspective or inverted perspective will depend on the object to be drawn and the exemplars available in the child's pictorial environment.

Children's Drawings from Other Cultures

All the evidence I have given for this account of the developmental changes in children's drawings has been derived from drawings produced by American and English children. To what extent can this account be used to describe children's drawings from other cultures? This question is difficult to answer because of the paucity of evidence bearing on the subject. In an experiment similar to the table experiment described above, Court (1989, 1990, 1992) asked rural Kenyan school children aged 6 to 18 years to draw a table with three objects on it. Court's experiment was carried out in a classroom situation, however, and the children did not draw from a fixed viewpoint. This experiment was a component in a larger study involving children from three groups (Kamba, Luo, and Samburu) representative of the country's ethnic diversity. These groups have distinct traditions in the visual arts, none of which include drawing on paper. However, since 1985 these children had been required to draw as part of the school syllabus.

The table drawings were assigned to classes generally similar to those used by Willats (1977a) but with two additions. One was a class for drawings in which the table top was drawn as a true shape, but showing multiple viewpoints. These drawings can be regarded as versions of fold-out drawings. The other was for drawings in inverted perspective, and fig. 2.26 shows an example of a drawing in this class.

Court's results cannot be compared directly with those obtained by Willats; the experimental conditions were not the same, and the level of schooling was found to have a greater influence on performance than age.

However, Court's study shows that, with the exception of the two classes described above, drawings by rural Kenyan children could be categorized in the same way as drawings by English children and that, broadly speaking, the developmental sequence seemed to be very much the same. The main difference between these two studies was that Court found that the commonest drawing system used by the oldest group of Kenyan children was inverted perspective rather than perspective. Court suggested a number of possible explanations for this finding, but pointed out that not only is inverted perspective a popular east African convention, it is also used in formal education and is seen regularly on chalk boards in classrooms.

Another relevant study is that of Jahoda (1981), a replication of Willats (1977a) carried out with schooled and unschooled adults in Ghana. In his introduction Jahoda expressed his initial skepticism of Willats' claim, as he saw it, that "the development of at least the earlier stages of drawing development is independent of cultural influences" (p. 133). In his discussion of the results of the experiment, however, he remarked that "given the radical disparities in cultural background and age between Willats' original and the present sample, the broad congruence of the findings is remarkable," that "it was feasible to apply the analytical scheme to the Ghanaian subjects," and that "the whole range of drawing systems was represented" (pp. 140, 140). Jahoda found that there was no significant difference between the patterns of drawing systems used by unschooled and schooled adults, most of whom produced drawing in classes 1, 2, and 3, but that there was a significant tendency for university students to produce drawings in the higher classes (oblique projection and perspective). Jahoda concluded that "the boundary between Classes 3 and 4 [vertical oblique projection and oblique projection] represents a critical divide; in the absence of an environment rich in perspective drawings, it is not crossed" (p. 142).

Studies of figure drawings by children having no tradition of pictorial art are also fairly scarce. One key study is that of Deregowski (1978), who reexamined drawings collected by Fortes (1940). In Deregowski's study, spontaneous drawings made by African adults and children (the Tallensi of northern Ghana) who had never drawn before, obtained by Fortes in the 1930s, were compared with drawings made by subjects coming from the same population who had learned to draw under Western influence. Deregowski reproduced a number of drawings made by Tale children "unfamiliar with the art of drawing," and some of these are reproduced here (fig. 13.8). Deregowski called these "ideographic" drawings and noted that figures of this type are not unique to the Tallensi: similar figures were obtained by Degallier (1904) from subjects in the Congo, by Dennis (1960) from Syrian Bedouin, and by Haddon (1904) from three subjects in New Guinea. These drawings are also similar to the stone age rock engravings of people and animals in Camonica Valley (fig. 1.5). A comparison between the drawings obtained by Fortes from unschooled adults and children in the 1930s with drawings obtained at the same time from schooled subjects, and drawings obtained within the same population a generation later, showed that these "ideographic" drawings were rapidly superseded by "Western style" drawings as a result of schooling and cultural exposure.

Deregowski claimed that these children did not produce scribbles or tadpole figures as Western children do, and concluded that "it would be erroneous to suggest that a universal 'grammar of drawing' can be derived by examination of drawings obtained from Western populations only" (p. 479). However, in a more recent study, Martlew and Connolly (1996) questioned the validity of Deregowski's conclusions. It seems that some of Fortes's children did produce scribbles, and that Fortes drew a picture himself to show the children what to do, so that some of them may have imitated his drawing. The study by Martlew and Connolly was based on an analysis of 287 human figure drawings collected from schooled and unschooled children aged 10 to 15 years living in the Jimi Valley, a remote region of Papua New Guinea. All the children attending school produced conventional Western-type drawings, but the unschooled children produced drawings corresponding to the whole range of drawing types usually associated with Western children, including scribbles, tadpole figures, Western stick figures, and conventional figures. These children produced comparatively few elongated microcephalic drawings of the type described by Fortes (fig. 13.8), but they did produce a relatively high proportion of a type described by Martlew and Connolly as "Jimi Contour" (fig. 13.9c). It seems that these

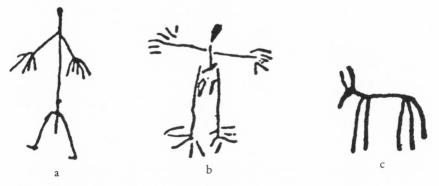

FIG. 13.8. Drawings by Tale children unfamiliar with drawing: (a) a man; (b) a woman; (c) a cow. From Deregowski (1978, fig. 2). Courtesy of Pion Ltd., London.

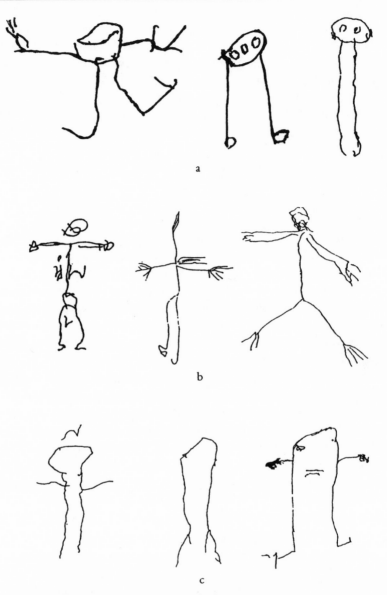

FIG. 13.9. Drawings by children from the Jimi Valley in Papua New Guinea: (a) tadpole figures; (b) Jimi stick figures; (c) Jimi contour figures. From Martlew and Connolly (1996). Copyright the Society for Research in Child Development.

children may have been attempting to use lines to denote true contours, but without having seen any more advanced exemplars: hence the relative crudity of these figure drawings, compared with drawings produced by Western children, such as the drawings shown in fig. 13.7d and (in part) fig. 13.7c, which are based on a denotation system in which lines stand for contours. These drawings may, however, be related to the early contour drawings by 4-, 5- and 6-year-olds described by Reith (1988).

Martlew and Connolly remarked that the range of drawings found in their study was strikingly similar to that found in the developmental sequence of figure drawings by Western children, and they concluded, as did Golomb (1992), that each child finds his or her solution to a drawing problem within a general set of rules. They also concluded that learning took place very rapidly among these teenagers when suitable exemplars were available.

It seems reasonable to conclude that, in the absence of evidence to the contrary, the classification schemes that I have proposed can be applied to children's drawings in all cultures, not just Western cultures. Moreover, in cultures where there is any evidence of a developmental sequence, drawings in the different classes appear in very much the same sequence. That is not to say that there are not considerable differences in drawings from different cultures, but these differences appear to be relatively superficial. The difference between perspective and inverted perspective, for example, is relatively superficial compared with the difference between both these systems and vertical oblique projection: in both these systems the orthogonals are represented by oblique lines and the shapes of the side and top faces of objects are distorted, whereas in vertical oblique projection the orthogonals are represented by vertical lines and the top face is represented as a true shape. Progression to the higher classes of systems in which objects are shown from a general direction of view is evidently very dependent on schooling and the presence of exemplars in the pictorial environment.

Mental Processes

What account of the mental processes underlying the development of drawing ability can be inferred from this account of developmental changes in the representational systems? If there is one single phrase that has been used over the past hundred years to sum up the development of drawing ability, it is that "young children draw what they know and older children draw what they see." One problem with this phrase is that it is so ambiguous that it can be used to cover almost any theory of drawing development.

However, as I remarked above, many writers now interpret this to mean that young children derive their drawings from object-centered internal shape descriptions, and older children derive their drawings from viewer-centered descriptions. The evidence obtained from the experiment described above in which children were asked to represent foreshortening seems to support this: most of the 4-year-olds did not change their drawings in order to represent foreshortening, suggesting that they were basing their drawings on object-centered descriptions, while a majority of the 7-year-olds and nearly all the 12-year-olds changed their drawings in response to a change of view from nonforeshortened to foreshortened, suggesting that they were basing their drawings on viewer-centered descriptions. However, these results were obtained in an experimental situation in which it was possible to compare *changes* in drawings in response to a change of view. It is dangerous to assume that just because a single, finished drawing provides a possible view it must therefore be derived from a viewer-centered internal description. For example, drawings of cubes in oblique projection are routinely described as representing the stage of visual realism (Phillips et al., 1978), and Nicholls and Kennedy (1992, p. 240) maintained that such drawings are produced by "matching directions from a vantage point." But as I have argued, such drawings can equally well be produced by applying a rule like "Draw the front face as a true shape and represent side edges by oblique lines" to an object-centered description of a cube. Without experimental evidence of the type described above, it is not safe to assume that just because an individual drawing provides a possible view, or even a general view, it must necessarily have been *derived* from a view.

Having said this, it is probably true to say that there *is* a general developmental change in the mental processes underlying children's production of drawings which can be captured by saying that young children base their drawings on object-centered descriptions and older children base their drawings on viewer-centered descriptions. The main evidence for this is the characteristic anomalies that appear in children's drawings, such as the fold-out drawings, and drawings of cubes containing the "flat bottom error," that are very difficult to explain except in terms of their derivation from object-centered descriptions.

It is important to distinguish between the mental processes underlying picture production and those underlying picture perception. The human visual system is designed to take in visual information in the form of views, and drawings that do not provide possible views do not look "right," at least to Western, adult eyes. It is sometimes suggested, however, that young children might prefer other types of drawing—fold-out drawings, for example—either because they provide information that the child regards as important, such as the true shapes of faces, or because they share common features with the child's own drawing. A number of studies have examined the relationship between children's drawings and their picture preferences, and most of these have found that children prefer drawings in which the representation of shape and space is more advanced than it is in the drawings they produce (Moore, 1986b, cites: Cox, 1981; Freeman, 1980; Golomb, 1973; Kosslyn, Heldmeyer, and Locklear, 1977; Lewis, 1963; Piaget and Inhelder, 1956; and Taylor and Bacharach, 1981). For example, Kosslyn et al. (1977) found that the overwhelming majority of 6-, 8-, and 11-year-olds, and three-quarters of their 4-year-olds, preferred "conventional perspective" drawings to "diagrammatic" drawings (that is, fold-out drawings). Moore (1986b) questioned these results, and found in her own study that children of all ages preferred drawings that had most features in common with their own productions. However, Moore's study only compared drawings (of a house) in perspective with drawings in orthogonal projection, both of which showed possible views.

Looking at the sequences of drawings produced by children of different ages, sequences like those exemplified by the children's drawings of tables shown in fig. 13.1, or the drawings of an unfamiliar object shown in figs. 13.2 and 13.3, or the drawings of sticks and discs in foreshortened positions shown in figs. 13.4 to 13.6, or the drawings of people shown in fig. 13.7, it is obvious that the drawings by older children are more *effective as shape representations* than the drawings by younger children. Luquet suggested that what children are trying to do when they are learning to draw is produce *recognizable representations,* that is, drawings in which the objects they intend to portray can easily be recognized. However, if the main way in which we recognize objects is through their shapes, then if children are to produce drawings that are recognizable as representations, they have to learn ways of producing effective representations of their *shapes.* Doing this necessarily involves learning the appropriate drawing and denotation systems.

This still leaves open the question of whether the main factor involved in drawing development is the growing child's intention to produce pictures that are more like adult pictures, or the intention to produce pictures that are more effective as representations, but this question is almost impossible to answer in Western cultures because both factors point in the same direction. What evidence we have from other cultures suggests that the early stages of drawing development are broadly similar across cultures, and this in turn suggests that development in these early stages is driven by innate mechanisms. If we can legitimately speak of a language instinct (Pinker, 1994), it seems equally legitimate to speak of a "drawing instinct." Beyond these early stages, however, further development takes place only when adult models are present as exemplars in the pictorial environment. When such models are introduced to cultures without a pictorial tradition, the adoption of a more advanced style appears to take place very rapidly. This does not mean that children necessarily copy such models directly; rather that they provide answers to drawing problems that children are already trying to solve.

The mechanism behind the developmental sequence I have described can be seen as a series of interactions between picture production and picture perception (Willats, 1984). In the early years of drawing development, most drawings are derived from object-centered internal descriptions. As a result, drawings are produced at each intermediate stage that may *be* right, in the sense of being the outcome of sensible and logical solutions to drawing problems, like the problem of showing more than one face in the drawing of a rectangular object; but such drawings do not necessarily *look* right. If the application of particular drawing and denotation rules results in drawings that look right, these rules will be retained; if not, they will be changed.[11] For example, fold-out drawings provide a sensible way of showing all three of the visible faces of a cube, but they look "wrong" to adults—and, the results of Kosslyn et al. (1977) would suggest, even to the children producing them. In order to produce drawings in oblique projection that show all three faces but also look "right," children have to abandon a denotation system in which regions denote faces, and adopt a new system in which lines denote edges.

In theory, this mechanism would be sufficient to enable a talented individual child, working in isolation, to reach the stage of oblique projection or perspective. In practice, children need to see how particular drawing problems are solved by seeing the solutions in pictures by adults or other children. For example, the change from fold-out drawings to oblique projections is a difficult transition to make, and Jahoda's results suggest that children are unlikely to make this transition unless they are brought up in a rich pictorial environment, or given some specific teaching, or both.

Doubtless, children need to become aware, consciously or otherwise, that there are such things as views of objects to be drawn in order to acquire the intention to draw them; and doubtless they need the necessary motor skills in order to put their intentions into effect. However, the results of the experiment described above in which children were confronted with the problem of representing foreshortening show quite clearly that seeing a view, and being able to reproduce its geometry correctly, is not all that is necessary in order to produce an effective representation of a foreshortened shape. Learning to draw involves learning the appropriate drawing and denotation rules, and children do this by seeking solutions to specific drawing problems.

CHAPTER FOURTEEN

Historical Changes

In the previous chapter, I described the developmental changes that take place in children's drawings. Children begin by basing their drawings on topological relations and the representation of extendedness, and a denotation system in which regions stand for whole volumes, and end by combining oblique projection or some form of perspective with line drawing, including the use of T- and end-junctions to represent points of occlusion. I argued that these changes in the drawing and denotation systems take place because children want to produce pictures in which objects such as tables and people can be recognized; and the only way in which they can do this is to discover more effective ways of representing the shapes of such objects and the spatial relations between them.

In this chapter I shall describe the use of representational systems, and the changes in these systems, during two periods in art history. The first period covers the development of Greek vase painting from the eighth to the fourth century B.C. The second includes Orthodox Christian art from the fifth to the fifteenth century A.D.

In the earliest period of Greek vase painting the paintings are pure silhouettes: areas of paint on a lighter ground. Although there may be some indication of a ground line suggesting the use of orthogonal projection, the spatial relations are essentially topological and the denotation system is one in which regions denote either volumes or regions in the frontal plane. In the final period the drawing systems used are either orthogonal projection or oblique projection and naive perspective, while the denotation systems are either pure line drawing, including the use of T- and end-junctions denoting points of occlusion, or a combination of line drawing with silhouette.

The pattern of development in Greek vase painting is thus in some ways quite similar to the pattern of development in children's drawings, but there are some significant differences. The first is that the use of orthogonal projection persisted throughout the whole period of development: even relatively late and sophisticated paintings, like the *Leave-taking* shown in fig. 11.3, are often based on orthogonal projection rather than oblique projection or perspective. Second, there is little or no evidence of the presence of anomalous drawing systems in Greek vase painting, such as the fold-out drawings and drawings containing the flat bottom error which are quite commonly found in children's drawings. The third difference is that the Greek vase painters began by using areas of paint as marks, and this confronted them with problems, such as the problem of representing details within the outline, which children, who use lines as marks from the very beginning, do not have to face. As a result there is one important change that took place during the course of the development of Greek vase painting— the change from the black-figure style to the red-figure style—which has no counterpart in children's drawing development.

Having said this, there is still a remarkable similarity between the patterns of development in children's drawings and Greek vase paintings. I shall argue that this similarity does not occur because children's drawing development recapitulates art history in some biological sense, but because the Greek vase painters were trying to solve very much the same drawing problems as those that confront children: the problems that confront any artist or draftsman who is trying to produce pictures that provide effective shape representations.

The pattern of development in Orthodox art is radically different: in fact the most striking characteristic of Orthodox art is its relative lack of change, compared with the huge changes that took place in Greek vase painting. That is not to say, of course, that there were no stylistic differences within Byzantine art or Greek or Russian icon painting during the period from the fifth to the fifteenth century.[1] But during this period there were no changes in the drawing and denotation systems used by Orthodox artists that can be seen to form a significant pattern of development in any one direction, comparable to the changes that took place in Greek vase painting over a much shorter period. The commonest drawing systems used in Orthodox art are inverted perspective and horizontal oblique projection. Individual rectangular objects such as tables or buildings are normally depicted in horizontal oblique projection, oblique projection, or inverted perspective, and where a number of objects are shown together the orthogonals commonly diverge. Where buildings are depicted in horizontal oblique projection they are commonly set on a ground plane that is folded down, so that the geometry of the depiction is similar to that of the fold-out pictures found in children's drawings. The denotation systems in Orthodox art vary a good deal. The element of silhouette is often emphasized, but the predominant system within the silhouette is either line drawing, or line drawing with the addition of tonal modeling; cast shadows are rare or nonexistent. The way in which line drawing is used is, however, often anomalous. In contrast with the way in which line drawing was used in Greek vase painting, and is normally used in Western "realistic" line drawings, like the drawing of a boy analyzed by Guzman (fig. 4.1) or the Japanese woodcut of wrestlers (fig. 5.9), the line drawing in Orthodox art often contains forbidden configurations, like those shown in fig. 1.14, and the direction of tonal contrast is often reversed, so that the line drawing is carried out using light lines on a darker ground. Thus the characteristic features of Orthodox art are a general lack of developmental change, and the use of anomalous drawing and denotation systems.

I shall argue that these characteristic features are present in Orthodox art because they serve quite specific functions. It was important that the faithful should be able to recognize the figures portrayed in Byzantine mosaics and Greek and Russian icon paintings, but it was also important, in order to avoid the dangers of idolatry, that these figures should not be seen to inhabit a world that could be confused with the everyday world of time and space inhabited by the worshiper. I shall argue that this representational problem was solved by the use of anomalous drawing and denotation systems; and I shall also argue that once this problem had been solved, as it effectively had been by the fifth century, there was no further necessity for any form of developmental change.

It should be possible to apply the categorization schemes I have described to the analysis of pictures from any period in art history, although such an undertaking would of course be far beyond the scope of this book or the abilities of any one author. Faced with the problem of choosing examples of how this might be done, I have chosen to describe the representational systems in Greek vase painting and Orthodox art for the following reasons. First, explaining the existence of anomalous representational systems provides a test for the adequacy of any theory of pictures. The existence of inverted perspective in artists' pictures, especially, is difficult to explain within purely optical theories such as those of J. J. Gibson and Margaret Hagen. Inverted perspective is found in Cubist paintings, in Chinese and Japanese paintings, and in Orthodox art; but Cubism was a relatively short-lived movement, and the use of inverted perspective in Oriental art is relatively uncommon, so it is possible to dismiss its appearance in these instances as the result of either incompetence, or "simple experimentation with layout techniques on the part of isolated artists" (Hagen, 1986, p. 149).

It is, however, much more difficult to apply this argument to the use of inverted perspective in Orthodox art, where it persisted for over a thousand years and formed the basis for such masterpieces as the Ravenna mosaics and Rublev's *The Holy Trinity.*

Second, the similarity between the patterns of development in children's drawing and Greek vase painting is so marked that it cries out for an explanation. If evolutionism is dead, and it is no longer possible to claim that child art recapitulates art history, providing an alternative explanation for this similarity poses a second test for any proposed theory of pictures. Again, the explanation I propose is that the patterns of development are similar in these two cases because the representational systems involved are intended to serve similar functions.

Together, descriptions of the drawing and denotation systems employed by artists in these two periods provide evidence for a theory of pictures that avoids the difficulties of an evolutionary theory of art history as well as the problems associated with purely optical theories of representation that predict no significant patterns of development. Different ages and different nations have represented the visible world in different ways because the representational systems used in these ages and nations have served different functions.

The Development of Greek Vase Painting

In his description of the spatial systems employed in Greek vase painting, White (1967) restricted his analysis to an account of the ways in which rectangular objects were represented. The reason White gave for adopting this restriction was that an analysis of this kind can be relatively objective: "the distortions of all angles and surfaces can be measured exactly, and the accuracy of construction in relation to vanishing points and the like can be assessed in detail" (p. 21).

Although I have a certain sympathy for this approach, I shall, instead, begin my account of the changes in the spatial systems in Greek vase painting by describing changes in the denotation systems employed in the representations of smooth objects, especially the human figure. The human figure, rather than rectangular objects, is the main subject matter in Greek vase painting: there are relatively few representations of rectangular objects in the earlier paintings. Moreover, it is possible to be just as objective about the changes in the denotation systems as it is about changes in the drawing systems. Regions either have internal structures or they do not, and it is usually possible to be confident about whether line drawings do or do not contain T- and end-junctions. Moreover, as I have tried to show in my account of children's drawings, a precondition for the discovery of more complex *drawing* systems in the representation of rectangular objects is the adoption of more developed *denotation* systems. An artist or draftsman who is tied to a denotation system in which regions in the picture are used to stand for volumes or faces in object-centered descriptions (as they are in fold-out drawings, for example) cannot use systems such as oblique projection or perspective because the shapes of the faces of rectangular objects represented in these systems have to be distorted out of their true shapes. I shall, therefore, take changes in the denotation systems rather than changes in the drawing systems as the primary indicators of developmental change.

If we look at the whole course of the development of Greek vase painting from the geometric period to the fourth century B.C., it is obvious that the paintings at the end of this period provide more effective shape representations than the paintings at the beginning. In Chapter 13, I made very much the same observation about the development of children's drawings. The drawings of rectangular objects by the older children shown in fig. 13.2 are better as representations than the drawings by the younger children, and the *Self-Portrait with Dogs* by Joanne shown in fig. 1.7 is clearly better in its representation of the shapes of smooth forms than the tadpole drawing by a 5-year-old shown in fig. 1.12. Of course, the later Greek vase paintings, such as the painting of *Woman Handing a Garment to a Girl* by the Achilles painter (fig. 11.4), show far greater technical sophistication and psychological penetration than the *Self-Portrait with Dogs*. But on a purely formal level it would not be unreasonable to compare these two pictures. Both are, in effect, line drawings, and both contain numerous T- and end-junctions correctly representing points of occlusion.

On the other hand, the three figures in the vase painting from the geometric period shown in fig. 14.1 look very different from the tadpole figures shown in figs. 1.12 and 13.7a. One obvious difference is that the body proportions in this vase painting are much more realistic than they are in the children's drawings. The other obvious difference is that marks in the early Greek vase paintings are silhouettes, whereas in most children's early drawings the marks are lines.

However, I argued in previous chapters that although most young children use lines as marks, the fundamental denotation system in children's early drawings is one in which the picture primitives are *regions* rather than lines. For example, I argued that the outline of the head or head/body in the drawing by the 5-year-old boy shown in fig. 1.12 ought not to be understood as representing a contour, at least in picture production. Instead, I suggested in the analysis given in fig. 4.5 that the picture primitives in this drawing are regions: the large round region stands for the head or head/body as a round volume, and the lines representing the legs are best understood as long regions standing for the legs as long volumes. The marks employed in the early Greek vase paintings—areas of dark paint on a lighter ground—thus reveal what the lines in children's early drawings disguise: the picture primitives in these paintings are regions, and in early paintings of this type it is the shapes of these regions that are significant, rather than the shapes of their outlines.

Greek vase painting began in about 1000 B.C. with the geometric style, so-called because much of the surface of the vase was covered with geometric patterns. At the height of the style, figure subjects began to appear, painted in pure silhouette without any internal lines or other marks. In the earliest of these paintings there is no foreshortening and no representation of occlusion. A colossal amphora in the National Museum in Athens dating from the eighth century B.C., for example (Pfuhl, 1955), shows a mourning scene with the dead person on a bier and the mourners ranged on either side with their arms raised: there is no representation of occlusion and no foreshortening. The bodies of the figures are represented by triangular regions, the heads by round regions with a protrusion for the chin, and the arms by long thin regions. The shapes of the legs are a little more complex: long regions thickened in two places to represent the thighs and calves, and with smaller regions at the end to represent the feet.

It is difficult to be sure about the spatial systems in pictures of this kind, but the absence of any representation of foreshortening or occlusion suggests that the regions in these very early paintings were intended to denote whole volumes, as they do in children's early drawings. The shapes of the regions in these paintings are, however, more complex than they are in most tadpole figures, suggesting that a number of shape modifiers like "having bumps" (for the nose and chin) and "being narrow at the bottom" (for the upper part of the body) have been added to the basic representation of extendedness. As in children's early drawings, however, these individual body parts are joined to each other by the topological relation "being connected."

Fig. 14.1 shows a painting of *Three Men, One Standing on His Head,* from about the same period. The style of this painting is similar to that of the painting described above, but the brushwork of the upper parts of the bodies of the standing figures flows into that of the lower body and legs, so that the outline of each figure forms a more coherent whole. The arms, however, are still represented separately by long bent regions. There is, in addition, some tentative representation of occlusion, most noticeably where the arms of the standing figures overlap their bodies. Perhaps it would be reasonable to say that the shapes of the painted regions are beginning to resemble the shapes of regions in the frontal plane, and that although the shapes of these individual regions are still important, the shapes of the outlines of the regions are beginning to resemble contours. A painting of this kind represents the beginning of the transition from a denotation system in which regions denote volumes to a system in which regions denote regions in the frontal plane.

Fig. 14.2 shows a vase painted in the late geometric style, c. 700 B.C. In the scene illustrated in this painting, one arm of the figure driving the chariot is shown overlapping the body, the chariot pole overlaps the legs of the horses, and one of the figures is shown astride a horse. The representation of occlusion in pure silhouette necessarily involves some ambiguity, although in this painting the ambiguity is kept to a minimum by ensuring that the

FIG. 14.1. Attic oinoche, *Three Men, One Standing on His Head,* geometric style, eighth century B.C. Ceramic, ht. 18 cm. Richard Norton Memorial Fund. Courtesy of Museum of Fine Arts, Boston.

beginnings and ends of all the overlapping forms are shown and that the area of overlap is as small as possible. For example, the chariot pole crosses the back legs of the horses at a point where we can see it crossing a gap in the legs. However, there is a limit to what can be done in this respect, and the relatively wide area of overlap where the rider's body and legs overlap the horse is beginning to cause a problem. An additional problem is that details within the outlines of the regions, such as the eyes and details of clothing, cannot be shown in pictures painted in pure silhouette.

These problems can be solved in two ways: by introducing additional regions in different colors or tones within the outlines of the main silhouette, or by introducing interior lines. Additional regions within the silhouette seem to have been introduced first: in the vase painting shown in fig. 14.2 the eyes of the figures and the horses, and the ends of the axle-trees, are shown using separate regions; but there are no interior lines.

In vases painted during the next phase of development, the orientalizing period, both techniques were combined, enabling relatively complex arrangements of figures or parts of figures to be shown overlapping each other, and details such as the eyes and clothing to be shown within the silhouette. The background of the painting was filled with ornament. Fig. 14.3 shows a

FIG. 14.2. Amphora, dipylon, *Procession of Two Horse Chariots,* late geometric style, eighth century B.C. Ceramic, ht. 77.7 cm. Metropolitan Museum of Art, New York, Rogers Fund, 1910.

vase painted in the black–and–white style in which both lines and areas of white in silhouette appear within the main outlines of the figures. Most of the lines are used to represent surface details, such as the feathers of the owl, rather than shape features, and most of the white areas are used either for decorative purposes or to depict separate parts of the figure within the main silhouette. However, the regions representing the arms and legs of the centaur kneeling in front of Herakles are outlined in white; and because one of the front legs is shown overlapping the other, a T-junction appears within the silhouette. Similarly, the regions representing Herakles' legs are filled in with white, leaving the outline of the silhouette as a black line. Although these lines still essentially represent the outlines of regions, they are beginning to play a first tentative role in the representation of occluding contours.

As time went on, the ornamental backgrounds of these paintings began to disappear, and the use of interior lines began to predominate over the use of areas of different colors, leading eventually to what is called the "black-figure" style. Fig. 14.4 shows an early example of a black-figure vase painting, together with a detail of the painting redrawn in pure silhouette. This redrawing shows that it is now the shapes of the outlines of the silhouette that are important rather than the overall shapes of the regions.

FIG. 14.3. Pro-Amphora, *Herakles and Nessos,* Attic, orientalizing style, second quarter of the seventh century B.C. Ceramic, ht. 108.5 cm. Metropolitan Museum of Art, New York, Rogers Fund, 1911.

The convexities and concavities of the outline correspond to the shapes of the contours, and thus to the surface shapes, of features like the nose and mouth, as they do in the portrait silhouette of a *Lady Taking Tea* shown in fig. 5.1; they are no longer just bumps or dents added to the shapes of the regions as they are in the paintings of the geometric period. The picture primitives in paintings of this type are thus lines rather than regions, and it is obvious from the redrawing that without the addition of interior lines within the silhouette, parts of this image would be very ambiguous. Moreover, some of these interior lines clearly denote occluding contours: the underarm of the seated figure facing forward ends correctly in an end-junction denoting a point of occlusion.

Although the introduction of interior lines would have allowed the effective representation of foreshortening, as it did in the 12-year-olds' drawings of the arms and the plate shown in fig. 13.6, no such foreshortening appears in this painting. The wheel of the chariot and the wreath are both shown in nonforeshortened positions, the heads are shown in profile, and none of the limbs of the figures is foreshortened.

Some time toward the end of the sixth century B.C. a dramatic change took place in the *mark* system used in Greek vase painting: the invention of the red-figure style. In this technique the figures were silhouetted in red (the natural color of the clay), while the background was filled in with a lustrous

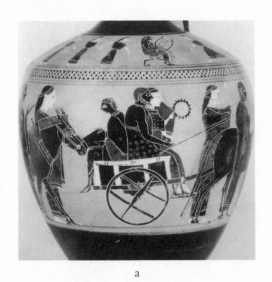

a   b

FIG. 14.4. Amasis painter, *Wedding Ceremony*, black-figure style, c. 550 B.C. Metropolitan Museum of Art New York. (a) Detail of vase painting. (b) Silhouette of subject, with internal lines and regions removed.

black glaze. Internal lines were added within the silhouette, using either thin lines of pure black glaze in slight relief, or lines of varying thickness carried out in diluted glaze giving a tonal range from dark brown to translucent yellow (fig. 14.5). The denotation system, however, remained essentially the same as it was in the later black-figure paintings: regions with interior lines, with the lines denoting edges and occluding contours.

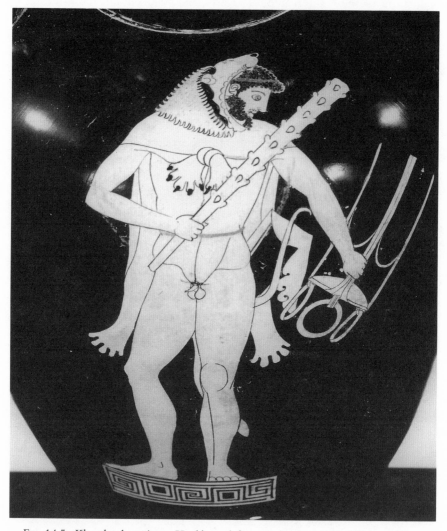

Fig. 14.5. Kleophrades painter, *Herakles,* red-figure style, about 490–480 B.C. Metropolitan Museum of Art, New York.

What was the motive behind this change? Gombrich (1960/1988) illustrated two sides of a late-sixth-century vase showing two identical scenes of *Herakles and the Cretan Bull,* one side of which is painted in the black-figure style and the other in the red-figure style, and he suggested that the direction of tonal contrast—light on dark or dark on light—was relatively unimportant; and it is true that the black-figure style continued to be used by some painters for another hundred years. Von Bothmer (1987), however, suggested that the red-figure style offered two advantages compared with the black-figure style: first, that the picture carried better over a greater distance; and second, that because the black of the background merges with the parts of the vase that have no figures painted on them, the outlines of the vase were less eroded by the decoration, and the integrity of the shape of the contour of the vase was preserved.

It seems possible, however, that a more direct perceptual factor is involved, and that line drawings carried out in a dark tone against a light background are more effective as representations per se than similar drawings carried out in a light tone against a dark background. The evidence for this is provided by an experiment carried out by Pearson et al. (1990). In Chapter 5, I described the method they used to derive line drawings from gray-scale images, which involved the use of a feature detector which they called a "cartoon operator." This operator scanned the gray-scale image in order to pick out a combination of "luminance valleys" and "luminance steps," and these features were then represented by lines. Pearson et al. used a feature detector of this kind because they proposed that luminance valleys in the cross-section of the light from a scene correspond to occluding contours; and they were able to show that this operation does in fact result in acceptable line drawings (fig. 14.6a).

Their earliest drawings were produced in white on a black background as shown on the left in fig. 14.6d. However, they noticed that when these drawings were inverted electronically, turning black to white and white to black, they looked more natural. For example, the drawing shown on the right in fig. 14.6a, which is carried out using black lines on a white background, looks more natural than the drawing on the left in fig. 14.6d. Why is this?

It is generally agreed that it is easier to recognize a person in a photographic positive than it is to recognize the same person in a photographic negative. Pearson et al. acknowledged that this might be due simply to our greater familiarity with photographic positives, and that recognition with negatives might improve with training. A similar argument might also apply to white-on-black line drawings. However, they suggested that the effect

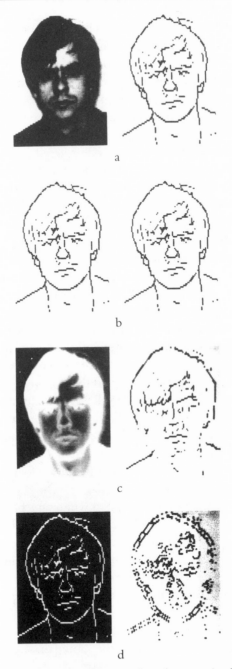

FIG. 14.6. The significance of the direction of tonal contrast in photographs and line drawings. The drawings on the right in figs. (a) to (d) show the results of passing the photographs and drawings on the left through a "cartoon operator" with a primary sensitivity to luminance valleys. From Pearson et al. (1990), courtesy of Don Pearson.

might be better explained by supposing that the early stages of the human visual system involve a feature detector, similar in its operation to their cartoon operator, which has its primary sensitivity to luminance valleys. In a drawing made up of black lines on a white ground the luminance valleys of the original image, derived from occluding contours in a view of the scene, are preserved as luminance valleys in the drawing; as a result, the drawing looks "natural." In a drawing carried out in white lines on a black background, however, the luminance valleys are turned to luminance *ridges:* bands of high light intensity with a low intensity on either side. These ridges would, if they had been derived from a real scene, represent entirely different surface shapes. By virtue of its flexibility and powers of high-level processing, however, the human visual system still interprets the drawing as a representation of a face, so there is, in drawings of this kind, a conflict between the representation of surface shape actually provided by the lines in the drawing, and our knowledge of the surface shapes of faces stored in long-term memory. As a result, white-on-black drawings look unnatural or anomalous compared with black-on-white drawings.

To test this argument, Pearson et al. passed the four images shown on the left in fig. 14.6 through their cartoon operator, and the results of these operations are shown in the images on the right. The result of putting the photographic positive through the operator was to produce the black-on-white line drawing shown in fig. 14.6a. When this drawing was itself used as the input for the operator, it passed through *unchanged,* as shown in fig. 14.6b. This suggests that a black-on-white line drawing produces a response in the early stages of the visual system that is very similar to that which would have been obtained from a full gray-scale view of a real scene. This would explain why black-on-white line drawings, like Picasso's drawing of Stravinsky (fig. 1.6), provide such effective shape representations, even though the actual array of light from such a picture is quite different from that which could be obtained from a real scene.

When the photographic negative and the white-on-black line drawing were put through the same operator, however, the results, shown in figs. 14.6c and 14.6d, were very different: neither operation resulted in an acceptable image. This suggests that neither photographic negatives nor white-on-black line drawings produce similar early visual responses to those that could be obtained from real scenes. This experiment thus suggests a possible physiological basis for the intuition that black-on-white line drawings are better as representations than white-on-black line drawings: the early stages of the human visual system may contain a feature detector that responds to luminance *valleys* but not luminance ridges.

The element of silhouette in both the red-figure and black-figure styles in Greek vase painting can correspond to reasonably natural lighting conditions—figures lit from behind, or from in front, both of which might be encountered in views of real scenes—and the visual system is presumably designed to accept both these kinds of images. So far as the element of *silhouette* in Greek vase painting is concerned, therefore, the alternative directions of tonal contrast—light-on-dark or dark-on-light—can seem equally natural. However, both our intuitions and the experiment described above suggest that the direction of tonal contrast in the line drawing *within* the silhouette in the black-figure paintings is unnatural, compared with the direction of tonal contrast in the red-figure paintings. This may be the reason why the black-figure style eventually came to be replaced by the red-figure style. In fig. 14.7 the direction of tonal contrast in the red-figure painting shown in fig. 14.5 has been reversed for comparison, and it does seem to be the case that the original red-figure painting provides a more effective shape representation than its counterpart in which the direction of tonal contrast has been reversed.

In previous chapters, I drew attention to the difficulty of portraying the foreshortening of sticks and discs in pictures based on regions as primitives. Line drawing, or a combination of line drawing with silhouette, makes possible the effective representation of foreshortening in a way that is not possible with silhouette alone. However, showing discs in foreshortened positions is easier than showing sticks in foreshortened positions, even within pure line drawings. As fig. 3.5 shows, both round regions and long regions provide about equally effective representations of discs, and the addition of an element of line drawing within the silhouette is sufficient to make clear the shape that the artist intends to portray. In contrast, a round or nearly round region, as a representation of a foreshortened or nearly fore-shortened stick, provides only a very poor representation, and even in pure line drawing the round shape of the outline of the drawing is in conflict with the extendedness of a stick in three-dimensional space, as it is in the child's drawing shown in fig. 13.5c. When line drawing is combined with the use of silhouette, as it is in both the black-figure and red-figure styles, the difficulty of showing the foreshortening of long shapes like arms and legs is increased, because the use of silhouette will tend to emphasize the shape of the outline, and thus the shape of the region it encloses, at the expense of the interior lines—especially, of course, if the painting is seen from some distance away. In the red-figure painting of Herakles shown in fig. 14.5, the foreshortening of the bowl and the partial foreshortening of the side rings of the tripod are both represented in a completely successful way, but the foreshortening of Herakles' left foot seems rather awkward, perhaps because the use of silhouette reduces the shape of the outline of the foot to a shape that is about equally extended in both directions, rather than a long shape. In contrast, the representation of the foreshortening of the left foot of the warrior in *Leave-taking* (fig. 11.3a) seems completely successful, presumably because this is shown using pure line drawing rather than a combina-

FIG. 14.7. Red-figure painting of *Herakles* (fig. 14.5) in which the direction of tonal contrast has been reversed photographically so as to simulate a black-figure painting. Photograph by Simon Ferguson.

tion of line drawing and silhouette. Perhaps for similar reasons many Greek vase painters persisted in showing heads in profile (a technique very well suited to a representation in pure silhouette or a combination of silhouette and line drawing) even when the use of interior lines within the silhouette would have enabled them to show three-quarter views. The shape of the

FIG. 14.8. Apulian volute krater, *Phoenix and Achilles,* red-figure style, South Italian, 350–340 B.C. Ceramic, ht. 2.46 m. Courtesy of Museum of Fine Arts, Boston, Francis Bartlett Fund.

outline of a head painted in profile represents the head as a "lump with a bump," thus reflecting its extendedness together with "having a bump" (the nose) as one of its nonaccidental shape properties. In contrast, the outlines of the silhouettes in the three-quarter views of the heads of the figures shown in fig. 14.8 represent the heads as "lumps"; it is only the inclusion of interior lines within the silhouettes that enables us to recognize their features.

White (1967) has described the development of the representation of rectangular objects in Greek vase painting, and there is no need to repeat this story in any detail. In most early Greek vase paintings, rectangular or nearly rectangular objects such as chairs and tables are shown in orthogonal projection in unforeshortened positions, and the ground plane is represented by a single line, as in the red-figure painting of *Herakles Feasting* shown in fig. 1.3. According to White, foreshortened settings first appeared in red-figure paintings from the beginning of the second quarter of the fifth century B.C.: in these paintings, objects such as chairs or stools are shown in slightly foreshortened positions, so that first one and then two of the rear legs appear. In later versions it is sometimes possible to catch a glimpse of the underside of a chair or stool, suggesting the use of perspective; but in most of these drawings the element of perspective is very slight, and they are probably better regarded as showing foreshortened views in orthogonal projection. There is no element of perspective in the relatively late and very carefully drawn chair in *Leave-taking* (fig. 11.3a), for example. True horizontal oblique projections (White calls them "complex frontal settings"), in which both the side and front faces of objects are shown as true shapes, are very rare in Greek vase painting, and I know of no examples of vertical oblique projections. Thus when drawings of rectangular objects in oblique projection began to appear, they had no obvious precursors in the form of horizontal or vertical oblique projections or fold-out drawings, as in the development of children's drawings. Finally, by combining representations of the undersides of temple ceilings in oblique projection with representations of their bases seen at eye level, the Greek vase painters were able to evolve a simple form of perspective (fig. 14.8).

All these developments in the representation of both smooth and round objects were critically dependent on changes in the denotation systems used in Greek vase painting. In the earliest vase paintings, figures are represented in pure silhouette. There are no surface details within the silhouette, no representation of occlusion, and no foreshortening. In the early black-figure vases, the use of some internal lines made possible the representation of occlusion and a limited amount of foreshortening. In the later black-figure vases, and with the invention of the red-figure style, the element of line drawing became more dominant and the foreshortening of smooth forms such as the limbs of figures was represented more freely. Finally, in the fifth century B.C., pure line drawing began to be used for the tomb lekythoi, while the red-figure technique continued to be used for more robust subject matter. In these later paintings the foreshortening is completely assured, and end-junctions are used freely and correctly for the points where contours end. In the earlier paintings, rectangular objects are shown in pure frontal settings in orthogonal projection. In the red-figure paintings and the tomb lekythoi, such objects are often shown in gently foreshortened positions, turned about a vertical axis. Finally, oblique projection was discovered, together with a simple form of perspective, so that rectangular objects could be shown from a completely general direction of view.

Comparing the later Greek vase paintings with the earlier ones, we can thus say, as we can of drawings by older children, that the later paintings are more effective as shape representations: the three-dimensional shapes of objects, and their orientations, can be seen more clearly and unambiguously in the later paintings than they can in the earlier ones. Consequently it is possible to recognize objects more readily in the later paintings than in the early paintings.

The actual course of development of Greek vase painting is, however, different in detail from that of children's drawings. The most important difference is that children use lines as marks in their early drawings, whereas the early Greek vase painters used areas of black paint on a red ground. No doubt this difference is due in part to the fact that children are provided with crayons, pencils, ballpoint pens, and felt pens with which to draw, all of which make lines rather than areas as marks, and in part to the fact that children are surrounded by line drawings in their pictorial environment. As a result, children use lines as marks even though, as I have argued, their earliest drawings such as the tadpole figures are based on an underlying denotation system in which regions denote volumes. Using lines as marks confers a great initial advantage on children, because it enables them to represent features such as eyes and details of clothing within the outlines of even their earliest figure drawings.

In contrast, the natural instrument for the Greek vase painters was a brush, and there were no line drawings in their pictorial environment. Consequently, the early Greek vase paintings exemplify in a pure form the use of a denotation system based on regions as primitives, whereas in children's drawings the presence of this system is disguised by the instruments they use and their familiarity with the mark system used in adult line drawings.

The other major difference between the development of children's drawings and Greek vase painting is that there are none, or hardly any, of the anomalous constructions such as the fold-out drawings so common in children's drawings of rectangular objects. At first one is tempted to think that the Greek vase painters might have made their mistakes in trial drawings and corrected them in the finished paintings, but this does not seem very likely. The reason for the absence of anomalies of this kind is probably due to the fact that the Greek vase painters continued to use orthogonal projection throughout the whole period of development: the use of oblique projection is actually quite uncommon, even in the later paintings. Consequently, the anomalies that arise in children's drawings as a result of their attempts to depict three or more sides at once, first in the form of fold-out drawings and then in the near-obliques, simply do not arise. Why the Greek vase painters persisted in the use of orthogonal projection, even in their most sophisticated drawings such as *Leave-taking,* is another matter. Probably it was, as White suggested, to avoid disrupting the picture surface: the examples of oblique projection or perspective that appear in the later paintings do not seem to sit comfortably on the curved surface of the vase. Moreover, it must be remembered that the Greeks had no examples of oblique projection in their pictorial environment, whereas children are constantly presented with examples of rectangular objects shown from a general direction of view which they naturally wish to emulate. Against this background the discovery of oblique projection by the Greek vase painters was a very significant development in the history of painting: as significant in its way as the discovery of perspective, to which it is an essential precursor.

The course of development of Greek vase painting thus suggests that a primary aim of the Greek vase painters was, as it is with children, to produce pictures that are more effective as shape representations. Each successive change, from pure silhouette, to the orientalizing style, to black-figure painting, to red-figure painting, and finally to pure line drawing in the white-ground style, was prompted by the need to solve quite specific representational problems; and each change resulted in pictures that were more effective as representations. Thus in at least one period of art history it is possible, as it is in the acquisition of drawing ability in children, to demonstrate the existence of a systematic pattern of development which might justly be called progress.

Orthodox Art

In contrast, Orthodox art shows no such pattern of development. The term *Orthodox art* is used here to include the Christian religious art of the Byzantine Empire and the icon paintings of the Orthodox Church. The history of the Byzantine Empire began in A.D. 330, when Constantine the

Great founded a new capital for the Roman Empire, and ended with the sack of Constantinople by the Turks in 1453. With Constantine's conversion to Christianity the age of martyrdom and persecution ended, and within fifty years of Constantine's death Christianity became "not merely the most highly favored but the only recognized religion of the Empire" (Ware, 1993, p. 18). The establishment of what became the Orthodox Church resulted in the first golden age of Byzantine art, which reached its climax in the sixth century with the building of St. Sophia and the mosaics at Ravenna. During the eighth and ninth centuries the Iconoclast controversy raged between those (the "Iconodules") who supported the use of representations of Christ and the saints for purposes of worship and as part of the liturgy, and the "Iconoclasts" who were opposed to representational art on the grounds that it led to idolatry.[2] This controversy lasted for about 120 years and ended in 843 with the victory of those who supported the use of icons, an event often referred to as the "Triumph of Orthodoxy." The period that followed, known as the second golden age, took place when the empire was at the height of its power, while the third golden age coincided with its political decline. However, this decline was not reflected in its art, which influenced artists throughout Europe and as far as Russia.

After the fall of Constantinople, Russia was the only nation capable of assuming the leadership of eastern Christendom, and people came to think of Moscow as "the third Rome," the center of Orthodoxy.[3] The two centuries from 1350 to 1550 marked the high point of Russian icon painting: during these years the Russian painters perfected the traditions they had taken over from Byzantium, and *The Holy Trinity* (color plate 1) by Andrei Rublev (c. 1360–1430) is widely regarded as the finest of all Orthodox icon paintings.

From a formal point of view, what strikes the nonspecialist most about Orthodox art is its use of anomalous representational systems and its relative lack of change. Whereas there is an obvious developmental sequence in the way spatial relations are represented in Greek vase painting, and equally obvious changes in painting during the Renaissance period, through the Baroque and Neo-Classical periods, through Impressionism and Cubism to the present day,[4] much the same drawing and denotation systems seem to have been employed in Byzantine art and Russian icon painting during a period of well over a thousand years.

Moreover, this period was not just a pause for breath between two stages in the development of representational systems. By the fourth century B.C. the development of line drawing had been taken about as far as it could go in terms of straightforward shape representation, and in the succeeding

Hellenistic period this was extended, by the addition of cast shadow and tonal modeling, into an illusionistic optical system. For the representation of rectangular objects the later Greek vase painters were able to employ oblique projection and a simple form of perspective, and during the Hellenistic period the use of something approaching Renaissance linear perspective was probably quite common.

But Byzantine art did not simply adopt these systems and keep them unchanged. Instead, the drawing and denotation systems used during this period are, above all else, anomalous; and these anomalous systems did not develop, as they do in children's drawings, into more "correct" forms. Instead, they appeared in the mosaics at Ravenna in the fifth and sixth centuries, persisted in Byzantine art until the fourteenth century, were adopted in Russian icon painting, and are still used in Orthodox icon painting at the present time.

Probably the most commonly used drawing system in Orthodox art is inverted perspective, although it is very often employed in combination with other systems. In this system the orthogonals diverge, instead of being parallel as they are in oblique projection, or converging as they do in perspective. However, it is not possible to define this system in terms of a single, consistent rule. The orthogonals do not normally diverge from a single point, either within individual objects or within the picture as a whole; and when objects are shown in a landscape there is normally no general tendency for objects in the background to be represented to a larger scale than objects in the foreground. Within individual objects, however, the orthogonals often diverge (figs. 2.24 and 2.25), and where two or more objects are shown together in oblique projection the orthogonals diverge within the picture as a whole (color plate 1). Just as there are many variants on the system I have referred to in children's drawings as "near-oblique," so there are many variants in the system generally referred to as "inverted perspective."

Another common drawing system used in Orthodox art corresponds to what in children's drawings would be called "fold-out" drawings. Very often, particularly in the background in icon paintings, two sides of a building are shown as true shapes, as they would be in horizontal oblique projection, and the ground plane is folded down (fig. 8.13).

Fig. 14.9 shows the mosaic in the left lunette in the presbytery of San Vitale at Ravenna, illustrating two episodes in the life of Abraham. The hut on the left, in the doorway of which Sarah is standing, is in horizontal oblique projection with the ground plane folded down. In the center of the composition, three angels are seated at a table: fig. 14.10 shows a detail of this part of the composition. The orthogonals of the table top are almost parallel, as they would be in oblique projection, but the orthogonals on the right-hand side diverge. The cakes on the table, however, are shown as true shapes, as if seen from above. On the right of the composition is an altar at which Abraham is shown sacrificing his son, Isaac; like the table, the altar is drawn in inverted perspective, and the orthogonals of both the top and the sides of the altar diverge. All these objects are set in a landscape, but although there is a suggestion of a horizon, with the sky above, and the hand of God emerging from the clouds, there is no representation of a coherent ground plane.

Thus although the ways in which the individual objects in this mosaic are represented give a quite strong impression of three-dimensional shape, the spatial system as a whole is not consistent; and this is true of the rest of the mosaics in San Vitale. On the other side of the presbytery is another, similar lunette showing Abel and Melchizedek sacrificing at an altar, also in inverted perspective, with buildings on either side in horizontal oblique projection. In fact, the only geometric objects not represented in either inverted perspective or horizontal oblique projection in the mosaics in San Vitale are the walls of Jerusalem and Bethlehem at the top of the apse, and they are

FIG. 14.9. San Vitale, Ravenna, *Scenes from the Life of Abraham*. Photo Alinari.

Fig. 14.10. *The Three Angels* (detail of fig. 14.9).

shown in a confused mixture of oblique projection and horizontal oblique projection.

Moreover, the ways in which such objects are represented in San Vitale are in no way exceptional when compared with the mosaics in other buildings in Ravenna. In the basilica of St. Apollinare Nuovo (sixth century) the throne on which the Virgin sits, in the main mosaic on the left-hand wall, is in inverted perspective. In the panels above, showing Christ's miracles and parables, the house in which the paralyzed man is lowered from the roof is in inverted perspective, while the tomb from which Lazarus is rising is in a combination of oblique projection and horizontal oblique projection. In the mosaics on the right-hand side of the nave, Christ's throne is, exceptionally, shown in perspective, but nearly all the other objects in the scenes in the panels above are either in inverted perspective or horizontal oblique projection. The mosaics in the apse of St. Apollinare in Classe show mainly figure subjects, but the most conspicuous rectangular object, the altar in the scene showing the three sacrifices of the Old Testament, is in inverted perspective.

The spatial systems in these mosaics, which were produced in the fifth and sixth centuries A.D., may be compared with the spatial systems in one of the masterpieces of the last period of Byzantine art, the mosaic of *The Numbering of the People* in St. Saviour in Chora in Istanbul (fig. 14.11a). Again, it is not only the drawing systems of the individual objects that are inconsistent but the spatial system of the picture as a whole. The top half of the throne on the left is in an approximation to isometric projection, while the bottom half is in an approximation to oblique projection (fig. 14.11b). Most of the building on the right is in an approximation to oblique projection, but the bottom meets the ground plane in a straight line, as it would in orthogonal projection. In the scene as a whole the main orthogonals of these objects run upwards and outwards from the center of the picture, giving an effect of inverted perspective, while the orthogonals of the small building on the extreme left run downwards toward the center of the picture.

Finally, the drawing systems in all these pictures may be compared with the drawing systems in Rublev's *The Holy Trinity* (color plate 1). The subject of the scene depicted here is, in fact, the same as that shown in fig. 14.9, the Three Persons of the Trinity being represented in the guise of the three angels who appeared to Abraham and Sarah. At first sight it looks as if the table at which the angels are seated is in inverted perspective, because the outlines of the region representing the visible part of the table top, one of the most conspicuous features of the picture, diverge to the right and left. In fact, the side edges of the table are not visible. However, the impression of inverted perspective given by the shape of this region is repeated in the

a

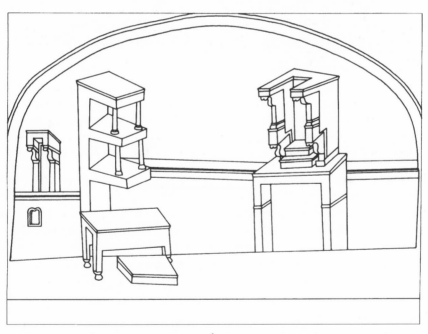

b

FIG. 14.11. (a) St. Saviour, Istanbul, *The Numbering of the People,* 1300–1320. From Dubery and Willats (1972). (b) An analysis of the drawing systems used.

directions of the orthogonals of the seats and footstools on either side of the picture. Although both seats and footstools are represented in approximations to oblique projection, the orthogonals to the right and left diverge from the center of the picture, giving an effect of inverted perspective to the picture as a whole. The open cavity for the drawer in the table, and the building in the background, are in normal oblique projection. Ouspensky and Lossky (1994), who refer to these last two features as being in "direct perspective," remark that: "This method of combining the two perspectives is not rare in ancient icons; still, preference is always given to inverse perspective" (p. 41).

It is, of course, impossible to illustrate here more than a few examples of Orthodox art. These examples are not, however, untypical. Anyone who is able to spend a few days at Ravenna will soon be convinced that the use of inverted perspective, together with the use of inconsistent mixtures of horizontal oblique projection or fold-out drawing, and oblique projection, is the norm, rather than the exception.[5] Similarly, even a brief look at any book on icon painting, such as Ouspensky and Lossky (1994), will soon persuade the reader that the same is true of Orthodox icon painting.

It is necessary to insist on this because it is often suggested that inverted perspective is rarely, if ever, used as the basis for a consistent art style, or that if it is used, it is used mistakenly or unintentionally. Gibson, for example, said:

> I do not know why Oriental painters (and Medieval painters and sometimes children) often represent the edges of table-tops and floors as diverging upward on the picture surface instead of converging upwards but I do know that they do not have a *system*. I suspect that this so-called inversion of linear perspective was quite unintentional and that the explanation is not simple. (Gibson, 1971, p. 30)

Hagen was even more positive: "It was never adopted anywhere with enough consistency to be called a style of spatial depiction. . . . Whatever the reasons for the occasional appearance of divergent perspective, it is never characteristic of any coherent art style" (Hagen, 1986, p. 149). In fact, this is not the case. Although the spatial systems in Orthodox art are not in themselves consistent, their *use* is consistent during an era that lasted far longer than the period (often taken to represent a coherent period of development) that extended from the beginning of the Renaissance to the beginning of the twentieth century.

Moreover, it is not just the drawing systems in Orthodox art that are anomalous: the denotation systems are also often anomalous. In the detail of the mosaic at San Vitale shown in fig. 14.10, the angels' legs are intertwined with the legs and rungs of the table in a way that reverses the normal rules for the representation of occlusion; and the lines of mosaic standing for the edges of the rungs of the table meet in ways that are not compatible with the denotation rules for line drawings of objects having plane faces described in Chapter 5. Similarly, although the drapery of these figures looks quite solid in some places, in other places the lines representing the contours come together in ways that are implausible. Looking at these mosaics is rather like looking at the pictures of impossible objects illustrated by Clowes and Huffman (fig. 1.14): the objects depicted in these mosaics look solid, but when we attempt to analyze them in detail the eye is baffled. Similarly, the representation of the contours of drapery in Orthodox manuscripts (figs. 2.24 and 2.25) and icon paintings (color plate 1 and fig. 11.5) is usually quite unrealistic, judged in terms of the normal rules for the representation of smooth objects given in Chapter 5, as exemplified in both Western line drawings and Japanese prints.

In addition, in icon painting, the normal direction of tonal contrast in line drawings is often reversed. The fundamental denotation system used in Byzantine art is line drawing, usually dark lines on a lighter ground with the addition of some fairly rudimentary tonal modeling (fig. 14.10). In Orthodox icons a similar system is used, although in many icons the element of silhouette seems just as, or even more, important. In addition, however, icons often contain areas in which some or all of the line drawing is carried out in a light tone, or gold (*assist*), on a darker ground, so that the normal direction of tonal contrast is reversed. For example, the lines representing the contours of the drapery in the figure of Christ in the *Noli me Tangere* icon shown in fig. 11.5 are carried out in gold on a dark ground. In the Rublev *Trinity* (color plate 1), some of the contours of the drapery are represented using dark lines on a lighter ground, but others are represented using light lines on a dark ground. Effects of this kind are quite common in Orthodox icon painting. Moreover, while the reversal of what the human visual system seems to accept as the natural direction of tonal contrast in line drawings is usually confined in these icons to the areas of drapery, the tonal modeling and highlights of features such as the head and hands in some icons, though difficult to analyze, seem quite unnatural, as if the figures were glowing with light.

Finally, icon paintings very often contain examples of false attachments between the depicted objects and the margin, very much as Gris's *Breakfast* contains instances of false attachments or near false attachments between the depicted objects and the frame. In Rublev's *Trinity,* for example (color plate 1), the edges of the far legs of the stools on which the angels are seated, the bottoms of the near legs of these seats, and the bottom edges of the footstools are all falsely attached to the margin. In a version in the Russian

Museum, Leningrad, painted about fifty years later (illustrated in Ouspensky and Lossky, 1994, p. 203), the legs of the stools and the top of the building on the left of the picture are falsely attached to the margin. In the magnificent Novgorod *Trinity* painted in the mid-sixteenth century (illustrated in Grierson, 1994a, p. 115), the building on the left, the tree, the mountain, the angels' wings on the left and right, one of Abraham's feet, one foot of the sacrificial calf, and both of Sarah's feet are falsely attached to the margin. Similarly, in representations of the Mother of God in the "Lovingkindness" icons, the sides of the body and the crown of the head are often falsely attached to the margin: numerous examples could be given.

From the standpoint of the tradition of Western, optically realistic painting, the use of anomalous drawing and denotation systems in Orthodox art can seem either perverse or incompetent. Many icon paintings would be classed in the West as examples of naive or folk art, and no doubt some of the incongruities in some of these pictures are simply mistakes, as they are in some Western paintings. In addition, some of the instances of false attachments may simply have arisen as a result of the artist's desire to make an economical use of the whole field of the picture. But it is hard to believe that the consistent, systematic use of anomalous drawing and denotation systems by artists who were capable of the dazzling technical brilliance exemplified by the Ravenna mosaics or the Rublev *Trinity* could be the result of mere incompetence, or ignorance of normal "scientific" perspective.[6] What purpose, then, did the employment of these anomalous drawing and denotation systems serve in Orthodox art?

Orthodox art is often said to be "symbolic." One of the functions of Orthodox art was to translate Orthodox doctrine into paint or mosaic, in order to complement and reinforce the verbal teaching given by the church, and many of the pictorial devices used in Orthodox art can be related to this teaching function. On a purely visual level, the emphasis on silhouette which is characteristic of many Russian icon paintings has an obvious practical value because it enables images to be recognized and understood more clearly in the interiors of dimly lit churches. On a symbolic level, many of the pictorial devices used in Orthodox art, especially some of the anomalous devices, have been given a doctrinal interpretation. One example is the very general omission of cast shadows in Byzantine art and Russian icon paintings. There are no shadows in Orthodox art because "The Divine Light permeates all things, so there is no source of light, which would illumine objects from one side or another; objects cast no shadows, for no shadows exist in the Kingdom of God" (Ouspensky and Lossky, 1994, p. 40). Moreover, as Waltz (1975) demonstrated (fig. 6.6), adding cast shadows to a picture can show that objects are anchored to the ground rather than floating freely in air, and in Western art shadows were routinely used for this purpose. In the *Pastoral Scene* shown in fig. 6.8, for example, the shadow cast by the figure of the shepherd shows that he is reclining on a bank. In Orthodox art, in contrast, figures are shown floating, free from their attachment to earthly time and space. Speaking of two icons of St. Basil and St. George, Ouspensky and Lossky (1994) remark that "They tread lightly, barely touching the ground with their feet and if it were not for the high line of the ground [shown in vertical oblique projection] their figures would appear separated from the earth and floating above it" (pp. 124–125).

Similarly, the reversal of the direction of normal tonal contrast can also be given a symbolic or doctrinal interpretation: light is represented as shining *out* of the figures of Christ and his saints and angels, rather than *on* them. According to Lazović and Frigerio-Zeniou (1985), the open wounds and the golden lines representing the folds of the drapery in the figure of Christ in the *Noli me Tangere* icon shown in fig. 11.5 are signs of his death and resurrection. Finally, the false attachments between the objects in the picture and the margin can be seen as a metaphor for the links between the spiritual and material worlds provided by Christ's Incarnation and the intercession of the Mother of God. As Averintsev (1994, p. 11) put it: "The icon lies on the border between the material and the immaterial, between the visible and the invisible. If one may so express it, the icon is focused on the point where the boundary between these two worlds is transcended through the Incarnation."

However, the very characteristic use of anomalous pictorial structures in Orthodox art has, I believe, an even more fundamental significance. The real heart of the dispute between the Iconoclasts and the Iconodules was about the nature of the relation between the material and spiritual worlds. The Iconoclasts repudiated pictorial representation because they wanted a religion free from all material defilement;[7] but the Iconodules argued that God can be represented in the person of Christ because he became human and took flesh in the Incarnation. Icons were therefore intended to represent, in the union between wood and paint and the holy images they depict, the union between God and man and, by extension, the sanctification of the material world. "God has 'deified' matter, making it 'spirit-bearing'; and if flesh has become a vehicle of the Spirit, then so—though in a different way—can wood and paint" (Ware, 1993, p. 33). Icons depict a spiritual world, not an earthly one, but they are nevertheless very much physical objects; and this is, in part, due to the use of anomalous pictorial devices like inverted perspective and incongruous mixtures of drawing systems which flatten the image and draw attention to the plane of the picture.

Nevertheless, the representation of the holy images in pictorial form brought with it the danger of idolatry: the danger that the faithful would worship the images themselves rather than the persons they represent. Thus as well as providing a metaphor for the union between the material and spiritual worlds, Orthodox art also demanded a form of depiction that fulfilled the first condition of pictorial representation as I have described it in Chapter 9, but not the second. It was important that the faithful should be able to *recognize* in these pictures the figures and objects that the artist intended to portray; but it was equally important that they should not be depicted as inhabiting a real, corporeal world. By using anomalous drawing and denotation systems the Byzantine artists, and after them the Orthodox icon painters, were able to reconcile these apparently contradictory aims.

Thus although there are considerable stylistic differences in Byzantine art and Orthodox icon painting from one period and country to another, Orthodox art as a whole is characterized by the use of anomalous representation systems. Rather than being the result of incompetence, these anomalous constructions served very specific ends: they allowed the artists and icon painters to represent the subjects of theology in a way that enabled them to be recognized, but prevented them from having a merely corporeal reality. Once this solution had been found, there was no point in changing it; and once the Orthodox artists had found a pictorial style suited to the needs of their culture, it persisted in a form that remained essentially unchanged for more than a thousand years.

The Direction of Art-Historical Changes

For many art historians in the nineteenth century the pattern of art history was a simple one: evolutionary progress from savagery to civilization, savagery being equated with the art of earlier ages, and civilization with the use of perspective and the art of the High Renaissance (Zerffi, 1876). Moreover, this development, or at least the direction of this development, was inevitable: "The 'will to form,' the *Kunstwollen,* becomes a ghost in the machine, driving the wheels of artistic development according to 'inexorable laws'" (Gombrich, 1960/1988, p. 16).

Evolutionary progress in the arts was often associated with what was called the "theory of recapitulation": the belief that the history of mankind can be discovered in the personal history of the child. In embryology, where the theory originated, recapitulation was abandoned before the end of the nineteenth century, but not before it had been extended to psychology; and this led many nineteenth-century scientists, including Darwin, to investigate aspects of the psychology of childhood (the development of language, for example) in the hope that they might throw some light on the evolution of the human species.[8]

Because of the many apparent similarities between children's early drawings and the art of "primitive" peoples, and the apparent similarities between the history of the discovery of perspective during the Renaissance and the acquisition of the ability to draw in perspective by older children, child art and art history tended to become confused. However, the theory that art history recapitulated the history of the child can be, and has been, interpreted in two quite different, and entirely contradictory, senses. Whereas earlier theories of evolution in art had led to the progressive view that civilization (represented by Western realistic art) was the ultimate destiny of all peoples, the theory could also be used to support the contrary view that drawings by older children and the later phases of art history represented a decline from an earlier golden age. The main evidence for this, it was claimed, was provided by early drawings and paintings by primitive peoples, such as the cave paintings of Lascaux. These paintings are the oldest we know, and they are highly realistic. How was this possible? The explanation was that in the childhood of mankind the eye itself was innocent, and able to see things as they really are, uncluttered by intellectual concepts (Bühler, 1949).

Ruskin used this theory of the "innocent eye" to defend Turner's paintings against an unsympathetic public, and Roger Fry hailed Impressionism as its final vindication. Art education, too, was profoundly influenced by this theory. Instead of primitives and children slowly and painfully making their way toward civilization and the ability to use perspective, children and primitive races were seen as able to express themselves in a free, original, and creative way until their work was spoiled by intellectual concepts and socialization; and this led educationalists such as Franz Cizek and Marion Richardson to attempt to protect children from any kind of art teaching.

Few art historians today would subscribe to any simple evolutionary theory of development or to the idea that the history of the race can be discovered in the history of the child. But as Gombrich has pointed out, the facts that gave rise to these myths are still there to be accounted for. One of these facts is, as I have tried to show, that there are certain similarities between children's early drawings and the art of some early cultures. Another is that there is a definite pattern in the development in children's drawings, and that there are some periods of art history in which development in a similar direction seems to have taken place.

I hope that it is clear by now that I am not arguing that the similarities between the patterns of development in children's drawings and the patterns of development in art history, where they occur, are due to some evolution-ary will to form. But if evolutionism is dead, how can these facts be accounted for? Throughout this book I have argued that the kinds of pictures that both artists and children produce are determined partly by the constraints im-posed by the design of the human visual system, and partly by the functions that their pictures are intended to serve. Because there are certain formal constraints on pictures if they are to provide effective shape representations, the development of children's drawing and the development of Greek vase painting have certain features in common. But representation in this re-stricted sense is far from being the only function of pictures, and the attempt to produce pictures that serve different functions will result in different kinds of pictures and different patterns of art-historical change, or lack of change, as it did in Byzantine art and Russian icon painting.

Art history within a particular culture is often seen in terms of progress toward some single coherent style; but does any such style now exist? I suggest that it does not, and that if there is any pattern in the history of depiction during the last two hundred years it is one of increasing *diversity* of styles. Attempts are sometimes made to identify a single style such as Cubism or nonrepresentational art as characteristic of the twentieth century.[9] Be-cause the Cubists rejected perspective, and Cubist paintings look so dramatically different from either Impressionism or the work of academic painters like Bouguereau that existed alongside Impressionism, Cubism has sometimes been taken as *the* typical artistic style of the first half of the twentieth century (Hagen, 1986). But this is very much an oversimplifi-cation. To begin with, Cubism was a very short-lived style: twenty years at the most, from 1909 to the late 1920s. Moreover, Cubism was seen by its initiators as an avant-garde style, not as typical of mainstream French art; and in its own time Cubism was even regarded as a relative failure compared with its more conservative opponents (Green, 1987). Cubism is a convenient landmark in the history of art, but it was hardly an enduring movement and was never widely adopted by the majority of artists. Nor does it seem possible to identify any other style as the dominant artistic style of the twentieth century. It is only necessary to list the names of some of these styles—Fauvism, Surrealism, Dada, German Expressionism, Futurism, Rayonnism, Orphism, Neo-Impressionism, Constructivism, Social Realism, Socialist Realism, Abstract Expressionism, Geometric Abstraction, Concep-tual Art, Minimalist Art, Op Art, and Pop Art—to indicate the fragmentation of style that occurred in the twentieth century. Marcel Duchamp, a leading force in Dada, has often been called a one-man movement, and this seems to be the condition to which most artists currently aspire. What seems to be characteristic of art in the twentieth century was that there *was* no characteristic style.

Moreover, it is no longer possible, as it was in previous periods and cultures, to equate the history of art with the history of depiction. A good case could be made, at least in the popular and commercial arts, for the dominance of an illusionistic pictorial style based on the use of perspective and optical denotation systems: for the very good reason that most pictures in circulation—snapshots, TV pictures, films, newspaper and magazine illustrations—are photographs of one kind or another. So far as most children are concerned, it is probably true to say that their pictorial environment is dominated by TV and comic books like *Superman:* in other words, pictures in perspective, based on either some optical, photographic technique or on straightforward line drawing. In this respect, the dominant pictorial style in pictures that tell a story has not changed all that much since the Renaissance.

But in addition to telling a story there are other, perhaps more important functions that pictures can serve. A historian of pictures looking back to our own period from a millennium ahead might well conclude that the most important changes that took place in pictorial styles since the discovery of perspective were the changes that took place in engineering and technical drawing. Artists' pictures, especially the pictures of the avant-garde, hardly touch the lives of most people, and pictures produced to serve the needs of journalism and mass entertainment are ephemeral by their very nature; but without engineering drawings modern civilization in its present form could quite literally not exist. Moreover, although it is probably true to say that most engineering drawings today are line drawings in orthogonal projection, this would be to ignore the great range of other technical drawing techniques currently in use: electrical circuit diagrams, for example, usually represent topological rather than projective spatial relations.

The truth is that any attempt to find a simple theory of change or lack of change in the history of depiction is likely to be inconclusive. Different pictorial styles are not like different languages: some styles are better suited than others to perform particular functions. Nor is it true to say that there is one best style to which all cultures have attempted to aspire: photographs are better than silhouettes at providing an illusion of reality, but they would be ineffective as road signs. Different pictorial styles—that is, different combinations of drawing and denotation systems—are best suited to different needs; and as these needs change, so the pictorial styles adopted by a culture, a period, or a discipline change with them. The pattern of development in children's drawings is determined by what it is that children are trying to do when they are learning to draw; and the history of art and, more generally, the history of depiction can only be understood in relation to the different functions that representational systems can serve.

Notes

Chapter One

1. I am indebted to Richard Wollheim for this formulation (personal communication). Clearly, the design characteristics of the human visual system have evolved in response to the need to interpret views of real scenes, not pictures of scenes.
2. In Willats (1984, p. 111) I discussed, very briefly, two other possible answers to the question: "When children are learning to draw, what is it that they are trying to do?" One answer was that children are trying to make their drawings look like adult pictures; the other, that they are trying to make them look like the real world. Possible answers to this question are further discussed in Chapter 13.

Chapter Two

1. The classification scheme described in this chapter is exhaustive: it includes all possible types of projection onto a flat surface. Various other schemes have been proposed for classifying the spatial systems in pictures, for example, White (1967) and Hagen (1985, 1986), but these are generally incomplete. White described various types of perspective, differing mainly in the degree of foreshortening of rectangular objects relative to the picture plane, and he described two other systems, which he called "frontal" and "complex frontal," that correspond to orthogonal projection and horizontal oblique projection. He also described a type of perspective—"synthetic perspective"—which corresponds to perspective projection onto a curved or spherical picture plane. However, he did not include vertical oblique projection or oblique projection in his scheme. Hagen's scheme is more complete than White's, and she used it to classify children's drawings as well as artists' pictures, but she failed to distinguish between orthogonal projection and horizontal and vertical oblique projection, or between oblique projection and isometric projection. Because her scheme was framed entirely in terms of primary geometry, she was also unable to include accounts of naive perspective or inverted perspective.

2. Maynard (1996) gives an excellent critique of traditional accounts of the projective geometry of perspective.

3. The inclusion of the word "oblique" in the names of these systems now seems rather misleading. Dubery and Willats (1972) coined the names "horizontal oblique projection" and "vertical oblique projection" for these systems because their definitions were given mainly in terms of primary geometry, and in these systems the projection rays intersect the picture plane at an oblique angle in the horizontal and vertical directions.

4. The mapping rules given in the text are very much simplified and are only intended to serve as examples, compared with the much more precise rules that would have to be used in a computer program intended to produce actual pictures.

Chapter Three

1. D'arcy Thompson (1917/1977) gave a well-known account of topological transformations in a biological context. Gombrich (1960/1988) and Stafford (1991) discuss Francis *Grose's Rules for Drawing Caricatures* (1788), which are, in effect, topological transformations. Neither of these accounts, however, is applicable to the kind of transformations in children's drawings in which enclosure within a volume in three dimensions is represented by enclosure within a region in two dimensions.

2. Light and MacIntosh (1980) tested 6-year-old children's responses to this distinction by asking them to draw a model house presented to them *inside* and *behind* a transparent glass beaker. They found that all the Inside Glass drawings showed the model house within the outlines of the drawing of the glass, but that half of the Behind Glass drawings showed the house to one side of, or above, the glass. This suggests that many of these children were basing their drawings on topological rather than projective relations (Willats, 1992c).

3. Overextensions are said to occur in children's early speech when the child's meaning of a word overlaps with that of an adult but extends beyond it: for example, when a child uses *bow-wow* to include horses and cows as well as dogs. Not all overextensions are based on the shape property of extendedness, although many are: Clark (1976) also gives examples of overextensions based on size, texture, movement, and function.

4. According to the method used in the British army for reporting on a landscape, there are only three kinds of trees: fir trees, poplar trees, and trees that have bushy tops. "Poplar trees" are a good example of one of Rosch's "clearest cases," used by the army to define the category of trees that are saliently extended in only one dimension, while "trees with bushy tops" are trees whose tops are saliently extended in all three dimensions. "Fir trees" are presumably bushy trees (or perhaps poplar trees) with the addition of the shape modifier "being pointed."

Chapter Four

1. I am indebted to an anonymous reviewer for this information.

Chapter Five

1. Huffman's picture grammar is not, in fact, powerful enough to label all the examples given because one of the interpretations of fig. 5.6b contains a false attachment (marked with an asterisk).
2. All pictures are formally ambiguous: the analyses given depend on various assumptions, such as the assumption that straight lines do in fact represent straight edges, and that there are no hidden complications on the other side of the object.
3. The picture grammar given here is a simplified version of that given by Huffman (1971). Huffman's version includes drawings of objects (such as drapery) whose surfaces are bounded by smooth edges.
4. The example of a line drawing given in fig. 5.11b is rather a simple one. In Pearson et al. (1990) more complex examples are compared with drawings of the same subjects made by a professional cartoonist.

Chapter Seven

1. Notable exceptions are Reith (1988) and Smith and Fucigna (1988).
2. In his Futurist Manifesto, Severini (1913/1973) declared, under the heading of FORM, that "our Futuristic artistic expression will be purely qualitative . . . Suppression of the straight line which is as static and formless as a colour without tonal gradations, and of parallel lines" (p. 123). This appears to be tantamount to saying that the formal properties represented would be topological rather than projective. Under the heading of COLOUR, Severini said: "Complementarity in general or Divisionism of analogous colours makes up the technique of colour analogy. . . . All sensations, when they take artistic form, become immersed in the sensation of *light*" (pp. 123, 124, original emphasis). "Divisionism" is another name for Seurat's version of Pointillism (Anfam et al., 1987, p. 334).
3. Transcription ought to be distinguished from pastiche. In a transcription of a picture the subject matter remains the same but the style is altered; in a pastiche the style remains the same but the subject matter is altered.

Chapter Eight

1. Examples of photographs in systems approximating to many of the projection systems can be found in the work of André Kertész (Kertész, 1984), including horizontal oblique projection (*New York, 30th November 1971*), oblique projection (*Paris, 1929*), axonometric projection (*Cross-road Square, Blois, France, 1930*),

and even inverted perspective (*Melancholic Tulip, 1939*). Kertész's work also includes an example of the reversal of normal atmospheric perspective (*Homing Ship [Central Park], New York, 1944*). Kertész left Budapest for Paris in 1925, and his friends included Leger, Chagall, and Vlaminck. His interest in the projection systems was perhaps prompted by his contacts with Cubist painters.

2. Hagen's position would be tenable if it were intended to apply to picture perception only, but it is clear that she intended it to apply to both production and perception: "This system reaffirms natural perspective as the explanatory structural umbrella for *production and perception* of representational pictures because all the geometries are present in natural perspective" (Hagen 1986, p. 114, my emphasis).

3. For example:

> Although the 36 geons have a clear subjective volumetric interpretation, it must be emphasized they can be uniquely specified from their two-dimensional image properties. Consequently, recognition need not follow the construction of an "object-centered" (Marr, 1982) three-dimensional interpretation of each volume. (Biederman, 1987, p. 122)

See also Costall (1993).

4. Two examples of systematic errors from my own children's early speech: one from my daughter ("If I go down there [onto the London Underground electric rails] I shall be all deaded and died"), and one from my son, who referred to "a place where you keep guns" as "an engunment."

5. Mitchelmore (1978) suggests that such drawings may represent either one face of the model, viewed orthogonally, or an outline of the whole object.

6. Kemp (1992) gives numerous other examples.

7. An essential component in this process would be the ability of the artist or draftsman to recognize three-dimensional shapes in the emerging picture. Van Sommers (1995) gives an account of a test in which twelve normal adults were asked to add the missing lines to incomplete pictures of three-dimensional objects such as folding screens. Two of the subjects could not get a single item correct, and another four had as many wrong as right. "Seeing in" is something that cannot necessarily be taken for granted.

Chapter Nine

1. Zerffi (1876), in his account of *The Historical Development of Art,* divided humanity into three ethnic groups. (Zerffi was a lecturer at the National Art Training School, South Kensington, later to become the Royal College of Art.) Negro art was associated with savagery. The Chinese he described as "childish" (p. 59) and "altogether deficient in painting, because they have no idea of perspective or shading" (p. 55), although he did acknowledge that they excelled in ceramic art. The mosaics of San Vitale (figs. 14.9 and 14.10) were described as being "gorgeous without refinement; and the technical treatment rough and

defective" (p. 280). The highest form of art he considered to be the Aryan art of the High Renaissance.

2. In a review of Hagen (1986), Costall (1988) remarked that "she [Hagen] seems to treat the existence of divergent perspective as a personal affront, and dismisses its perpetrators as either incompetent or frivolous" (p. 138).

3. Biederman (1987) and Biederman and Ju (1988) have suggested that the critical features for object recognition are shape properties, and that other properties such as color, brightness, and texture are of secondary importance. In their experiments, subjects were asked to identify brief presentations of slides of pictures of common objects. Each slide was presented in two versions: a line drawing of the object, and a full color photograph. They found that overall performance levels (measured in terms of errors, and delays in identifying the objects) were much the same for the two versions. As a result they argued that line drawings and full color photographs were about equally good for object recognition purposes.

4. Strictly speaking, the silhouette of an object cannot reveal any "dents" in the surface: convex curves in the outline of a silhouette correspond to convex surfaces in a body, and concave curves correspond to saddle-shaped surfaces. Only line drawings or line drawings with shading can reveal the presence of dents.

5. "Counting generously, experts can come up with about a dozen, but by such standards English would not be far behind" (Pinker, 1994, p. 64). What Pinker calls "the Great Eskimo Vocabulary Hoax" is derived from Benjamin Lee Whorf's hypothesis that language channels thought, and its corollary that some languages are better than others for talking about certain things. The current position is perhaps best summed up by Denny (1979a, p. 97):

> Interest in the Whorfian hypothesis seems to be a permanent feature of our intellectual life. In talking to scholars from other disciplines I find that they are very curious about whether language channels thought. In answering their questions I try to outline the weak version of the Whorfian hypothesis, which I take to be that languages facilitate certain patterns of thought by making available efficient coding mechanisms for them, whereas other thoughts may require greater effort at coding. But I try to make clear that the strong Whorfian hypothesis is a dead issue—no one believes that language coerces thought—if we make the effort we can encode any thought in any language.

Chapter Ten

1. But see Allen (1988) and his distinction between iconoclasm and *aniconism* (the nonuse of images) in Islamic art.

2. In *Cartesian Linguistics,* Chomsky (1966) described the origins of the idea that language, which is shared by all human beings, is essentially "creative." He also traced the argument by which Schlegel related the creative aspect of language to creativity in the arts (pp. 17, 18).

Chapter Eleven

1. The stage properties of *The Mystery and Melancholy of a Street*—the arcades, the empty van, the Victorian statue (here represented only by its shadow), and the rounded tower, all bathed in a raking light—are typical of those employed by de Chirico in his paintings of Italian squares during his "metaphysical" period (1911–1917). The girl rolling a hoop is, however, unique to this painting: Soby (1966) relates this figure to the figure of the little girl in the background of Seurat's *A Sunday Afternoon on the Island of La Grande Jatte*, 1886. De Chirico was much influenced, not only by Nietzsche's philosophy, but by the poetic quality that he claimed to find in his work. De Chirico wrote in his memoirs:

   > This novelty is a strange and profound poetry, infinitely mysterious and solitary, which is based on the *Stimmung* . . . of an autumn afternoon, when the sky is clear and the shadows are longer than in the summer, for the sun is beginning to be lower. . . . the Italian city *par excellence* where this extraordinary phenomenon appears is Turin. (Crossland, 1962/1971, p. 55)

   The origin of de Chirico's melancholy can perhaps be traced to the death of his father, but also to his intestinal troubles.
2. A contemporary critic, writing in the same year in which The *Mystery and Melancholy of a Street* was produced, wrote: "geometry and the effects of perspective are the primordial elements of his art, his usual means of expressing emotion" (Solfici, 1914, quoted in Soby, 1966, p. 47). Soby commented that "De Chirico proposed as early as 1912–13 to recapture through predominantly linear methods an illusory atmosphere of infinity, wherein architecture, figures, object and statuary would appear utterly detached from a near and present reality. 'Who can deny,' he was later to write, 'the troubling connection between perspective and metaphysics?'" (Soby, 1966, p. 41).
3. De Chirico wrote that "In Giotto, too, the use of architecture is highly metaphysical. All the openings—doors, arches, windows—while closely related to the figures, induce a foreboding sense of cosmic mystery" (de Chirico, 1920, quoted in Soby, 1966, p. 38).
4. Fig. 11.3, which is taken from Pfuhl (1955), appears to have been "unrolled" by some photographic process from the cylindrical surface of the vase on which it appears. I have been unable to discover the origin of this illustration, but inspection of the original vase painting suggests that the illustration is faithful to the original.
5. This painter can perhaps be identified with the Florentine monk Don Silvestro dei Gherarducci, who was attached to the monastery of Santa Maria degli Angeli, Rome (Kantner, Boehm, Strehlke, et al., 1994). I am indebted to Susan Frances Jones, assistant curator of Early Italian Painting, National Gallery, London, for this information.
6. I am indebted to Louise Williams of the Photographic Library and Dr. Dillian Gordon, curator of Early Italian Painting, both of the National Gallery, London, for pointing out to me the changes made by the artist during the course of the painting process.

Chapter Twelve

1. This is not, of course, the case: photographs are subject to human intervention at virtually every stage of the photographic process. Kertész's photograph *Melancholic Tulip, 1939,* which is in inverted perspective (note 1, Chapter 8) provides a good example.

2. Edmund Gosse, in his autobiographical *Father and Son,* relates how his father allowed him to read the poetry of Sir Walter Scott, but not his novels:

   > He refused to permit this, on the ground that those tales gave a false and disturbing picture of life, and would lead away my attention from heavenly things. I do not fully apprehend what distinction he drew between the poems, which he permitted, and the novels, which he refused. But I suppose he regarded a work in verse as more artificial, and therefore less likely to make a realistic impression, than one in prose. (Gosse, 1907/1976, p. 162)

   Gosse's father, the famous marine zoologist, was a founding member of the Plymouth Brethren, an extreme Protestant sect. This prohibition provides a rare example of iconoclasm directed toward words rather than pictures. I am indebted to my wife, Ruth Willats, for drawing my attention to this example, which seems analogous to the distinction I have made between illusionistic pictures and the more obviously artificial quality of icon paintings.

3. In Russian icon paintings the central area of the panel is typically hollowed out with an adze to form a slight recess, leaving a raised margin or border at the edges of the icon. According to Maltsevna (1994) this recess was derived from the Hellenistic niche, and the margin marked the transition between the two-dimensional world of the icon and the world inhabited by the viewer.

4. De Chirico's *The Double Dream of Spring,* 1915, contains a picture within a picture, and there are false attachments both between features of the inner picture and the inner frame, and between features of the outer picture and the inner frame. Soby commented that "this device (the picture-within-the-picture) will become a frequent element in the art de Chirico produced after his return to Italy in the summer of 1915" (Soby, 1966, p. 98).

5. Hofstadter (1979, p. 701), commenting on *The Two Mysteries,* remarks:

   > Focusing on the inner painting, you get the message that symbols and pipes are different. Then your glance moves upward toward the "real" pipe floating in the air—you perceive that it is real, while the other one is just a symbol. But that is of course totally wrong: both of them are on the same flat surface before your eyes. The idea that one pipe is in a twice-nested painting, and therefore somehow "less real" than the other pipe is a complete fallacy. Once you are willing to "enter the room," you have already been tricked: you've fallen for the image as reality.

6. Maynard (1996, p. 29) pointed out that most accounts of linear perspective confuse the idea of representations in perspective as projections *on* to a transparent window with the experience of viewers looking *through* a picture in perspective at a depicted scene:

Those who look through glazed windows see glass, and they see scenes beyond. They do not however see those scenes *projected* on the glass. Likewise, those who look at perspective pictures see picture surfaces, and (often) imagine seeing depicted scenes behind them. By analogy, they would not imagine those scenes as projected into patterns on the picture surfaces.

Hockney's *Play within a Play* emphasizes the role of the glass as a surface *separating* the picture domain from the object domain—but at the same time the face and hands of his portrait of John Kasmin form a painted pattern *on* the glass.

Chapter Thirteen

1. Clark (1897) asked North American children aged 6 to 16 years to draw an apple with a hat pin stuck through it. He divided the drawings into three groups, which he described as "pin clear across," "pin stopping on edges," and "pin as it appeared." He concluded that the 6-year-olds "draw things as they are known to be, not as they appear" (p. 287). Clark's illustrations suggest that the youngest children (mean age about 8 years) were basing their drawings on a denotation system in which regions denote volumes, that the intermediate group (mean age about 12 years) was using a denotation system in which regions denote regions in the visual field, and that the oldest group (mean age about 14 years) was using a denotation system in which T- and end-junctions denote points of occlusion.
2. Piaget and Inhelder (1956) were obviously puzzled by this mismatch between theory and practice, and attempted to get over the difficulty by collapsing the three classes based on projective, affine, and Euclidean-metrical geometry into a single class corresponding to Luquet's stage of visual realism.
3. Hagen's own evidence shows a clear age-related sequence in the drawing systems children used when she asked them to draw a model house, following the order: Orthogonal (orthogonal projection), Affine (oblique projection), and Projective (perspective) (Hagen, 1985, p. 70).
4. But see note 1, Chapter 7.
5. Willats (1977a) gives $r = 0.926, P < 0.01$.
6. Angles of convergence between $+20°$ and $-20°$ were deemed to represent parallel orthogonals.
7. Willats (1977a) gives $r = 0.0965, P < 0.001$.
8. In the event, nobody ever did suggest this.
9. McNemar's test gave the following results: for the 7-year-olds, $\chi^2 (1, N = 32) = 7.56, P < 0.005$; for the 12-year-olds, $\chi^2 (1, N = 32) = 9.6, P < 0.005$.
10. For example, Nicholls and Kennedy (1992) found relatively few drawings of cubes in horizontal oblique projection or vertical oblique projection in their experiment, whereas I found vertical oblique projection to be the most commonly used system in children's drawings of tables (Willats, 1977a). Lee and Bremner (1987), in a partial replication of this experiment with a much larger number of subjects, found the use of vertical oblique projection to be less

common than in Willats (1977a). It was still the system most commonly used by children between the ages of 7 and 10 years, however.

11. This is, of course, very similar to Gombrich's (1960/1988) theory of "schema and correction" as a mechanism for art-historical change.

Chapter Fourteen

1. I am not suggesting, of course, that there were no stylistic changes in Orthodox art. Kitzinger (1977) described the course of stylistic changes in early Byzantine art, and there were very obvious changes in Russian icon painting during the eighteenth century, largely as a result of the Westernizing influence of Peter the Great. What I am suggesting is that there was no obvious single direction of developmental change, as there was in Greek vase painting.

2. Sendler (1993) gives an excellent account of the political and religious disputes that surrounded the iconoclastic controversy.

3. Franklin (1994) argued that the importance of the notion of Moscow as the Third Rome, taking over the providential mission and universal status of Constantinople and establishing Muskovite legitimacy and identity, has often been exaggerated. According to Ouspensky and Lossky (1994), the Cretan School of icon painting became the principal successor to Byzantine painting after the fall of Constantinople. It was, however, greatly influenced by Western painting, as in the icon shown in fig. 11.5.

4. These changes were primarily changes in the denotation systems used rather than the drawing systems. Perspective was invented or rediscovered in the early Renaissance and continued in use until the early twentieth century; it could, indeed, be argued that it is still the most commonly used system in painting. There were some significant changes that took place in the drawing systems during this period: the changes in the varieties of perspective used by Italian painters during the fourteenth and fifteenth centuries described by White (1967) and, of course, the abandonment of perspective by the Cubists. But the most significant changes that took place during this period were changes in the *denotation* systems. The early Renaissance paintings were essentially line drawings representing shape features such as edges and contours, with the addition of some tonal modeling. In succeeding periods, more and more pictorial devices related to the optical denotation systems and the play of light were added—cast shadows, highlights, and atmospheric perspective—so that the array of light that could be obtained from the picture approximated more and more closely to the array that could be obtained from the scene. This pattern of development culminated in the invention of photography and television, and is, indeed, still under way with virtual reality. The invention of photography was a *chemical* invention; machines for capturing the perspective projections of scenes had been in use since the beginning of the Renaissance.

5. The Ravenna mosaics are illustrated in Bovini (1956) and Bustacchini (undated).

6. Grierson (1994b, p. 20) has questioned whether, in the absence of examples of normal linear perspective in the pictorial environment, Byzantine artists could have used inverted perspective deliberately in order to depict a supernatural world:

> While Byzantine artists did display sophisticated techniques to avoid optical distortion on curving surfaces, and neither their technical skill nor the complexity of contemporary optical theory should be underestimated, in the absence of any examples of scientific perspective it is difficult to understand how an artist for whom this technique was simply not available would have had the option of rejecting it in order to make a statement about his intentions.

Difficult perhaps, but not impossible. In Chapter 11, I drew an analogy between the deliberate use of ungrammatical constructions in poetic speech, for expressive reasons, and the use of anomalous pictorial constructions for similar reasons. The analogy ought not to be carried too far, however. In order to use and appreciate the significance of ungrammatical constructions in poetic speech, it is necessary to know the correct rules of language, even though this knowledge is likely to be, for the most part, at an unconscious level. Moreover, in order to acquire this knowledge it is necessary to have been brought up in an appropriate linguistic community in which the use of correct constructions is the norm (Chomsky, 1965/1972). However, whereas the rules of language are conventional, the rules of perspective are not conventional: they depend on physical optics and the design features of the human visual system. Thus it ought to be possible to recognize that pictures in inverted perspective do not depict a real, corporeal world, even in the absence of examples of the use of "scientific" perspective in the pictorial environment. A similar argument would apply to the use of other anomalous pictorial devices: the reversal of the normal rules for the direction of tonal contrast in line drawings, for example.

7. Iconoclasm was actually a much more complex phenomenon than this very brief account suggests, and included both religious and political elements (Sendler, 1993, p. 21). The theological argument against the use of images put forward by the Iconoclasts at the Council of Hiera (754) was that if we attempt to represent the divinity of Christ we claim to be able to represent what cannot be expressed. If, on the other hand, we represent the humanity of Christ we separate the humanity from the divinity, and divide what must be united. In addition, the association between the material nature of the wood and paint used to make the images, and the spiritual nature of what they represent, would degrade the holiness of the original model (ibid., pp. 26, 27). Against this, St. John of Damascus argued that

> Of old God the incorporeal and uncircumscribed was not depicted at all. But now that God has appeared in the flesh and lived among humans, I make an image of the God who can be seen. I do not worship matter but I worship the Creator of matter, who for my sake became material and deigned to dwell in matter, who through matter effected my salvation. (Quoted in Ware, 1993, p. 33)

Ware comments that "the Iconoclast controversy is thus closely linked to earlier disputes about Christ's person. It was not merely a controversy about religious art, but about the Incarnation, about human salvation, about the salvation of the entire material cosmos" (p. 33).

8. Although Piaget is best known as a child psychologist, he saw himself as engaged in what he called "genetic epistemology," a general explanation of human knowledge; and he saw his studies of childhood as a convenient, if indirect, route to this larger goal. In accordance with this program, Gablik (1977) used Piaget's account of child development as a model for art-historical changes. The Modern period, which she equated with late Impressionism, Cubism, and Nonfigurative Art, is identified with Piaget's formal-operational stage. Pariser (1983) gives a penetrating critique of this approach.

9. See Gablik (1977, p. 43), Hagen (1985, table 3.1; 1986, table 9.1) and note 8 above.

Glossary

Accidental alignment   The accidental alignment of unrelated features in a view of a scene as the result of choosing a particular viewpoint: as when two corners, separated in the scene, occupy the same location in a view.

Bodies   Three-dimensional scene primitives whose only attributes are such abstract properties as texture and three-dimensional shape.

Canonical view   A view that reveals all (or as many as possible) of the undulations in the three-dimensional surface of an object (Richards et al., 1987, p. 1169).

Contours   The projection in the frontal plane of the locus of points where the line of sight just grazes the surface of a smooth object. Such contours are sometimes referred to as "occluding contours" in order to distinguish them from surface contours.

Denotation systems   The representational systems that map scene primitives into corresponding picture primitives.

Description   The result of applying a representation to an entity or set of entities (Marr, 1982, p. 363).

Dimensional index   The number of dimensions of space within which a scene or picture primitive can potentially be extended. Thus a *line* has a dimensional index of one because it can be extended in only one dimension on the picture surface.

Domain   The scope of a representational system. Three kinds of domains are normally considered in the analysis of pictures: the object domain whose primitives are entities such as tables and people; the scene domain whose primitives are entities such as edges and surfaces; and the picture domain whose primitives are entities such as regions and lines. In addition, picture primitives are represented by physical marks, such as blobs of paint or pigment.

Drawing systems   The representational systems that map spatial relations in the scene into corresponding relations on the picture surface.

Edges   Surface discontinuities such as the edges of cubes, and the projections of such features in the frontal plane. Edges (but not contours) can thus form part of both object-centered and viewer-centered representations.

End-junction   The point at which a line representing a contour ends.

Extendedness   The extendedness of a primitive specifies its relative extensions in different directions. The terms *round, flat,* and *long* provide informal descriptions of the extendedness of bodies. More formally, the extendedness of a scene or picture primitive can be described by specifying its dimensional index together with its index of extension. For example, round, three-dimensional bodies or lumps, which are about equally extended in all three dimensions, can be described as 3_{111} volumes.

False attachment   False attachments in pictures represent accidental alignments in views of scenes: for example, a line junction representing two otherwise unrelated corners which occupy the same location in a view.

Frontal plane   The plane lying perpendicular to the viewer's line of sight (Marr, 1982, p. 364).

Generalized cone   The three-dimensional shape swept out by moving a cross-section of fixed shape but smoothly varying size along an axis (Marr, 1977, pp. 442, 443).

General position   A position for the viewer such that accidental alignments are avoided.

Index of extension   The subscripts "1" or "0" added to the dimensional index of a scene or picture primitive in order to denote relative extension or lack of extension in a particular direction.

Line   A one-dimensional picture primitive.

Line junction   The point where a line representing a contour ends, or the point where two or more lines meet.

Local color   The term used by artists to describe the intrinsic color of a surface irrespective of the lighting or viewing conditions: synonymous with *object color,* the term used in psychology (Sutherland, 1991, p. 286).

Local tone   The term used by artists to describe the intrinsic tone (along a scale from black to white) of a surface irrespective of the lighting or viewing conditions.

Luminance step edges   A linear pattern in the cross-section of an array of light bounded by slightly darker elements on one side and slightly lighter elements on the other. A pattern of this kind in an image might correspond to a feature such as the projection of the boundary of a cast shadow (Pearson et al., 1990, p. 47).

Luminance valleys   A pattern in the cross-section of an array of light in which a column of slightly darker elements appears against a surround of slightly lighter elements. A pattern of this kind in an image might correspond to a contour (Pearson et al., 1990, p. 50).

Lump   An informal name for a volumetric scene primitive that is about equally extended in all three dimensions.

Marks   The actual physical entities, such as blobs of paint or pigment, used in drawings, paintings, and so on to represent picture primitives.

Nonaccidental properties   Properties in an image or picture, such as straightness and curvilinearity, which are taken by the visual system as strong evidence that the corresponding feature in the scene shares the same properties. For example, if there is a straight line in the image or picture representing an edge, the visual system infers that the edge is also straight.

Object-centered description   A shape description specified relative to the intrinsic coordinate system of an object or scene (Marr, 1982; Sutherland, 1991, p. 286).

Objects   Entities such as tables and people, whose attributes are less abstract than those of bodies.

Occluding contours   A term sometimes used to distinguish the contours of an object—the locus of points where the line of sight just grazes the surface—from surface contours.

Occlusion   If an object is hidden by another object relative to a particular viewpoint, it is said to be occluded by it. The representation of this relation in drawings is often called "overlap," a misleading term because there is usually no physical overlap. Rather, those parts of the drawing depicting objects or parts of objects which would be occluded relative to a given viewpoint are eliminated from the drawing, a process known in computing as "hidden line elimination" or HLE.

Orthogonals   Lines in the picture representing edges in the scene that lie perpendicular to the picture plane.

Outline   The boundaries of the regions in a silhouette, or the lines in a line drawing representing the boundaries of an object.

Picture   A two-dimensional representation of a three-dimensional scene.

Picture plane   Pictures produced by projection are imagined as resulting from the intersection between lines or rays from the scene and a plane, known as the picture plane, located between the scene and the viewer (Maynard, 1996).

Picture primitives   The most elementary units of shape information in a picture. Picture primitives may be zero-dimensional (points or line junctions), one-dimensional (lines), or two-dimensional (regions).

Point of occlusion   The point in a view of a scene where an edge or contour passes behind a surface.

Primary geometry   The geometry of the projection of lines or rays from objects in the scene and their intersection with the picture plane to form an image or picture (Booker, 1963).

Primitives   The most elementary units of information available in a representation.

Recapitulation   According to the theory of recapitulation, the development of an individual repeats the evolutionary history of the species. The theory is sometimes summed up by saying that "ontogeny recapitulates phylogeny." In the late nineteenth and early twentieth centuries it was thought that children's drawing development could provide a model for the history of art.

Regions   A term used to describe both two-dimensional shape primitives in views of scenes, and two-dimensional picture primitives.

Representation   A formal scheme for representing a set of entities and their relations (Marr, 1982, p. 366). Sometimes used more loosely here and elsewhere (e.g., Wollheim, 1977) as synonymous with "description."

Representative view   A view that reflects the extendedness of an object or body (Willats, 1992a, p. 488).

Rim   The locus of points on the surface of an object where the line of sight just grazes the surface (Koenderink and van Doorn, 1982, p. 132).

Saliency of extension   The significant extension of a shape primitive in a given direction, compared with its lack of extension in other directions.

Saturation   In painting, the purity of the hue of a pigment. A "fully saturated" red is redder than one that has been adulterated with an admixture or black or white. In vision, the subjective richness or purity of a color; in general, the more white light is present, the less saturated the color (Sutherland, 1991, p. 388).

Scene   A three-dimensional representation of the object domain.

Scene primitives   The most elementary units of shape information in a scene. Scene primitives may be three-dimensional (bodies such as lumps, sticks, and slabs), two-dimensional (surfaces and faces), one-dimensional (edges), or zero-dimensional (corners).

Secondary geometry   The two-dimensional geometry of the picture surface, obtained without recourse to the idea of projection. For example, pictures in perspective may be obtained by letting the orthogonals converge to a vanishing point (Booker, 1963).

Secondary shape properties   Shape properties of scene primitives (such as "being pointed at one end") that are less elementary than their extendedness.

Shape   The geometry of an object, or a scene or picture primitive.

Shape modifier   A means of representing secondary shape properties such as "having plane faces" or "being pointed" added to a picture primitive to modify its extendedness (Willats, 1992a, p. 493; cf. Hollerbach, 1975).

Slab   An informal name for a volumetric scene primitive that is saliently extended in two dimensions but not the third.

Smooth object   An object whose surface is without edges, creases, or other abrupt surface discontinuities.

Stick   An informal name for a volumetric scene primitive that is saliently extended in only one dimension.

Surface contours   One-dimensional shape features on the surface of a smooth object, or the projections of such features: such as the lines in a picture representing the intersections between an object's surface and a set of parallel planes, or the lines connecting points of equal surface curvature.

Tadpole figure   Children's early figure drawings that lack a trunk, or in which the trunk is amalgamated with the head.

T-junction   A line junction in the form of the letter T, normally representing a point of occlusion.

View   The projection of a scene in the frontal plane; in engineering drawing, the representation of such a projection.

Viewer-centered description   A shape description specified relative to a coordinate system centered on the viewer (Marr, 1982; Sutherland, 1991, p. 470).

Viewpoint   The notional position occupied by a monocular viewer at the point of projection in the primary geometry of a projection of a scene; also referred to as the "station point" or "spectator point."

Visual field   A term used by Gibson (1950) to describe the introspective experience of seeing the world as a perspective projection. "The attitude you should take is that of the perspective draughtsman. It may help if you close one eye. If you persist, the scene comes to approximate to a picture" (p. 27).

Visual world   A term used by Gibson (1950) to describe the introspective experience of seeing the world as extended in depth, and as containing three-dimensional objects that remain constant in size whatever their distance from the viewer.

Volumetric primitive   A three-dimensional scene primitive. The simplest possible volumetric primitive specifies only a location and an extent. At the next level of complexity the primitive may be specified in terms of its relative extendedness in each of the three dimensions of space. At further levels, secondary shape properties may be specified, such as "being curved" or "being pointed at one end."

References

Adams, K. L., and Conklin, N. F. (1973). Toward a theory of natural classification. *Papers from the 9th Regional Meeting, Chicago Linguistic Society,* 1–10.

Allen, T. (1988). *Five Essays on Islamic Art.* n.p. [USA?]: Solipsis Press.

Alpers, S. (1983). *The Art of Describing: Dutch Art in the Seventeenth Century.* Chicago: University of Chicago Press.

Ames-Lewis, F. (1986). *The Draftsman Raphael.* New Haven, Conn.: Yale University Press.

Anati, E. (1964). *Camonica Valley.* London: Jonathan Cape.

Anfam, D. A., Beal, M., Bowes, E., et al. (1987). *Techniques of the Great Masters of Art.* Secaucus, N.J.: Chartwell Books.

Arnheim, R. (1954). *Art and Visual Perception.* Berkeley: University of California Press.

Arp, J. (1948). *On My Way: Poetry and Essays 1912 . . . 1947.* New York: Wittenborn, Schultz, Inc.

Averintsev, S. (1994). Visions of the invisible: the dual nature of the icon. In R. Grierson (ed.), *Gates of Mystery: The Art of Holy Russia* (pp. 11–14). Cambridge: The Lutterworth Press.

Barasch, M. (1990). *Giotto and the Language of Gesture.* Cambridge: Cambridge University Press.

Baron-Cohen, S., Campbell, R., Karmiloff-Smith, A., et al. (1995). Are children with autism blind to the mentalistic significance of the eyes? *British Journal of Developmental Psychology,* 13, 379–398.

Baron-Cohen, S., Riviere, A., Fukushima, M., et al. (1996). Reading the mind in the face: a cross-cultural and developmental study. *Visual Cognition,* 3(1), 39–59.

Baxandall, M. (1985). *Patterns of Intention.* New Haven, Conn.: Yale University Press.

———. (1988). *Painting and Experience in Fifteenth Century Italy: A Primer in the Social History of Pictorial Style.* Oxford: Oxford University Press.

Biederman, I. (1987). Recognition-by-components: a theory of human image understanding. *Psychological Review,* 94, 115–147.

Biederman, I., and Ju, G. (1988). Surface vs. edge-based determinants of visual recognition. *Cognitive Psychology,* 20(1), 38–64.

Blank, P., Massey, C., Gardner, H., and Winner, E. (1984). Perceiving what paintings express. In W. R. Crozier and A. J. Chapman (eds.), *Cognitive Processes in the Perception of Art* (pp. 127–143). Amsterdam: North-Holland.

Blau, E., and Kaufman, E. (eds.) (1989). *Architecture and Its Image: Four Centuries of Architectural Representation: Works from the Collection of the Canadian Centre for Architecture.* Montreal: Centre Canadien d' Architecture/Canadian Centre for Architecture.

Booker, P. J. (1963). *A History of Engineering Drawing.* London: Chatto and Windus.

Bovini, G. (1956). *San Vitale.* London: Andre Deutsch.

British Standard 1192 (1969). *Projection.* London: Her Majesty's Stationery Office.

Bühler, K. (1949). *The Mental Development of the Child.* London: Routledge and Kegan Paul.

Bunge, W. (1966). *Theoretical Geography.* Lund, Sweden: C. W. K. Gleerup.

Bustacchini, G. (undated). *Ravenna: Capital of Mosaic.* Bologna: Italcards.

Cahill, J. (1985). *Chinese Painting.* New York: Rizzoli.

Carroll, L. (1962). *Through the Looking-Glass and What Alice Found There.* London: Macmillan.

Cennini, C. d'A. (fifteenth century/1954), trans. D. V. Thompson, Jr. *The Craftsman's Handbook (Il libro dell'arte).* New York: Dover Publications.

Chomsky, N. (1957/1972). *Syntactic Structures.* The Hague: Mouton.

———. (1965/1972). *Aspects of the Theory of Syntax.* Cambridge, Mass.: MIT Press.

———. (1966). *Cartesian Linguistics: A Chapter in the History of Rationalist Thought.* New York: Harper and Row.

Clark, A. B. (1897). The child's attitude toward perspective problems. *Studies in Education,* July, 283–294.

Clark, E. V. (1976). Universal categories: on the semantics of classifiers and children's early word meanings. In A. Juilland (ed.), *Linguistic Studies Offered to Joseph Greenberg on the Occasion of His Sixtieth Birthday* (vol. 1, pp. 449–462). Saratoga, Calif.: Anma Libri.

Clowes, M. B. (1971). On seeing things. *Artificial Intelligence,* 2(1), 79–116.

Cooper, D., and Tinterow, G. (1983). *The Essential Cubism: Braque, Picasso and Their Friends (1907–1920).* London: Tate Gallery Publications.

Cortazzi, H. (1983). *Isles of Gold: Antique Maps of Japan.* New York and Tokyo: Weatherhill.

Costall, A. (1988). Review of *Perspective and Other Drawing Systems* (Dubery and Willats, 1983) and *Varieties of Realism: Geometries of Representational Art* (Hagen, 1986). *Perception,* 17, 137–140.

———. (1993). Beyond linear perspective: a cubist manifesto for visual science. *Image and Vision Computing,* 11(6), 334–341.

Court, E. (1989). Drawing on culture: the influence of culture on children's drawing performance in rural Kenya. *Journal of Art and Design Education,* 8(1), 65–88.

————. (1990). Poster presented at the IVth European Conference on Developmental Psychology, University of Stirling, Scotland, August 27–31.

————. (1992). Researching social influences in the drawings of rural Kenyan children. In D. Thistlewood (ed.), *Drawing Research and Development* (pp. 55–67). Harlow, Essex: Longman.

Cox, M. V. (1981). One thing behind another: problems of representation in children's drawings. *Experimental Psychology,* 1, 275–287.

————. (1985). One object behind another: young children's use of array-specific or view-specific representations. In N. H. Freeman and M. V. Cox (eds.), *Visual Order: The Nature and Development of Pictorial Representation* (pp. 188–201). Cambridge: Cambridge University Press.

————. (1992). *Children's Drawings.* London: Penguin.

Crook, C. (1985). Knowledge and appearance. In N. H. Freeman and M. V. Cox (eds.), *Visual Order: The Nature and Development of Pictorial Representation* (pp. 248–263). Cambridge: Cambridge University Press.

Crossland, M. (trans.) (1962/1971). *The Memoirs of Giorgio de Chirico (Memorie della mia vita).* London: Peter Owen.

Crystal, D. (1971). *Linguistics.* Harmondsworth, Middlesex: Penguin.

Darwin, C. (1872). *The Expression of Emotions in Man and Animals.* Chicago: University of Chicago Press, 1965.

Davis, M. (1988). *The Early Italian Schools before 1400.* (Revised edition by D. Gordon.) London: National Gallery Publications.

Degallier, A. (1904). Notes psychologiques sur les Nègres pahouins. *Archives de psychologie,* 4, 362–368.

Dennis, W. (1960). The human figure drawing of the Bedouins. *Journal of Social Psychology,* 52, 209–219.

Denny, P. J. (1979a). The "extendedness" variable in noun classifier semantics: universal features and cultural variation. In M. Mathiot (ed.), *Ethnolinguistics: Boas, Sapir and Whorf Revisited* (pp. 97–119). The Hague: Mouton.

————. (1979b). Semantic analysis of selected Japanese numeral classifiers for units. *Linguistics,* 17, 317–335.

Deregowski, J. B. (1977). Pictures, symbols and frames of reference. In G. Butterworth (ed.), *The Child's Representation of the World* (pp. 219–235). New York: Plenum Press.

————. (1978). On reexamining Fortes' data: some implications of drawings made by children who have never drawn before. *Perception,* 7, 479–484.

Deuchar, M. (1990). Are the signs of language arbitrary? In H. Barlow, C. Blakemore, and M. Weston-Smith (eds.), *Images and Understanding* (pp. 168–179). Cambridge: Cambridge University Press.

Dubery, F., and Willats, J. (1972). *Drawing Systems.* London: Studio Vista; New York: Van Nostrand Reinhold.

————. (1983). *Perspective and Other Drawing Systems.* London: The Herbert Press; New York: Van Nostrand Reinhold.

Elkman, P. (1973). Cross-cultural studies of facial expression. In P. Elkman (ed.), *Darwin and Facial Expression* (pp. 169–222). New York: Academic Press.

———. (1992). An argument for basic emotions. *Cognition and Emotion, 6*, 169–200.

Farr, D., and House, J. (1987). Catalog entries in: *Impressionist and Post-Impressionist Masterpieces: The Courtauld Collection.* New Haven, Conn.: Yale University Press.

Fazzioli, E. (1987). *Caractères chinois.* Paris: Flammarion.

Fong, W., and Hearn, M. K. (1981/1982). *Silent Poetry: Chinese Paintings in the Douglas Dillon Galleries.* New York: Metropolitan Museum of Art. Reprinted from the *Metropolitan Museum of Art Bulletin* (Winter 1981/1982).

Fortes, M. (1940). Children's drawings among the Tallensi. *Africa, 13*, 239–295.

Franklin, S. (1994). The origins of Russia and its culture. In R. Grierson (ed.), *Gates of Mystery: The Art of Holy Russia* (pp. 27–36). Cambridge: Lutterworth Press.

Freeman, N. H. (1972). Process and product in children's drawings. *Perception, 1*, 123–140.

———. (1975). Do children draw men with arms coming out of the head? *Nature, 254*(5499), 416–417.

———. (1980). *Strategies of Representation in Young Children.* New York: Academic Press.

———. (1986). How should a cube be drawn? *British Journal of Developmental Psychology, 4*, 317–322.

———. (1987). Current problems in the development of representational picture-production. *Archives de psychologie, 55*, 127–152.

Freeman, N. H., Evans, D., and Willats, J. (1988). Symposium overview: the computational approach to projection drawing-systems. Paper given at the Third European Conference on Developmental Psychology, Budapest, June 15–19.

Freeman, N. H., and Janikoun, R. (1972). Intellectual realism in children's drawings of a familiar object with distinctive features. *Child Development, 43*, 1116–1121.

Gablik, S. (1977). *Progress in Art.* New York: Rizzoli.

Gardner, H. (1980). *Artful Scribbles: The Significance of Children's Drawings.* New York: Basic Books.

Gibson, J. J. (1950). *The Perception of the Visual World.* Boston: Houghton Mifflin.

———. (1954). A theory of pictorial perception. *Audio-visual Communications Review, 1*, 3–23.

———. (1971). The information available in pictures. *Leonardo, 4*, 27–35.

———. (1978). The ecological approach to the visual perception of pictures. *Leonardo, 11*, 227–235.

Golomb, C. (1973). Children's representation of the human figure: the effect of models, media and instruction. *Genetic Psychology Monographs, 87*, 197–251.

———. (1992). *The Child's Creation of a Pictorial World.* Berkeley: University of California Press.

Gombrich, E. H. (1960/1988). *Art and Illusion: A Study in the Psychology of Pictorial Representation.* Oxford: Phaidon Press.

Goodenough, F. L. (1926). *Measurement of Intelligence by Drawings.* New York: Harcourt, Brace and World.

Goodman, N. (1968). *Languages of Art.* Indianapolis: Bobbs-Merrill.

Gosse, E. (1907/1976). *Father and Son.* Harmondsworth, Middlesex: Penguin.

Gowans, A. (1979). Child art as an instrument for studying history: the case for an "ontology repeats phylogeny" paradigm in universal history. *Art History,* 2(3), 247–274.

Green, C. (1987). *Cubism and Its Enemies: Modern Movements and Reaction in French Art, 1916–1928.* New Haven, Conn.: Yale University Press.

Gregory, R. L. (1970). *The Intelligent Eye.* London: Weidenfeld and Nicholson.

Grierson, R. (ed.) (1994a). *Gates of Mystery: The Art of Holy Russia.* Cambridge: Lutterworth Press.

————. (1994b). The death of eternity. In R. Grierson (ed.), *Gates of Mystery: The Art of Holy Russia* (pp. 15–26). Cambridge: The Lutterworth Press.

Guzman, A. (1968). Decomposition of a visual scene into three-dimensional bodies. *Proceedings of the Fall Joint Computer Conference,* 291–304.

————. (1971). Analysis of curved line drawings using context and global information. In B. Meltzer and D. Mitchie (eds.), *Machine Intelligence,* vol. 6 (pp. 325–375). Edinburgh: Edinburgh University Press.

Haddon, A. C. (1904). Drawings by natives of New Guinea. *Man,* 4, 33–36.

Hagen, M. A. (1985). There is no development in art. In N. H. Freeman and M. V. Cox (eds.), *Visual Order: The Nature and Development of Pictorial Representation* (pp. 59–77). Cambridge: Cambridge University Press.

————. (1986). *Varieties of Realism: Geometries of Representational Art.* Cambridge: Cambridge University Press.

Hambledon, F. C. (1948). Locomotives worth modelling. *Model Engineer,* 98(2447), 404–407.

Harris, D. (1963). *Children's Drawings as Measures of Intellectual Maturity.* New York: Harcourt, Brace and World.

Hayes, J. (1978). Children's visual descriptions. *Cognitive Science,* 2, 1–15.

Hockney, D. (1976). *David Hockney by David Hockney.* London: Thames and Hudson.

Hofstadter, D. R. (1979). *Gödel, Escher, Bach: An Eternal Golden Braid.* Hassocks, Sussex: Harvester Press.

Hogarth, B. (1981). *Dynamic Light and Shade.* New York: Watson-Gupthill.

Hollerbach, J. M. (1975). Hierarchical shape description of objects by selection and modification of prototypes. MIT. Artificial Intelligence Laboratory Technical Report No. 346 (pp. 1–237). Cambridge, Mass.: MIT Press.

Horn, B.K.P. (1975). Obtaining shape from shading information. In P. H. Winston (ed.), *The Psychology of Computer Vision* (pp. 115–155). New York: McGraw-Hill.

Huffman, D. A. (1971). Impossible objects as nonsense sentences. In B. Meltzer and D. Mitchie (eds.), *Machine Intelligence,* vol. 6 (pp. 295–323). Edinburgh: Edinburgh University Press.

Jahoda, G. (1981). Drawing styles of schooled and unschooled adults: a study in Ghana. *Quarterly Journal of Experimental Psychology,* 33A, 133–143.

Kahnweiler, D. H. (1969). *Gris.* London: Thames and Hudson.

Kantner, L. B., Boehm, B. D., Strehlke, C. B., et al. (1994). *Painting and Illumination in Early Renaissance Florence, 1300–1450.* New York: Metropolitan Museum of Art.

Kemp, M. (1989). *Leonardo on Painting.* New Haven, Conn.: Yale University Press.

———. (1992). *The Science of Art: Optical Themes in Western Art from Brunelleschi to Seurat.* New Haven, Conn.: Yale University Press.

Kennedy, J. M. (1974). *A Psychology of Picture Perception.* San Francisco: Jossey-Bass.

———. (1983). What can we learn about pictures from the blind? *American Scientist,* 71, 19–26.

Kennedy, J. M., and Ross, A. S. (1975). Outline picture perception by the Songe of Papua. *Perception,* 4, 391–406.

Kerschensteiner, G. (1905). *Die Entwicklung der zeichnerischen Begabung.* Munich: Carl Gerber.

Kertész, A. (1984). *The Manchester Collection: Catalogue of the Retrospective Exhibition of the Work of Andre Kertész at the National Museum of Photography.* Bradford: National Museum of Photography.

Kitzinger, E. (1977). *Byzantine Art in the Making.* London: Faber and Faber.

Klee, P. (1961). *Notebooks (The Thinking Eye),* vol. 1. (J. Spiller, ed.) London: Lund Humphries.

———. (1965). *The Diaries of Paul Klee, 1898–1918.* (F. Klee, ed.) London: Peter Owen.

Koenderink, J. J. (1984). What does the occluding contour tell us about solid shape? *Perception,* 13, 321–330.

———. (1990). *Solid Shape.* Cambridge, Mass.: MIT Press.

Koenderink, J. J., and van Doorn, A. J. (1982). The shape of smooth objects and the way contours end. *Perception,* 11, 129–137.

———. (1992). Surface shape and curvature scales. *Image and Vision Computing,* 10(8), 557–565.

Kosslyn, S. M., Heldmeyer, K. H., and Locklear, E. P. (1977). Children's drawings as data about internal representations. *Journal of Experimental Child Psychology,* 23, 191–211.

Lazović, M., and Frigerio-Zeniou, S. (1985). *Les icones du Musée d'art et d'histoire Genève.* Geneva: Musée d'art et d'histoire.

Le Corbusier (1923/1981). *Towards a New Architecture.* London: Architectural Press.

Lee, M., and Bremner, G. (1987). The representation of depth in children's drawings of a table. *Quarterly Journal of Experimental Psychology,* 39A, 479–496.

Lewis, H. P. (1963). Spatial representation in drawing as a correlate of development and a basis for picture preference. *Journal of Genetic Psychology,* 102, 95–107.

Light, P. H. (1985). The development of view-specific representation considered from a socio-cognitive standpoint. In N. H. Freeman and M. V. Cox (eds.), *Visual Order: The Nature and Development of Pictorial Representation* (pp. 214–230). Cambridge: Cambridge University Press.

Light, P. H., and MacIntosh, E. (1980). Depth relationships in young children's drawings. *Journal of Developmental Child Psychology,* 30, 79–87.

Loehr, M. (1980). *The Great Painters of China.* Oxford: Phaidon Press.

Lowe, D. G. (1987). Three-dimensional object recognition from single two-dimensional images. *Artificial Intelligence,* 31, 355–395.

Luquet, G.-H. (1913). *Les dessins d'un enfant.* Paris: Alcan.

———. (1927). *Le dessin enfantin.* Paris: Alcan.

Maltsevna, D. (1994). The technique of Old Russian painting. In R. Grierson (ed.), *Gates of Mystery: The Art of Holy Russia* (pp. 314–317). Cambridge: Lutterworth Press.

Marr, D. (1977). Analysis of occluding contour. *Proceedings of the Royal Society of London, Series B,* 197, 441–475.

———. (1978). Representing visual information: a computational approach. In A. R. Hanson and E. M. Riseman (eds.), *Computer Vision* (pp. 61–80). New York: Academic Press.

———. (1982). *Vision: A Computational Investigation into the Human Representation and Processing of Visual Information.* San Francisco: W. H. Freeman.

Marr, D., and Nishihara, H. K. (1978). Representation and recognition of the spatial organization of three-dimensional shapes. *Proceedings of the Royal Society of London, Series B,* 200, 269–294.

Martlew, M., and Connolly, K. J. (1996). Human figure drawings by schooled and unschooled children in Papua New Guinea. *Child Development,* 67, 139–158.

Matthews, J. (1994). *Helping Children to Draw and Paint in Early Childhood.* London: Hodder and Stoughton.

Matthews, R. H. (1956). *Chinese-English Dictionary.* Cambridge, Mass.: Harvard University Press.

Maynard, P. (1996). Perspective's places. *Journal of Aesthetics and Art Criticism,* 54(1), 23–40.

Minsky, M., and Papert, S. A. (undated). *Artificial Intelligence Report, Artificial Intelligence Memo. No. 252.* Cambridge, Mass.: Massachusetts Institute of Technology.

Mitchelmore, M. C. (1978). Developmental stages in children's representation of regular solid figures. *Journal of Genetic Psychology,* 133, 229–239.

Moore, V. (1986a). The use of a colouring task to elucidate children's drawings of a solid cube. *British Journal of Developmental Psychology,* 4, 335–340.

———. (1986b). The relationship between children's drawings and preferences for alternative depictions of a familiar object. *Journal of Experimental Child Psychology,* 42, 187–198.

Moskowitz, B. A. (1978). The acquisition of language. *Scientific American,* 239, 82–96.

Nagel, E., and Newman, J. R. (1964). *Gödel's Proof.* London: Routledge and Kegan Paul.

Nakayama, K., and Shimojo, S. (1992). Experiencing and perceiving visual surfaces. *Science,* 257, 1357–1363.

Nicholls, A. L., and Kennedy, J. M. (1992). Drawing development: from similarity of features to direction. *Child Development,* 63, 227–241.

Offner, R. (1981). *A Critical and Historical Corpus of Florentine Paintings: A Legacy of Attributions,* vol. 5. Locust Valley, N.Y.: J.J. Augustin.

Orwell, G. (1980). *Decline of the English Murder and Other Essays.* Harmondsworth, Middlesex: Penguin.

Ouspensky, L., and Lossky, V. (1994). *The Meaning of Icons,* translated by G. E. H. Palmer and E. Kadloubovsky. Crestwood, N.Y.: St. Vladimir's Seminary Press.

Pariser, D. (1983). The pitfalls of progress: a review and discussion of Gablik's *Progress in Art. Visual Arts Research,* 9(1), 41–54.

Parker, D. M., and Deregowski, J. B. (1990). *Perception and Artistic Style.* Amsterdam: North-Holland.

Pearson, D., Hanna, E., and Martinez, K. (1990). Computer generated cartoons. In H. Barlow, C. Blakemore, and M. Weston-Smith (eds.), *Images and Understanding* (pp. 46–60). Cambridge: Cambridge University Press.

Perez, B. (1888). *L'art et la poésie chez l'enfant.* Paris: Alcan.

Perkins, D. N. (1972). Visual discrimination between rectangular and nonrectangular parallelopipeds. *Perception and Psychophysics,* 12(5), 396–400.

Pfuhl, E. (1955). *Masterpieces of Greek Drawing and Painting.* London: Chatto and Windus.

Phillips, W. A., Hobbs, S. B., and Pratt, F. R. (1978). Intellectual realism in children's drawings of cubes. *Cognition,* 6, 15–33.

Piaget, J., and Inhelder, B. (1956). *The Child's Conception of Space.* London: Routledge and Kegan Paul.

Pinker, S. (1986). Visual cognition: an introduction. In S. Pinker (ed.), *Visual Cognition* (pp. 1–63). Cambridge, Mass.: MIT Press.

————. (1994). *The Language Instinct.* London: Penguin.

Rawson, P. (1969). *Drawing.* London: Oxford University Press.

Reith, E. (1988). The development of use of contour lines in children's drawings of figurative and non-figurative three-dimensional models. *Archives de psychologie,* 56, 83–103.

Ricci, C. (1887). *L'arte dei bambini.* Bologna: Zanichelli.

Richards, W., Koenderink, J. J., and Hoffman, D. D. (1987). Inferring three-dimensional shapes from two-dimensional silhouettes. *Journal of the Optical Society of America A,* 4, 1168–1175.

Rintelen, F. (1923). *Giotto und die Giotto Apokryphen.* Basel: n.p.

Rivière, J. (1912). Sur les tendances actuelles de la peinture. *Revue d'Europe et d'Amérique,* 1, 384–406.

Robinson, B. W. (1967). *Persian Miniature Painting.* London: Her Majesty's Stationery Office.

Rosch, E. (1973). On the internal structure of perceptual and semantic categories. In T. E. Moore (ed.), *Cognitive Development and the Acquisition of Language* (pp. 111–144). New York: Academic Press.

Scharf, A. (1979). *Art and Photography.* Harmondsworth, Middlesex: Penguin.

Sendler, E. (1993). *The Icon: Image of the Invisible.* Torrance, Calif.: Oakwood.

Severini, G. (1913/1973). The plastic analogies of dynamism—Futurist manifesto. In U. Apollonio (ed.), *Futurist Manifestos* (pp. 118–125). London: Thames and Hudson.

Seymour, C. (1964). Dark chamber and light-filled room: Vermeer and the camera obscura. *Art Bulletin,* 46, 323–331.

Smith, N., and Fucigna, C. (1988). Drawing systems in children's pictures: contour and form. *Visual Arts Research,* 14(1), 66–76.

Soby, J. T. (1966). *Giorgio de Chirico.* New York: Museum of Modern Art.

Spencer, J. R. (1966). *Leon Battista Alberti on Painting.* New Haven, Conn.: Yale University Press.

Sprigg, J., and Larkin, D. (1987). *Shaker: Life, Work, and Art.* London: Cassell.

Stafford, B. M. (1991). *Body Criticism: Imagining the Unseen in Enlightenment Art and Medicine.* Cambridge, Mass.: MIT Press.

Steadman, R. (1983). *I, Leonardo.* London: Jonathan Cape.

Steiner, G. (1977). *The Tower of Babel: Aspects of Language and Translation.* Oxford: Oxford University Press.

Stern, W. (1930). *Psychology of Early Childhood.* London: George Allen and Unwin.

Sully, J. (1895). *Studies of Childhood.* London: Longmans.

Sutherland, S. (1991). *Macmillan Dictionary of Psychology.* London: Macmillan.

Taylor, B. (1719). *New Principles of Linear Perspective; or the Art of Designing on a Plane the Representations of all sorts of Objects, In a more General and Simple Method than has been done before.* London: Printed for R. Knaplock at the Bishop's Head in St. Paul's Church-yard.

Taylor, M., and Bacharach, V. R. (1981). The development of drawing rules: metaknowledge about drawing influences performance on non-drawing tasks. *Child Development,* 52, 373–375.

Teuber, M. (1976). *Blue Night* by Paul Klee. In M. Henle (ed.), *Vision and Artifact* (pp. 131–151). New York: Springer-Verlag.

———. (1980). Paul Klee—between art and visual science. Paper read at the 12th annual meeting of the Cheiron Society, Bowdoin College, Brunswick, Maine.

Thompson, D. (1917/1977). *On Growth and Form,* rev. ed. Cambridge: Cambridge University Press.

Thorne, J. P. (1972). Generative grammar and stylistic analysis. In J. Lyons (ed.), *New Horizons in Linguistics* (pp. 185–197). Harmondsworth, Middlesex: Penguin.

Tredgold, T. (1838). *The Steam Engine.* London: J. Weale.

Van Sommers, P. (1995). Observational, experimental and neurophysiological studies of drawing. In C. Lange-Kuttner and G. V. Thomas (eds.), *Drawing and Looking* (pp. 44–61). Hemel Hempstead, Herts.: Harvester Wheatsheaf.

Von Bothmer, D. (1987). *Greek Vase Painting.* New York: Metropolitan Museum of Art.

Vredeman de Vries, J. (1604–1605/1968). *Perspective.* New York: Dover.

Waltz, D. (1975). Understanding line drawings of scenes with shadows. In P. H. Winston (ed.), *The Psychology of Computer Vision* (pp. 19–91). New York: McGraw-Hill.

Ware, T. (1993). *The Orthodox Church.* London: Penguin.

Wertheimer, M. (1923). Untersuchung zur Lehre von der Gestalt, II. *Psychologische Forschung,* 4, 301–350.

White, J. (1967). *The Birth and Rebirth of Pictorial Space.* London: Faber and Faber.

Willats, J. (1974). Computers and the structural analysis of pictures. *Mathematical Education,* 5(4), 743–744.

———. (1977a). How children learn to draw realistic pictures. *Quarterly Journal of Experimental Psychology,* 29, 367–382.

———. (1977b). How children learn to represent three-dimensional space in drawing. In G. Butterworth (ed.), *The Child's Representation of the World* (pp. 189–202). New York: Plenum Press.

———. (1980). On the depiction of smooth forms in a group of paintings by Paul Klee. *Leonardo,* 13(4), 276–282.

———. (1981). Formal Structures in Drawing and Painting. Unpublished Ph.D. thesis, Council for National Academic Awards (North East London Polytechnic).

———. (1983). Unusual pictures: an analysis of some abnormal structures in a painting by Juan Gris. *Leonardo,* 16(3), 188–192.

———. (1984). Getting the drawing to look right as well as to be right: the interaction between production and perception as a mechanism of development. In W. R. Crozier and A. J. Chapman (eds.), *Cognitive Processes in the Perception of Art* (pp. 111–125). Amsterdam: North-Holland.

———. (1985). Drawing systems revisited: the role of denotation systems in children's figure drawings. In N. H. Freeman and M. V. Cox (eds.), *Visual Order: The Nature and Development of Pictorial Representation* (pp. 78–100). Cambridge: Cambridge University Press.

———. (1987). Marr and pictures: an information-processing account of children's drawings. *Archives de psychologie,* 55, 105–125.

———. (1990). The draughtsman's contract: how an artist creates an image. In H. Barlow, C. Blakemore, and M. Weston-Smith (eds.), *Images and Understanding* (pp. 235–254). Cambridge: Cambridge University Press.

———. (1992a). Seeing lumps, sticks, and slabs in silhouettes. *Perception,* 21, 481–496.

———. (1992b). The representation of extendedness in children's drawings of sticks and discs. *Child Development,* 63, 692–710.

———. (1992c). What *is* the matter with Mary Jane's drawing? In D. Thistlewood (ed.), *Drawing Research and Development* (pp. 141–152). Harlow, Essex: Longman.

———. (1995). An information-processing approach to drawing development. In C. Lange-Küttner and G. V. Thomas (eds.), *Drawing and Looking* (pp. 27–43). Hemel Hempstead, Herts.: Harvester Wheatsheaf.

Wilson, B., and Wilson, M. (1977). An iconoclastic view of the imagery sources in the drawings of young people. *Art Education,* 30(1), 4–6.

———. (1981). The case of the disappearing two-eyed profile; or how little children influence the drawings of little children. *Review of Research in Visual Arts Education,* 15, 1–18.

————. (1984). Children's drawings in Egypt: cultural style acquisition as graphic development. *Visual Arts Research,* 10(1), 13–26.

Winner, E. (1982). *Invented Worlds.* Cambridge, Mass.: Harvard University Press.

————. (1986). Where pelicans kiss seals. *Psychology Today,* 20(8), 24–35.

Witkin, A. P., and Tennebaum, J. M. (1983). On the role of structure in vision. In P. H. Winston (ed.), *The Psychology of Computer Vision* (pp. 157–209). New York: McGraw-Hill.

Wollheim, R. (1973). *On Art and the Mind.* London: Allen Lane.

————. (1977). Representation: the philosophical contribution to psychology. In G. Butterworth (ed.), *The Child's Representation of the World* (pp. 173–188). New York: Plenum Press.

————. (1987). *Painting as an Art.* London: Thames and Hudson.

Zerffi, G. G. (1876). *A Manual of the Historical Development of Art.* London: Hardwicke and Bogue.

Index

Page numbers in *italics* denote pages on which illustrations appear. Color plates follow page 146.

methodology compared with that of art history, 16–17
Mondrian, Piet, 58
Monet, Claude
  Rocks at Port Coton, with the Lion Rock, 232
  Seine at Giverny, Morning Mist, The, 233
  Waterlily Pond (Japanese Bridge), 231
motor skills, 165, 166, 318
Mountain Landscape, 244
M.S.L., *South View of Fen End Farm,* 18, 49, 195
Music Lesson (A Lady at the Virginals), The, 60, 193, 221
Mystery and Melancholy of a Street, 250, 360

naive perspective, 9, 63–65
  in children's drawings, 10, 65, 293
  in folk art, 10, 64–65
  in Greek vase painting, 320, 337
Naked on the Bed, 29, 267, *color plate 5a*
Nash, John, *Canal Bridge, Sydney Gardens, Bath,* 234–35, *color plate 3*
Nash, Paul
  Landscape of the Moon's Last Phase, 235
  Monster Field, 235
  Pillar and Moon, 235, *color plate 9*
natural categories, 78
natural symbols, 79–80
near-oblique drawings, 178, 182–83, 196–98
Necker cube, 210, 294
Neo-Impressionist painting, 144, 222, 352
Nicholson, Ben, *Girl in a Mirror, 238*
Noli me Tangere (Creto-Venetian), *259,* 347
Noli me Tangere (Giotto), *260*
Noli me Tangere (Master of the Lehman Crucifixion), 29, 259, 261, 262, 263, *color plate 4*
Noli me Tangere, representations of, 261–62
nonaccidental shape properties, 86–87, 113, 309
noun classifiers, 78, 84
Nude in a Bathtub, 226
Numbering of the People, The, 26, *345*

object-centered descriptions, 18–20, 115, 151–53, 316
object language, 269–70
object recognition, 19–22, 123, 207
  in Catholic painting, 25

dependent on shape recognition, 123, 207
in Orthodox art, 34, 350
related to context, 94–96
in road signs, 21, 239
objects, 8, 19–20
oblique projection, 2, 12, 37–38, 52–55
  cabinet oblique projection, 55
  in cast shadows, 139
  cavalier oblique projection, 55
  in children's drawings, 10, 41–42, 183–84, 293, 299
  in Chinese painting, 2, 9, 55, 242
  in engineering drawing, 9
  in Greek vase painting, 241, 320, 337, 339
  in icon painting, 9, 346
  in Japanese prints, 9, 55
  in medieval painting, 9
  in Persian painting, 9, 228
occluding contours, 97. *See also* contours
occlusion, 25, 325
  points of, 25, 97, 293–94, 309. *See also* T-junctions
  reversal of the normal rules for, 278
Oh, but oh! 280
one-square drawings, 179–82. *See also* orthogonal projection
optical denotation systems, 4, 98, 128–46, 353
optical fusion, 128, 144, 222
Orchard Pavilion, The, 234, 237, 243
orientalizing style, 327–28
Orthodox art, 26–27, 339–50
  absence of change in, 321–22, 340
  anomalies in, 322, 340–41, 348–49
  doctrinal interpretation in, 348–49
  false attachment in, 347–49
  horizontal oblique projection in, 9, 12, 26–27, 48, 321, 342
  inverted perspective in, 12–13, 26–27, 66, 321, 323, 341–46, 349
  reversal of direction of tonal contrast in, 28, 322, 347–49
orthogonal projection, 2, 12, 38, 43–46
  in children's drawings, 10, 41–42, 44, 179–82, 293, 298
  in Egyptian painting, 46
  in engineering drawing, 4, 9, 21, 44, 205, 353
  in Greek vase painting, 9, 46, 240–41, 320–21